TOMBS, TEMPLES AND THEIR ORIENTATIONS

TOMBS, TEMPLES AND THEIR ORIENTATIONS

A New Perspective on Mediterranean Prehistory

Michael Hoskin

Churchill College, Cambridge

Ocarina
Books

Bognor Regis

Published by Ocarina Books Ltd.
27 Central Avenue, Bognor Regis, W Sussex PO21 5HT
United Kingdom
www.ocarinabooks.com

First published 2001

Printed and bound in the United Kingdom by Information Press,
Southfield Road, Eynsham, Oxford OX8 1JJ

Available from Oxbow Books, Park End Place, Oxford OX1 1HN, United Kingdom
www.oxbowbooks.com

British Library Cataloguing-in-Publication data

A catalogue record for this book is available
from the British Library

ISBN 0–9540867–1–6

Contents

Preface

This book brings together the fruits of a dozen years of fieldwork among the prehistoric sanctuaries and communal tombs of the central and western Mediterranean. Its kernel consists of the Corpus Mensurarum, a list of the orientations of approaching three thousand monuments, which I hope will enable archaeologists to take into account what was evidently a consideration of significance to the builders: namely, which way is the monument to face. The first two chapters set the scene, but the rest are essentially commentaries on the data in the Corpus. The data themselves are uncontroversial, and there will likewise be little argument about the presence of patterns in the data; but there is room for debate when we discuss the possible motivations in the minds of the builders that resulted in the patterns we uncover. I offer my own inferences from the patterns, but I hope that archaeologists who have read the first two chapters and at least sampled the rest will be able to come to their own conclusions.

Hundreds of friends have helped me in the field, for most of the tombs are small, ruined, and overgrown with vegetation, and when this is the case, to locate them calls for patient teamwork. I cannot list all my collaborators, but there are some whose omission would cause the very stones to cry out. They are Renate Gralewski of Cologne, Elizabeth Allan of Cambridge, and Silvia Gibbons of London, who each accompanied me on numerous expeditions. At first my colleagues and I depended on passing shepherds and goatherds to help us locate our tombs; but as time went on we received increasing support from local archaeologists, some of them the most eminent in their profession. They spared time to work with us in the field and they contributed to the resulting publications, and I have tried to mention them in the relevant chapters. But even they often needed to call on local enthusiasts, and at times our little party grew to the size of a small army as we spread out in search of tombs. To all my most grateful thanks.

Five other close friends deserve special mention. Giorgia Foderà Serio of Palermo Observatory worked with me in Sicily, Pantelleria, Malta and Tunisia, sometimes in fraught circumstances. Mauro Peppino Zedda of Isili in Sardinia was a relentless taskmaster in our study of the great Nuraghic monuments. Fernando Pimenta of Lisbon organized his fellow countrymen into a series of efficient collaborations. Juan Antonio Belmonte of the Astrophysical Institute of the Canary Islands, who is pioneering the archaeoastronomy of North Africa and the Middle East, read this work in draft and is responsible for notable improvements. And it was Clive Ruggles of Leicester University, the world's only Professor of Archaeoastronomy, who originally proposed that I should assemble my data into an organized book, and then subjected it to a ferocious line-by-line critique.

Fieldwork costs money, and I am grateful to Churchill College, Cambridge and to the Foreign Travel Fund of Cambridge University for their support.

Lastly, I thank my son Bernard, who undertook the layout of my recalcitrant manuscript with its many pages of tables, for his patience and forebearance.

The interested reader can find out more about my Mediterranean odyssey by turning to the articles in *Journal for the history of astronomy* (*JHA*) and its *Archaeoastronomy* supplement (*AA*) that are listed under Further Reading. With the completion of my work in the Mediterranean, I am currently extending the geographical coverage northwards, into the rest of France, and across the seas, to Cornwall and Ireland. Details of articles reporting on this fieldwork, together with the whole of the present Corpus Mensurarum in electronic form, can be found in the Web site of Science History Publications Ltd, the publishers of *JHA*: http://www.shpltd.co.uk.

1

Origins of an Odyssey

Television is not all bad. In the winter of 1970, as editor of the newly-founded *Journal for the history of astronomy*, I found myself watching a fascinating programme in which an elderly Scots engineer named Alexander Thom[1] discussed the purpose of the great rows of menhirs that march across the countryside of Carnac in Brittany. They were, it seemed, astronomically motivated, part of a complex of stones which the prehistoric builders could have used for high precision observations of the moon. In particular, a huge stone some 20 metres in height and weighing over 340 tons had been erected as a sort of universal foresight, related to a number of backsights located in various directions many kilometres distant. Megalithic Man, according to Thom, had stood at one of these backsights at a critical time of the lunar cycle, and watched the moon as it rose or set behind the great foresight. Backsight and foresight together formed an observing instrument built on a vast scale and therefore offering great accuracy, and this (he claimed) had enabled the constructors to monitor the cycles in sufficient detail for them to predict lunar eclipses.

This reminded me vividly of a suggestion of Galileo's.[2] Around a solstice the sun sets in almost the same position night after night, so that the actual day of the solstice is difficult to determine; but on one particular occasion, around midsummer, Galileo had noticed that the sun had set that evening behind a distant mountain in a position that was noticeably different from its setting point the night before. The mountain was in effect the foresight of an observing instrument whose length was so great that even the tiny movement of sunset around the solstice could be detected. Thom, though unaware of Galileo's suggestion, believed that Megalithic Man had done exactly the same thing.

The claim that there had been a prehistoric science of astronomy was clearly relevant to my journal. I wrote to Thom and invited him to submit an article on Carnac, and there began a partnership that resulted in the publication of no fewer than twenty articles. It was a partnership because Thom was an engineer unused to literary argumentation and no longer young, and he would send me a draft which I would then work up into publishable form. Now Thom was not only a great fact-gatherer, a meticulous and indefatigable surveyor of sites, but he was also an uninhibited theorizer, and his claims aroused immense interest among historians of astronomy and no less alarm among archaeologists.

A decade passed, and I found myself President of the history section of the International Astronomical Union, and so expected to organize a conference in the middle of my term of office. What better topic than this contentious subject of 'archaeoastronomy'? — for I was now receiving so many articles on prehistory that I had been forced to dedicate whole issues to the theme. Oxford seemed a suitable location, for the colleges were well used to hosting conferences and the city was near enough to great monuments like Stonehenge and Avebury for us to visit them on the final day. And so, in September 1981, astronomers, historians, ethnographers and even one or two archaeologists converged on Queen's College for what was to prove a lively meeting. The students of the Maya and other Mesoamerican cultures had ample evidence of the obsession with astronomical cycles on the part of the peoples they studied. They possessed written documents, admittedly few in number; they could decipher carvings on the walls of buildings; they could question descendants now living; and they could measure the alignments of structures. Theirs was a multidisciplinary approach, and they were scandalized at the gulf between Thom and his sympathizers on the one hand and European archaeologists on the other.

The reason for the gulf was clear: most Old World archaeologists found Thom's conclusions repellent and his astronomical and statistical arguments incomprehensible. But at least the Thomists, having little other than the stones to work with, measured these stones with care and precision. Their New World counterparts, blessed with a variety of evidence, were much more cavalier. And so each party had much to teach, and much to learn.[3] The New World participants agreed to host a return match in the Yucatan which they named 'Oxford 2', and to date six 'Oxford' meetings have been held and there is a standing international committee to perpetuate the series.

At the time of Oxford 1 I was an editor struggling to assess articles offered for publication in a field largely alien to me. This was about to change. I enjoyed holidays in Menorca and spent much time in a cove with numerous large caves in the cliffs. From an archaeological map for tourists I learned that these included ancient burial caves. My interest aroused, I eventually made contact with William Waldren, an American who had excavated an important site on Menorca and who enjoyed an attractive lifestyle whereby he wintered in Oxford and summered on Mallorca where he had been excavating for many years. We formed a firm friendship, and under his guidance I had my first experiences of practical archaeology. Then, in 1987, Waldren took me to visit an excavation directed by Antonio Arribas Palau, professor of archaeology in the University of the Balearics. Arribas, hearing of my background in astronomy, suggested that I investigate the orientations of the Bronze Age sanctuaries of Menorca. This in turn led to an invitation from the University of Granada to measure the orientations of the tombs at the great site of Los Millares in Almería; and so one thing led to another, and the result is this book.

My primary purpose is to make available to prehistorians of the Mediterranean the many hundreds of orientations I have measured (what a friend has generously termed "un espectacular corpus de información", "una mina de oro"[4]), so that they may take orientations into consideration along with all the other evidence. For it has never been my belief that the 'archaeoastronomer' can go it alone; I do not see the student of orientations as a *deus ex machina*, able single-handedly to resolve confusion. However, I believe that every archaeological team not only should have experts in flint and pottery and bones and radiocarbon dating and so forth, but that, where appropriate, it should include someone who knows how to measure orientations and inter-pret them. For it is now indisputable that around the Mediterranean most of the prehistoric tomb and temple builders were following customs in the orientation as well as in the structure and location of their monuments; and the modern investigator needlessly impoverishes his enquiry if he ignores these customs of orientation.

The most that could be claimed for this book is that, like the proverbial curate's egg, it is good in parts. Today I normally work and publish in collaboration with archaeologists, but even so the archaeological context I offer for my measurements will inevitably be sketchy and inadequate — the range of cultures whose orientation customs it has been my privilege to investigate is so great that to ensure that the purely archaeological content was always of professional standard would have delayed publication by years. I took retirement from my university post nine years before the normal age partly in order to have unrestricted time for fieldwork. Typically, to locate three or four tombs will occupy a complete day (at an average cost of perhaps £25 per tomb). An archaeolo-gist in university or other professional employment is unlikely to be able to spend so long in the field, even if his research interests made it appropriate for him to range so widely and yet to focus on so limited an aspect of prehistoric cultures. In any case, as I point out in the next chapter, tombs are being destroyed on a vast scale, and in all-too-many cases my measures can no longer be repeated. It therefore seems preferable to assemble my measures — hitherto scattered across numerous journal articles — between the covers of a single book, and to attempt an overview of the results, even if the archaeological context leaves much to be desired. I cite archaeological publications which the interested reader may care to pursue, and meanwhile beg indulgence for any shortcomings.

The focus of this book is on the islands and European mainland of the central and western Mediterranean. After an introduction to motives and methods we discuss in Chapter 3 the great temples of Malta and Gozo, which were at their peak around 3000 BC. They seem to be among the secrets of archaeology, for they predate the pyramids of Egypt and were in their time the greatest buildings on the face of the earth. I offer a tentative explanation for their orientations, but much more interesting is the discussion of the tally stones on the entrance pillars of one of the temples. This, according to my colleagues and me, represents the numbers of days in the intervals between one notable heliacal rising (that is, a star's appearance in the dawn sky after weeks of absence lost in the glare of the sun) and the next; if we are right, then the traditional calendars based on heliacal events, used by farmers to the present day and which we first find expressed in written form in Hesiod's *Works and days* in about the eighth century BC, go back a further two millennia.

In Chapter 4 we investigate the Bronze Age sanctuaries of Menorca, which were at their height around 1000 BC, and also those of Mallorca, which are Iron Age, from the middle of the first mil-lennium. I propose a theory that provides an explanation for a number of hitherto puzzling facts established by excavators working on Menorca, and which parallels our tentative explanation for the orientations of the Maltese temples. As a result, I offer a consistent explanation of the orienta-tions of the temples and sanctuaries of the Maltese and Balearic islands, even though construction

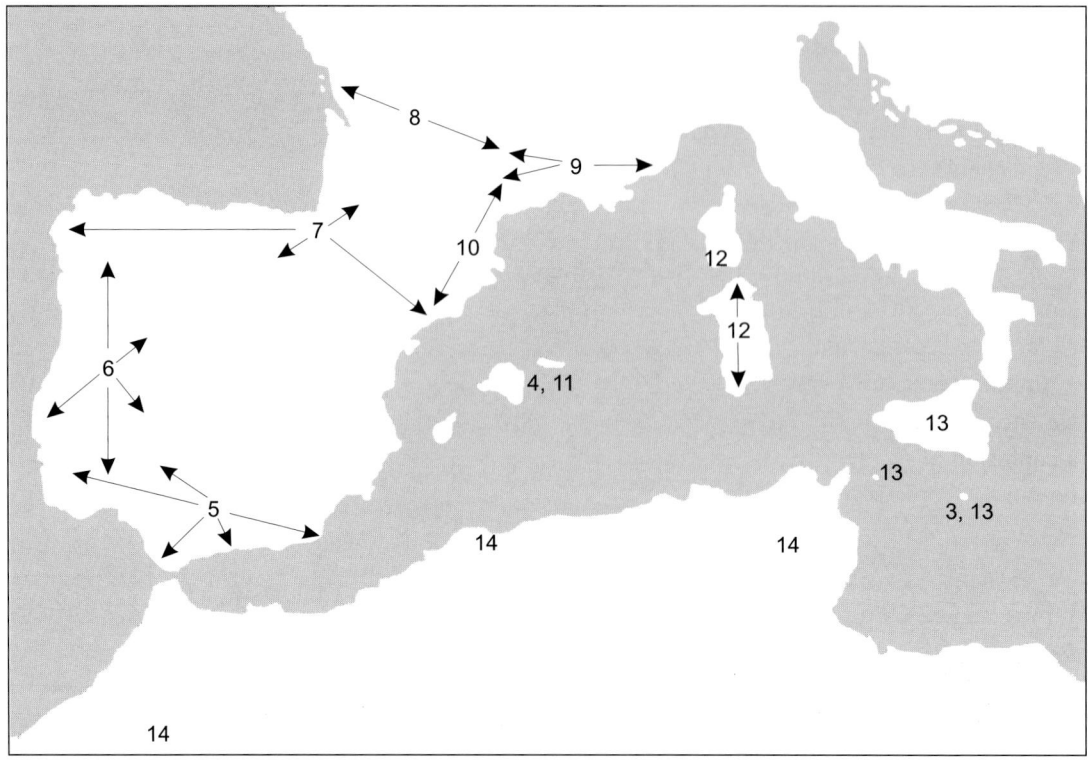

A schematic representation of our coverage of the central and western Mediterranean, with the numbers of the relevant chapters.

of the buildings was spread over three millennia.

Temples and sanctuaries dedicated to cult are rare in Mediterranean prehistory, whereas communal tombs, multipurpose structures that must often have been used for ritual, are very numerous. In Chapter 5 we begin, in Almería and the Costa del Sol, a clockwise progress around three-quarters of Iberia (the remaining quarter being devoid of monuments), during which we shall measure approaching one thousand tombs. The final stage of our journey, in Chapter 7, takes us across northern Spain and along both sides of the Pyrenees, until we are almost within sight of the Mediterranean coast again. We find that almost every one of the tombs faces the eastern half of the horizon, and to the south of midsummer sunrise.

In Chapter 8, we cross into France, and in imagination follow the great band of limestone plateaux or Causses that stretches from the Bay of Biscay southeastwards towards the Mediterranean. "In imagination" for myself as well as for the reader, because to visit many hundreds of these mostly inconspicuous tombs, in a country where the cost of living is higher than elsewhere, would have been extremely expensive in both time and money; and in any case many of the tombs have been destroyed in recent years.

A major gap in my coverage of the western Mediterranean threatened. However, it was clear from the published thesis of a French archaeologist, Yves Chevalier, that he had already carried out much of the necessary fieldwork; but only a handful of the orientations were explicitly cited in his book. It took some time to track down his address, but when contact was made he gladly agreed to publish his data in full. Most unfortunately, Chevalier had by now fallen ill, and before he could fulfil his undertaking he met an early death. However, in implementation of his wishes his family made his manuscripts freely available to me, and from these and from two magnificent inventories published by the French archaeologist Jean Clottes it proved possible to assemble a paper listing in all the orientations of nearly one thousand French dolmens. From the dense concentrations of tombs in the central Causses we have six hundred measures, and again almost all faced the eastern half of the horizon.

In Chapter 9, however, in Provence and east Languedoc, not far from the Mediterranean coast, we encounter for the first time westerly-facing tombs, and then in Chapter 10 we are faced with a confusion of easterly and westerly customs as we investigate southwest France and the neighbouring region of Cataluña. After this it is a relief, on revisiting the Balearic Islands in Chapter 11, to find that all the tombs face westerly.

In Chapter 12 we pass to Corsica and Sardinia. There we once more find easterly customs: the early dolmens on both islands, and (on Sardinia) the *corridoi dolmenici* that succeeded them as well as the hundreds of later *tombe di giganti*, almost all faced eastwards and south of midsummer sunrise. The rare exceptions are almost exclusively to be found in the south of Sardinia.

In Chapter 13 we discuss briefly the modest tombs of various types that are to be found on the islands of Malta, Sicily and Pantelleria, and then, to complete our coverage of the west Mediterranean basin, we turn in Chapter 14 to north Africa, and specifically to Tunisia, Algeria and Morocco. There had seemed every reason to expect to find on these southern shores of the Mediterranean, prehistoric tombs whose builders were following customs similar to those familiar to us from the islands and European mainland; and in Tunisia we did indeed find many hundreds of dolmens. But these are mostly very late, from the last centuries before Christ, and many of them are Punic or Roman. Furthermore, in my opinion their orientations were usually chosen to suit the lie of the land rather than in response to what was to be seen in the sky. Algeria we could not visit because of the present unrest, and what we can say about its tombs is based on the publications from a generation ago. Finally, Morocco has been investigated by intrepid colleagues and we report on their work, although the monuments they have visited prove to be culturally remote from the Iberian tombs across the water.

So far in this book the eastern Mediterranean has not been mentioned, though there are many areas there that offer the archaeoastronomer the prospect of rich harvests. As an encouragement to other investigators, we conclude this volume with a study of the Minoan cemetery at Armenoi in Crete, where we had the privilege of measuring over two hundred tombs excavated out of the bedrock, still in excellent condition and with orientations measurable to an accuracy of minutes rather than degrees.

Notes and references

1   His principal writings are: *Megalithic sites in Britain* (Oxford, 1967); *Megalithic lunar observatories* (Oxford, 1971); and *Megalithic remains in Britain and Brittany* (with A. S. Thom, Oxford, 1978). In addition he published many articles, some twenty of them in *Journal for the history of astronomy* (hereafter *JHA*) and its supplement, *Archaeoastronomy* (hereafter *AA*).

2   Galileo, *Dialogue on the great world systems*, transl. and ed. by G. de Santillana (Chicago, 1953), 398.

3   The proceedings appeared in two volumes: *Archaeoastronomy in the Old World*, ed. by D. C. Heggie (Cambridge, 1982), and *Archaeoastronomy in the New World*, ed. by A. F. Aveni (Cambridge, 1982).

4   J. A. Belmonte, *Las leyes del cielo: Astronomía y civilizaciones antiguas* (Madrid, 1999), 75.

2

Measuring Orientations: Why, Where, and How

It is not, I think, inapposite to consider these [prehistoric] monuments in the same terms as one would the churches of Christendom or the mosques of Islam, had the religions to which these afford architectural witness wholly vanished from our knowledge.
                                                                                                                   Stuart Piggott, 1965[1]

Then to her Patron Saint a previous rite
Resounded with deep swell and solemn close,
Through unremitting vigils of the night,
Till from his couch the wished-for Sun uprose.

He rose, and straight — as by divine command —
They, who had waited for that sign to trace
Their work's foundation, gave with careful hand
To the high altar its determined place.
                                                                                                                   William Wordsworth, 1823[2]

One end of every Church doth point to such a Place, where the Sun did rise at the time the Foundation thereof was laid, which is the Reason why all Churches do not directly point to the East; for if the Foundation was laid in *June*, it pointed to the North-east, where the Sun rises at that time of the Year; if it was laid in the Spring or Autumn, it was directed full East; if in Winter, South-east; and by the standing of these Churches, it is known at what time of the Year the Foundations of them were laid.
                                                                                                                   Sir Henry Chauncy, 1700[3]

Why

We imagine we are in the far distant future, and the mosques and churches of the Middle Ages have long since fallen into ruin and their purposes have vanished from the written record. Archaeologists are studying these ruins. They establish the layout of the buildings, and they lovingly identify and list the various artefacts found there. But, with one exception, they pay no attention to the orientations of their axes. The buildings appear ritualistic in purpose, but the remains seem to offer few clues to the religions they served.

There is one archaeologist, however, who makes it his business not only to measure the orientation of each of the ruins, but to assemble and collate this information. This archaeologist finds that the axes of the mosques converged on a city in the Middle East; and he concludes that this cannot have come about by chance, but that this city must have been of special significance in the religion served by the mosques.

Turning his attention to the churches, our archaeologist finds a pattern of a wholly different kind. Their axes face within a range centred around east, and a little calculation shows that this range was identical with the range of sunrise at the time when the churches were constructed.

This (he finds) is true of the churches of England, and the churches of Portugal, and the churches of Russia, and so on. Clearly this repeated coincidence of the range of church orientation with the range of sunrise cannot be the result of chance: sunrise must have played a fundamental role, at least in the symbolism of the religion served by these churches.

We see that in this imaginary scenario of the future, these significant aspects of the religions served by the mosques and churches have not vanished from the face of the earth. On the contrary, they are preserved in the ruins; but they are accessible only to the archaeologist of the future who makes it his business to measure and collate large numbers of orientations. All his colleagues pay dearly for their lack of interest in such measurements.

Why should not the same be true of present-day archaeologists who study prehistoric tombs and temples?

Where, when, and in which direction

In the chapters that follow we present and discuss the orientations of many hundreds of prehistoric communal tombs, and a smaller number of sanctuaries, from the central and western Mediterranean. Nearly two thousand of our measures are of communal tombs of Iberia and the south of France, and they will serve to illustrate our procedures.

Most of these tombs belong to the period from the late Neolithic to the early Bronze Age. It was during the Neolithic (the last era of the Stone Age) that peoples learned to herd animals and cultivate the land, and so they could enjoy a settled and relatively-assured existence denied to their hunter-gatherer ancestors. Even so, for most of the Neolithic, the emphasis was on herding rather than cultivation — and on the herding of the highly mobile flocks of sheep and goats, rather than the slower-moving pigs and cattle. People moved with their animals; dwellings were improvised out of caves; and the dead were often deposited in the caves where they had lived.

In the late Neolithic, cultivation grew in importance, and pigs and cattle became more common. As a result people became less mobile, and this gave them the incentive to build themselves permanent dwellings in the open air. Trade began on a significant scale, and new burial customs emerged: the dead were to be buried in specially-constructed stone tombs. These tombs were sometimes no more than the little cists for individual burial already known from earlier times, but usually they were larger structures to serve an entire family or clan. Some were prominent, territorial markers suitable for decades and even centuries of use.

Burial in communal tombs continued throughout the Chalcolithic or Copper Age, though it became increasingly confined to the re-use of existing tombs, and fewer and fewer new ones were built. Then, in the early Bronze Age, the use of communal tombs itself was gradually replaced by individual burials once more. The tombs of Iberia and France to which we dedicate six chapters are, therefore, mainly of the Neolithic and Chalcolithic, with some from the early Bronze Age: the period during which communal tombs were constructed had a beginning and an end.

The overwhelming majority of these tombs have (or had) a well-defined axis of symmetry, and it is the orientation of this axis that we measure. In order to permit the deposition of further bodies whenever deaths occurred, and the placing of offerings, the tomb had a means of access, and this

The measurement of the orientations of tombs is less routine than might be supposed. The beehive-shaped ('tholos') tomb no. 30 at Los Millares in Almería (*above*) has a well-defined centre to the circular chamber and an equally well-defined mid-point between the two entrance stones to the corridor. The same cannot be said for the tholos tomb (*below*) at Ourique in southern Portugal.

was normally an entrance at ground level; we choose to measure the orientation in the direction from the interior outwards through the entrance. That is, our measured orientation reflects the view the dead would have, were they still to possess the power of sight (and were there to be no physical obstacle obstructing their vision). Why we select this direction rather than the opposite is not easy to put into words, but fortunately this seems to be one thing on which all agree.

Temples and sanctuaries are very much rarer, and we shall meet them mainly on the tiny islands of Malta, where great temples were built around 3000 BC, and Menorca, where small but beautiful sanctuaries were erected around 1000 BC. On Malta the definition of the orientation of a temple is less straightforward because of the complexity of the structures; and to complicate matters further a group of archaeologists has expressly challenged our opinion that the sense is again from the interior looking out. In Menorca the axis of symmetry is clear, and the inside-to-outside direction evident from the lie of the land.

How

In an ideal world, where the sun always shone, tombs were exempt from destruction, archaeologists had the strength of packmules and lived forever, and funds for this work were unlimited, orientations would normally be measured by theodolite. A compass is vulnerable to magnetic anomalies in the rock, and also to the presence of man-made complications, such as concealed metal used by archaeologists to reinforce the tomb now being measured. But a theodolite can be used only when the sun is shining, for it measures the horizontal angle between the axis of the monument and the direction of the sun at the moment when the measurement is taken, this direction being known from calculated tables. Sadly, the sun does not always shine: I visited Sicily for a week to measure by theodolite the orientations of Greek temples, but clouds persisted and much time and money were wasted, and not a single measure resulted.

Equally importantly, time is not on our side. Not only do we as individuals age and decline (and this fieldwork calls for health and agility), but the destruction of tombs is appalling and relentless. In measuring orientations we are in fact engaged in rescue archaeology, for vandalism by individuals, and corporate vandalism in the form of new roads, new buildings, and especially the mechanical clearance of land for eucalyptus and other cultivation, is destroying tombs on a tragic scale. In central Portugal a local archaeologist acting as our guide frequently was reduced almost to tears when, of a dozen or so tombs existing at the time of his last visit, only one or two were now to be found. In Huelva in southwest Spain we visited one major tomb, spoke to the man clearing adjacent land with massive machinery, and found that had our visit been 24 hours later the tomb (whose presence was unknown to him) would have been destroyed. And at the other end of the spectrum, some well-meaning archaeologists intent on 'restoration' will not hesitate to set about rearranging the monument to conform with their ideas; sometimes the liberties they take are so great that for 'restored' we should read 'vandalized'.

Measurement by theodolite is indeed appropriate in certain circumstances, particularly when *both* the care that was lavished on the construction of a monument *and* its present condition are of unusual quality, and measurements are therefore possible to an accuracy of better than one

(*Left*) A typical dolmen, with an orientation defined to no better than two or three degrees: Mascortejo I in Huelva, which we visited only hours before the area was due to be cleared for agriculture. (*Right*) Precision construction that merits precise measurement, by theodolite: the Greek temple at Segesta in Sicily.

degree. This is most obviously the case with Greek and Roman temples, constructions built to a high precision. Other investigations, for example into the precise relationship of a monument to a distant horizon feature, may also call for exact measurement. But very few prehistoric tombs have an axis that we can define to better than two or three degrees. If, say, we put one pole in the middle of the backstone, and another in the middle of the corridor, and seek to measure the orientation of the line joining them, it will normally be the case that either pole could with equal justification be placed several centimetres to one side or the other. Why then spend time measuring the orientation to an accuracy of minutes with a theodolite, when a repeat measurement next day with repositioned poles may give an orientation that differs by two or even three degrees?[4] In such a situation, to use a theodolite purely on principle makes as much sense as employing a scalpel in an abattoir.

Nor is measurement by theodolite itself immune from mistake: in one recent article three experienced professors of astronomy admitted measuring the same poles with two different theodolites, and deriving orientations that differed by more than one degree.

It is when the rock is igneous and liable to generate magnetic anomaly that the best justification can be advanced for the use of a theodolite to measure the orientation of a monument. But this is very unusual. Huge areas of the western Mediterranean are limestone, and there the creation of natural caves by the erosion of rainwater encouraged early settlements. If the investigator, before visiting a new region, consults geologists as to where, if any, the rock may give rise to magnetic anomaly, he will normally find these problem areas are limited and were often unattractive to early inhabitants. If there is an anomaly, it will often reveal itself if the measures are taken from different positions along the axis, for example from opposite directions. And where a problem does arise, it may be possible to solve it by measuring the axis of the monument relative to the direction of a distant feature of known position. Thus, when measuring a peak sanctuary in Crete built on igneous rock, we measured the angle between the axis of the sanctuary and the direction of an observatory on a distant mountain-top, and we were able later to calculate the orientation of the sanctuary itself.

The compass I use is of the 'off-shore' type, intended for sailors. This incorporates a simple prism. As a result, when one looks over the top of the compass towards the alignment of the two surveying poles that defines the orientation, one sees floating in front of one's eyes the number of degrees (from magnetic north), so that when in a couple of minutes the needle has settled, one has a value that can be read with an accuracy of better than one degree. If all members of the team take their turn to make the measure, any discrepancy of, say, half a degree can be discussed and resolved. Of course my compass, like every measuring instrument, has an error of construction; but this I determined once and for all, by carefully observing one geodesic point from another and using the officially-stated coordinates to establish what the correct reading would have been. The error proved to be about 40', and this I must always allow for.

So, of course, must we allow for the difference between magnetic and true north; that is, the difference in the current calendar year for the particular region where we are working. The necessary information is usually available in the margins of Ordnance Survey and similar maps.

Granted this, the compass must be the instrument of choice. It can be used in all weathers. If the lie of the land and the vegetation allow the human operator to place himself in line with the poles, he is able to utilize the compass; whereas frequently it would be impossible to position a theodolite because of dense undergrowth, precipitous terrain, and so forth. Some might think that the theodolite is used by serious professionals and the compass by cavalier amateurs. But almost all our tombs were irregular when first constructed and have suffered damage over the millennia, and if so the compass can normally give all the orientation information that survives. While the theodolite user spends valuable time struggling to position his instrument on the axis of the monument, and waiting for the sun to appear, and writing grant proposals to support this wasteful procedure, tombs are being destroyed and his own productive years are ebbing away.

The great majority of our tombs are megalithic, and the great majority of these have a backstone which was usually the first slab to be erected and which normally faces along the axis of symmetry, towards the entrance or passage opposite. The orientation of such a tomb is then from the centre of the backstone to the centre of the entrance or passage — if the entrance is destroyed, the direction faced by the backstone will itself give a reasonable indication. Very occasionally, however, there are problems, as when the axis is not orthogonal to the backstone, or the passage changes direction.

When this happens the orientation of the tomb may not be well-defined, and we may puzzle over the motive for the apparent change of mind on the part of the constructors.

Archaeotopography and archaeoastronomy

Archaeoastronomy has become an accepted term, and as the founder of a journal with that name the present writer is as much to blame as anyone. Yet it suggests that, come what may, the measurer of orientations is determined to identify an astronomical motivation in the minds of the prehistoric builders, and that he had this intention even before he got anywhere near the site. Given the extravagant claims made a generation ago for Stonehenge and for the stone circles of Britain — claims that not unreasonably continue to arouse scepticism and even hostility among British archaeologists — this is doubly unfortunate; for the example of the mosques shows that motivations for the choice of orientation that are of great significance may in fact have nothing whatsoever to do with the sky.

Francis Bacon, the early seventeenth-century author whose methodology was later to be adopted by the infant Royal Society, argued that fact-collecting should precede theorizing, for only thus would prejudice be avoided. Modern philosophers of science view this approach with disdain, pointing out that the very choice of which facts to collect (to say nothing of the language in which the facts are described) involves theory: facts are 'theory-laden'. But there are merits in adopting something of a Baconian approach to the measurement of orientations. True, our decision to make quantitative measures, and our choice of what to measure, reflect expectations as to what will prove significant. Yet there is much to be said for suspending judgement, first, as to whether or not the tomb constructors were constrained to follow some custom of orientation (though we shall find that they nearly always were); and second, as to whether that custom was motivated terrestrially (as with mosques) or celestially (as with churches). An example of how not to proceed was given by an article on the orientations of five megalithic tombs published a few years ago. From five tombs in one field it is scarcely possible to establish that the builders were following a custom, certainly not that the custom was astronomical, and most definitely not that the 'targets' were two specific stars and the sun and the moon.

Instead we shall attempt, in successive chapters, to present the data from our various regions before going on to interpret them. Criticisms of Bacon notwithstanding, the orientation of a tomb is normally an uncontroversial fact. That is, given that we are agreed that we wish to measure the azimuth (angle measured clockwise from true north) of the axis of the tomb in the direction from the inside out, any half-competent measure will yield approximately the same answer. Likewise, the existence of a range of orientations for tombs of this type and culture will (if it exists) be an uncontroversial fact, though there may be discussion as to the limits of the range — some may prefer a narrow range and accept several anomalous orientations, whereas others may opt for a wider range and fewer anomalies. Archaeologists can scarcely do other than welcome these facts, and in my experience this approach has formed the basis of delightful collaborations with leading archaeologists of many countries. Indeed, I have sometimes been invited to lecture to students of archaeology, and have then taken them out into the field and shown them how to measure orientations.

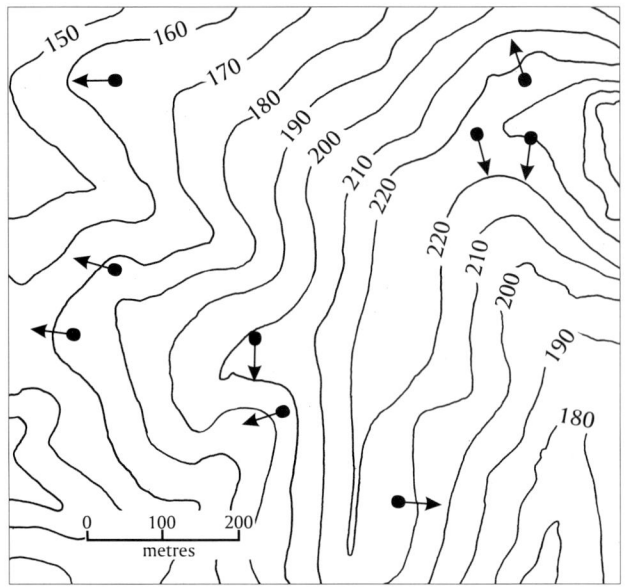

The topography of Mycenae, the nine tholos tombs being indicated by circles, with arrows to show the orientations of their passages. These orientations are in all directions, but we see that eight of the nine tombs face downhill. The three tombs in the upper-right of the plan are immediately west of the Lion Gate, the main entrance to the Citadel. (Orientations courtesy of Amanda-Alice Maravelia.)

The systematic measurement of orientations, and the establishment of the (approximate) ranges that reflect the customs followed by the prehistoric builders, I call *archaeotopography*, a term coined for me by a colleague in Classics. Archaeotopography alone can contribute in important ways to archaeological debate, and I give two examples of this.

Near the citadel of Mycenae in southern Greece, in the third quarter of the second millennium BC, nine great tombs were built to house royal burials. These tombs have an approach passage leading to an entrance, inside which is a false-cupola, beehive-shaped chamber or 'tholos'. A Mycenaean tholos is constructed of stones arranged in a series of circular courses, each course on top of the preceding one, the diameter reducing as the height above ground level increases. These are majestic monuments: the so-called Treasury of Atreus has 33 courses of hammer-dressed ashlar blocks rising to a height of no less than 13½ metres and creating the inspiring effect of a cathedral. Only an obsession with the belief that enlightenment must have come from the east — *ex oriente lux* — could have led archaeologists of the early twentieth century to see the great Mycenaean tholoi as the models for the modest and crudely constructed Spanish tombs pictured on pages 9 and 57 and discussed in Chapter 5. Nevertheless, Mycenaean colonizers were imagined to have settled at Los Millares in Almería, and to have followed the customs they had known back home when building tholoi in their new colony.

Had one of these archaeologists practised archaeotopography, their successors would have been spared embarrassment when radiocarbon dating revealed that the Almerian tombs in fact were a millennium and a half *older* than those of Mycenae — for an analysis of the orientations shows that the Mycenaean tombs face downhill, while 60 out of 66 tholoi at Los Millares face easterly, between 62° and 117° (Table 5.1): not only had the supposed colonizers forgotten how to build in enduring blocks of stone, but they had apparently changed their religion into the bargain.

The second example concerns the relation between the Nuraghic culture of Sardinia which, as we shall see in Chapter 12, flourished during the second millennium, and the Bronze Age 'talayotic' culture of Menorca (Chapter 11), which was at its height around the end of the same millennium. Both cultures take their name from the truncated conical stone towers that are prominent in the landscapes, and a photograph of a 'nuraghe' can look very much like a photograph of a 'talayot'. Furthermore, with a little imagination one might persuade oneself that the Nuraghic communal tombs, which are known as *tombe di giganti* or 'tombs of giants', bear some similarity to the Menorcan 'navetas', communal tombs so called because of their resemblance to upturned boats. Does this warrant the conclusion that the talayotic culture was established on Menorca by Sardinians who arrived by boat and who proceeded to build in accordance with the customs they had known back home? Thus Juan Comas writes: "The analogy between *talayots–nuraghi* and *navetas–tombe di giganti* has come to be generally accepted among archaeologists ... [who] conclude that towards 1200 BC an invasion of Sardinians arrived on Menorca and covered the island with talayots and navetas."[5]

Most archaeologists of the region know one of the islands involved but have only a passing acquaintance with the other, and this may explain the dubious claims of similarity. A typical Menorcan talayot is simply a mass of boulders, with only a tiny passage leading to a cramped chamber. But a nuraghe is a complex structure with a lofty central chamber made of false-cupola construction of the highest quality. Its similarity to a crude Menorcan talayot is very far from obvious.

Still less obvious is the parallel between a *tomba di giganti* and a naveta, for the typical *tomba di giganti* has a narrow chamber from whose entrance two imposing arms extend in a curve to either side, as though to embrace the sacred ground in front of the tomb. By contrast, a naveta, as its name implies, is a spacious chamber which a dozen people can occupy without crowding, and it is often built on two floors with a substantial ceiling of flat stones in between.

But whether the constructions are similar might be thought a matter of opinion. By contrast, orientations being quantitative, it is an undeniable matter of fact that the customs of orientation were utterly different, the Sardinian tombs facing easterly and the Menorcan westerly; and so presumably were the underlying religious beliefs. Archaeotopography thus poses a severe difficulty for those who claim Sardinian origins for the talayotic culture of Menorca; and the problem arises from the basic, uncontrovertible measurements. The contrast between the ranges of tomb orientations in the two cultures is a fact beyond all dispute.

Motivations

When the data have been collected, the first question is whether the orientations fall within a range. In the little island of Pantelleria, as we shall see in Chapter 13, the passages in the burial mounds known as 'sesi' display no evident pattern of orientation. In Tunisia (see Chapter 14) there are vast (and very late) necropolises in which it seems that the tombs look downhill simply because this was the least laboursome way to lay them out. But if the data do reveal the existence of a range of preferred orientations, then this range is a clue to the motivation in the minds of the prehistoric builders when they chose the directions in which their monuments were to face.

What was this motivation? In reasoning from the effect (the range) to the cause we loosen our grip on certainty; we speculate, and opinions among us may reasonably differ. The fundamental question will be, whether or not the motivation originated in the sky (as with churches), or whether (as with mosques) it was terrestrial, or even meteorological — to face the warmth of the sun or to shelter from the prevailing wind.[6]

But in many of the cultures that we shall study, there is a consistency of orientation over a wide geographical region, and it seems that only in the sky can we find the means by which such uniformity could have been achieved. A striking example of this phenomenon is displayed by the seven-stone 'antas' of Portugal and adjacent regions of Spain, which we discuss in Chapter 6. We have measured 177 of these tombs over an area that extends across central Portugal and into the neighbouring Spanish provinces, and every single one is oriented around east or east-southeast, within a range of less than 60°. Central Portugal is flat, and there is certainly no geographical feature that could explain such extraordinary consistency over such a vast area. Instead, we have here a most compelling proof of the presence of an astronomically-motivated custom, and so we can be confident, indeed certain, that we are engaged in archaeoastronomy.

Some simple astronomy

Whenever an astronomical interpretation is a possibility, the investigator must measure not only the direction of the axis of the tomb or temple but also the angular altitude (in degrees above the horizontal) of the skyline towards which the monument looks. This is necessary because in Mediterranean latitudes, astronomical bodies never rise or set vertically but do so along inclined paths. So for example at the (astronomical) equinoxes, the sun is crossing the celestial equator and from a flat terrain (or at sea) is seen to rise almost due east. But if instead there is a hill to the east of the monument, the sun must climb behind the hill and reach the summit before it first becomes visible; and while climbing it is also moving south, so that its eventual appearance, even though this is the day of the equinox, is some way to the south of east.

The angular altitude of the skyline can be measured with a theodolite or with various other instruments, in particular with a hand-held clinometer. Unfortunately those admirable archaeologists who make careful compass measures (and even meticulously record the date of each so that the appropriate correction can be made for the difference between magnetic and true north) are usually unaware of the need to measure angular altitudes. This is regrettable, especially when the labour and cost of revisiting the sites is prohibitive (if, indeed, the tombs still exist); in such cases we shall be forced to assume a typical altitude for the purposes of calculation, consoling ourselves with the knowledge that in moderate terrain an error in angular altitude is only of secondary importance, and that in any case we usually have no way of knowing the height of the surrounding trees when the tomb was built.

The third datum needed for an astronomical interpretation is the latitude of the site. This is needed because, for example, the direction of sunrise on a given day of the year varies with latitude (with the result that the amplitude of the range of sunrise increases as we move further north). Fortunately our calculations are not sensitive to minor changes in latitude, and a latitude accurate to one-tenth of a degree (easily found from maps) is entirely sufficient.

Given azimuth, angular altitude of the skyline, and latitude, the corresponding astronomical 'declination' is easily found from a simple trigonometrical formula or, better still, by obtaining from Clive Ruggles of Leicester University a copy of his computer program that does the calculation and also takes atmospheric refraction into account (see his Web site http://www.le.ac.uk/archaeology/rug/). Declination is the angular position of a heavenly body north (positive) or south (negative) of the celestial equator. This is a matter of astronomy and has nothing to do with the location of any particular archaeological site. At a given 'epoch', such as AD 2000 or 2000 BC, each star has a given declination; and the declinations of all the brighter stars for present, past and future epochs can most easily be found by consulting a published catalogue. The individual ('proper') motion of a given star across the sky is invariably tiny and the change this produces even after centuries is usually negligible for our purposes (though it was in fact taken into account by the authors of the catalogue we recommend[7]); but the star's declination, being measured north or south of the celestial equator, changes dramatically with time because the earth is not a perfect sphere, and so the gravitational pull of the moon and sun causes its axis to wobble (taking the celestial equator with it), with a period of nearly 26,000 years. What today we see as the Pole Star (and to which we therefore currently assign a declination of nearly +90°) will be the Pole Star again around AD 28,000, but not in the intervening millennia. This wobble, or 'precession', means that in prehistoric times the axis of the Earth was tilted in a direction different from the one it has today, and so the prehistoric Menorcans (for example) were looking towards a somewhat different region of the heavenly sphere from that seen by the modern inhabitants of the island. In consequence the Southern Cross, though today invisible from Menorca, could be seen there in talayotic times, a fact that will prove to be of significance for our understanding of the talayotic sanctuaries and their orientations.

Perhaps surprisingly, the dramatic change over time in the stars visible from a given place is not matched by comparable changes in the sun and the moon. The sun today has declination +23½° at the summer solstice (that is, on midsummer's day) and −23½° at the winter solstice, while about 2900 BC the corresponding values were ±24°. As a result, as seen from a given site, the sun now rises at midsummer in a position marginally south of where it rose in prehistoric times, and the total range of sunrise has correspondingly shrunk; but the change is small, indeed negligible for many purposes, as modern druids attending sunrise at Stonehenge on midsummer's day, or the privileged few packed inside Newgrange at dawn in midwinter, will testify.

No one doubts the great significance for prehistoric Mediterranean peoples of the winter solstice. As the solstice approached, the sun's rising point had for almost six months been moving south along the horizon, and of late the days had been getting alarmingly short and gloomy. Unless the sun called a halt and reversed the movement of sunrise, darkness and cold would take over, and human life would cease. Happily, at the solstice, and no doubt in response to ritual appeals, the sun did stop its alarming southwards progress and began its return with the promise of a new year. The Romans celebrated this with the feast of Sol Invictus, the Unconquered Sun, and since the actual date of Christ's birth was unknown, early Christians made this their feast of Christmas. No such life-threatening crisis surrounds the summer solstice, but Christians have made this the feast of John the Baptist, who was to decrease as Christ increased.

The significance for prehistoric peoples of the two equinoxes — when Christians celebrate the conceptions of Christ and of John the Baptist — is more problematic. The scientific definition is impossibly abstract for our present purposes: the days when the sun crosses the equator and so has 0° declination; the days when on an atmosphere-free earth and with a level horizon and accurate clocks, night and day would be shown to be equal. On the real earth, with its atmosphere, night and day are far from equal ('equinox') at the equinoxes.[8]

If our prehistoric peoples did see the equinoxes as significant, there are perhaps three ways in which they could have determined them. The first is by counting the days between one solstice and the next, and reckoning the middle day between these two events. But it is very difficult to identify the actual day of a solstice, since the movement of sunrise along the horizon slows as the sun nears the solstice, and for several days around that time it rises at almost the same point of the horizon. Any error in the identification would undermine the calculation of the equinox, and this would have major consequences for the inferred direction of equinox sunrise, since around equinox the position of sunrise changes substantially from one day to the next. The method also presupposes the ability to count into the hundreds.

The second method (assuming the horizon is level) is by bisecting the angle between the solstice sunrises. But the Greek geometers arrived at the concept of bisecting an angle only after a long process of abstraction, and it seems unlikely that prehistoric peoples could have matched this.

The third method, again assuming a level horizon, involves positioning two poles in the ground each morning so that they are aligned with the sunrise. Equinox is then the day when the same two poles, viewed in the opposite direction the same evening, are found to be aligned with sunset. This is indeed a simple and practical procedure. But just why prehistoric peoples should have found these alignments of interest is not obvious, and we shall maintain a lively scepticism towards claims of an equinox alignment.

The moon's cycles are more complex than those of the sun. Not only does it go through its monthly cycle, giving welcome illumination during the night for part (but only part) of each four weeks, but moonrises span their full range over this period (rather than taking a year to move from north to south and back, as does the sun). Furthermore, the range of moonrise itself expands and contracts over a period of 18.6 years, and it did the same in prehistoric times. For nine years or so its range is greater than that of sunrise, and then for nine years it is less. At maximum the moon's declination is 5° greater in each direction than that of the sun at its extremes (that is, at the solstices), and at monthly intervals around this time it rises (and sets) several degrees further north than the sun does at midsummer and (two weeks later) correspondingly further south than the sun does at midwinter. Watchers in any given location will see the full moon nearest midsummer rising (and setting) further south on the skyline than it has been seen for a generation, and that nearest midwinter correspondingly far north; and it could be that these extreme limits — known as the major lunar standstills — seemed to certain prehistoric peoples so remarkable as to call for tombs or sanctuaries to be aligned in those directions.

Then, somewhat over nine years later, the range shrinks to a minimum, when the moon rises and sets at the so-called minor lunar standstills. It could be that these horizon positions too were of such interest as to be the 'targets' of prehistoric structures; but since the moon rises and sets at these positions every month, this is inherently less plausible, and to establish the claim requires correspondingly more convincing evidence.

Because for half of the moon's 18.6-year cycle the range of moonrise is (and was) greater than the range of sunrise, during this time any tomb that faced sunrise (twice a year) also faced moonrise twice a month. This can make it difficult to distinguish between the sun and moon as 'targets' of orientations. However, the southern limit of the range of tomb orientation frequently coincides with midwinter sunrise, and if so, this encourages us to think of sunrise as the target.

In Mesoamerica we know from written evidence that intense interest was taken in cycles of planets. But their motions are complex, and their cycles difficult to perceive without the ability to keep written records and to make arithmetical calculations. If therefore the planets were of interest to prehistoric peoples of the Mediterranean, it was probably simply as 'stars' that moved among the other stars, and any trace of this is more likely to be found in rock art than among alignments.

In conclusion, then, we can be sure that the winter solstice was of great concern to the peoples whose structures we study, because of its decisive importance to the continuation of human life. The summer solstice, the equinoxes, the major and minor lunar standstills, may possibly have been of interest to our monument builders; and if so, this may reveal itself to us in alignments to sunrise and sunset (or moonrise and moonset) at these times. But following William of Ockham, we shall not "multiply entities without necessity": we shall favour the simplest possible explanation of astronomical alignments.

Some practicalities

Our measurements of monuments (azimuth, angular altitude, latitude, and corresponding declination) are set out in the Corpus Mensurarum at the end of this volume. But lengthy tables of numbers do not easily convey the picture that is emerging, and so in the successive chapters we give visual summaries of the relevant data.

These take two forms. If the data are few in number, we present them in the form of a circle or part thereof, with north at the top and lines radiating from the centre to indicate the various azimuths. So ingrained is the convention that 'north is up', that such a chart instantly conveys whether the orientations are easterly or southerly or whatever. However, if the data are numerous and the lines crowded, it is easy to underestimate the number of tombs that face in the most usual directions — and one is tempted to give undue attention to any anomalous orientations. In such cases we present the data in the form of a histogram, with a horizontal axis measured in 5° intervals and vertical bars whose heights correspond to the numbers of tombs whose azimuths fall within the particular 5° intervals.

In describing the customs embodied in these charts, we find it convenient to use a small number of acronyms. This is because four patterns occur over and over again. The overwhelming majority of orientations of tombs in the west Mediterranean face the eastern half of the horizon, while a minority — in Mediterranean France and adjacent Cataluña, and in the Balearics — face the western half. Of those that face easterly, some groups of tombs have orientations within the range 60°–120° or thereabouts, while others have a wider range, from 60° to due south or thereabouts. The former we term SR and the latter SR/SC. Similarly, tombs that face the western half of the horizon sometimes have orientations within the range 240°–300° (these we term SS), and sometimes within the wider range from due south to 300° (SD/SS). It will emerge that these acronyms have been chosen because they are abbreviations for 'sunrise', 'sun-climbing', 'sunset' and 'sun-descending', respectively, but we shall of course have to justify this astronomical interpretation of the motivation underlying the custom embodied in the data.

Azimuths of Solar and Lunar Events

Azimuths (in degrees) of sunrise and moonrise for sites with a level horizon, in 2900 BC, when the sun had dec. ±24° at the solstices, and the moon had dec. ±29° at the major standstills and ±19° at the minor standstills. These declinations were (and are) slowly diminishing, and today they are about ±23½°, ±28½° and ±18½° respectively. That is, the same events now take place marginally closer to due east than they did in prehistoric times. The effect of an elevated horizon is to move each of the events further south. The corresponding azimuths for sunset and moonset are obtained by taking 360° and subtracting the listed quantity.

lat.	30°	32°	34°	36°	38°	40°	42°	44°	46°
MLS (north)	56	55½	54½	53½	52½	51	49½	48	46½
SS (summer)	61½	61	60	59½	58½	57½	56	55	53½
mls (north)	68	67½	67	66½	66	65	64½	63½	62½
mls (south)	112½	113	113½	114	114½	115½	116½	117½	118½
SS (winter)	117½	118½	119	119½	120½	121½	122½	124	125
MLS (south)	124½	125	126	127	128½	129½	131	133	135

MLS: moonrise at major lunar standstill
SS: sunrise at solstice
mls: moonrise at minor lunar standstill

Further reading

C. Ruggles, *Astronomy in prehistoric Britain and Ireland* (New Haven and London, 1999).

J. A. Belmonte, *Las leyes del cielo: Astronomía y civilizaciones antiguas* (Madrid, 1999).

Notes and references

1   S. Piggott, *Ancient Europe* (Edinburgh, 1965), 60.

2   William Wordsworth, "On seeing the Foundation preparing for the Erection of Rydal Chapel, Westmoreland", 1823.

3   Sir Henry Chauncy, *The historical antiquities of Hertfordshire* (London, 1700), i, 88.

4   An extreme example of this occurred in a recent paper in which the authors found a difference of over 3° in their two measures by theodolite of the orientation of a tomb, which "can be explained by the fact that the corridor ... deviates to the south". This is precisely why use of a theodolite was inappropriate for this tomb — or, in plain English, a waste of time.

5   J. Comas, *Aportaciones al estudio de la prehistoria de Menorca* (Madrid, 1936), 21–22. More recently L. Pericot García (*The Balearic Islands* (London, 1972), 79) has commented: "The 'giants' tombs' of Sardinia have always

been mentioned as possible prototypes for navetas, for the building techniques employed are similar."

6   Y. Chevalier, *L'architecture des dolmens entre Languedoc et centre-ouest de la France* (Bonn, 1984), 32, suggests that the Languedoc-type dolmens that we discuss in Chapter 9 "semblent avoir été dirigés le plus souvent le dos aux vents dominants qui viennent du Nord et du Nord-Est dans la région languedocienne".

7   G. S. Hawkins and S. K. Rosenthal, "5,000- and 10,000-year star catalogs", *Smithsonian contributions to astrophysics*, x/2 (1967).

8   On this see C. L. N. Ruggles, "Whose equinox", *AA*, no. 22 (1997), S45–50. This topic, along with the other issues discussed in this chapter, are treated at length in his *Astronomy in prehistoric Britain and Ireland* (see above), the first purchase for any serious student of Old World archaeoastronomy.

I

ORIENTATIONS OF TEMPLES AND SANCTUARIES

The Temples of Malta and Gozo

There is little doubt that the communal tombs to which our later chapters are dedicated not only enshrined the religious beliefs of the builders, but were themselves places of ritual. But two of the cultures of the central and western Mediterranean went further, and systematically constructed for themselves sacred buildings whose primary purpose was ritual. Both cultures developed on small islands: on Malta and neighbouring Gozo, which lie between Sicily and north Africa; and on Menorca and Mallorca, two of the Balearic Islands. In the present chapter we discuss the temples of Malta and Gozo, and try to unravel the mystery of the tallies engraved on the entrance to one of them.

The temples

The temples of Malta and Gozo are perhaps the best-kept secret in Mediterranean archaeology. Only a generation ago, they seemed unremarkable when compared with the great cultures of the eastern Mediterranean: archaeologists put the arrival of man on the islands at perhaps 2300 BC, and so the islands' temples were thought to be later than many of the great monuments of

The main façade of the temple at Hagar Qim, with the subsidiary temple in the right foreground

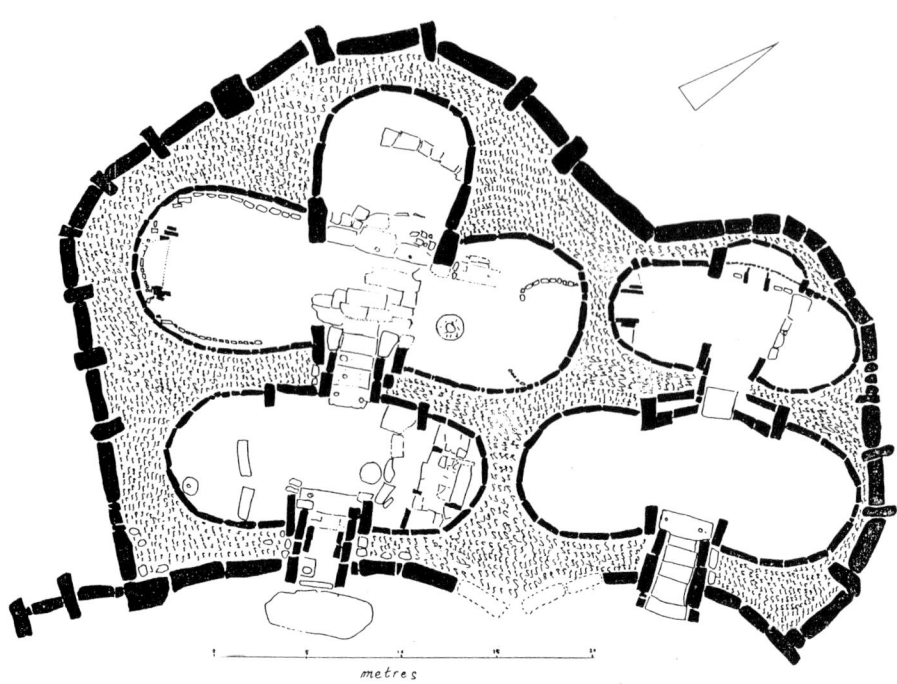

The twin temples at Ggantija. Ggantija I, to the left, was built before Ggantija II, which faces 9° further south. (Courtesy of J. D. Evans.)

Egypt and possibly contemporary with the palaces of Minoan Crete, neither of which they rival. However, in an astonishing rewriting of prehistory, radiocarbon dating has since put the arrival of man at around 5000 BC, and the introduction of pottery characteristic of the Temple Period earlier than 4000 BC. Temple construction began about 3600 BC and was already drawing to a close when the Great Pyramid of Giza was completed in the middle of the third millennium BC. The complex and magnificently-worked twin temples of Ggantija on Gozo, for example, date from the middle to late fourth millennium BC, and one wonders if there was then a structure of comparable grandeur anywhere on earth. Yet these remarkable monuments remain relatively unknown.

Within the Temple Period, archaeologists propose 'phases' of temple construction on the basis of development in the plan of temple structures, increasing sophistication in building technique, stone dressing and decoration, and evidence from pottery and other finds. But the sequence is not always secure, and for our purposes it will be sufficient to rely on structural evidence of priority (as, for example, when a later temple is erected against the side of an existing one) and on the two broadest phases, which are securely established: the Ggantija Phase, 3600–3000 BC, and the Tarxien Phase, 3000–2500 or a little later. Temple building then came to an abrupt end, for reasons that remain shrouded in mystery.

Most (but not all) of the temples were built in groups of two or more on the same site, in

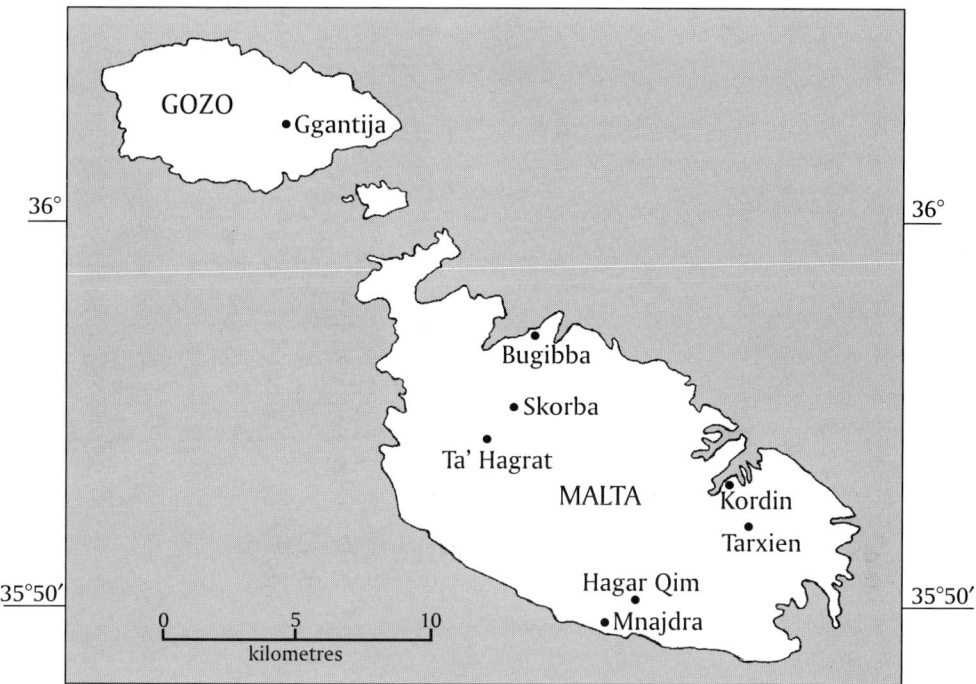

The temples of Malta and Gozo.

successive stages. A glance at the site-plan of the twin temples at Ggantija shows that they were constructed around axes that are well-defined (and in this instance nearly parallel). Were the Ggantija axes, and those of other temples, selected for reasons astronomical? The question was seriously discussed in print for the first time in 1980, by two members of staff from the University of Malta, George Agius and Frank Ventura.[1]

A fundamental problem they faced was that the clarity of structure we see in Ggantija is far from typical. At Hagar Qim, for example, in addition to the original main axis, we find an interlocking network of structures, with axes leading in all manner of directions, some through an entrance leading to the exterior, but others purely internal to the building. Which of these should be taken into account?

The answer adopted by Agius and Ventura was what one might describe as *maximal*. That is, an axis was given the benefit of the doubt if it was clearly a feature of the construction, even if it was not a true axis of symmetry. At Hagar Qim, they accepted the main axis in both directions together with four unidirectional axes (measured from the perspective of those within and looking out), and so they derived for this temple no fewer than six azimuths. In this way, for Malta and Gozo they accumulated a total of 26 azimuths. Among these there was a clear concentration of 20 azimuths between 128° and 230° — roughly, between southeast and southwest — but the remaining six (including four from Hagar Qim) showed no pattern.

This seemed to call for further investigation, and so in June 1991 Giorgia Foderà Serio of

The temple complex at Mnajdra. Mnajdra III, to the right, is the earliest, and its inner entrance pillars are engraved with the tallies that we discuss below. Mnajdra I, to the left, is anomalous in facing almost due east. (Photograph courtesy of the Museum of Archaeology, Malta.)

Palermo Observatory and I sailed to Malta where we were met by Frank Ventura. In place of the earlier maximal approach, we adopted instead a *minimal* one — for in the study of orientations it is difficult enough to make sense of authentic measures, and well-nigh impossible if the authentic measures are contaminated by spurious ones. In the present case this meant that we admitted an axis into consideration only if we were convinced that it was an unequivocal axis of symmetry. In consequence we accepted the two at Ggantija and the three at Mnajdra, but at Hagar Qim we rejected all except the principal axis, and even this we accepted only in the direction towards the main doorway (because only in this direction does the axis lead to what was probably an open forecourt). We were able to obtain an orientation for the axis of a second, subsidiary temple at Hagar Qim, despite its poor condition. At Skorba one of the two axes has a bend near the entrance and so its orientation is less well-defined than elsewhere. At Ta' Hagrat we accepted the principal axis; but not that of the side-temple (which is probably later), because it leads into the main temple rather than to the exterior. The minimal remains at Bugibba, where the monument now adorns the grounds of a tourist hotel, provided another axis, as did Kordin III. All the other temples were rejected, usually because of their ruinous condition, with the exception of the complex and difficult structures at Tarxien. There the elaborate Temple I is clearly admissible, as is Temple III. The early Temple IV, ruined though it is, has a clear axis of symmetry and is also included. Temple II, however, is problematic. It was evidently built *after* Temple I and integrated

Orientations of 15 temple axes.

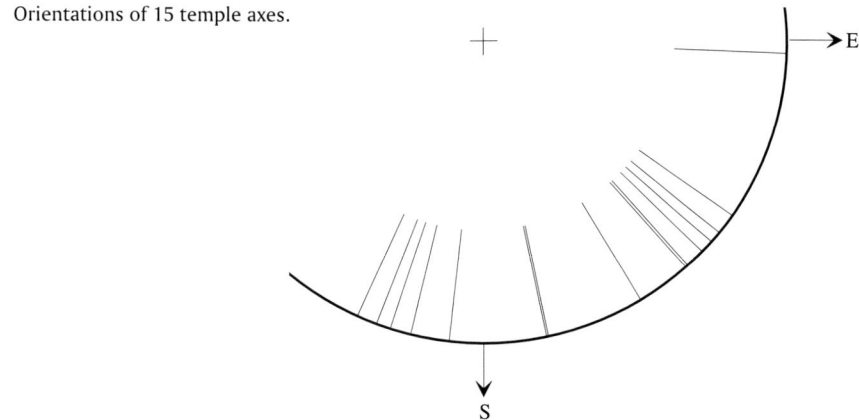

into it; and although it is on slightly higher ground, it seems doubtful whether it allowed a view of the sky to the observer looking along the axis (a surviving prehistoric clay model of the structure implies that the walls were high). We therefore rejected Temple II.

This left us with 15 orientations to determine. The 1980 Agius/Ventura azimuths had in most cases been measured with a theodolite, but a few had been estimated from published charts. We could safely use our compass, since Malta and Gozo are formed of coralline and globigerina limestone together with blue clay and greensand, and there is no reason to expect any magnetic anomaly. The azimuths listed in Table 3.1 of the Corpus Mensurarum at the end of this book are the directions from a pole placed on the temple axis near the axis's interior end (the pole being located midway between the side-walls at this point), to a pole at the midpoint of the entrance. The data are based on the compass alone in those cases where Agius and Ventura relied on charts; on the 1980 theodolite measure at Kordin, where in 1991 we were thwarted by the padlock which declined the respond to the key; and on a combination of theodolite and compass measures in other cases. The only non-trivial discrepancy was at Skorba, where the orientation is not well-defined.

The cited azimuth is that of the axis itself, but an observer within the temple who looked out through the entrance was of course able to see some distance to left and right, the width of his angle of view increasing the nearer he stood to the entrance. This means that we must regard the cited azimuth not as a precise orientation, but as a *guide* to the direction in which the monument was presumably intended to face.

When we examine the list of orientations, we note that Mnajdra I is exceptional. The azimuths of the remaining 14 axes are highly non-random, for the arc from Ggantija I (125½°) to Mnajdra III (204°) measures less than a quadrant of a circle. Such a concentration of axes cannot have come about by chance. Furthermore, the temple builders' interest in the sky is attested by the 'Tal-Qadi stone', a slab of globigerina limestone found at the Tal-Qadi temple and now in the Museum of Archaeology in Malta. Radial lines divide this surviving fragment into five segments, four of which are incised with symbols that appear to represent stars and the fifth with a lunar crescent. The declinations in the table show that all 14 axes are too far south ever to face the rising or setting sun, and that 12, if not 13, are too far south ever to face the rising or setting moon. Of course all the axes would have faced the sun daily as it was climbing or descending in the sky, and all or nearly all would have similarly faced the moon.

What of the stars? The Pleiades, a cluster known to be of keen interest to early cultures worldwide,[2] rose close to due east throughout the Temple Period, and so is a possible 'target' for Mnajdra I, but not for the 14 axes now under consideration. Sirius, the brightest star in the heavens, had declination −22½° in 3000 BC, within the range of sunrise, and so is again too far north. Canopus, the second brightest star in the heavens, was south of declination −55° throughout the Temple Period, and hence invisible from the islands. α Cen, the third brightest star, however, merits further consideration. Because of the precession of the earth's axis discussed in the last chapter, α Cen has been below the Maltese horizon throughout the Christian era; but in the early Temple Period it was prominent, being some 20° above the horizon when due south. It was preceded some 40 minutes earlier by the bright star β Cen, which itself was preceded an hour or so earlier by the Southern Cross, a star group that today is considered so striking as to be portrayed on the national flags of both New Zealand and Australia.[3] These stars of Centaurus and the Cross would have

The Tal-Qadi stone (photograph by Salvatore Serio, taken by permission of the Museum of Archaeology, Malta). Note the incised lunar crescent and star-like symbols.

Declinations of bright southern stars during the Temple Period.

	3500 BC	3000 BC	2500 BC
	°	°	°
α Cru	−35.97	−37.85	−39.89
β Cru	−32.01	−33.97	−36.08
γ Cru	−29.71	−31.57	−33.61
β Cen	−31.35	−33.67	−36.12
α Cen	−33.24	−35.68	−38.20
Canopus	−57.37	−56.35	−55.43

formed an impressive procession across the southern sky in the Temple Period.

The stars' declinations are listed above. At the beginning of the Temple Phase, the first star of the Cross, γ Cru, rose behind the hill opposite Ggantija with azimuth 128° (though it would have needed to climb higher before becoming visible above the atmosphere). This is just 2½° south of the axis of Ggantija I, an acceptable amount in the light of our earlier remarks about the width of the field of view through the entrance to the temple. We see from Table 3.1 that Ta' Hagrat would have faced the rising of γ Cru in 3500 BC, that γ Cru rose slightly south of Hagar Qim I when it was built early in the third millennium, and that at all the other temples the Cross and the two bright stars of Centaurus would be well above the horizon when they appeared over the axial line of the temple.

When, in the next chapter, we come to consider the southerly orientations of the (much later) sanctuaries of Menorca, we shall have stronger arguments in favour of the hypothesis that the sanctuaries faced the Cross-Centaurus star group. The star group was then much lower in the sky and closer to the horizon, and we shall argue that this must be the reason why the locations chosen for the sanctuaries always had an uninterrupted view to the south — for otherwise the star group would not have been visible. Two thousand years earlier, the star group was sufficiently high in the sky to be easily visible from most locations on the flat islands of Malta and Gozo, and therefore — *if* the temples did indeed face the Cross-Centaurus group, as I suggest — there was no need for them to be built in carefully chosen sites; which unfortunately deprives the modern investigator of persuasive evidence. We can therefore do no more than offer the Cross-Centaurus stars as a *possible* reason for the southerly orientations.

The suggestion does, however, account for the surprising construction of twin temples at Ggantija, where examination of the dividing wall shows that Ggantija I, seen in the site-plan to the left (that is, south), was built first, and Ggantija II was added alongside at a later date, to face 9° further south. We have seen that, when Ggantija I was first constructed, the Cross-Centaurus group would have been glimpsed rising in the entrance to the temple. But precession, decade by decade, would have carried the rising positions of the stars further and further south, and the time would have come — all too quickly — when Ggantija I faced unacceptably far north of these positions and the stars could no longer be seen in the entrance. The modified orientation incorporated in Ggantija II would have rectified this mistake.

We have assumed throughout that the temple orientations were chosen to meet the requirements of the élite who were within the temple and looking out through the entrance. A similar 'inside-out' orientation is virtually certain in the case of the Menorcan sanctuaries, many of which are on a downward slope. It must however be reported that five eminent archaeologists of Malta have taken our data (of course, with acknowledgement) and given it an 'outside-in' interpretation, from the viewpoint of the 'many' gathered outside the temple and looking inwards.[4] They write that

> a more probable orientation for the vast majority of the congregation would have been towards the focus of liturgical intensity, that is into the interior of the monument itself.... In the model of orientation we have proposed above, the primary orientation of most temples was towards the north-west rather than to the south-east. Given the cultural context of the Maltese islands, this might be interpreted both as an orientation towards Sicily in terms of ancestral origins and towards Pantelleria, Sicily and Lipari in terms of the exotic products brought into the island.[5]

They conclude in eirenic fashion:

> The alternative interpretations of orientation, although geometrically opposed, are not necessarily mutually exclusive. We suggest that the temples in their later complex form emphasize the presence of two principal perspectives in society: that of the priests and that of the congregation. The priests inside might have elaborated a protected and exclusive astronomical lore derived from observations over the shoulders of the congregation. The congregation could have retained a more general concept of a broadly conceived ancestral direction given distant but tangible form by the precious exotic fragments housed in the inner recesses of the temple.[6]

Whatever the truth of the matter, it is heartening to find archaeologists taking on board the factual, 'archaeotopographical' elements of our investigation and using these data in their own researches.

The anomaly of Mnajdra I

But what of the exceptional (easterly) orientation of Mnajdra I? When we take the skyline altitude into account, we find that the temple faced the rising of celestial bodies with declination almost exactly 0°. This is, of course, the declination of the sun at what we moderns term the equinoxes. However, as we saw in the previous chapter, the nominal equality of night and day is an abstract concept that supposes a level horizon on an atmosphere-free earth (and accurate clocks to confirm the equality), and this has no relevance to prehistory. We also considered there the possibility that prehistoric peoples may have seen a special significance either in the direction that (geometrically) bisected the directions of sunrise at the solstices, or in the days of the year that were (arithmetically) midway between the solstices.

It seems unlikely that the concept of the bisection of an angle existed in Malta two-and-a-half millennia before Euclid. But perhaps this should not be ruled out entirely, and accordingly, in 1981, Ventura and Agius organized a systematic search of the hill facing the temple, for any indication of a marker that might have been used to record the position of a solstice sunrise.[7] They were rewarded with the discovery of a hole some 35cm in diameter and of similar depth, on the horizon as seen from the temple. It was impossible to demonstrate that the hole was man-made, still less to date it. Nevertheless, theodolite measures and calculations showed that at the time of the winter solstice around 3000 BC, at the moment when the lower edge of the sun touched the skyline, its right (southern) edge would have touched a pole inserted in the hole; and this would have given observers at the temple a fair indication of when the sun had reached its extreme position.

Was there a matching hole for the summer solstice? Investigations were hampered by unhelpful landowners who use the land partly for cultivation and partly for hunting and bird-trapping, and who did not welcome intruders. Nevertheless, the only hole that was a possible candidate proved to be 3° out of position.

The hypothesis of a geometrical determination of 'equinox' was therefore rejected. The counting of days, however, did remain a possibility, and we shall shortly come to evidence from Mnajdra itself that the temple builders were fully able to handle the simple arithmetic involved in counting days of the year. The 'winter solstice' post could have been used to determine the (approximate) day of the winter solstice; and from this a people with sufficient ability in counting could have determined the number of days in the year, and therefore the number of days in one-quarter of the year. After all, a contemporary culture, the Egyptian, was able to do that and much more besides.

However, as we saw in Chapter 2, establishing the exact day of a solstice is a difficult task, for the sun rises in almost the same place for several days around the actual solstice; and an error in the determination of the solstice would be reflected in an error in the day supposedly midway between the solstices, when the position of sunrise is changing rapidly and the error would result in a significant displacement of the supposed direction of sunrise at equinox.

A difficult task, but not perhaps an impossible one. Counts averaged out over a number of years could have yielded an equinox day of the required accuracy; but perhaps this is too much to expect. Alternatively, a post 3° south of the azimuth of the summer solstice would provide a marker for the sun's movement northwards as the solstice neared, and for its movement southwards after the solstice. If an observer kept tally of the number of days between the sun's touching the post before the solstice and its touching the post after, then the day midway between these two events would be the solstice.

It is therefore not impossible that Mnajdra I did indeed face the equinox sunrise. However, an alternative hypothesis is to hand, for around the time that Mnajdra I was built, the Pleiades had declination 0°, and we have already remarked on the significance of this asterism to early peoples in both the Old and the New World. Did the temple perhaps face, not the equinox sunrise, but the rising of the Pleiades?

The tally stones of Mnajdra III

Surprisingly, evidence in support of this is engraved in the very pillar stones that flank the entrance to the inner chamber of the earlier Mnajdra III. The westerly of these two pillars was re-erected early in the present century, while the easterly is *in situ*. Each is some 1½ metres

The view from the interior of Mnajdra III, with Mnajdra I in the right background. The two pillars flanking the entrance in the foreground are engraved with tallies.

high, and around 70cm in width, and each has rows of drilled holes that very strongly suggest tallies. But what tallies could have been of such permanent significance that they were drilled into temple stones that have survived five millennia?

That we might be dealing with tallies of *days* occurred to us when Giorgia Foderà came down to breakfast one morning and pointed out that the total number of holes on each stone was roughly equal to the number of days in half a year. But if the tallies were of intervals of days, what events did these intervals separate?

The west pillar, which had been re-erected, has some damage to a limited area of the inner face, and this interferes with the rows of holes in some places. The top three rows are made respectively of 12, 19 and 7 deeply incised holes, while above them are 16 faint dots each about 5mm wide. The fourth and fifth rows undulate somewhat but they run fairly parallel to each other. In two places the face of the stone is eroded and there is some uncertainty in the count. Thus the fourth row clearly contains 30, but possibly 31 holes, while the fifth row contains 31, or possibly 32 holes. The next two rows are the most problematic since damage to the stone surface blots out the middle section of both rows and possibly the left-hand part of the seventh row. In the case of the middle sections, we made a careful estimate of the number of holes in the gap, by measuring the length of the gap and comparing it to the undamaged part of each row. The sixth row thus consists of two parts with 12 holes each, separated by a gap which could have contained 11 holes, for a total of 35 holes. The seventh row has a part with 17 holes, a gap which could have contained 9 holes, and another part with 11 holes, bringing the total to 37 holes. The last row consists of 12 or 13 narrower holes.

The east pillar, never having fallen, is free from such damage. The upper part of its inner face still carries the pitted decoration which is characteristic of the Ggantija phase. Its middle part contains nine horizontal rows of deeply incised holes and a column of slightly shallower holes. In this case the record is very clear with an uncertainty of only 2 holes. The first three rows contain 19, 13 and 16 holes respectively. The fourth row has 3 holes and the fifth row consists of 4 holes, a long empty space, and 3 holes on the same level. The sixth row has 24 holes, but possibly it could have had 25. The seventh row has 11 and the eighth 25 holes. The ninth row runs from one edge

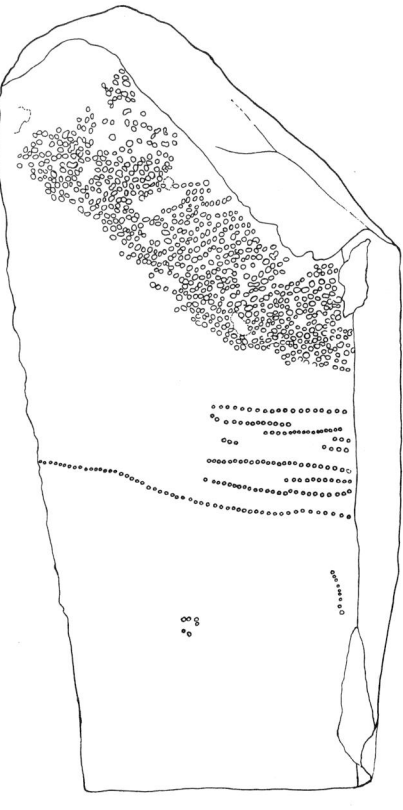

The east pillar of the entrance to Mnajdra III (drawing by Frank Ventura).

The proposed interpretation of the tallies, compared with dates of heliacal risings calculated for the latitude of Mnajdra, a star limiting magnitude of 6.0, and extinction factors of 0.20 and 0.25 mag/air mass (corresponding to good nights at a dry sea-level site and in a humid climate, respectively).

Interval (days)	Observed day	date	Star/Group	Calculated Day $k = 0.20$	$k = 0.25$
	96	6 Apr	Pleiades	96	100
19					
	115	25 Apr	α Tau	113	116
13					
	128	8 May	Hyades	125	128
16					
	144	24 May	α Ori	142/147	144/149
3					
	147	27 May	γ Ori	144	147
4 + 3					
	154	3 Jun	β Ori	155	158
24					
	178	27 Jun	α CMa	176	177
11					
	189	8 Jul	β CMa	186	188
25					
	214	2 Aug	α Boo	212	214
53					
	267	24 Sep	γ Cru	264	267
8 or 9					
	275/276	2/3 Oct	β Cen	277	279

of the slab to the other and it contains 53 holes. The column, part of which can be seen behind a smaller standing stone, contains 8, possibly 9 holes. (We might mention that away from the rows, in a lower part of the pillar, is a curious pattern of six smaller holes arranged in a roughly circular fashion, and it is not impossible that this represents the Pleiades; certainly it is quite different from the rows of holes.)

Comparing the clarity, layout and uniformity of the rows on the two pillars, one gets the impression that the record of the east pillar may be a 'fair copy' of that on the west stone.

Once the possibility had occurred to us, that the tallies represented day counts, and given the potential involvement of the Pleiades, we considered the possibility of day counts beginning with the heliacal rising of the Pleiades (the reappearance of the asterism in the dawn sky following a period of absence while lost in the glare of the sun). Bradley Schaefer of Yale University, who has made a special study of the dating of heliacal events, kindly computed the most likely date for the heliacal rising of the Pleiades in Malta in the Temple Period; but he pointed out that a small difference in air pressure alone could alter the date by as much as eight days.

On the other hand, the intervals *between* heliacal events are less affected, and although we could never expect an exact match between the tallies and such calculated intervals, we might find a match close enough to constitute convincing evidence in favour of such an interpretation.

We were of course well aware of the fundamental role of the heliacal rising of Sirius, the celestial embodiment of Isis, in the contemporary Egyptian calendar: the star rose (in mid-July) around the time of the flooding of the Nile, and if necessary, steps were then taken to adjust the calendar by means of an extra ('intercalary') month, so as to ensure that Sirius rose in the final month not only of the current year, but also of the year to come. To mark the 36 'weeks' of ten days each, other star groups or 'decans' were chosen: every ten days a new decan rose heliacally.[8] We also knew of the traditional folk-lore used even today by peasant farmers, whereby heliacal risings and settings mark the stages in the agricultural year. In written form this goes back to the eighth century BC, when the Greek poet Hesiod incorporated such a calendar in his poem, *Works and days*. When "rosy-fingered dawn gazes on Arcturus", for example, the grapes should be cut.[9] Clearly, Hesiod did not invent this calendar; he was availing himself of the wisdom acquired by farmers through long centuries of experience. Might our tallies be a calendar of heliacal events, perhaps listing the numbers of days between festivals that marked the reappearances in the dawn sky of important stars or asterisms?

We therefore established, with the help of Bradley Schaefer, the most likely dates for the heliacal risings of stars of magnitude 2 or brighter, and also the Pleiades and the Hyades, as seen from Malta in the Temple Period.[10] We included the Hyades despite their relative faintness, because of their mention by both Hesiod and Homer. Hesiod says that when, towards the end of October, "the Pleiades and the Hyades and the might of Orion set",[11] the farmer's year is ended and so the farmer must think again about ploughing. In Homer's *Iliad*, when Hephaistos made the shield of Achilles, "he wrought thereon Earth and Heaven and Sea, and the unwearied sun and the full moon and all the signs wherewith the Heaven is crowned, the Pleiades and the Hyades and the might of Orion and the Bear which also men call the Wain...".[12]

On the basis of these dates we were able to suggest a sequence of heliacal risings at intervals that correspond to the number of drilled holes in each row of the east pillar. The sequence started with an observation of the heliacal rise of the Pleiades, which on a good dry night occurred on 6 April (day 96 of the year). Nineteen days later, on 25 April (day 115), the heliacal rise of Aldebaran (α Tau) was observed and the interval between the first and second observation was (we suggest) recorded as a row of drilled holes. According to this reasoning, the next notable heliacal rise occurred thirteen days later, on 8 May (day 128). This date does not correspond to the heliacal rising of a bright star, but it does tie in with the estimated heliacal rising of the Hyades. The observations continued sixteen days later with the heliacal rise of α Ori on 24 May (day 144), followed by γ Ori on 27 May (day 147) and seven days (4 + 3 holes) later by β Ori and the stars of the belt of Orion. Each time, we suggest, the interval between one event and the next was recorded as a series of holes in a separate row on the stone pillar. The next heliacal rise of importance came twenty-four days later when Sirius (α CMa) rose on 27 June (day 178), close to the summer solstice. Eleven days later, on 8 July (day 189), β CMa joined Sirius in the pre-dawn sky, and the heliacal rising of Arcturus (α Boo) was noted on 2 August (day 214), after an interval of twenty-five days. A long period of fifty-three days then passed before the next notable heliacal rising, which was that of γ Cru on 24 September (day 267). If we are right in thinking that the temples were with one exception oriented to the Cross-Centaurus group, then this event would have been of special significance.

The record of drilled holes stops at this point (although the column of 8, or possibly 9, small holes elsewhere on the stone could correspond to the heliacal rising of β Cen, observed on 2 or

3 October (day 275 or 276)). The table shows the number of holes in each row of the tally (the numbers that we interpret as the intervals between heliacal risings), the dates of the presumed observations as derived from the tally, and the calculated dates of observation. Despite the lack of information concerning atmospheric conditions at the time of temple building, and the difficulties of calculating exact dates of heliacal risings, the correspondence between the presumed dates of observation and the calculated dates is remarkable.

Just how remarkable was shown when we experimented with other correlations. First, we attempted to fit the tally intervals with the comparable sequence of days of heliacal *settings* of the stars in the table. Second, we scrambled the order of tally intervals and compared the numbers thus derived against the calculated dates of heliacal risings. The poor correlations that resulted soon persuaded us of how striking is the fit generated by the scenario we have proposed.

To conclude: the drilled holes permanently incised on the stones at the entrance to the temple seem clearly to be tallies, and tallies of lasting importance and of religious significance. We think the evidence that the tallies were counts of days between heliacal risings is reasonably convincing, given (i) the match between the tallies and the calculated dates of rising, (ii) the known importance of heliacal risings in the Egyptian calendar during the Maltese Temple Period, and (iii) the enduring importance of heliacal events to agricultural communities.

If we are right, and the tally sequence on Mnajdra III began with the rising of the Pleiades, this suggests that the anomalous orientation of Mnajdra I was because it faced the rising of this same asterism.

Further reading

J. D. Evans, *The prehistoric antiquities of the Maltese islands* (London, 1971).

G. Foderà Serio, M. Hoskin and F. Ventura, "The orientations of the temples of Malta", *JHA*, xxiii (1992), 107–19.

D. H. Trump, *Malta: An archaeological guide* (1st edn, London, 1972; 2nd edn, Valetta, 1988).

F. Ventura, G. Foderà Serio and M. Hoskin, "Possible tally stones at Mnajdra, Malta", *JHA*, xxiv (1993), 171–83.

Notes and references

1 G. Agius and F. Ventura, *Investigation into the possible astronomical alignments of the Copper Age temples in Malta* (Malta, 1980). This booklet, published by Malta University Press, was republished in revised form in *Archaeo-astronomy* [bulletin], iv (1981), 10–21.

2 On this see A. F. Aveni, *Skywatchers of ancient Mexico* (Austin, Texas, 1980): "This star group has been of such great importance to nearly every developing civilization that a digression on Pleiades observations in general may be worthwhile" (p. 30). Similarly, D. R. Dicks, in *Early Greek astronomy to Aristotle* (London, 1970), remarks that the Pleiades star group "has been used by various people all over the world to mark the passage of time and the seasons of the year" (p. 36).

3 Aveni writes of the importance of the Southern Cross in Mesoamerica (*Skywatchers*, 252).

4 S. Stoddart *et al.*, "Cult in an island society: Prehistoric Malta in the Tarxien Period", *Cambridge archaeological journal*, iii (1993), 3–19.

5 *Ibid.*, 15–16.

6 *Ibid.*, 17.

7 Agius and Ventura, *Investigation*.

8 A good account of Egyptian calendarics is R. A. Parker, "Egyptian astronomy, astrology, and calendrical reckoning", *Dictionary of scientific biography*, xv (New York, 1978), 706–27.

9 Hesiod, *Works and days*, 609–11.

10 For these dates and for a full discussion of our procedures, see Ventura *et al.*, "Possible tally stones".

11 Hesiod, *Works and days*, 615.

12 Homer, *Iliad*, xviii, 483.

4

The Sanctuaries of Menorca and Mallorca

In 123 BC the Romans occupied the islands of Menorca and Mallorca and quickly extinguished what remained of the talayotic culture (which, as we saw earlier, takes its name from the truncated conical towers or 'talayots' that are the culture's largest monuments). However, the talayotic culture had long been in decline: the arrival of iron in the first centuries of the first millennium BC had been accompanied by the introduction of alien customs, and later the impact of Rome and Carthage had further disturbed the indigenous way of life. The golden age of the talayotic civilization had coincided with the Copper/Bronze Age on the islands, from around 1300 to around 800 BC. During this period innumerable settlements developed, in conditions that were evidently peaceful enough to permit the inhabitants to embark on the daunting task of the construction of a massive talayot without fear of attack. So crowded was the southern, limestone half of Menorca that a settlement was often only a few hundred metres from its nearest neighbours, from which a hostile band would have been able to arrive within minutes.

The purpose of a talayot is obscure. Its name derives from the Arabic for 'watchtower', but there are many ways of looking out (for enemies?) that would have been equally effective and would have involved only a tiny fraction of the labour. It cannot have been for defence, for a fire lit outside by besiegers would quickly render conditions within intolerable for defenders. In any case, while the typical Mallorcan talayot had a perimeter wall and a roof supported by a central column, and therefore provided protected space in an emergency for a goodly number of people, the typical Menorcan talayot had only a tiny chamber accessed via a narrow corridor, and so could accommodate only a tiny handful. The most plausible suggestion has come from William Waldren, that the construction of a talayot was a form of peaceful competition for prestige between villages, as in the Middle Ages a town demonstrated its status by the splendour of its cathedral (or today by the success of its football team).

Further evidence of just how organized and peaceful was the Menorcan way of life comes from the Bronze Age burial caves at Calas Covas, on the south coast. In the remote past Menorca and Mallorca were joined, and glaciers from the mountains of Mallorca sometimes entered the sea in what is now Menorca, cutting clefts in the cliffs as they did so (and thus providing the modern holiday-maker with a beach). Two of these glacial ravines meet at Calas Covas just before they

(*Left*) The taula sanctuary of Sa Torreta. The taula itself is *in situ*, but the entrance (in the foreground) is now much reduced. The talayot is glimpsed above and to the left. (*Right*) The taula sanctuary of Bella Ventura, the only one whose entrance survives intact. The taula itself has lost the upper (horizontal) stone, and a corner is broken from the vertical component.

enter the sea, so creating extensive cliff faces. In these cliffs more than a hundred natural lime-stone caves were enlarged in the first millennium BC to provide burial places for a great number of men, women and children.[1] Yet there is no sign of habitation at Calas Covas, and certainly there was no settlement large enough to require a hundred burial caves. Instead, it must be that the vil-lages in that part of the island collaborated to make Calas Covas a great necropolis, testimony to the peaceful conditions then prevailing. Only later in the first millennium do we find fortifications thrown up around settlements, perhaps reflecting social disturbance resulting from the growing practice whereby local men left the island for a time to serve as mercenaries in one or other of the opposing armies of Rome and Carthage.

The taula sanctuaries of Menorca

Talayots are by far the most obvious feature of the prehistoric settlements on Menorca, and because the island is flat there is frequent intervisibility between them, so much so that it is not uncommon for the observer on top of one talayot to see eight or ten other talayots on the surrounding skyline. More interesting to us, however, are the 'taula' precincts that take their name from the Catalan for 'table'. Each taula consists (or consisted) of two massive stones that together have the appearance of a capital letter T: a vertical supporting slab with near-rectangular faces, and, balanced on top of it, a horizontal slab, also nearly rectangular.

It seems that a major settlement on Menorca normally possessed a single taula, which was surrounded by a precinct wall. Originally this wall had an entrance with a lintel, though that at Bella Ventura is the only one that survives intact. One face of the vertical stone, which we shall term the front face, looked towards the entrance. This face was carefully fashioned into a flat surface; the reverse face was sometimes similarly fashioned, but sometimes it was left rough.[2]

To either side of the entrance, along the front of the precinct, the wall was slightly concave (as indeed were the façades of the temples of Malta). The taula precinct bears almost no other resemblance to the Maltese temples, but this has not prevented speculators from claiming that the taulas derived directly from the temples. This suggestion, never plausible given the distance

The taula of Torralba, the masterpiece of talayotic architecture. The horizontal (upper) stone is not rectangular; instead, each side slopes upwards and outwards to create an aesthetically pleasing effect. The precinct wall survives to a height of some 1½ metres, and many of the pilasters are present.

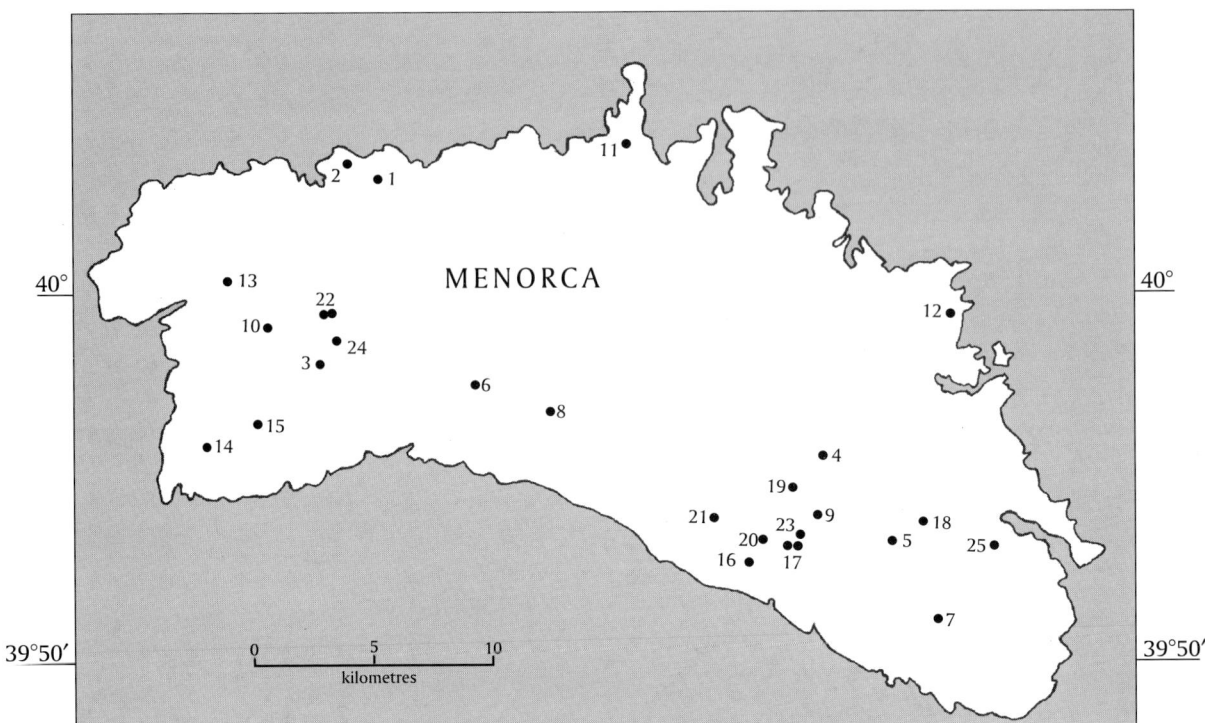

The taula sanctuaries of Menorca.

1 Alfurinet	8 Binicodrell Nou	15 Son Catlar	22 Torre Llafuda E, W
2 Algairens	9 Cotaina	16 Son Rotger	23 Torre Llisa Vell
3 Bella Ventura	10 Es Tudons	17 Sonacasana E, W	24 Torre Trencada
4 Biniac	11 Sa Cavallería	18 Talatí de Dalt	25 Trepucó
5 Binimaimut	12 Sa Torreta	19 Torralba d'en Salort	
6 Binimassó	13 So N'Anglado	20 Torralbec Vell	
7 Binissafullet Nou	14 So N'Olivaret Nou	21 Torre d'en Gaumes	

between the islands and (more especially) the great differences in structure and scale between the two types of monument, became even more fanciful when radiocarbon dating established a minimum time-gap of over a millennium between the latest of the temples and the earliest of the taulas. The concave façades may however have served similar purposes, to define a sacred area in front of the monument, as was likewise the case with the *tombe di giganti* of Sardinia that we shall discuss in Chapter 12.

From either end of the façade the precinct wall extended backwards, and then curved in the manner of a horse-shoe as it surrounded the central taula. Inset into the wall were pilasters, which defined subordinate spaces. In addition, certain locations within the interior of the precinct seem to have had a special significance.

Was the purpose of a taula religious or secular? This controversy from past decades has long since been resolved by the discovery by excavators of cult objects in various taulas, and by the

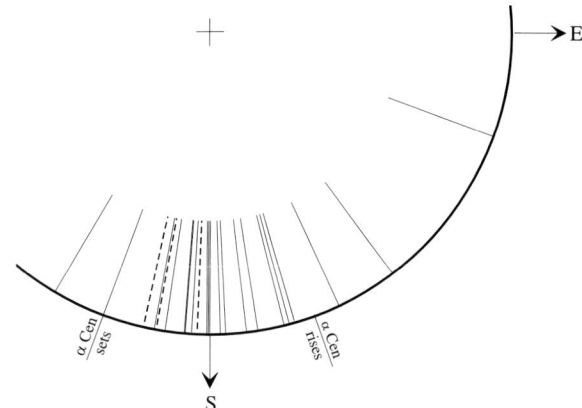

The orientations of the taulas in the southern half of the island. The three broken lines represent orientations (at So N'Angladó, Sonacasana (west), and Biniac) that take into account the actual fields of view from the taulas. Also shown is the rising and setting of α Cen in 1000 BC.

presence in many precincts of great numbers of bones of sacrificed animals: there is no doubt that a taula was a sanctuary. There are still some who argue that the precinct was wholly roofed-in, but if this was done in stone then the great quantity of stone involved has in every case mysteriously disappeared.

My first measurements of taula orientations were carried out in the summer of 1988, in the mistaken belief that the vertical stone of the central feature rested on top of the bedrock and therefore may have rotated slightly in the course of the three millennia since it was erected. Later, however, archaeologists who had excavated taulas told me that the vertical component was in fact dropped into a slot in the bedrock prepared to receive it, which of course is why so many of these uprights are still *in situ*. In July 1989, therefore, I revisited every one of the sites and took measures of the orientation of the vertical component as near to the bedrock as practicable.[3]

In subsequent campaigns the fieldwork was extended to other taulas,[4] including the few scattered ones in the northern part of the island,[5] an enterprise not without incident. A large area in the northwest was in the possession of an owner hostile to all strangers, and measurement of his taulas therefore called for a long and distinctly low-profile detour across country. On arrival at one of these taulas I found a crack in the vertical component, and in the crack were two scraps of paper inside a plastic envelope. Both were addressed to me, and both had been placed there a year earlier in the expectation that the Englishman would reach the site sooner or later. One, the earlier of the two, offered an archaeological interpretation of the precinct. The other had been written the very next day, by another visitor to this remote site; he had read the first note, disagreed with the interpretation, and set out his own view of the matter.

The orientations of the numerous taulas in the south of the island are shown in Table 4.1. As in Malta — and perhaps this is no coincidence — the monuments face southerly. As in Malta, and this must be by coincidence, there is one anomalous measure: a single monument that faces easterly instead.

In measuring the orientations I noticed an aspect of the locations of the taula precincts that was to prove of crucial significance: in every case, the site offered an uninterrupted view to the horizon. Sometimes the taula simply looked out to sea; at other times it might be looking across a plain from the southerly slope of a little rise, on the top of which, behind the taula, was the talayot. In no case did the taula look towards any sort of hill. While Menorca is indeed flat, in striking contrast to Mallorca, it has many undulations; and if one makes a parallel study of other monuments of the same culture, such as the burial navetas (see Chapter 11), one quickly finds examples where the monument faces rising ground and the view to the south is impeded.

Clearly, then, when the prehistoric inhabitants of a village decided to build a taula, they felt it necessary to select a site with a perfect and uninterrupted view to the (southerly) horizon. Why should this be so? There is no land visible to the south, indeed no land nearer than distant Africa. And today there are no stars of interest low in the sky to the south. But if we calculate backwards the effect of precession, the wobble of the earth's axis that we discussed in Chapter 2, then we discover that at the period of taula construction, which was at its height around 1000 BC, the Southern Cross and the two following bright stars of Centaurus were visible in the southern sky — but only just. In 1300 BC, for example, the very bright star α Cen climbed above the horizon to the respectable height of 6° (that is, twelve solar diameters), having risen some 25° east of south (and being about to set some 25° west of south). But in 600 BC the star rose only 15° east of south and climbed little more than 2° above the horizon, so that even though it is one of the brightest stars it would barely have been glimpsed through the atmosphere. Around 1000 BC, α Cen and the preceding stars of this Cross-Centaurus group would have been seen framed in the precinct entrance of a southerly-facing taula; but only if the site commanded a wholly uninterrupted view to the south.

There seems to be no plausible alternative explanation for the requirement that the site for a taula should have offered an unimpeded view of the southern horizon. Does the Cross-Centaurus hypothesis also serve to explain other puzzling facts connected with taulas?

First, although there was a parallel talayotic culture on Mallorca, which is separated from Menorca by less than 40km of sea, the talayotic sanctuaries on Mallorca are (as we shall see) few and later and quite different in form. Why, then, are there numerous taulas on little Menorca and none on Mallorca? Because, we suggest, Menorca is flat and near every prehistoric village there was a site that offered a good view to the south, so that the Cross-Centaurus group might be seen framed in the precinct entrance. But Mallorca is very mountainous, and settlements were in the fertile valleys and plains, and so it was frequently impossible to find a site that offered a good view to the south.

Second, excavators at the taula sanctuary of Torralba d'en Salort in southern Menorca found a plinth with three holes on the upper surface.[6] Each hole contained a fragment of bronze in the shape of a hoof that had been secured in its hole with molten lead, the rest of the statue no doubt having been broken off and plundered long ago. This presented a problem of interpretation because, although totems in the form of horses are not uncommon, there was no known horse-god in Mediterranean cultures.

Excavators at the sanctuary of Torre d'en Gaumes made a still more remarkable find: a little statue in bronze of a man sitting on a throne with an inscription *in Egyptian hieroglyphics* that declared the man to be Imhotep, the god of medicine.[7] Why should someone — perhaps a passing Egyptian sailor — have placed a statue of his god of medicine in a taula sanctuary?

The prehistory of the constellations is a matter of lively debate, but in the *Almagest* of Ptolemy, the late Greek work written in the second century AD that incorporated both the Greek and the Babylonian achievement in astronomy, the Southern Cross and the following bright stars were all part of the constellation of Centaurus. Indeed, the constellation is very ancient, going back at least to the famous Babylonian astronomical compendium MUL.APIN written around the beginning of the first millennium BC.[8] In Greek mythology the centaur in question was Chiron, who taught medicine to the Greek counterpart of Imhotep, namely the god Asclepius.[9] Now it is well known that in Egypt of the period, gods and goddesses were routinely identified with constellations.[10] So, for example, the goddess Isis was identified with the star Sirius, and similarly the god Osiris was identified with the constellation of Orion; Isis followed Osiris as Sirius followed Orion across the sky. Suppose that in talayotic Menorca, the stars of Centaurus were identified, if not at first with the actual teacher of the god of medicine, at least with a manifestation of medicine in some form. Then a taula, oriented towards this celestial embodiment of medicine, would doubtless be itself a place of healing, and an appropriate place for an Egyptian to deposit a statue of his god of medicine.

If belief in the Centaur and his role in medicine also reached Menorca, than we have an easy explanation for the bronze hooves at Torralba. They are not part of some horse-god, but of the centaur Chiron, who had the head and trunk of a man but the body of a horse, and whose representation in the sky this taula alone failed to face.

The hypothesis that the taulas were places of healing, looking southerly towards the celestial representation of the teacher of the god of medicine, therefore explains a number of hitherto-puzzling facts. But do the measured orientations (other than that of anomalous Torralba) conform to such an hypothesis?

The view that taula construction reached its peak around 1000 BC depends in part on radio-carbon studies of material from the precinct wall of Torralba, whose elegant upper stone is not the routine rectangular block but has sides that incline upwards and outwards. Torralba represents the artistic peak of talayotic building, and cannot be the earliest taula. It is entirely possible that taula construction had been in progress elsewhere for three or even more centuries. Other than Torralba, only one taula faces more than 30° from south, namely Torre Trencada (36/37° east of south), and even this would have faced the rising of γ Cru, the 'uppermost' star of the Cross, a little before 1400 BC. We must also bear in mind that the entrance to a taula precinct was relatively wide and located a very short distance from the taula itself. At Torre Trencada, for example, the field of view for someone with his back to the taula and looking out through the entrance would extend much further south than the simple orientation would suggest.

Our conclusion, then, is that, provided Torre Trencada was constructed early, from all the southern taulas save Torralba the stars of the Cross-Centaurus group would have appeared framed by the lintel and side-pillars of the entrance, during their shallow arc of passage across the southern horizon.

What, then, of Torralba? One would prefer not to have to give an explanation (a critic might say, invent excuses) for an anomalous orientation, but unfortunately this is unavoidable. The precinct has been fully excavated, and the bedrock is exposed. It is therefore possible to measure the orientation of the actual slot cut into the bedrock to receive the vertical stone, and this faces between 110° and 111°. In 1000 BC, about the time Torralba was constructed, Sirius, the brightest star in the sky, rose at azimuth 112° as seen from the taula. Rigel (β Ori, the sixth brightest star visible to the talayotic observer) rose at azimuth 111°; and the constellation of Orion was seen on the horizon northwards from Rigel, to due east and beyond. We are dealing, uniquely, with a site with a known date of construction, one that has a vertical taula stone of exceptional quality and perfection of shape and where the slot in the bedrock is accessible to measurement. It would be a remarkable coincidence if Torralba faced so exactly towards the point on the horizon where Rigel rose, shortly to be followed by Sirius. We therefore examine the possibility that Torralba was dedicated to Sirius and/or Orion.

We have already mentioned the special significance of Sirius and Orion in contemporary Egypt, and we have discussed the Egyptian statue of Imhotep found at Torre d'en Gaumes. Are there any other clues to possible Egyptian influence in Menorca?

In the central Mediterranean, Egyptian influence in late talayotic times is well attested: the worship of Isis became so prevalent in Rome in the last centuries before Christ that the Roman authorities were unable to stamp it out. More immediately relevant to the period of taula construction are the mysterious Sea Peoples, of whom *The Cambridge ancient history* speaks as follows:

> Among the 'peoples of the sea' who made raids on the coasts of the Mediterranean and against Egypt in the period 1400 to 1190 BC and who were employed as mercenaries in the Egyptian army soon after the middle of the second millennium BC, were a people calling themselves Sherden. There are two main views about the origin of these people. One is that they come from Sardinia itself, in a word that they are Nuraghic heroes campaigning in the east Mediterranean, already well known to them by trade. The other view is that they came … from Sardis and the Sardinian plain. This second view would appear to be the more likely.
>
> We can then see in the period 1400–1190 BC groups of people led by warlike chieftains, themselves expert sailors and with a knowledge of the routes between the east Mediterranean and the west, setting out from some such area as Sardis and, after periods of harassing Egypt, ending up in the island of the west Mediterranean which was eventually called after them, Sardinia.[11]

If, therefore, there was intense influence from the eastern Mediterranean on the culture of Sardinia (as is confirmed by finds now in Sardinian museums[12]), it is far from impossible that this influence extended to the next island, Menorca, and at just the time when taula construction began.

This may help us to understand, not only the orientation of taulas towards star groups, but finds at Torralba other than the bronze hooves. These included a bronze bull. In later Egypt, when the Apis bull died in the temple of Ptah near Memphis, the corpse of the animal was mummified and identified with Osiris.[13] We have seen that Torralba faced the rising of the constellation Orion which the Egyptians identified with Osiris, and it may be that the bronze bull of Torralba represents Osiris.

Also found at Torralba were figurines of the Punic fertility goddess, Tanit. The Carthaginians never settled Menorca (as they did Ibiza and, to a much lesser extent, Mallorca), but they traded extensively with the islanders. Boats would arrive at Calas Covas, and an archaeological team that excavated the sea bed in the cove recovered a pottery figure of Tanit. From Calas Covas a Punic road led up to the talayotic settlements. It is entirely possible that if Torralba was dedicated to Sirius/Isis (rather than, or in addition to, Orion/Osiris), then Punic traders would think to place there figurines of their own goddess.

The suggestion that Torralba was oriented on Sirius, the star whose heliacal rising (its reappearance in the dawn sky after some weeks' absence lost in the glare of the sun) controlled the beginning of the Egyptian calendar year, helps to explain another curious fact uncovered by the excavators of the sanctuary. My first public presentation of the suggestion that Torralba faced the rising point of Sirius was made at a 1988 conference, and in the audience was the late Edward Sanders, who had been responsible for analysing the bones of the animals sacrificed at Torralba. He remarked on the curious fact that these animals seemed all to come from either the second half of their first year of life or the second half of their second year. Now if Torralba was indeed dedicated to Sirius, then by far the most notable event of the year would have been the star's heliacal rising, which took place some three weeks after midsummer.[14] Sanders considered that November would have been the peak month for the birth of the animals sacrificed; if, therefore, they were sacrificed at the time of the heliacal rising, then their bones would indeed have conformed to the pattern he had discovered.

The Torralba orientation falls outside the pattern of the other taulas; and although the explanations we offered for both were in terms of sky-beings — the centaur Chiron, and Sirius/Isis — we knew of no association between the two. A link was to be provided by a member of the audience on another occasion, Roger Ceragioli. He pointed out that, in his geography/travel guide, Heraclides Criticus (third century BC) gives details of the ritual that took place on Mount Pelion, where Chiron had lived. This ritual, according to Heraclides, took place "at the [heliacal] rising of Sirius during the peak season of heat",[15] and it may have been a sacrifice to Chiron. In a letter Dr Ceragioli summarizes the situation thus:

> It appears that there was a class of hereditary medicine men at Mount Pelion, who claimed to be Chiron's descendants. The people of the region sacrificed to Chiron by offering medical plants as firstfruits. It seems reasonable to suppose that they did so under the guidance of the hereditary medicine men, since only they knew how to use the plants. In addition, at Sirius's heliacal rising, the upper-class men were slaughtering sheep, skinning them and donning skins for a procession up to the cave of Chiron. The slaughtering must be a sacrifice, perhaps to Chiron, perhaps to Zeus Actaeus whose shrine was close by, perhaps to both. It could also be that all the above-mentioned gods, people and activities belong to a single ritual, but it is impossible to say.

It is perhaps difficult to believe that in distant Menorca, as early as 1000 BC, there was already an association between the Centaur and Sirius; but the suggestion that one taula faced Sirius and the rest faced Centaurus (Chiron) had been made in print long before Dr Ceragioli pointed out the mythical link between them.

As the work proceeded, my colleagues and I extended our measures to include the field of view as one looked from the central taula towards the entrance, for it is on this field of view (and not the simple orientation of the central stone) that our explanation focuses. We systematically measured the orientation of the line-of-sight of an observer standing with his back to the left edge of the taula stone and looking past the right upright of the entrance, and of an observer with his back to the right edge of the stone and looking past the left upright of the entrance.[16] The most significant datum to emerge concerned Biniac, whose westerly orientation (22° west of due south) is exceeded only by Torre d'en Gaumes. Yet the entrance at Biniac is not directly opposite the taula: it is so located that an observer with his back to the taula and looking through this entrance would have to look somewhat left, that is, more southerly, between about 169° and 195°. It is as though the taula — either when erected, or later, when precession had reduced the arc traced by the stars — was found to face too far west, and the axis of the monument was adjusted in a southerly direction by unorthodox placement of the precinct entrance.

The talayotic sanctuaries of Mallorca

In Mallorca there are no taulas, but sanctuaries of a different form were built there later, following the introduction of iron in the late ninth and early eighth centuries. They seem to have appeared around the sixth century, although we have radiocarbon dates from only one site, Son Mas near Valldemossa on the north coast,[17] and must otherwise rely on pottery and other materials recovered during excavations. In form these structures were apsidal, or else square, in which case the corners were rounded. The exterior face of the perimeter wall was in most cases built of fitted orthostats (vertical slabs) that were typically 120cm high and 90cm wide. At the entrance was either a threshold or steps leading down into the interior.

These sanctuaries are scattered all over the island, in the plains as well as in the mountains, and both near the coast and in the interior. Some, such as Son Marí, are isolated; others, such as S'Illot, are inside villages; and others again (such as Capocorb d'en Jaquetó and Es Pedregar) are part of more extensive and complex settlements. Most are free-standing structures, whether inside the villages or outside, so that the space surrounding the sanctuary, and especially that in front of it, could be used for ritual.

A striking feature in each of the sanctuaries that have been excavated is a burnt layer formed of carbon, ash, and huge quantities of bones of sheep, goats and pigs. These layers are not limited to particular areas, where there might have been altars, pyres, or ritual places, but are spread in varying degrees throughout the whole of the sacred precinct.

Of the indigenous pottery found in the sanctuaries, the most striking are the 'crested cups'. Such pottery seems to have been specially identified with the sanctuaries, but it is also associated

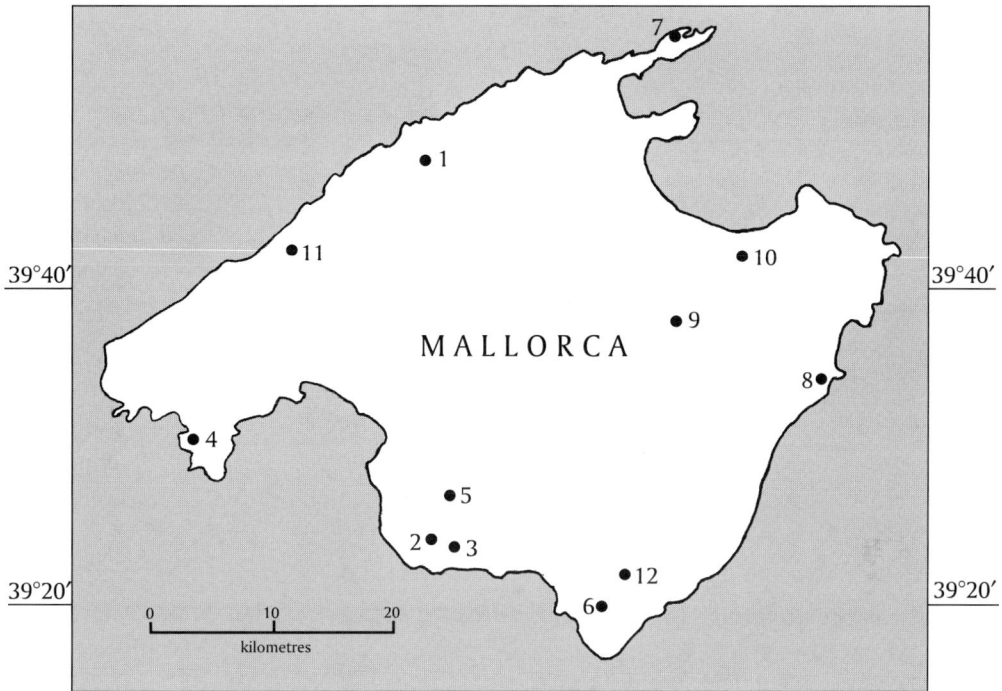

The sanctuaries of Mallorca discussed in the text.

1	Almallutx	5 Es Pedregar	9 Son Ferragut
2	Capocorb d'en Jaquetó	6 Ets Antigors	10 Son Marí
3	Capocorb Vell	7 Ses Arenes de Formentor	11 Son Mas
4	Es Fornets	8 S'Illot	12 Talaies d'en Clar

with burials of the period, which suggests a link between the dead and the worshippers in the sanctuaries. Imported pottery, whether Punic or Roman, is also commonly found, and this allows us to date the abandonment of the sanctuaries to the second century BC. But the most remarkable discoveries have been of bronze statues, some of them of nude warriors with lances while others are of the heads, or simply the horns, of bulls.[18]

In May 1997, two young Mallorcan archaeologists, Jaume García Rosselló and Joan Fornés Bisquerra, joined me in measuring a number of the surviving Mallorcan sanctuaries, as a contribution to the first day of a visit to Son Mas and associated sites by a group involved in the "Time Team" series for British television. Unfortunately most of the sanctuaries are in poor condition or worse, and on occasion we had to reject measures because we were uncertain even of the correct identification of the monument. The remaining sanctuaries with measurable orientations were investigated by my Mallorcan colleagues in the succeeding months.

One curious feature of the Mallorcan scene is the existence of pairs of sanctuaries facing in opposite directions. Two such pairs are measurable:

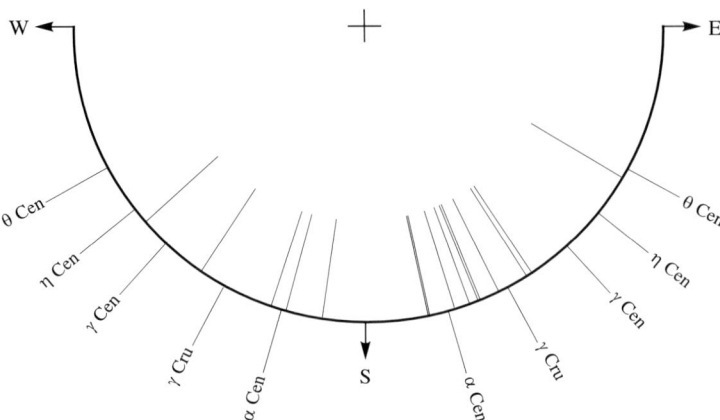

The orientations of the Mallorcan sanctuaries listed in Table 4.2, with an indication of the directions in 600 BC of the rise and set of stars of the ancient constellation of Centaurus, assuming a skyline with zero altitude. If the skyline was elevated, the directions would have been further to the south.

S'Illot 1 and 2: both are apsidal in shape and are located inside a village. They face each other. Their orientations are 53° (skyline altitude 0°) and 234° (alt. 0°).

Son Ferragut 1 and 2: the first is apsidal in shape, but internal walls were later inserted to divide it into three. The second is some 15 metres away. Their orientations are 49° (alt. 0°) and 244° (alt. 1°).

The remaining 15 measurable sanctuaries are listed in Table 4.2. Their orientations extend over a range of only a little over a quadrant, and so are far from random. Ten faced between 121° and 168°, and the remaining five between 188° and 228°, which may be thought of as two octants, one in which certain stars rose and the other where the same stars set. If for calculation we assume a skyline altitude of 3° when the actual figure is not available, we find that the corresponding declinations varied between −21½° and −46° for the easterly range, and between −29° and −47° for the westerly. There are naturally many stars whose declinations in the middle of the first millennium BC fell within these ranges, but in the light of our interpretation of the Menorcan taulas, the constellation Centaurus is an attractive candidate, even if the evidence is far from conclusive. On mountainous Mallorca, as we mentioned earlier, settlements were often in fertile valleys and plains, from which stars low in the southern sky would have been hidden by the mountains. In particular, by 600 BC α Cru had declination −49° and was invisible from Mallorca (latitude just under 40°N). But under favourable conditions and with a low horizon to the south, α Cen (dec. −48°, mag. 0.06) might just have been visible, and γ Cru (dec. −43°, mag. 1.60) could have been seen if the skyline altitude was no more than moderate. Other stars of the ancient constellation of Centaurus could have been viewed from most of our sites. Thus θ Cen, the third brightest star of the modern constellation (mag. 2.26) had declination −22°, γ Cen (2.38) had declination −35°, and η Cen (2.65) had declination −29°. It is therefore possible that the Mallorcan sanctuaries faced the rising or setting of Centaurus, even though the Cross itself was no longer visible.

The pre-talayotic sanctuary at Son Mas

My visit to Mallorca with the Time Team yielded unexpected evidence that a very much earlier (pre-talayotic) sanctuary may have had the Cross-Centaurus group as an object of cult. William Waldren's excavations at the talayotic sanctuary of Son Mas near Valldemossa in the north of the island had brought to light surprising quantities of high-quality pre-talayotic pottery, and this led him and his associates to conclude that "the site was already used as a ritual area in Chalcolithic [that is, Copper Age] times". They were able to obtain a number of radiocarbon dates, but there was a lengthy and inexplicable gap in these dates: "This would imply that the site was probably abandoned for several centuries in late pre-talayotic times",[19] around 1700 BC. If so, the site was later reoccupied, and the talayotic sanctuary constructed on what had long been sacred ground. But since these investigators could imagine no explanation for the abandonment, they continued to hope for further radiocarbon dates that would fall into the missing centuries and so relieve

The sanctuary of Son Mas (photograph by Mark Van Strydonck).

The boulder in front of the Son Mas sanctuary, with the valley beyond (photograph by Mark Van Strydonck).

them of the need to find such an explanation.

In front of the talayotic sanctuary of Son Mas is a huge boulder with a groove that Waldren believes is artificial. This groove points up a valley to the south. On the second day of the Time Team visit, I was asked to measure the profile of the valley as seen from the sanctuary, and I found that the valley floor lay in a direction with azimuth 189°, and had skyline altitude 5°, thus corresponding to declination −44°. Being convinced that the Menorcan taula sanctuaries faced the Cross-Centaurus group of stars, and suspecting that the much earlier temples of Malta had also done the same (see Chapter 3), I was struck by the thought of the brilliant spectacle that the Cross would have made around 2000 BC as it crossed the valley, framed by hills to left and right. My problem was that precession would have caused the Cross to sink steadily lower in the sky, until around 1700 BC the lowest star of the Cross would have disappeared from view. If the Cross was indeed an object of cult, this would presumably have provoked a crisis; but being wholly unaware of the gap in the radiocarbon dates, I knew of no evidence for any such abandonment.

As it happened, the Time Team had also brought to Mallorca Mark Van Strydonck of the Royal Institute for Cultural Heritage at Brussels, who had himself been responsible for processing the radiocarbon samples, and I confided in him my pressing need for a crisis around 1700 BC. Astonished, Van Strydonck pulled from his pocket the draft of the latest paper on the radiocarbon dating, which again proposed a (hitherto inexplicable) site abandonment around 1700 BC. He and I were able next day to explain on camera our combined interpretation: that (as the high-quality pottery showed) the pre-talayotic site had been a sanctuary; that (as the astronomy associated with the groove suggested) this may have had the Cross-Centaurus stars as its object of cult, in which case one would expect a crisis around 1700 BC; that the radiocarbon evidence implied the abandonment of the site around 1700 BC; and that the site was later reoccupied by a different people who built their own sanctuary there.

Some implications

We have seen that a *possible* explanation of the southerly orientations of the Mallorcan talayotic sanctuaries, as of the temples of the Malta, is that they faced the ancient constellation Centaurus. For the taulas of Menorca we can put the case more confidently: the very special choice of location for a taula seems to lead to the conclusion that they did indeed face the Cross-Centaurus group of stars, which would have been seen framed in the entrance of most of the sanctuaries; and this would account for a range of objects uncovered by excavators. Finally, the wholly unexpected convergence of the archaeological, astronomical and radiocarbon evidence concerning a pre-talayotic sanctuary at Son Mas that was abandoned at the very time when the Cross-Centaurus group sank out of sight is, as the senior archaeologist of the Time Team commented, almost too good to be true.

Further reading

J. García Rosselló, J. Fornés Bisquerra and M. Hoskin, "Orientations of the talayotic sanctuaries of Mallorca", *AA*, no. 25 (2000), S58–64.

M. Hoskin, "The talayotic culture of Menorca: A first reconnaissance", *AA*, no. 9 (1985), S133–51.

M. Hoskin, "The orientations of the taulas of Menorca (1):

The southern taulas", *AA*, no. 14 (1989), S117–36.

M. Hoskin, P. Hochsieder and D. Knösel, "The orientations of the taulas of Menorca (2): The remaining taulas", *AA*, no. 15 (1990), S37–48.

M. Hoskin, "The orientations of taulas: Addenda", *AA*, no. 16 (1991), S89–90.

Notes and references

1 Cristóbal Veny Meliá, *La necrópolis protohistórica de Cales Coves (Menorca)* (Madrid, 1982).

2 An excellent guide to the layout of the taula sanctuaries is to be found in P. Hochsieder and D. Knösel, *Les taules de Menorca* (Menorca, 1995). However, the authors, who are teachers of art, are out of their depth in questions of mathematics, and the archaeoastronomical hypotheses they advance are totally misconceived.

3 Hoskin, "The orientations of the taulas of Menorca (1)".

4 Hoskin *et al.*, "The orientations of the taulas of Menorca (2)"; Hoskin, "The orientations of taulas: Addenda".

5 There are four possible taula sites in the north of the island, widely separated from the southern taulas and from each other, of which two are included in Table 4.1: Sa Torreta and Algairens. Sa Torreta is normal except that it faces 125°, too far north for the Cross-Centaurus

group of stars, but not too far north for the constellation of Centaurus. Algairens is normal except that it faces across a valley towards a low range of hills with non-zero altitude, though given the loss of light in the atmosphere of the earth close to the horizon, this makes no practical difference. Sa Cavalleria is a maverick site that has been described as "a fortified sanctuary", while the layout of Alfurinet makes no sense at present and the Director of the Museum of Menorca recommends that judgement on it be suspended until the site is excavated.

6 Details of the finds at Torralba are given in the *DAMARC underground news*, i, no. 1 (October, 1980), published by the Deya Archaeological Museum and Research Centre on Mallorca.

7 G. Rosselló-Bordoy, *El poblado prehistórico de Torre d'en Gaumes (Alaior)* (Palma de Mallorca, 1986); *idem*, R. Sánchez-Cuenca and P. de Montaner Alonso, "Imhotep, hijo de Ptah", *Mayurqa*, no. 12 (1974), 123–42.

8   H. Hunger and D. Pingree, MUL-APIN: An astronomical com-
    pendium in cuneiform (Archiv für Orientforschung, xxiv;
    Horn, Austria, 1989), 138 etc.

9   J. Lemprière, A classical dictionary (2nd edn, London,
    n.d.), 19.

10 R. A. Parker, "Egyptian astronomy, astrology, and cal-
    endrical reckoning", Dictionary of scientific biography, xv
    (New York, 1978), 706–27.

11 The Cambridge ancient history, ii/2, 3rd edn (Cambridge,
    1975), 741–2. A standard work on the Sea Peoples is N.
    K. Sanders, The Sea Peoples, rev. edn (London, 1985).

12 F. Barreca, La civiltà fenicio-punica in Sardegna (Sassari,
    1988), chap. 4, espec. pp. 147–8.

13 P. Johnson, The civilization of ancient Egypt (London,
    1978), 148.

14 According to Parker (op. cit., 707), the heliacal rising
    of Sirius fell around 17/19 July in the Julian calendar
    throughout Egyptian history.

15 Heraclides Criticus, [De Graeciae urbibus], ed. by F. E.

Pfister (Vienna, 1951), II.8. See also Plutarch, Moralia
646f–647a.

16 Full details of the field of view from each taula are
    given in Hoskin et al., "The orientations of the taulas of
    Menorca (2)".

17 W. Waldren and M. Van Strydonck, Prehistoric sanctuary
    of Son Mas: A radiocarbon analysis survey dating the activ-
    ity sequences of the prehistoric sanctuary of Son Mas,
    Valldemossa (5th edn, DAMARC Series 24; Deya Archae-
    ological Museum and Research Centre, 1995). For fur-
    ther details of our work on the Mallorcan sanctuaries,
    see García, Fornés and Hoskin, "Orientations of the
    talayotic sanctuaries of Mallorca".

18 These figures of warriors have been named "Mars Bal-
    earicus": J. Gual, Figures de bronze a la protohistòria de
    Mallorca (Conselleria de Cultura, Palma, 1993).

19 M. J. Y. Van Strydonck, W. H. Waldren and V. Hendrix,
    "The ¹⁴C chronology of the Son Mas sanctuary site
    (Valldemossa, Mallorca, Spain)", Radiocarbon, xl (1998),
    735–48, p. 747.

II

ORIENTATIONS OF COMMUNAL TOMBS

5

Easterly-facing Tombs (I): South Iberia

My fieldwork in Menorca had brought me into contact with Margarita Orfila, whose family owned the land at Calas Covas with its hundred Bronze Age burial caves, and who was herself an archaeologist on the staff of the department in the University of Granada. The Granada department had had the privilege of excavating one of the most famous prehistoric sites in Spain, at Los Millares, not far from the port of Almería on the Mediterranean coast. Through the good offices of Margarita Orfila, in September 1991 I was invited by the department to measure the orientations of the tombs of Los Millares; and when we finished this work ahead of schedule, I was taken to measure the numerous sepulchres at Montefrío, a hilly site to the west of Granada. At both places, as we shall see, I found clear evidence that the builders were following a well-defined custom: nearly all the tombs faced easterly — indeed, within the range of sunrise.

This was more than encouraging, and so I decided to extend my efforts, first to the remaining tombs of the 'autonomous region' of Andalucía, and then to those in other parts of the Mediterranean; these tombs occupy the rest of this book.

In Almería our fieldwork was enlivened by a brush with the local constabulary. One day we were measuring the orientation of a tomb when two policemen arrived and demanded to see our permit. They saw that we were engaged in some form of archaeological research, and not unreasonably assumed we must be excavating, for which of course a permit is essential. Clearly, we needed to convince them that in fact our research involved no interference with the monuments; and the only way to do this was to give them a seminar on archaeoastronomy and explain just what we were about, and why it was likely to shed light on the monuments of which they, as local residents, were rightly proud. Adrenalin gave fluency to my Spanish for the next ten minutes, during which time the atmosphere improved considerably, and before long the two policemen were offering us helpful suggestions as to the steps we might usefully take to achieve our archaeological goals. The meeting concluded with handshakes all round.

A confrontation of another kind was only just avoided when we were later working in the province of Sevilla (Seville). Northwest of the city of that name, at El Castillo de las Guardas, is a modest group of tombs, some of which are on land belonging to a *rancho* dedicated to the breeding of bulls for the bullring. In search of these tombs, we found a field gate with no more than a simple catch to keep it closed. Erroneously interpreting this as a sign that no valuable animals

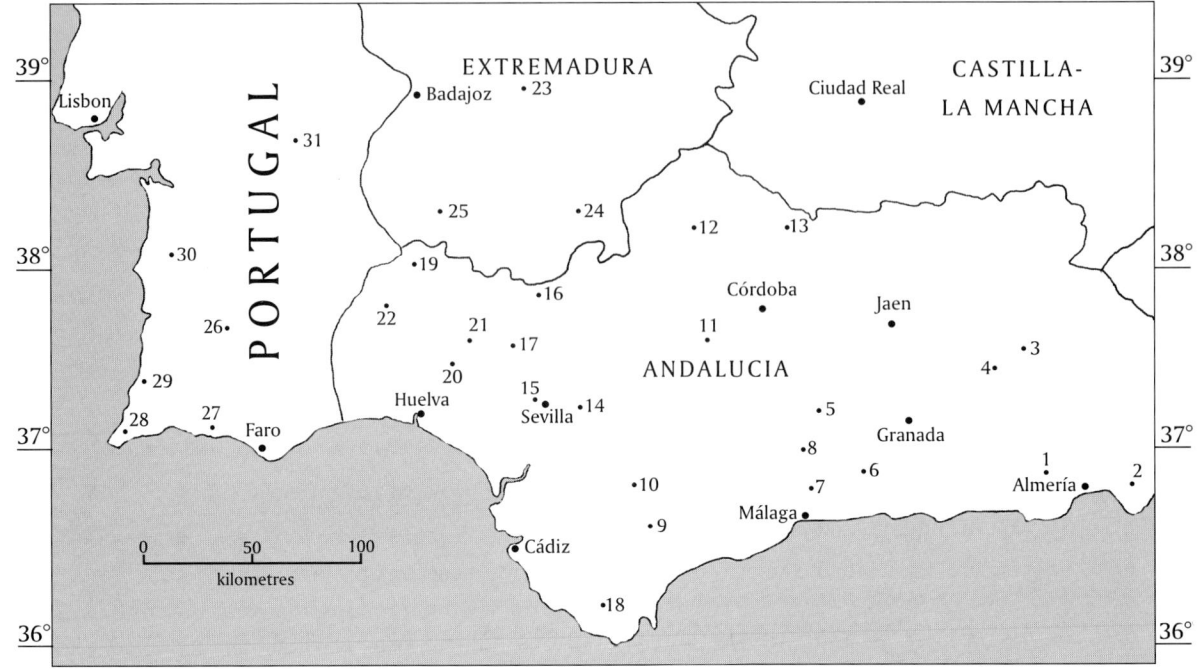

South Spain and Portugal, with the principal sites discussed in this chapter.

1 Los Millares, Alhama de Almería	11 Sierra Zuela de Posadas	22 Santa Bárbara de Casa
2 Barranquete	12 The Upper Guadiato	23 Mérida
3 Río Gor, Baños de Alicún, El Baúl	13 Villanueva de Córdoba	24 Llerena
4 Fonelas	14 El Gandul	25 Jerez de los Caballeros
5 Montefrío	15 Valencina de la Concepción	26 Ourique
6 El Pantano de los Bermejales	16 Almadén de la Plata	27 Portimão
7 Chaperas, Tajillo del Moro	17 El Castillo de las Guardas	28 Vila do Bispo
8 Antequera	18 La Laguna de la Janda	29 Aljezur
9 Encinas Borrachas	19 Aroche	30 Santiago do Cacém
10 Los Gigantes, La Angostura,	20 Valverde del Camino	31 Évora
El Moral	21 Zalamea la Real	

were confined within, we entered and climbed the rise in front of us. On cresting the hill we found we were in fact sharing the field with a great number of bulls; fortunately we had seen them before they saw us. Since (a) a statistical enquiry does not require the accumulation of every possible datum, and (b) we had no wish to spend a couple of hours up a tree with an angry bull below, we felt it appropriate to withdraw.

Stones large and small

Megalithic tombs — communal tombs built from a small number of large stones — will be the central concern of this and the next ten chapters of this book: this form of construction is near-universal in the central and west Mediterranean, despite the physical challenge of erecting slabs that were always sizeable and sometimes huge. The tombs take many forms, and there is no agreed terminology for them. They are sometimes spoken of collectively as 'dolmens', but this term is best reserved for major monuments that were often prominent in the landscape. Smaller, family-sized tombs we shall speak of as 'megalithic sepulchres' when the distinction is significant.

We shall encounter communal tombs built with large numbers of small stones only twice: in Provence and east Languedoc (Chapter 9), where many of the tombs had dry-stone walls and used megaliths only for the backstone and entrance pillars, and in the present chapter. For whatever reason, across south Iberia from Almería in the east to the Atlantic coast of Portugal in the west, a minority of builders painstakingly used small stones to fashion monuments with circular chambers of false-cupola construction (the genuine cupola being built on more advanced mechanical principles). As the circular courses of stonework of the chamber increased in height from the ground, their diameters were steadily reduced, so that the chambers acquired the shape of a

A reconstructed tholos at Los Millares.

beehive. When the opening at the roof was small enough, the construction was completed with a slab placed across the gap.

As we saw in Chapter 2, archaeologists designated these structures 'tholoi' because this was the Greek word they were using for similar buildings found in ancient Mycenae, and the Iberian tholoi were thought by some to have been built by colonizers who had come from Mycenae. The advent of radiocarbon dating proved beyond doubt that the Iberian tholoi antedated those of Mycenae by many centuries, but the name has stuck. One does not need to invoke colonizers (or even influence) to explain the similarities of construction: the laws of mechanics ensure that any successful building of false-cupola form must be built to the same basic plan. Unfortunately, false-cupola construction, unless carried out with great skill as at Mycenae, is far from robust, and it takes little to bring the whole edifice crashing down. After this happens, the stones used in the construction are easily scattered by human or natural agents, leaving an ill-defined shape unhelpful for our purposes.

How the builders of megalithic tombs were related to the builders of tholoi remains moot. Were they different peoples following different customs? Or did the same population decide at some stage to abandon one custom and adopt another?

In a letter, Victor Hurtado of the University of Seville sums up the difference between the tholoi and the major dolmens thus:

> The dolmens are older constructions, many of the fourth and even fifth millennia BC, built by groups who followed a mixed agricultural and pastoral way of life, and who lived in regions with ample supply of stone. They should be seen not only as the focus for the cult of the ancestors, but as markers defining the territorial boundaries established by their builders. This form of construction calls for a major investment of manpower, which presupposes an extensive population and possibly the involvement of neighbouring groups who would join in ceremonies during the construction.
>
> Tholoi by contrast are later, being built in the third millennium. They were constructed close to settlements and therefore had lost any territorial function, this now being fulfilled by the settlements themselves. They represent a technical advance: physical power has been replaced by intellectual ability. They do not require a large manpower, but can be built even by a small population provided there are stones available.[1]

Peoples with the tradition of building communal tombs of stone, whether megalithic or tholos, did not penetrate into the deep interior of Iberia, which is almost empty of such monuments; and so our survey of the tombs of the peninsula in this and the two following chapters can conveniently proceed clockwise around the periphery. For some reason Murcia and Valencia, on the Mediterranean coast, have scarcely a tomb between them, and so it is convenient to begin our clockwise journey with Almería, which is on the coast to the southeast of this tombless region, and end with Cataluña, on the coast to its northeast. In the present chapter we explore the south of the peninsula, across Andalucía from Almería in the east to Huelva in the west,[2] into Badajoz, over the Portugese frontier, across the Algarve, and up the Atlantic coast to just beyond Lisbon.

Almería

There are just two major concentrations of tombs in Almería, at Los Millares and adjacent Alhama de Almería, and at Barranquete.

Los Millares and Alhama de Almería

Los Millares is situated on the easily-defensible headland above the confluence of two rivers, the Andarax and the Rambla de Huéchar, 15km northwest of the port of Almería. The triangular area of the settlement (which dates from the later centuries of the fourth millennium) was protected on its landward side by walls extending across the ground separating the two rivers. Small but sophisticated hill forts above the settlement eventually provided an outer ring of defences, and indicate a society of a complexity most remarkable for Spain in the third millennium BC.[3]

Collective burials took place in tombs located over a wide area of the settlement, almost all outside the defensive walls. The majority are tholoi, often with passages divided into segments by orthostats (vertical slabs) each pierced by a 'porthole'. A few are of different construction, including some that have the orthostatic side-walls and capstone of a megalithic sepulchre. However, the tombs of non-tholos construction are (like the tholoi) surrounded by sizeable tumuli of small stones. In consequence, the appearance even of those listed as 'megalithic sepulchres' in the literature was, or became, very different from the megalithic tombs in neighbouring Alhama de Almería. We shall therefore treat all the Los Millares tombs as though they were tholoi.

Because of the exceptional importance of the site, I made two completely independent measurements of the tombs, the first in 1991 and the second, with a different colleague, in 1993. Despite the presence of a passage, the orientation of a tholos is much more difficult to determine than is that of the typical megalithic tomb, not least because of the absence of any backstone. Where the condition of the tomb permitted, the orientation (see Table 5.1) was taken as the direction from a pole at the centre of the circular chamber to a pole in the middle of the passage, as shown in the photograph on page 9. Unfortunately not only is the tholos structure very fragile, but at Los Millares stones were plundered early in the twentieth century for use in road-building. As a result, the exact location of the centre of the chamber is often uncertain. Fortunately, it often happened that slabs lining one side (or both) of the passage were still *in situ*; if all else failed, we measured the orientation of these passage stones. The differences between the 1991 and 1993 measurements were usually no more than 1° when the condition of the tomb was good, but could be as much as 4° when the condition was poor.

In all, orientations could be quantitatively measured in the case of 48 tombs. No fewer than 42 of these face between 62° and 117°; this is within the range of sunrise, and as explained in Chapter 2, we characterize such orientations as 'SR'. In a further 18 tombs the condition was too poor to permit any quantitative measure, but in every single instance it was clear that the orientation was within the same range and so these are listed in the table as 'typical'. Interestingly, the tomb that faces 62°, by far the most northerly orientation, is exceptionally large: the chamber measures an impressive 5½ metres in diameter, and the passage is nearly 2 metres wide.

Measurement of Tomb 2 at Alhama de Almería, using poles placed one in the centre of the backstone and the other in the centre of the corridor.

There are two adjacent tombs whose orientations (212° and 216°) are highly anomalous, not to say maverick. Four others face between 127° and 150°, and we characterize them as 'SC', for they face in directions where the sun had risen and was climbing in the sky. All are situated on flat ground where the unusual orientation represented no saving in labour.

Of the 66 tombs, then, for whose orientations quantitative or qualitative measurements could be obtained, no fewer than 60 faced within the range of sunrise, most of them towards sunrise in the autumn, winter or spring. As to the handful of tombs with SC orientations, it seems that these were often unusual in other ways as well, sometimes being of non-tholos construction, or built into the side of a natural eminence rather than constructed on open ground, or yielding finds that link them with the megalithic sepulchres of nearby Alhama de Almería (where SC tombs are common). Perhaps these exceptions to the SR pattern had their origins in an earlier settlement on the site.

After our fieldwork was completed, our colleague Juan Antonio Belmonte revisited the site, and he noticed that there are concentrations of orientations opposite to the directions of distant mountain peaks. I agree with him that this may be more than coincidence, and that if the constructors noticed that a particular sunrise orientation happened to be aligned (in the opposite direction) with a mountain peak, then a later tomb may have been oriented opposite to the peak

(*Left*) The orientations of 48 tholoi and related tombs at Los Millares. A further 18 tholoi faced within the range of sunrise but were in too poor a condition to permit a quantitative measure. Note that of the 66, only 6 faced outside the range of sunrise. (*Right*) Orientations of 38 megalithic sepulchres at Alhama de Almería; not shown are three tombs with ambivalent orientations. 21 of the 38 faced outside the range of sunrise.

in the sure knowledge that it would thereby face within the range of sunrise.

On much higher ground two to three kilometres to the southwest, between Los Millares and the little town of Alhama de Almería, is an area once thickly sewn with the more familiar megalithic sepulchres, each having a polygonal chamber formed of orthostats, with a prominent backstone that faces a short entrance passage. A survey carried out in 1981 (but unpublished and not available to us) located some seventy such sepulchres. Since then agriculture and industry have extended their grip on the area, and many of the tombs are now lost while others are under immediate threat.

The surviving tombs are today concentrated in two zones, an upper and a lower, each being located near the edge of a plateau that overlooks a valley to the east. We succeeded in locating 25 sepulchres in the upper zone and 20 in the lower. Details of the 41 that yielded orientations are given in Table 5.2. In three cases the orientation is ambivalent because the backstone is not aligned orthogonally to the sides of the chamber.

The table shows that in the upper zone the orientations range from 97° to 158°. In the lower zone the range is from 76° to 132° (or to 141° if the more southerly value is adopted for one of the tombs with ambivalent orientation). In all, 19 (46·3%) of the tombs are SR but 22 (53·7%) are SC, and so we characterize the overall range as 'SR/SC'.

Archaeologists are not agreed as to the relationship between the tholoi of Los Millares and the megalithic sepulchres of Alhama de Almería, though finds from the two sites show that both belong to the early third millennium. Some see the contrast in tomb type as proof of the presence of two independent traditions in adjacent areas, while others ascribe it to social differences within the same community, the élite being buried in the more elaborate and sophisticated tholoi.

One might suppose that within the same community, the astronomical/religious motivations underlying the customs of tomb orientation would be the same, even if the forms of the tombs varied. What light do our data shed on this?

We saw above that at Alhama, rather more than half the tombs were SC. At Los Millares just down the hill, however, the distribution of orientations is very different. Of the 66 tholoi for which we have quantitative or qualitative orientations, 2 (3·0%) had anomalous southwesterly orientations, 4 (6·1%) were SC, but no fewer than 60 (90·9%) were SR. Put at its simplest, over nine-tenths of the Los Millares tholos tombs faced within the range of sunrise while over half the Alhama megalithic sepulchres faced south of sunrise. This suggests a significant difference in the astronomical/religious beliefs of those who occupied these adjacent sites, and although this is only one item of evidence among many, we think it lends support to archaeologists who favour the presence of two distinct customs.

Barranquete

The village of Barranquete lies 23km due east of Almería, and some 30km southeast of Los Millares. To the northwest of the village, on the west bank of the Rambla de Morales, lies a prehistoric settlement with a number of known or suspected tholos tombs to the north and south of the settlement. Eleven of these tombs have so far been excavated, and it is clear that the site is closely related to Los Millares and indeed is the other major example of the tholos culture of Almería.[4]

We visited the site in 1993. Tomb 10 is now ruined, and the orientation of Tomb 5 is ill-defined (but is certainly south of east). However, the remaining nine face within the range 95°–134° (Table 5.3). Four faced sunrise in the winter months, while four more faced a little outside the range of sunrise (but within or very near the range of moonrise); the ninth was measured as facing 134°, some 12° south of the range of sunrise, but it was in 'very poor' condition and the orientation is not secure. There are too few data to suggest a firm interpretation, but at least the east/southeast range seems established.

Granada and Murcia

Río Gor

Some 60km northeast of the city of Granada lies the valley of the Río Gor. To either side of the valley is a fertile plateau, high ground that in places is more than 1000m above sea level. The river itself is in summer no more than a stream easily forded or even jumped. Nevertheless, over

Tomb 65 at Río Gor.

the millennia it has cut deeply into the plateau, and the valley now has sides that are often alarmingly precipitous.

On a promontory overlooking the river, just south of the new motorway viaduct, there was a settlement whose inhabitants buried their dead in tholoi, but we could not find sufficient remains of these tholoi to yield an orientation. Megalithic sepulchres, however, are plentiful in the area, being located on the plateau or on the slopes of the valley for some 10km of the river's course, both north and south of the little town of Gorafe. Another group of sepulchres is located a further downstream, near the hamlet of Baños de Alicún de las Torres, and there is a scattering of others elsewhere in the area, notably at the village of El Baúl. In all, 198 sepulchres were described in 1959 by M. García and J.-C. Spahni, who also listed other sepulchres known to earlier investigators but of which they themselves were unable to find any trace.[5]

For the most part the Río Gor sepulchres are modest in size. The typical chamber has a back-stone and three, four or five other orthostats, and measures 2 metres or even less in maximum extent, though a few are significantly larger. There is usually a narrow passage constructed of orthostats to either side, and the entrance orthostat often has a semicircular hole in the centre of its base. On average a Río Gor sepulchre contained seven or eight burials, but tomb no. 84 contained no fewer than 22.

In 1992 and 1993 I visited the area twice, locating tombs partly through the indications given by García and Spahni, and partly with the help of local goatherds. In addition to tombs at Baños de Alicún and at El Baúl, which we discuss below, in these two campaigns we located 79 Río Gor tombs with measurable orientations, from an area where García and Spahni in 1959 found 127 with sufficient remains for their chambers to be classified. The orientations are listed in Table 5.4. All 79 tombs face between 67° and 177°, and so the range is clearly SR/SC.

Moratalla

In the extreme north of the autonomous region of Murcia, immediately east of Andalucía, there is an isolated megalithic tomb: Dolmen de Bagil (2°3′W, 38°14′N), in Moratalla.[6] Although it is no less than 125km northeast of the Río Gor, archaeologists associate it with the culture exemplified in the sepulchres of the Río Gor area, and so we list it in Table 5.4. It faces 91°.

Baños de Alicún

Baños de Alicún is a hamlet 6km northwest of Gorafe. The dozen tombs that exist or existed there are separated from the nearest of the Río Gor sepulchres by some 3km. Ten survive, one of which is now below ground. Although García and Spahni treat the Alicún tombs alongside those of the Río Gor, there are significant differences. The Alicún tombs are typically more ambitious and of greater size than the modest sepulchres hard by the river: four exceed 3½m in length and one reaches 5m. In construction, they favour sides formed of converging rows of aligned orthostats, a form that is unusual by the river, and they show no preference for high ground, a feature so characteristic of the sepulchres along the Río Gor.

These differences are reflected in their significantly different range of azimuths, which is noticeably more southerly than that of the riverside tombs: the orientations of the seven tombs we measured (see Table 5.5) are between 120° and 204°. Tomb 9, whose length of 5 metres makes it the biggest tomb of the region and which fortunately is in an excellent state of preservation, is oriented 204°, and unquestionably faces the western half of the horizon.[7] Its orientation may be genuinely anomalous; but it is just possible that it was deemed to lie within the arc where the sun was around culmination, and travelling almost horizontally before beginning its descent. If so, overall the range may be characterized as SC.

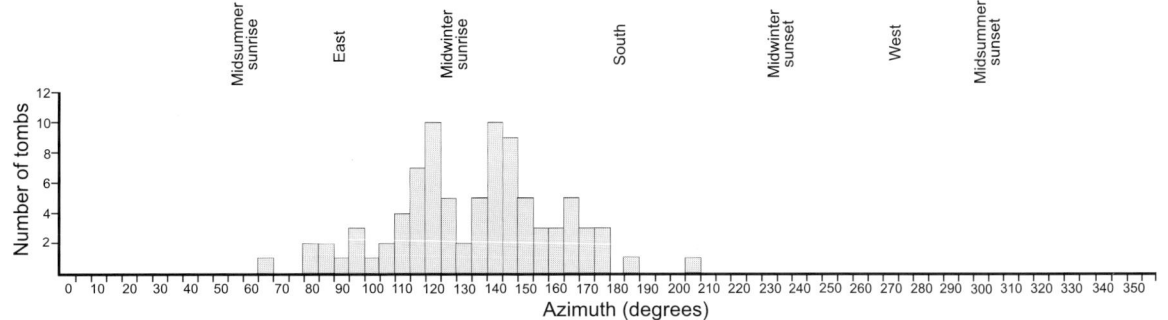

Histogram showing the orientations of 88 megalithic sepulchres along the Río Gor and at Baños de Alicún.

El Baúl

The gorge of the Rambla del Baúl lies some 7km to the east of the Río Gor and follows a parallel course. The village of El Baúl lies on the east bank of the Rambla, and on the opposite bank is a field containing half-a-dozen small megalithic sepulchres in poor condition. These we visited in March 1993.

García and Spahni again treat these sepulchres as part of the Río Gor complex, but again there are significant differences between the two groups. Whereas the Río Gor tombs invariably have a major orthostat that serves as backstone and apparently dictates the construction of the rest of the monument, the El Baúl tombs tend to be polygonal with no one stone pre-eminent; and whereas most Río Gor tombs cluster on the edges or upper slopes of the steep banks of the river, the El Baúl tombs turn away from the nearby gorge and seem, so to speak, to be unaware of its presence.

These differences are reflected in the orientations of the El Baúl tombs, which face well to the south. The absence of backstones and the tiny sizes of the chambers would in any case result in poorly-defined orientations, but the ruinous state of the monuments and the almost total absence of identifiable passages make quantitative measurements impossible. We had to content ourselves with the qualitative assessment, that all the orientations were southerly, around culmination.

Fonelas

On high ground above the modern village of Fonelas, 14km to the southwest of Gorafe, lies the best preserved of several necropolises that had survived in this immediate area into the present century.[8] The tombs were excavated in recent times; but unfortunately the excavators then left them to fall into ruin. As a result we found the orientations difficult to measure; even collation of the monuments with the excavators' reports was problematic, not least because the reports provide no plan of the site. We visited the area in March 1993, and were able to locate and measure ten tombs.

The tombs vary considerably in size. The larger ones have a relatively wide trapezoidal

Orientations of 8 megalithic sepulchres at Fonelas. The broken line indicates the probable direction of Tomb 7, which may however have faced in the reverse direction.

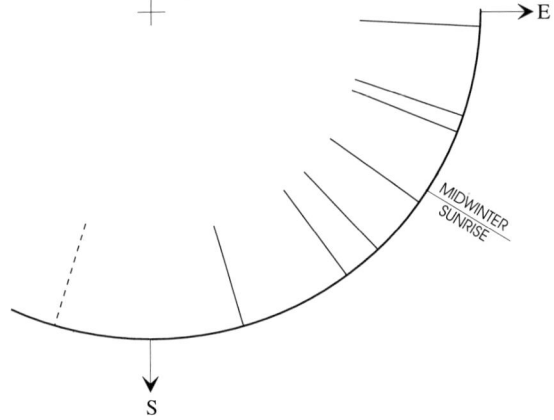

chamber, with a back-wall up to 2¾m in length and formed (unusually) of not one but several orthostats, while the sides are somewhat longer and converge gently towards the entrance passage; some of the chambers are known to have been subdivided. The smaller tombs are similar in shape, being merely scaled down, with chambers between 1m and 1¾m in width and of similar length. As at the Río Gor, the tombs are on high ground and sited in relation to the cliff edges.

The orientations are listed in Table 5.6. We see that, with the exception of Tomb 7, where doubts as to the location of the passage made the direction of the axis uncertain, all the tombs faced well within the southeast quadrant, so that the range may be characterized as SR/SC.

Montefrío

Near the town of Montefrío, some 40km west-northwest of the city of Granada, is an extensive cluster of megalithic sepulchres that have been excavated in recent years by teams from the University of Granada.[9] The tombs generally consist of a rectangular (or trapezoidal) chamber and a short passage — and this despite the fact that most contained the remains of only one individual (in a few cases, of two persons). Though rarely exceeding 8 metres in overall length, the tombs are significantly more substantial than those of the Río Gor area, both in overall size and in the weight of the individual stones.

We visited the site in 1991 and again in 1993, and measured almost all the tombs. The 41 orientations are listed in Table 5.7. All face between 74° and 159°, a range of less than a quadrant. But if we take the three most southerly-facing (SC) tombs to be exceptions, then we are left with 38 tombs (92·7%) that face in the narrow range between 74° and 128°. When the skyline altitudes are taken into account, we find that these tombs faced sunrise in the autumn, winter or spring, an SR pattern that we shall find repeated many times.

Orientations of 41 megalithic sepulchres at Montefrío.

Tomb 22 at Montefrío.

El Pantano de los Bermejales

Some 30km to the southwest of Granada, the Río Cacín runs in a northwesterly direction through fertile countryside. It feeds into an extensive dam or *pantano* around which are *bermejales*, areas thickly strewn with rock and often steep. Beside the dam, and near both banks of the river for some 5km downstream, are small groups of tombs and cave burials that first came to notice in 1964 when a drop in the level of the waters of the dam revealed a megalithic tomb of unusual construction, consisting of a long gallery that led to a relatively small, cubical chamber. The sides of the gallery were lined with orthostats, as were the walls of the chamber itself, and the roofs of both chamber and gallery were also made of flat slabs. The whole monument was covered with an earthen mound, whose perimeter was marked by small stones forming a retaining kerb. Unfortunately for our purposes, to save it from the waters the tomb had to be removed and reconstructed on higher ground, and so its original orientation can no longer be measured.

However, this discovery drew attention to the region, and by the end of the decade several more sepulchres had come to light. In all, some 22 tombs were located, and archaeologists divided them into seven little groups scattered along both banks of the river.[10] Most of the tombs have since been submerged in the waters of the dam or destroyed by farmers, but the survivors are remarkably varied in both type and size. For example, the pair that make up Group 3 of the tombs shared a tumulus some 25m in diameter. The larger and more conventional had been a substantial structure trapezoidal in shape and some 5½m long. Lying athwart the sometime entrance at the east end was a much smaller tomb (now almost vanished); this tomb was strangely L-shaped and had no clear orientation.

In 1992 we failed to find a sizeable tomb of Group 4 that had contained the remains of some 75 individuals. We therefore revisited the area in April 1993, and chanced to meet two elderly gentlemen who had once worked on the farm and who had witnessed the deliberate use of machinery to destroy the tomb. The space cleared by this act of vandalism was intended for use as part of the farm complex — but this complex had already been abandoned: a tomb that had survived for millennia was sacrificed to make space for buildings that were in use for only a decade or two.

In all, we identified and measured seven tombs, all of which were megalithic sepulchres, of varying shapes and sizes (Table 5.8). Despite this variety, six of the seven have orientations within a range of only 30° and are SR (to within a degree or two), having faced sunrise in the winter half of the year. The seventh, with orientation 145°, is clearly SC.

Málaga

In the province of Málaga[11] there are no great concentrations of small megalithic sepulchres as at Alhama de Almería, Río Gor and Montefrío, nor are there lesser groupings as at Fonelas or El Pantano de los Bermejales. Instead, the megalithic tombs of the province are large, isolated dolmens. Using information supplied by Ignacio Marques of the University of Malaga, we were able to visit ten of them during two visits, the first in 1992 and the second in 2000. The glory of the province, however, resides in the three monumental tombs at Antequera, one megalithic, one tholos, and one a galleried tomb similar in form to the rescued tomb at El Pantano de los Bermejales.

Chaperas and Tajillo del Moro

On the road leading north from the coastal city of Málaga is the little town of Caserbermeja. Some 6km south of the town, on a high crest separating two little rivers, are the two sepulchres of the Necropolis of Chaperas, and in April 2000 we located the first of these. It has an overall length of 6m, and is notable in having the corridor subdivided into segments by side pillars. It faces 81°.

Some 3km east of Casabermeja is the isolated sepulchre of Tajillo del Moro. It is 4m in length, and nearly 2m in width, and has orientation 97°.

Antequera

Near the town of Antequera, some 35km north of Málaga and at the intersection of routes important commercially in prehistoric times, are three of the most remarkable tombs of southern Spain. They are all built on a massive scale; indeed, it is as though giants had visited the area and decided to erect scaled-up versions of the tombs of mere humans. Yet all are of different form. Why each of three groups of builders, following wholly different customs, should have chosen to build once only (or so it seems) and on such a scale is a mystery.

(*Left*) The approach to Dolmen de Viera at Antequera; (*right*) the gallery, with the rectangular chamber beyond.

The first of the tombs is Dolmen de Viera,[12] which was discovered in 1905 and restored in 1941. It is a scaled-up version of the galleried sepulchre rescued from the waters of El Pantano de los Bermejales. The gallery (today nearly 10m long) leads to a relatively small rectangular chamber whose sides measure less than 2m. The axis, from the midpoint of the entrance to the chamber to the midpoint of the entrance to the gallery, has azimuth 96°; the side-walls of the gallery, however, are not perfectly straight and a section is aligned to 93°, which, when the skyline altitude is taken into account, happens to correspond to the equinox sunrise.

Dolmen del Romeral[13] is a tholos. Enclosed within a vast tumulus no less than 85m in diameter, it too was discovered in 1905 and restored in 1941. The passage is now 14½m long, but was originally of twice that length; it is uninterrupted by any of the pierced dividing slabs common in the tholoi of Almería, and the entrance to the chamber is formed of uprights and a lintel. This chamber itself is over 5m in diameter, and the false cupola ceiling is of exceptional size. An inner chamber, smaller but of similar design, is offset a little from the main axis. This axis, from the centre of the principal chamber along the centre of the passage, has a well-defined azimuth of 199° (skyline altitude 5°), and so faces west of due south, though it might be argued that the sun

Dolmen de Menga at Antequera. The achievement of the builders in lowering the huge capstones onto the sidestones and central supports is nothing short of amazing.

was then still around culmination.

Dolmen de Menga (sometimes, like the others, termed a 'Cueva', though 'cave' is a gross mis-nomer) is close by Viera.[14] Likewise restored in 1941, it is of staggering dimensions, being built of stones that would have dismayed an Egyptian. The chamber has the structure of a colossal mega-lithic sepulchre, each of the sides being formed of seven lofty orthostats; it is 18½m long, and 6m wide at its maximum. The passage is short by comparison: 5m long and 3½m wide. Chamber and passage are together roofed with five enormous slabs, the biggest of which is 2½m thick, 6m long, and at least 7m wide as it spans the chamber, giving a volume of over 100 cubic metres. These great stones had been fetched from a distance of over 1km. The irregular shape of the side-walls of the chamber, and the relative shortness of the passage, prevent the monument from having a precisely-defined orientation; but it faces close to northeast.

Such an orientation is most unusual — indeed, in facing north of midsummer sunrise it is unique among the numerous tombs we have so far studied in this chapter. As usual, one regrets having to invent an excuse for the anomalous orientation of a single monument, but a visitor to the site sees at once that the tomb faces a nearby mountain of bizarre shape: for the rock formation looks exactly like the face of a sleeping giant. Once one has noticed this, it is difficult to remember that this is no more than an odd quirk of geology. Not to put too fine a point upon it, the mountain gives you the creeps. I think it is the target for the orientation of the great tomb.

Encinas Borrachas

Further to the west, and not far south of the historic town of Ronda, is a scattered group of three megalithic sepulchres forming the Necropolis of Encinas Borrachas. Encinas Borrachas 1 has not been excavated, but has the familiar trapezoidal shape. It is 7 metres in length, and faces 132° in azimuth, towards where the sun rose at midwinter behind a steep hill. Encinas Borrachas 2 lies a little over 1km to the southwest. It is ruined and has been much disturbed by the pressure

The view from on top of the corridor of Dolmen de Menga, looking towards the mountain that resembles the face of a sleeping giant.

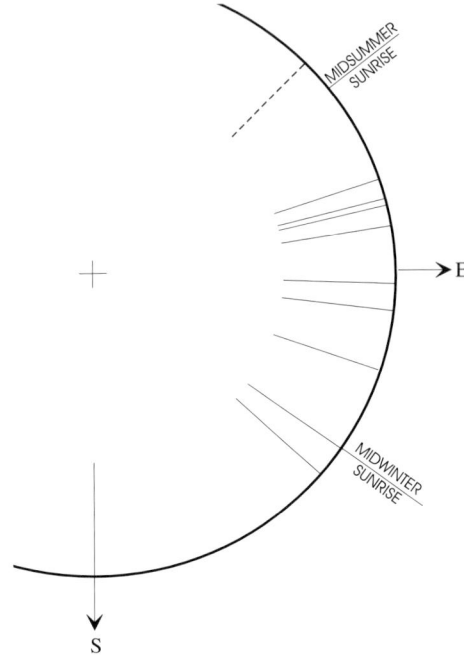

Orientations of 11 megalithic sepulchres in the province of Málaga. Menga is shown with a broken line.

El Sepulcro de La Giganta.

of earth, but the backstone appears to be *in situ* or almost so, and if so the tomb faced roughly
south. There is a further tomb, Encinas Borrachas 3, but this we did not locate on our first visit;
an attempt to do so in 2000 was frustrated by the high fence that has been erected by the landowner, as a result of which all three tombs are now inaccessible.

Los Gigantes

Some 10km northwest of Ronda lies a pair of megalithic sepulchres that came to light in 1941.
One, known as El Sepulcro de La Giganta, is near the farmhouse of El Chopo. There is no longer
any clear division between the chamber and the passage, but its length overall exceeds 12m, and
its orientation has azimuth 92°.

Nearly 3km to the east is El Sepulcro de El Gigante. It appears to be similar to La Giganta in
construction, but it is in a poorer state of preservation, and today is only about 5m in length. Its
orientation has azimuth 75°.

La Angostura

Some 8km further to the northwest lie the three sepulchres that form the Necropolis of La Angostura. They were excavated in 1975. La Angostura 1, or Sepulcro de El Charcón, is near the top of a very steep hill that rises to over 1000m. It is in a fair state of preservation, with much of the roof intact. The rectangular chamber and porch together measure 8½m overall, and the surrounding tumulus, now largely vanished, was some 21m in diameter. The tomb is oriented 77° in azimuth. La Angostura 2, Sepulcro de Algorrobales, is some 600m further south, in the garden of a house. The well-preserved chamber is nearly 6m in length and is oriented 109°. La Angostura 3, Sepulcro de Lagarín, has a rectangular chamber and a short porch, measuring 4½m overall, and is oriented 125°.

El Moral

3km to the east of La Angostura 3 and high above the farm of El Moral, is a tomb that was discovered and published by the owner, whose site plan suggested it had a wholly anomalous northerly orientation.[15] In fact it has a double backstone that faces a very normal 76°, though it is true that the corridor turns north, thereby avoiding the narrow strip of bedrock between the tomb and the steep downward slope it faces.

Leaving aside Menga, we measured in all the orientations of ten megalithic sepulchres in Málaga. Though they are widely dispersed, their orientations (Table 5.9) are remarkably consistent: with the exception of the ruined, south-facing Encinas Borrachas 2, all are SR.

Córdoba

For our statistical enquiry we need tombs in numbers, and if possible of uniform construction. As we have proceeded westwards through Andalucía, the extensive necropolises of Alhama de Almería, Río Gor and Montefrío have given place to scattered tombs. As we continue our clockwise journey around the peninsula we find that this continues to be the case in the next three provinces, Córdoba, Sevilla and Cádiz, which lie respectively north, west and southwest of Málaga.

Córdoba's tombs are modest in scale and widely-scattered, and nearly all are north of the Guadalquivir river (which flows from east to west through the modern city of Córdoba). Most are in groups and located near settlements, but some are isolated or in pairs. Those that are megalithic range from small tombs with near-circular chambers of slate and in some instances a corridor, to large sepulchres lined with orthostats that reduce in height towards the entrance. Some however are of varying forms of tholos construction; the chamber may be formed of orthostats or of drystone or of a combination of the two, while the roof is always false cupola, and in one there is even a side-chamber.

Most of the tombs are in poor condition, and few have been dated using modern techniques. The surviving grave goods show that the megalithic tombs were in use in the high Copper Age (first half of the third millennium), while the tholoi appear to be a little later.

Orientations of 15 tombs in the province of Córdoba.

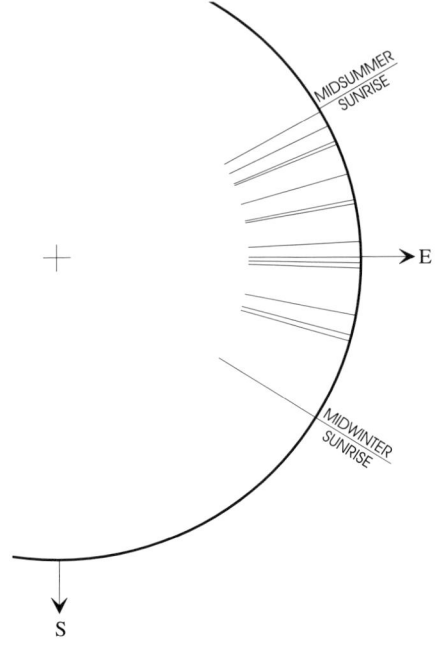

In April 2000 I was able to visit a representative sample of these monuments in collaboration with José Martín de la Cruz of Córdoba University, J. Carlos Vera Rodríguez of Huelva University, and a local carpenter who possessed the keys to the gates of even the most remote farms. Two of the tombs, the dolmens of La Sierra Zuela de Posadas, lay close to the Guadalquivir river, some 30km southwest of the city of Córdoba. The first is a small galleried tomb, and the second is doubtless of similar construction though only two of its sidestones are visible. Most, however, were some 50km north of the city, near Belmez and Fuente Obejuna, or a little further east, around Villanueva de Córdoba. Two, and probably three, of the Fuente Obejuna tombs are tholoi, as is Minguillo 4, south of Villanueva. The remainder are megalithic.

In all we measured fifteen tombs (Table 5.10), every one of which faced within the range of sunrise. No fewer than nine faced sunrise in the six summer months of the year, while all save one faced well to the north of midwinter sunrise, the exception being Delgados 2 at Fuente Obejuna, the tholos with side-chamber. This tomb, which is in poor condition, was oriented roughly towards midwinter sunrise.

Sevilla

A recent multimedia catalogue of the province of Sevilla has raised the number of known megalithic and tholos monuments to 65, all of them funerary in purpose. The megalithic tombs are found mainly on high ground, such as the northern and southern sierras that flank the Guadalquivir valley, whereas tholoi (and artificial caves) predominate along the valley itself. This is the opposite of what one might expect, since the valley communities were the largest and had the manpower needed to handle megaliths.

In visits in 1997 and 2000, we were able to investigate four isolated groups of tombs. The tombs of three groups are conventional in their orientations, but the two tombs that make up the fourth group are extraordinary both in scale and in their excellent state of preservation, and still more extraordinary in their possible implications for archaeoastronomy.

El Gandul

Some 15km southeast of the city of Seville is the hamlet of El Gandul, with its prison and military base, a truly unpromising start. However, by the Neolithic it had acquired the character of a sacred site, which it retained down to early historic times, and so perhaps it is unsurprising that we encounter there a remarkable miscellany of tomb types. I visited the area in June 1997 and measured five tombs (Table 5.11), all of them on farmland or on land used for military exercises. Las Canteras has a circular chamber excavated out of the bedrock, and this had a false cupola ceiling; the chamber of El Pedrejón is again circular; El Vaquero has an intact corridor some 15m in length leading to a tholos chamber that has a side-chamber; La Casilla is a conventional gallery, though its corridor is less straight than usual; and El Termino, the strangest of all, has a corridor leading to a circular chamber excavated out of the bedrock, and from the chamber a subsidiary corridor at right-angles to the first leads to a second and smaller chamber. All however have unexceptional orientations, three facing within the range of sunrise and the remaining two a little further to the south.

El Castillo de las Guardas

El Castillo de las Guardas is some 40km northwest of Seville and near the border with Huelva where, as we shall see, the tombs become frequent once more. It is home to a group of tombs located on a *rancho* dedicated to the breeding of bulls for the bullring. We found ourselves sharing a field with innumerable bulls, but the bulls were soon in undisputed occupation. Nearby is another group of tombs, Antón Núñez I–IV, tiny and in very poor condition, each best identifiable through the remains of its tumulus. Indeed, so poor is their condition that their authenticity is questioned, and so we omit them from Table 5.11. If genuine, two of them face 97° and 90° respectively; the condition of the third was so poor that its orientation was unmeasurable, and we were unable to locate the fourth.

Almadén de la Plata

The greatest concentration of tombs in the province is near Almadén de la Plata, in the Sierra Morena which runs east–west a hundred kilometres or so north of the city of Seville. In July 2000 I was invited to join a surveying team of students from the University of Bradford led by Leonardo García Sanjuán. We measured nine megalithic tombs (Table 5.11), modest in scale and in poor condition, but with sizeable corridors. Eight faced easterly, six of them within the range of sunrise. The most southerly-facing of the eight (az. 136°, and so some 15° south of the range

The view from the chamber of Matarrubilla, Valencina de la Concepción, looking along the corridor towards the modern entrance steps.

of sunrise) had a clearly identifiable chamber and, no less than 16 metres away, an equally clear corridor entrance, but nothing was visible of the rest of the corridor in the scrub separating them; it is just possible that the chamber faced within the range of sunrise but that the corridor later veered a little to the south.

Of greatest interest, however, was the ninth dolmen, which the team had identified the previous week and named Dolmen de Bradford. Only a few centimetres of the stones protruded from the ground and this made the authenticity of the 'dolmen' a matter of debate; furthermore, two trees had clearly disturbed the layout and compromised the measurement of the orientation. Nevertheless, we agreed that the odds were in favour of its authenticity, and if so, the dolmen's orientation was a very surprising 32° or so. However, when I calculated the corresponding declination, taking into account the unusually high skyline altitude of some 8°, I realized that the tomb would have faced the rising of Arcturus around 3000 BC, provided of course that it had been constructed by that date.

To give context and perhaps plausibity to such an orientation we need to investigate two great tombs at Valencina de la Concepción, located 10km west of Seville and now effectively a suburb; for the Valencina settlement may well have interacted with the smaller farming communities to the north, and the similarity between the (most unusual) orientations of Dolmen de Bradford and one of the Valencina dolmens may be a reflection of this.

Valencina de la Concepción

In the third millennium, when it was close to the sea, Valencina was the site of a vast settlement, a number of whose tombs survived into modern times. One, Ontiveros, is under a modern house, and only the beginning of the (lengthy) corridor is accessible even to the owners; it apparently faces east-southeasterly. Another was discovered during a recent rescue excavation, but its huge size called for greater resources than were then available, and so it has been covered over and preserved for future study. Two others are vast tombs that are cherished by the city fathers; they are among the treasures of Spanish prehistory — and they have orientations of exceptional interest.

The first is Matarrubilla, which has a tholos chamber, on the floor of which is a remarkable stone slab that appears to have been a table for offerings. Access to the chamber is along a perfectly-straight and uninterrupted corridor no less than 37 metres in length and 2 metres in height. The side-walls incline slightly, so that the width reduces from 140cm at the floor to 130cm at the ceiling.

When one is standing in the tholos chamber and looking along the vast, straight corridor towards the modern concrete steps built to allow safe entry down into the tomb, one cannot doubt that the builders had adopted an orientation that had significance for them. The layout seems to invite an astronomical motivation, although today, because of the steps and the farmer's olive trees immediately outside, it is no longer possible to glimpse the sky from the chamber. The orientation, which Victor Hurtado and I measured by compass in 1997 as carefully as possible, was wholly exceptional, just under 18° in azimuth. Only after perusing the chapters that follow will the reader appreciate just how very unusual is so northerly an orientation. But there is no escaping the fact that Matarrubilla, a magnificent tomb of unquestionable authenticity, faced far to the north of the ranges of the rising of sun or moon or planets. Could it be possible that the tomb faced the rising of an individual star, or even of a constellation, in the manner of Menorcan taulas?

I considered the possibility of a stellar orientation with great reluctance. As Anthony Aveni wrote in a review in *Nature*:

> There are several reasons why, when it comes to postulating theories of orientations, archaeoastronomers stay away from the stars. First of all there is the problem of selection — there are 6,000 points of light visible to the naked eye.... A second problem is that, unlike the sun and moon, the stellar changes in rise–set position are both highly dependent on the epoch [because of the precession of the earth's axis] and variable from star to star. Third is the so-called problem of extinction. Even under optimal conditions, only the two or three very brightest stars are visible all the way down to zero-degrees elevation, and the fainter the star, the higher above the horizon it will be seen to disappear.[16]

There are indeed archaeoastronomers who postulate stellar 'targets' for every tomb, and because the tombs are of uncertain date, and there are so many stars, whose risings and settings are ill-defined in azimuth as they fade from view in the atmosphere of the Earth, these claims can never be disproved. As Karl Popper taught us, a theory that cannot be falsified is of no value.

Nevertheless, as we saw in Chapter 4, in Egypt the brightest star Sirius was an object of cult, as was the constellation Orion, and so orientations on stars are not in themselves impossible, merely difficult to justify. Thus a claim that an entire constellation was the target of the single tomb Matarrubilla would be unfalsifiable, and so pointless; but might the tomb have faced the rising of one of the very brightest stars visible from Valencina, at a date acceptable for the construction of the tomb? Given the exceptional precision with which the great tomb can be measured, this seemed a challenging possibility.

Clearly measurement of the orientation by theodolite was called for, and in April 2000 Fernando Pimenta of Lisbon agreed to meet me in Valencina for the purpose. Alas, the heavens opened, and not only did the clouds make the use of a theodolite impossible but the very chamber of the tomb was flooded. Undeterred, Fernando Pimenta made a second journey from Lisbon, but this time his car broke down on the way. A third attempt, however, was successful, and yielded an azimuth of 17°48'. The corresponding point on the skyline was near where Arcturus rose late in the fourth millennium BC, Arcturus being then the third brightest star in the Valencinan sky, outshone only by Sirius and α Cen. Encouraged, we felt we must now make an equally accurate measurement of the limits in altitude of the sky that was once visible from inside the tomb. And so late in July 2000 my resolute Portugese friend set out from home at 3 a.m. to collect me from my base in the north of Sevilla province, so that we could work together at Valencina. To an observer in the chamber deep within the tomb, the lintel of the original entrance provided an upper limit to the external field of view, namely 1.1° above the horizontal. Today a lower limit of 0.9° is provided by the modern steps, but the distant skyline as seen from the entrance itself has altitude 0.6°, and it is very possible that in prehistoric times this skyline was also visible from the chamber. If so, the sky as seen from the chamber had an upper altitude of 1.1° and a lower altitude of 0.6°. As the tomb has latitude 37°25', these limits correspond to declinations +49°47' and +49°15' respectively. Arcturus had the latter declination just before 3100 BC, and the former just before 3200, and so it is a fact that the tomb (intentionally or otherwise) faced the rising of Arcturus when constructed, *provided* it was built in the decades immediately prior to 3100.

Before we consider the plausibility of this date, we must make a parallel study of nearby La Pastora. This too is a tholos approached via a long corridor, some 44 metres in length (of which the outermost section now lacks its roof). The corridor is markedly more cramped, being only 1½ metres in height, and there are three successive portals, each with a lintel and side-pillars that protrude from the walls. This makes it all the more remarkable that the sky is, even today, visible from the chamber. My compass measure of just under 243° was within the range of sunset, but by analogy with Matarrubilla it suggested instead the setting point of Sirius, the brightest star in the sky. (In the minds of historians of early astronomy, Sirius and Arcturus are already linked as being the only two individual stars mentioned by Hesiod in his poem on the agricultural calendar, *Works and days*, which we mentioned in Chapter 3 in connection with the tally on the Maltese temple of Mnajdra.) The theodolite gave an azimuth of 242°57′, and the lower limit of the visible skyline, defined by a nearby hill imagined without the hedge on its crest, has altitude 1.8°; the original upper limit is uncertain owing to the destruction of the roof near the entrance. The lower limit corresponds to a declination of –20°12′, and if we suppose that the original entrance lintel gave an upper limit of (say) 2° altitude, this would correspond to a declination of –20°03′. Sirius had declination –20°14′ in 2300 BC and –19°57′ in 2200 BC. La Pastora therefore faced the setting of Sirius when constructed, *provided* it was built in the 23rd century BC.

With more than a little interest I consulted my archaeological friends of nearby Seville University as to the likely construction dates of the great tombs. I was advised that they had little evidence to go on, though La Pastora was clearly later than Matarrubilla; and that as far as present knowledge goes, our proposed dates were perfectly possible. While encouraging as far as it went, this was in some ways a disappointing verdict, since (uniquely?) a stellar hypothesis had implied construction dates defined with an accuracy of only a few decades: we had expected a more challenging test of these dates.

Given the extraordinary lengths and straightness of the corridors of the two great tombs, it

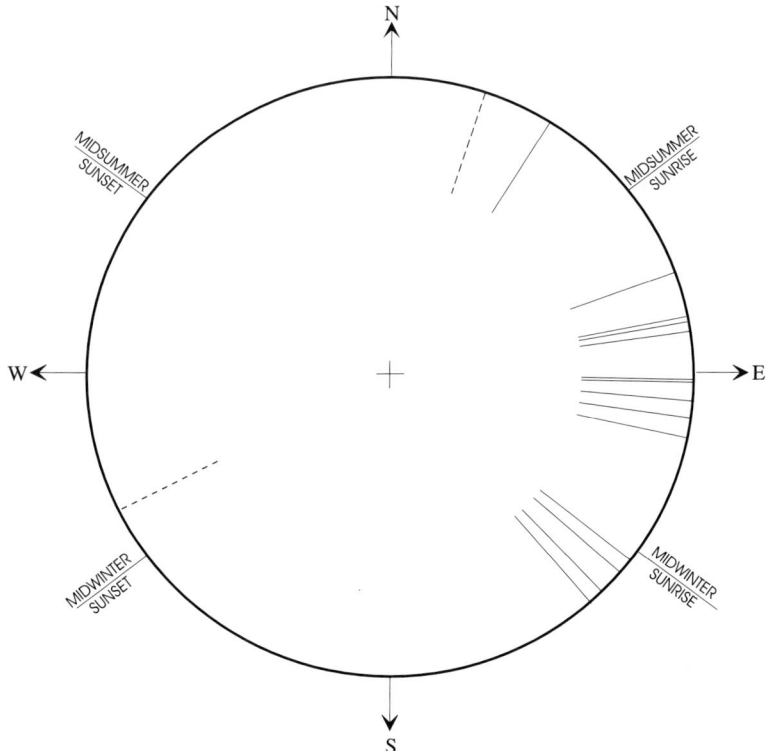

Orientations of 16 tombs in the province of Sevilla. Matarrubilla and La Pastora, Valencina de la Concepción, are shown with broken lines.

is difficult to suppose that their orientations were of scant significance to the builders. An astro-nomical interpretation seems almost inescapable, and we have seen that the archaeological evidence is compatible with the hypothesis that each tomb faced the rising or setting of one of the very brightest stars at the time it was constructed. Valencina was a settlement of vast extent and influence. Do we find, in neighbouring regions of Spain, any additional clues to stellar orientations?

Though orientations around north-northeast are almost unknown in southern Europe and the Mediterranean islands, there are three more such tombs not far from Valencina. We have already mentioned Dolmen de Bradford, which faced the rising of Arcturus around 3000 BC (though the imprecision of the orientation prevents us from being more specific). In the province of Badajoz, at Monesterio, some 30km northwest of Almadén, we came across another megalithic tomb, La Dehesa del Hospital (Table 5.14), that would have faced the rising of Arcturus around 2500 BC. A fourth tomb, Los Charcones at Benalup near the southernmost tip of the peninsula (Table 5.12), faced the rising of Arcturus towards the end of the third millennium. It is remarkable that orientation on the rising of Arcturus could provide a motivation for all four of these (most exceptional) north-northeasterly orientations — provided of course that the suggested construction dates continue to be archaeologically acceptable.

Cádiz

Cádiz is the southernmost province of Spain, and I learned from Carlos Vera of the existence there of a handful of tombs only in the summer of 2000. They were, according to publications written long ago,[18] westerly facing; if so, this was highly unusual for the Iberian peninsula, and it was therefore important to visit them and perhaps identify the motive that underlay the builders' choice of orientations.

La Laguna de la Janda lies a mere 20km or so from the very tip of the Iberian peninsula, and is to the west of Gibraltar. The lake in question existed in prehistoric times and is being studied by a group of palaeobotanists from the University of Córdoba. Some years ago the lake was largely drained and the land given over to agriculture, with disastrous consequences for the migrating birds who were using it as a staging post on their journey south. Some members of the aristocratic family who own the land favoured restoring at least part of the lake, but this was opposed by other members, and the resulting dissension poses problems for archaeologists who wish to cross parcels of land belonging to more than one owner. Five of us eventually set out, including Carlos Vera and members of the palaeobotany team who knew the area intimately, and we reached the tombs without incident.

The region, as it happened, was the very last piece of the geographical jigsaw surveyed in this book, and the tombs it contained were novel indeed. Located on sloping ground overlooking the plain that once contained the lake, they are galleries, only a metre or so in width but up to 7m in length, with parallel sides consisting of rows of orthostats. In structure their novelty consists in the extraordinary scale of the typical backstone in relation to the modest width of the chamber.

of the entrance, but the back of the chamber was formed of circular, drum-shaped stones incised with *cazoletas* or cup-marks — a curious method of defining the space within a chamber. Also, of the megalithic tombs of Huelva that we measured, it is the only one to face close to south.

If the structure of La Belleza was unfamiliar, that of the other two was so familiar — but so unexpected this far south in the peninsula — that each was greeted with the cry, "It's an anta!" In the Alentejo region of Portugal, as we shall see in the next chapter, there are great numbers of tombs built to a very distinctive pattern. Indeed, they are so characteristic of central Portugal that when we are in the field we speak of them as 'antas', using a generic Portugese term for 'dolmen', even though, strictly speaking, they are simply one form of anta; and for convenience we shall do the same in the pages that follow.

The constructors of an anta began by inserting a lofty orthostat into the ground to serve as the backstone. They then positioned two further lofty slabs to lean against it, one to the left and the other to the right. These slabs are not true orthostats set vertically in the ground, but are supported by the backstone on which they lean. The builders next placed two further slabs, one to left and the other to right, to lean against the last two; and then two more, to lean against these. The result is an octagonal-shaped chamber formed of seven stones, the eighth side (that opposite the backstone) opening to provide the entrance and often leading to a lengthy corridor.

The builders usually made little attempt to level off the tops of the lofty slabs. This, and the overlapping of the side-stones, none of them vertical but each leaning for support on one of its neighbours, create an instantly-recognizable construction. Happily for our enquiries, tombs of

The corridor of Los Gabrieles 4, Valverde del Camino, which begins (left foreground) in one direction and then veers sharply to the left.

El Pozuelo 6 at Zalamea la Real. The entrance corridor is at bottom left. The corridor then divides, with its left-hand branch seen in the centre of the picture; this branch itself divides, one part turning left and passing under the surviving capstone while the other part turns right and enters the reconstructed tumulus under another capstone. The right-hand branch of the original corridor passes behind the prominent stone in the right foreground, and then divides; one part does a U-turn to the left, to enter a chamber whose two backstones are seen at the upper right-hand edge of the photograph. These backstones therefore face in a direction opposite to that of the monument as a whole.

this form are widespread: they occur in the three Spanish border provinces of Huelva, Badajoz and Cáceres, and extend across a broad band of central Portugal as far as the Atlantic coast. They form a large and well-identified statistical population, certainly one of the finest in Europe for archaeoastronomical study. In this chapter we merely note the presence in our area of a handful of southerly outliers of this form of construction, reserving the analysis of the population as a whole for the following chapter.

I had visited Huelva out of duty, to complete my coverage of the tombs of the peninsula, and with no expectation of encountering wholly novel forms of construction. La Belleza was a 'one-off'; but the province had two other surprises in store.

The first surprise, embodied in two of the tombs at Los Gabrieles, Valverde del Camino, involved the sharp and unequivocal change of direction in the middle of the lengthy corridor that we mentioned above. The corridor of Los Gabrieles 4 begins with azimuth 104°, and suddenly alters direction no less than 50° to the north, towards azimuth 54°. The corridor of Los Gabrieles 6 begins with azimuth 90°, and ends with 61°. This latter direction is within the range of sunrise, but the 54° of Los Gabrieles 4 corresponds to declination +28° (a few degrees north of midsummer sunrise, and close to the extreme northerly rising of the moon).

The second surprise arose from several tombs that we might term 'hydra', to borrow the name of the many-headed monster of Greek mythology. To have two or more independent chambers within a single tumulus or mound is not unknown (indeed, as we shall see in Chapter 13, this is normal in the 'sesi' of Pantelleria, and it is found too in northern France); and side-chambers leading off the main chamber or off the corridor are common enough in Iberia. But in a hydra tomb of Huelva the tumulus has a single entrance, and the entrance corridor then divides into two, three or even four secondary corridors, each leading to a chamber, all of which seem to be of the same status. In tomb no. 6 at El Pozuelo, Zalamea la Real, for example, there are four chambers, and the access corridor to one of the four does a complete U-turn, so that the exit from this chamber at first leads westerly, in the opposite direction to the easterly (SR) orientation that the tomb as a whole shares with most of the megalithic tombs of the province. This suggests that here the symbolic direction of importance was that of the exit of the main corridor to the outside world, and not the exit from the chamber itself.

In addition to the south-facing La Belleza and the two antas, we measured 27 megalithic tombs (see Table 5.13), including the massive Dolmen de Soto 1 with its famous carvings. Of the

The chamber and corridor of Dolmen de Soto 1, a truly megalithic sepulchre.

27, no fewer than 25 were SR, while one faced a little too far north, and one a little too far south. In all, 27 (90.0%) of the 30 megalithic tombs were SR, a welcome return to normality after the west- and north-facing tombs of Sevilla and Cádiz.

A little cluster of tholoi, today three in number, are located near Santa Bárbara de Casa. One has the SR orientation of 85°, but the other two face far to the south, with SC orientations of 161° and 170°.

Southeast Badajoz

The Spanish province of Badajoz forms the southern half of the autonomous region of Extremadura, and lies immediately north of the Andalusian provinces of Sevilla and Huelva. It is bordered on the west by Portugal. The southeast of the province belongs archaeologically with the present chapter, while the eleven antas of the northwest belong to the chapter that follows. Here, therefore, we discuss tombs lying southeast of a line drawn between the towns of Mérida and Jerez de los Caballeros (see Table 5.14), for convenience deeming a twelfth anta, in Jerez itself, to lie northwest of this line.

We visited the area in September 1998 and worked with the assistance of three local archaeologists.[21] To the east of Mérida we were shown a tomb of most unusual construction, Dolmen de Megacela, whose subcircular chamber is formed of a ring of no fewer than twelve substantial orthostats of similar heights, with a gap in the ring for the entrance. Its orientation, however, was a very usual 86°.

Further southeast, in the region of Llerena near the province of Sevilla, the five tombs we measured were disappointing, being modest in scale, in poor condition, and difficult to interpret.

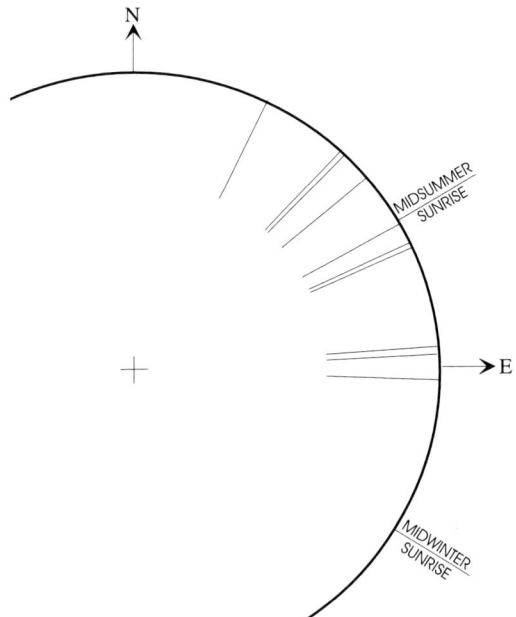

Orientations of 10 tombs of southeast Badajoz.

Dolmen de Magacela which, most unusually, has a circular chamber formed of twelve substantial orthostats.

One may be a tiny tholos: Dolmen de Veguilla 1, which has a chamber of only 1¾m diameter formed by a ring of seven small separated stones, none of them with more than 15cm showing above ground. We later learned that three of the five tombs were near to iron mines, and we cannot exclude the possibility of an anomaly affecting our compass. Yet the measurements, however insecure, lay within the range from northeast to east-northeast, which is unusually far north.

Near Jerez de los Caballeros, in the southwest of the province, our spirits were lifted by the magnificent tholos, Dolmen de la Grania del Toriñuelo. This vast tomb has a chamber nearly 5m in radius, and a corridor 25m in length; its orientation is an unexceptional 86°. Not far away is a galleried tomb that faces 92°.

When I revisited the province in July 2000, in addition to the tomb at Monasterio oriented 26° that we discussed in connection with the tombs at Valencina de la Concepción, we measured a dolmen, hitherto unknown but close to the Km 52 stone on the road Ex202, that faced 50°. Putting these data together, we find that of the ten tombs of several different types that we measured in southeast Badajoz, one faced sunrise around the equinoxes, while all the other nine faced further north: six towards sunrise in the summer months, and the other three well north of the range of sunrise. Even the Jerez anta that we postponed to the next chapter faced to the far north of the SR range. Such a pattern is very unusual.

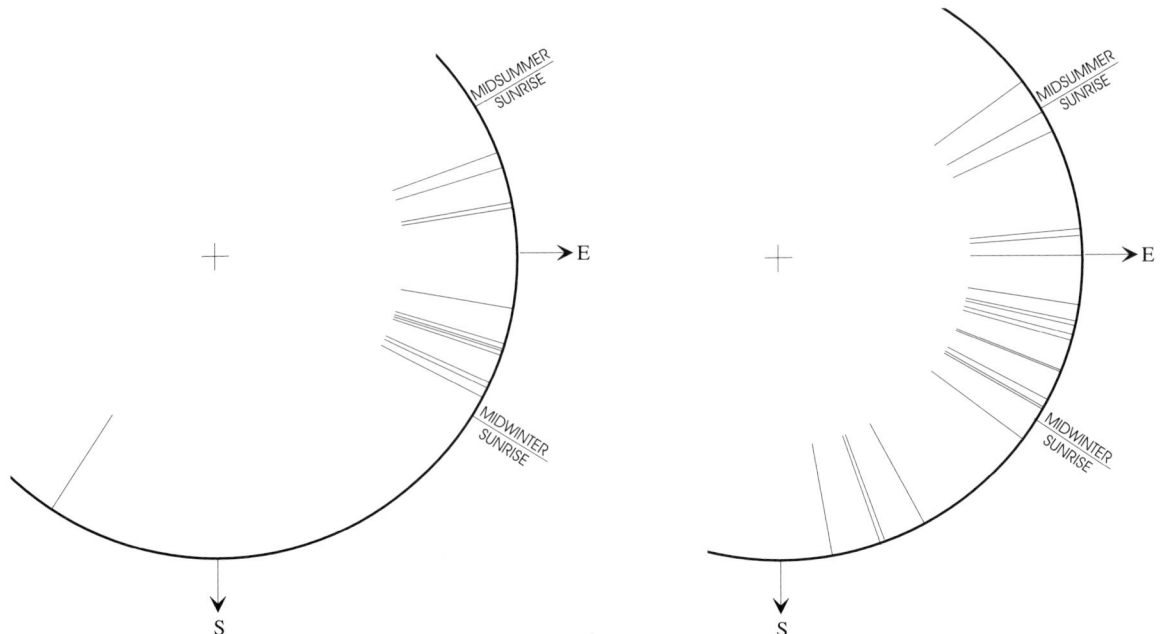

(*Left*) Orientations of 13 megalithic tombs of southern Portugal and the Lisbon area. Not shown are five antas, which are included in the histogram on p. 98. (*Right*) Orientations of 21 tholoi of southwest Iberia (Huelva, southeast Badajoz, southern Portugal, the Lisbon area, and the Alentejo).

Southern Portugal

The antas of central Portugal form one of the most impressive collections of prehistoric tombs in Europe. By contrast, in the south of the country (see Table 5.15) the tombs are widely scattered, the most notable concentration being near the town of Ourique, which lies some 60km from the south coast and 50km from the Atlantic away to the west. The region is known to have contained the remains of nearly fifty monuments, of various types and dates of construction, but the locations of a great many of them are unknown today. The surviving tombs include classic antas, tombs that are pear or horse-shoe shaped with no clear distinction between chamber and corridor, and tholoi.

I visited the area in September 1994, and again in March 1998.[22] Five of the tombs we measured are megalithic, and all faced sunrise. One, however, is in very poor condition and our measure is only approximate; the other four (which include one classic anta) have orientations in a northerly SR range, 70°–82°.

Four of the tombs near Ourique were tholoi, with orientations 65°, 103°, 106° and 127° respectively. The first three are of course SR and the fourth is only just outside the range.

Elsewhere in the south of Portugal, tombs are very thin on the ground, though almost all faced sunrise in the winter months. Fernando Pimenta located two megalithic tombs at Alcoutim near the Spanish frontier and two more at Tavira on the coast; they face between 108° and 118°, and three have subcircular chambers formed of nine orthostats. There is a tholos at Alcoutim facing

112°, and a group of tholoi at Alcalár near Portimão on the Algarve coast, most in poor condition. Of these, Tombs 4 and 7 have measurable orientations, while Tombs 3 and 9 are present in little more than outline; they face between 99° and 120°. The condition of Tomb 11 I classed as 'very poor'; it appears to have an orientation of about 54°, and if so it faced some 5° north of midsummer sunrise. Nearby is a megalithic sepulchre that faces 108°.

Another megalithic sepulchre is near the southwest tip of Portugal, on the southern coast at Vila do Bispo, and this faces 116°. Further north, near Aljezur, is Corte Cabreira, a tholos that is in unusually good condition; it faces 112°. Further north still, near Santiago do Cacém, is a pair of megalithic tombs; one is an anta and faces 108°, while the other faces 100°.

Although the Alentejo region of central Portugal belongs to the next chapter, it is convenient to mention its tholos tombs here, for we visited only one whose status is beyond dispute: Tholos de Escoural, near Évora, which faces due east. Anta do Caladinho, near Redondo, is of doubtful form. At Farisoa 1, near Reguengos de Monsaraz, a small tholos with its own corridor was later inserted into the megalithic tumulus, while Olival da Pega 2, a huge anta now under excavation, had small tholos chambers added to either side of the corridor and leading into it. Only Tholos de Escoural yielded a meaningful orientation.

The Lisbon area

The coastal region near Lisbon that is bordered on the west by the Atlantic and on the south by the River Tejo is an archaeoastronomer's nightmare. It is logistically awkward, as several of the tombs are being engulfed by suburban sprawl. It contains limited areas of magnetic anomaly (though we did not detect any actual effect of this). And it has — today — very small numbers of tombs of many different types, not all of them conventional in structure. I was able to visit most of them in April 1998 with the help of Teresa Simões of the museum at Odrinhas, and their orientations are listed in Table 5.16.[23]

Five of the tombs are authentic tholoi. That at Barro, some 20km northwest of Lisbon, has orientation 160°. Geographically this is the most northerly of the surviving tholos tombs, one that was still further north having been destroyed. Other tholos tombs in the region face 105°, 118° and 152°. The fifth, São Martinho 2, has been cut in half by farmers, but clearly faced south of east. All are SR/SC.

The region has a miscellany of other tombs. Praia das Maças is a tholos, but it is an extension of an artificial cave tomb and located hard up against the cliff, and so the builders were constrained in their choice of orientation. Bela Vista, which faces 80°, has a circular chamber but this is made of massive blocks and there is no sign of an attempt at false cupola construction. Pego Longo faces 347° (!), but it is not a true dolmen but rather a 'paradolmen', a tomb where advantage has been taken of a convenient natural rock structure; here a rock-face was adapted to form one side, and to this the builders added a facing side and a backstone. At Carenque, on high ground, three underground chambers have been cut out of the bedrock (with orientations 38°, 153° and 174° respectively).

Apart from this unpromising collection, we measured five megalithic tombs. One, Anta da

Anta de Estria, near Lisbon, perhaps the only westerly-facing tomb in Portugal (photograph courtesy of Fernando Pimenta).

Estria (Sintra), has since become the pride and joy of the company that owns the adjacent, newly-constructed filling station: customers are encouraged to visit the tomb after they have paid for their fuel. The tomb is of particular interest because in some ways it resembles an anta (in our restricted sense of the term), but its layout has features uncharacteristic of antas. Its orientation is 213°, so that it faces the western half of the horizon. Curiously, on the hill immediately above it is a conventional anta, Anta do Monte Abraão, one of four indubitable antas of the region. They face 98°, 98°, 110° and 111° respectively. Though they mark the westward limit of this form of construction, like most antas they faced sunrise in the winter months.

A pattern emerges

Although we have only just begun our circuit of the Iberian peninsula, some patterns are already emerging from the data. We have so far listed the orientations of 390 tombs. Of these, 10 (2·6%) faced between 0° and 60°, north of the range of sunrise. Two of the 10 are major monuments: the great tholos of Matarrubilla at Valencina, whose orientation is a wholly exceptional 17¾° and may have faced the rising of Arcturus, and the gigantic megalithic sepulchre of Menga at Antequera (45°), which we suggested faces the anthropomorphic mountain. Three others (Los Charcones at Benalup in Cádiz, 32°; Bradford at Almadén de la Plata in Sevilla, 32°; and La Dehesa del Hospital, Monesterio, Badajoz, 26°) we suggested may be culturally linked with Matarrubilla.

The other five are poor specimens: two little sepulchres in Badajoz (43°, 44°) where our measures may have been affected by magnetic anomalies; the little tomb that we spotted from the car near Km 52 on the Ex202 in southeast Badajoz (50°); a ruined tholos at Alcalár in the Algarve (54°); and a tomb in Huelva (52°) whose corridor may be partly bedrock and which perhaps should be considered a paradolmen.

No fewer than 368 (94.4%) were SR/SC and faced the range of sunrise, or the sun while it was climbing in the sky or around culmination (say, 60°–190°).

Finally 12 tombs clearly faced the western horizon (190°–360°): two of the tholoi at Los Millares (212°, 216°); the great tholoi of Romeral at Antequera (199°) and La Pastora at Valencina (242¾°); megalithic sepulchres at Baños (204°) and Fonelas (199°); five sepulchres in the far south of Cádiz (214°, 216°, 231°, 234°, 250°); and the quasi-anta near Lisbon (213°). Not a single tomb of the 390 faces the northwest quadrant.

When we restrict our attention to the 368 tombs that are SR/SC, we find that the major groupings belong to one or other of two types. Those of one type have tombs that are overwhelmingly SR: 60 out of 64 at Los Millares, 38 out of 41 at Montefrío. Provinces can display a similar pattern: 15 out of 15 in Córdoba are SR, 28 out of 31 in Huelva, and 17 out of 18 in south Portugal. We note that the data give us no reason to focus our discussion on moonrise rather than sunrise: the orientations are concentrated in the ranges of sunrise in the autumn, winter and spring, with midwinter sunrise as the cutoff point except for a very few anomalies.

Elsewhere, where SC tombs are present in quantity, they may equal or outnumber the SR. In Alhama de Almería, 19 are SR and 22 SC, while at the Río Gor (including Baños de Alicún), 36 are SR and 51 SC.

In south Iberia, then, tombs are overwhelmingly SR/SC, with nearly 95% of them facing between midsummer sunrise and culmination; but in some places nearly all the tombs faced sunrise, while in others a majority of tombs faced the sun while it was climbing in the sky. Will we find the same patterns in the rest of the peninsula?

Further reading

C. Cerdan Marquez and G. and V. Leisner, *Los sepulcros megalíticos de Huelva* (Madrid, 1952).

R. Chapman, *Emerging complexity: The later prehistory of south-east Spain, Iberia and the west Mediterranean* (Cambridge, 1990).

M. García Sanchez and J.-C. Spahni, "Sepulcros megalíticos de la región de Gorafe (Granada)", *Archivo de prehistoria Levantina*, viii (1959), 43–111.

A. Gómez Ruiz and M. Hoskin, "Studies in Iberian archaeoastronomy: (7) Orientations of megalithic tombs of Huelva", *AA*, no. 25 (2000), S41–50.

M. Hoskin, E. Allan and R. Gralewski, "Studies in Iberian archaeoastronomy: (1) Orientations of the megalithic sepulchres of Almería, Granada and Málaga", *AA*, no. 19 (1994), S55–82; "(2) Orientations of the tholos tombs of Almería", *AA*, no. 20 (1995), S29–40; "(3) Customs

and motives in Andalucía", *AA*, no. 20 (1995), S41–48.

M. Hoskin and C. Sauch i Aparicio, "Studies in Iberian archaeoastronomy: (6) Orientations of megalithic tombs of Badajoz and neighbouring Portugal", *AA*, no. 24 (1999), S35–40.

M. Hoskin and colleagues, "Studies in Iberian archaeoastronomy: (5) Orientations of megalithic tombs of northern and western Iberia", *AA*, no. 23 (1998), S39–87.

M. Hoskin and colleagues, "Studies in Iberian archaeoastronomy: (8) Orientations of megalithic and tholos tombs of southwestern Iberia", *AA*, no. 26 (2001), in press.

F. Jordá Cerdá *et al.*, *Historia de España*, i: *Prehistoria* (Madrid, 1986).

F. Molina González, *Prehistoria de Granada* (Granada, 1983).

Notes and references

1 Personal comm., 2000.

2 For an introduction to the prehistory of the region, with emphasis on the province of Granada, see Molina, *Prehistoria de Granada*.

3 The literature on this great site is very extensive. See Hoskin *et al.*, "Studies, (2)", ref. 4, and Chapman, *Emerging complexity*, *passim*.

4 Ma. J. Almagro Gorbea, *El poblado y la necrópolis de El Barranquete* (Acta Arqueológica Hispánica, vi; Madrid, 1973).

5 García and Spahni, "Sepulcros megalíticos de la región de Gorafe (Granada)".

6 Information from J. A. Belmonte (personal comm., 1999). A sepulchre with corridor is reported from the necropolis of Murviedro at Lorca, but this has been destroyed. On Copper Age burial customs of the region, see the chapter on "El Eneolitico en el sureste" by A. M. Muñoz Amalibia, in vol. ii of *Historia de Cartagena*, ed. by J. Mas García (Murcia, 1986), espec. pp. 152–5.

7 The 'south-east' orientation given by García and Spahni is a slip, as the north arrow of their figure shows.

8 J. E. Ferrer *et al.*, "La necrópolis megalítica de Fonelas", *Noticiario arqueológico Hispánico*, xxx (1988), 23–81 plus appendix.

9 For the extensive literature on Montefrío, see Hoskin *et al.* "Studies, (1)", ref. 11.

10 A. Arribas Palau and J. E. Ferrer Palma, "La necrópolis megalítica del Pantano de los Bermejales (Granada): Actuaciones arqueológicas", *Anuario arqueológico de Andalucía*, 1986, 307–10.

11 For further information and bibliography on the megalithic tombs of Málaga, see Hoskin *et al.*, "Studies: (1)".

12 On Viera, see S. Giménez Reyna, *Memoria arqueológica de la provincia de Málaga* (Madrid, 1946), 40–43 and Plates XXI–XXIII.

13 On Romeral, see Giménez, *op. cit.*, 31–37 and Plates XIII–XVII.

14 On Menga, see Giménez, *op. cit.*, 43–49 and Plates XXIV–XXVI.

15 A. Perez Aguilar, "La necrópolis prehistórica del Moral", *VIII Congreso Nacional de Arqueología, Sevilla–Málaga, 1963* (Zaragoza, 1964), 184–206.

16 Anthony F. Aveni, review of *Stonehenge* by John North, *Nature*, issue of 3 October 1996, 403–4, p. 404.

17 Juan de M. Carriazo, "El dolmen de Ontiveros (Valencina de la Concepción, Sevilla)", *Homenaje al Profesor Cayetano de Mergelina (Murcia, 1961)* (Murcia, 1962), 209–29.

18 H. Breuil and W. Verner, "Découverte de deux centres dolméniques sur les bords de la Laguna de la Janda (Cadix)", *Bulletin hispanique: Annales de la Faculté des Lettres de Bordeaux et des Universités du Midi*, xix (1917), 157–88; C. de Mergelina, "Los focos dolménicos de la Laguna de la Janda", *Memorias de la Sociedad Española de Antropología, Etnografía y Prehistoria*, iii (1924), 97–126.

19 In Brittany, however, tombs with corridors at right angles to the chamber are not uncommon.

20 For further information on the megalithic tombs of Huelva, see Gómez and Hoskin, "Studies: (7)".

21 José Iñesta Mena of Llerena, María Jesús Carrasco Martín of Jerez de los Caballeros, and Hipólito Collado of Mérida. For further details of our work in Badajoz, see Hoskin and Sauch, "Studies (6)".

22 For further information, see Hoskin and colleagues, "Studies (5)", Section P.

23 For further information, see *ibid.*, Section N.

6

Easterly-facing Tombs (II): West Iberia

In our clockwise progress around the Iberian peninsula, we have reached the latitude of Lisbon. The handful of tombs near the coast we have already discussed; next on our agenda is the Alentejo, the territory south of the Tejo river (which enters the sea at Lisbon). It is a region famous in European archaeology for its great concentration of seven-stone antas, whose instantly recognizable form of construction, whereby each sidestone leant against its predecessor, we described in the last chapter. We have already met outlying antas in Huelva, in southern Portugal, and near Lisbon itself. Now we shall meet many more: throughout the Alentejo, and across the Spanish frontier into Extremadura with its two provinces of Badajoz and Cáceres.

The central Alentejo and northwest Badajoz

The megalithic tombs of the central Alentejo fall into two groups. The first comprises tombs that have small funerary chambers (in most cases elongated) and are without clearly differentiated corridors, while the second consists of antas. We also find a handful of monuments that seem not to fall into either of these two groups, and so we list them separately, though they may in fact be transitional between the other two forms.

Most of the tombs are made of granite. Those made of schist (and this includes some antas) are, not surprisingly, more modest in height and have smaller chambers than those in granite. All the largest tombs of the Alentejo (some are 4 or even 5 metres in height) were built in granite.

Most researchers assign an earlier date to the small sepulchres without differentiated corridor. Today these tombs are relatively few in number, but this may be because they are more vulnerable to destruction, and also because, being small, some have yet to be identified. However, they do seem to be absent from many of the contexts in which the antas are to be found. It may well be that the sepulchres without corridor are located in areas where agricultural occupation of the Alentejo first took place. When, in later times, greater economic prosperity permitted the major effort needed to erect the massive antas, these monumental tombs would be built not only alongside their smaller predecessors, but also in other areas brought into cultivation around the end of the Neolithic, after construction of tombs of the first type had ceased.

I worked on a number of occasions in the central Alentejo in collaboration with Manuel

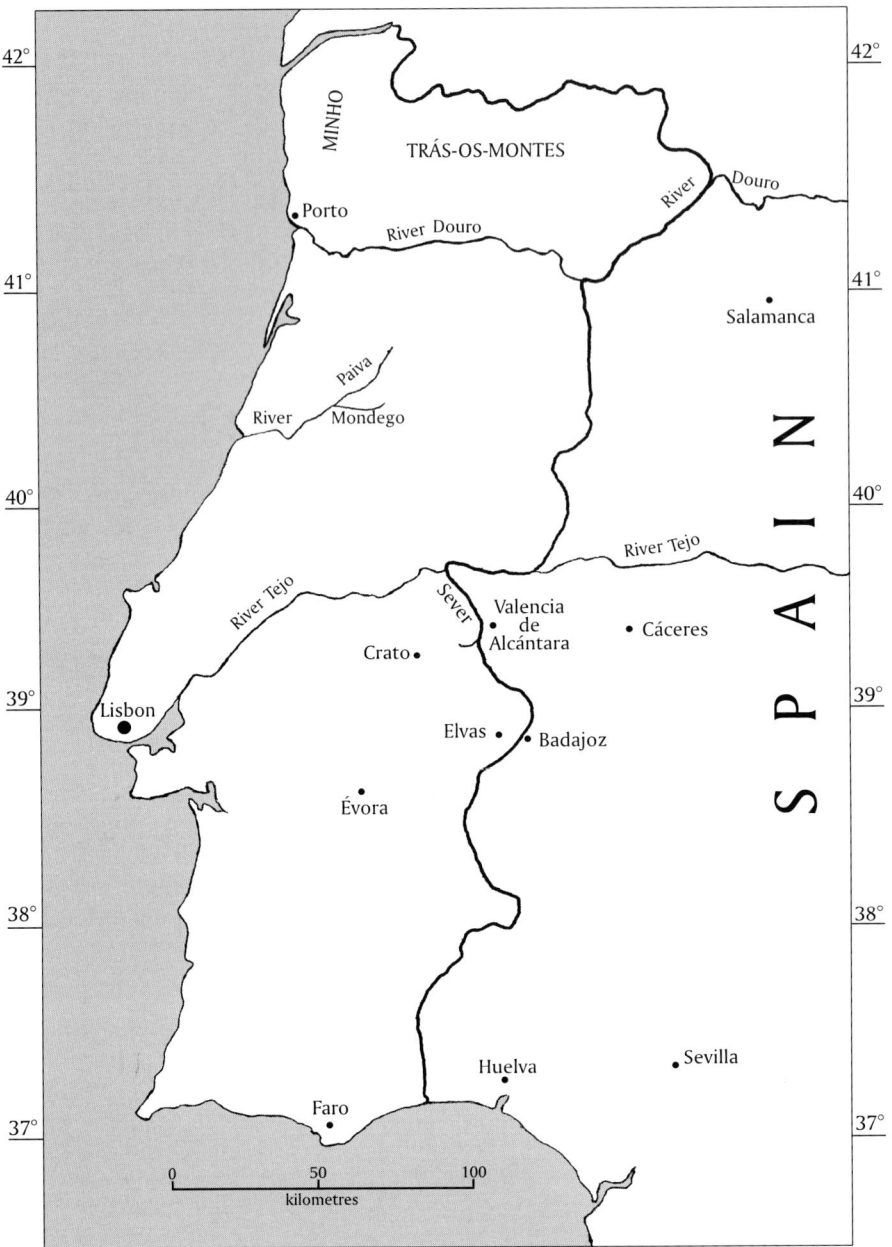

Portugal and neighbouring regions of Spain, with the principal places discussed in this chapter.

Calado, whose familiarity with the region is unrivalled (not least because of his microlight aircraft). Together we measured seven of the smaller tombs, 95 antas, and ten more of uncertain type.[1] The orientations of the smaller tombs and of those of uncertain type are listed in Table 6.1;

Caeira 2, one of the seven-stone antas at Mora in the Alentejo. In the foreground is the passage, and beyond we see the tall sidestones of the chamber, which originally leant inwards but which have been pushed out by the fall of the capstone. Antas are the tallest megalithic tombs of western Europe: the stones of the chamber of Anta Grande de Zambujeiro, south of Évora, are over 5 metres in height.

all faced sunrise. The orientations of the 95 antas are listed in Table 6.2, along with twelve antas in northwestern Badajoz that I measured in September 1998,[2] and the seven we have already encountered in Chapter 5 (two in Huelva, two from the south of Portugal, and three near Lisbon): a total thus far of no fewer than 114.

A little further north, near Elvas and close to the Spanish border, is a region that likewise has small tombs without corridor and antas with corridor. In July 1997, in collaboration with Miguel Lago, a local archaeologist, I measured a total of 25 tombs, four of which were 'small' and the other 21 antas.[3] Their orientations are listed in Tables 6.1 and 6.2, as appropriate.

Further north still, and towards the limit of the granite, there is a scattering of antas around the little Portugese town of Crato,[4] and a dense concentration of fine tombs straddles the frontier, around Marvão and Castelo de Vide and, across the Sever into Spain, near Valencia de Alcántara. They are mostly made of tall granite blocks, typically 3m in height, and they dominate the landscape. The Valencia tombs have been studied by Primitiva Bueno Ramírez,[5] and according to her the construction of those with short corridor began around 4000 BC while those with long corridor first appeared around 3200 BC. Not surprisingly, these impressive structures were re-used into the early Bronze Age. In some cases the entrance to the chamber was partly blocked by an eighth stone straddling the corridor stones; and the whole monument was covered by a tumulus of which few traces now remain.

Such a rich region called for careful study, and I visited it in 1994, 1997 and twice in 1998. These visits[6] yielded a total of 40 further antas, whose orientations are also listed in Table 6.2. Finally, in our work among the schist tombs in the far northwest corner of the province of Cáceres,[7] we encountered on a platform just above the Sever river a pair of antas, and these too are listed in the table.

In all, then, we have the orientations of no fewer than 177 seven-stone antas; and it is nothing short of astonishing to find that every single one is oriented within an arc of little more than one-sixth of a circle. The region occupied by these antas extends in an east–west direction for

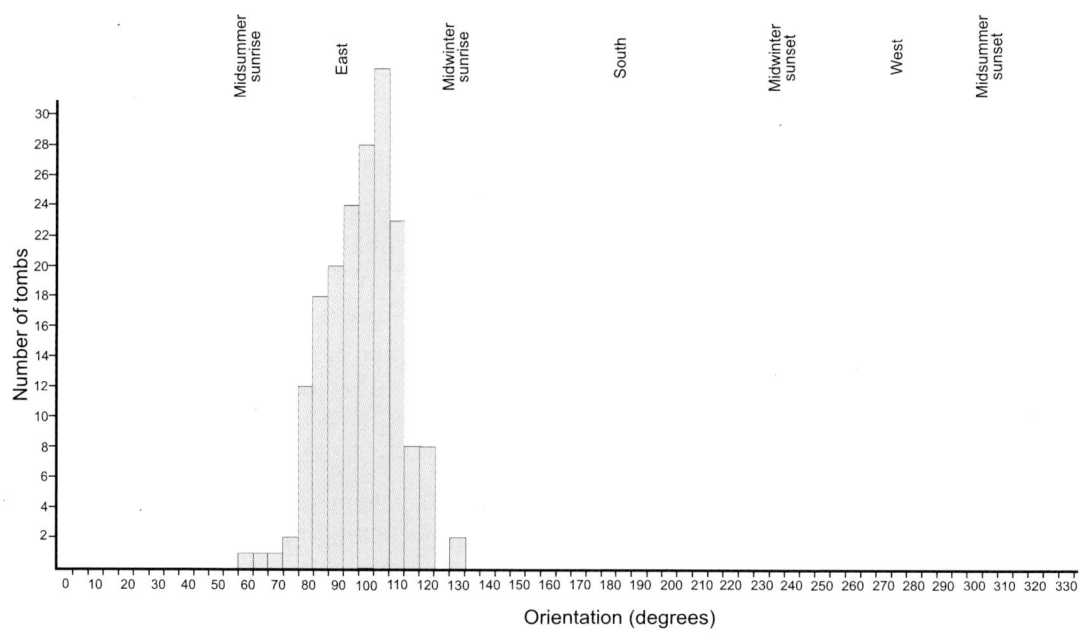

Histogram of 177 antas of central Portugal and neighbouring Spain. Two (La Tierra Caída 1 and 2, Cedillo) are oriented towards azimuth 128° and 129° respectively, but because they are in a valley with steep sides they too faced sunrise. Four have 'typical' orientations and these are distributed appropriately. Despite the great number of tombs and the vast area over which they are spread, every single one of the 177 antas faced sunrise (to within a couple of degrees), the majority in autumn/spring or winter.

over 200km, from the Lisbon coast to the Spanish border provinces, and a similar distance from north to south. This extraordinary consistency is arguably the most compelling proof we have from western Europe that tombs were oriented on the sky; for the Alentejo is very flat (as shown by the skyline altitudes in the table) and there is no prominent geographical 'target' for tomb orientations, even if it were possible to see the same mountain over such vast distances. Nor are there strong prevailing winds, or any of the other terrestrial motivations sometimes advanced for customs of orientation.

Furthermore, when we take the skyline altitudes into account, we find that the range of anta orientation corresponds to declinations between $+23°$ and $-25½°$, virtually identical with that of sunrise ($+24°$ to $-24°$ around the time the tombs were built). There is not a single anta that faced the western horizon; not a single anta that faced easterly and north of midsummer sunrise; and not a single anta that faced easterly and significantly south of midwinter sunrise.

We have seen (Chapter 2) that the builders of Christian churches often ensured that their buildings faced sunrise, by laying out the axis to face sunrise on the day that building began; and by measuring the orientation of the axis we can calculate which day of the year this would have been (subject to an ambiguity between spring and autumn). It seems very probable that the builders of antas likewise oriented their tombs on sunrise, and if so, we can perform the same calculation and determine when in the year these people had the leisure to engage in a major building project. Indeed, after proposing this to my Iberian colleagues, I found that French archaeologists had been coming to similar conclusions for many years.[8]

Interestingly, whereas nearly all Portugese tombs of whatever type faced within the range of sunrise, there are regions where the orientations fell within an altogether narrower band. Thus the seven antas near Crato face between 91° and 104°, which might suggest that construction began just after the autumn equinox or just before the spring equinox (but not in the winter months). Similarly, we shall find that the little schist tombs in Cáceres north of Valencia and in neighbouring Portugal almost always faced in the range from 86° to 114°.

Another curiosity is that of the 33 antas around Valencia de Alcántara, no fewer than 17 faced sunrise in the six summer months. This is strange since one might have expected the builders to have been preoccupied with food production during the time of year implied by the 'sunrise' interpretation of these orientations. Juan Antonio Belmonte, who collaborated in the measurements at Valencia and elsewhere, has rightly pointed out[9] that a tomb that faced sunrise necessarily faced moonrise, and has drawn attention to historical evidence (written, admittedly, very many centuries after the tombs were built) showing that the moon was, or became, an object of cult in Iberia. Thus Strabo, writing about the time of Christ, tells us: "The Celtiberians and their neighbours in the north offer sacrifice to a nameless god at the seasons of the full moon, by night, in front of the doors of their houses, and whole households dance in chorus and keep it up all night."[10] And one can see the attraction of having a party a dozen or more times a year.

The moon travels rapidly up and down the horizon each month, changing position markedly from one night to the next; and its rise is in any case invisible for part of the month when the moon is lost in the glare of the sun. It seems unlikely, therefore, that a tomb would simply be oriented on moonrise on whatever day construction began. A more plausible occasion would be a full moon, and no doubt the commencement of construction could always have been postponed until the next such moon. However, this by itself would not explain these narrow ranges of orientations, or the absence of tombs facing the extreme positions of moonrise, a few degrees in either direction beyond the range of sunrise. For this a further assumption is necessary; as, for example, that a certain full moon of the year may have been of special significance, rather as the full moon following the spring equinox is related to Easter and so has a special significance for Christians.

Given the number of times we encounter a range of orientations — not least, that of the antas as a whole — of which the southern limit virtually coincides with the southern limit of sunrise, it seems to me that in many contexts a sunrise interpretation is by far the most plausible; and if in some particular area the tombs faced sunrise in spring or autumn, or even summer, I prefer to ascribe this to the local rhythm of life, rather than invoking a different heavenly body for whose involvement I find no compelling evidence. Transhumance (the ancient, and modern, custom of moving flocks of sheep between highland summer pastures and lowland winter pastures) may be one factor; and even in a settled community, why should it not have been customary to embark on these often massive constructions in (say) the late autumn, when there were the winter months ahead in which the work could be carried through to a conclusion?

Small schist tombs of northwest Cáceres and the Portugese Upper Tejo

The River Tejo flows westerly while it marks the border between Spain and Portugal, with Spain to its south and Portugal to its north. But when the Tejo is joined by the River Sever, the border turns south and follows the Sever instead. In prehistoric times the rivers were highways rather than the frontiers they are today, and so in this section we study both the area of Cáceres in the angle formed by the two rivers, and the regions of Portugal on the opposite banks.

The tombs are most common in areas within reach of one or other river, and are often in twos and threes, though sometimes as many as ten may be found together. They are of schist, and the chambers have a variety of shape. On the Portugese side they were once numerous, but the survivors are few and the number is dimishing fast. The orthostats are rarely over a metre in height, the schist is fragile, and few of the tombs are easy to recognize; mechanical farming and the widespread plantation of eucalyptus is causing devastation on a tragic scale, sometimes intentional but often not. It is common for only one or two tombs to be identifiable today where once a dozen were known.

In Cáceres, archaeologists distinguish three architectural types: (i) chambers some 1½m to 2m in diameter, with long and clearly differentiated corridors; (ii) simple open chambers of rectangular (or trapezoidal) shape and no clear distinction between chamber and corridor; and (iii) rectangular closed tombs with chambers of less than two square metres.[11] The tombs were located in prominent positions, and were covered with tumuli formed of earth with pieces of white quartz and slabs of schist.

The fragility of the schist orthostats forming the chambers prevented the use of capstones in most cases, and it seems that the tombs were covered with wood in the form of poles and branches. In some cases this is confirmed by notches cut into the top edges of orthostats. Curiously, in those Portugese tombs where human remains have been found, they have been of one, or at most two persons. This would seem to suggest that the entrances were for offerings rather than for the insertion of further bodies; but in size the chambers are on a par with communal tombs elsewhere, and we therefore treat them as such. In date the Portugese tombs have been assigned to the Middle and Late Neolithic, although on the basis of finds from the Cáceres sepulchres Primitiva Bueno Ramírez places them around the beginning of the Copper Age and no earlier than 3000 BC.[12]

In June 1997 Socorro López Plaza of the University of Salamanca joined us in measuring eleven of the Cáceres tombs (Table 6.3).[13] Most were located on the highest ground available, but two, La Tierra Caída 1 and 2, were down a deep slope, on a platform just above the Sever. Although made of schist they are massive antas, and we mentioned them earlier in this chapter; they look in directions where the sun appeared a week or two either side of the winter solstice. Of the remaining nine tombs, eight faced in the very narrow range from 86° and 105° while the ninth, which had no clear symmetry, we estimated to face 112°.

In April 1998 we explored the Portugese area with Francisco Henriques, a noted amateur

Valle Pepino 1 in northwestern Cáceres, one of the more substantial of the small schist tombs.

Orientations of 34 small schist tombs in northwestern Cáceres and the Portuguese Upper Tejo.

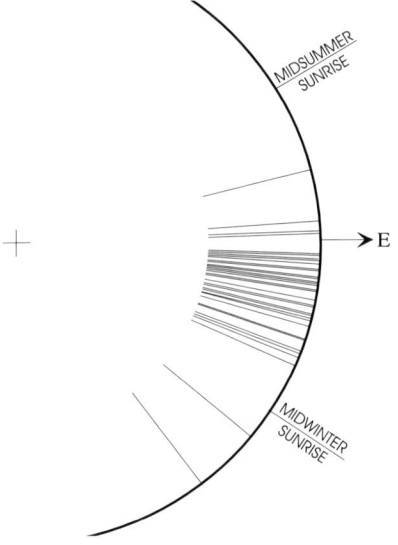

archaeologist, as our guide.[14] We measured a total of 26 tombs (Table 6.3), and although they were scattered over an area of many tens of square kilometres, 23 (88·5%) of the 26 lie within the range 88°–114°, virtually identical with that of the tombs across in Spain. Of the other three, Amieiro 8 is in poor condition but has a 'typical' orientation and Silveirinha faced marginally south of midwinter sunrise, so that Samarrudo 2 is the only one that is clearly not SR.

In total, then, and leaving aside the two antas, 32 (91·4%) of the 35 tombs face within the narrow range from 86° to 114°, and looked towards sunrise in the early spring or late autumn, while only one of the 35 faced clearly south of midwinter sunrise.

Tombs of Salamanca

The Spanish province of Salamanca borders north-central Portugal. It lies on the western edge of the high plateau (or *meseta*) that occupies the centre of Spain, and from the province the Douro river, and the Tormes river that joins the Douro, flow westwards into Portugal to enter the sea at Porto.

The megalithic tombs of the province[15] fall into three main types.

(a) Tombs with large chambers, formed of as many as a dozen or more orthostats, and often 4 or even 5 metres in diameter. In some cases (if not all) the chambers were partly covered by slabs of stone, the roof being completed with wood and branches packed with mud and slate. Access to the chamber was by means of a corridor that was clearly distinguished from the chamber both in width and height, and chamber and corridor were covered by a tumulus that was typically from 20 to 30 metres in diameter. No radiocarbon dates are available for these tombs, but comparison with related tombs elsewhere suggests that they were constructed in the last centuries of the fourth millennium BC, and they continued in use until the middle of the second millennium.

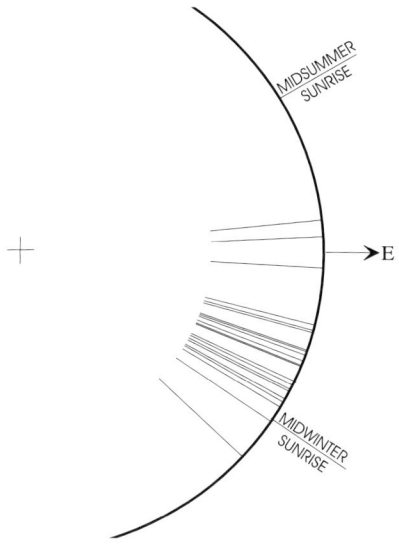

Orientations of 21 megalithic tombs of Salamanca. Two of the azimuths have been adjusted to reflect the high elevations of the skyline faced by these tombs.

(b) In the west of the province, poorly conserved tombs whose construction resembles that of the Portugese antas in which each sidestone leaned against its predecessor. In Salamanca, the corridor was often long and clearly distinguished from the chamber, and the stones forming the

La Navalito, Lumbrales, Salamanca, a tomb of type (b) resembling an anta.

103

sides of the corridor also leaned successively upon each other. The objects found in these tombs place them late in the fourth millennium.

(c) Small tombs, without corridor and with oval or rectangular chamber two metres or rather more in maximum diameter, or with a corridor barely distinguishable from the chamber. Only a handful of these tombs are known; they have been little studied, and no finds are recorded, so that their dates are very uncertain. They may be among the earliest megalithic monuments in Salamanca, but they may also be as late as the Bronze Age.

Some 80 tombs have been identified in the province, but the number whose orientations can be measured is only a small fraction of this. Many have disappeared, or are in such a ruinous state that not even their type can be established. In 1994 and 1995 Socorro López collaborated with us in measuring the orientations of 21 tombs,[16] and these are listed in Table 6.4. Two faced south of midwinter sunrise, but by negligible amounts; the rest all faced sunrise at some time of year, the majority between early November and the middle of February.

Tombs of the Mondego Plateau of central Portugal

The numerous megalithic tombs of this region are distributed between two cultural phases.[17] The first is known as Carapito/Pramelas, and in this the tombs have polygonal chambers without corridor (or at most with a short, token one), and they were built between 4100 and 3700 BC. In

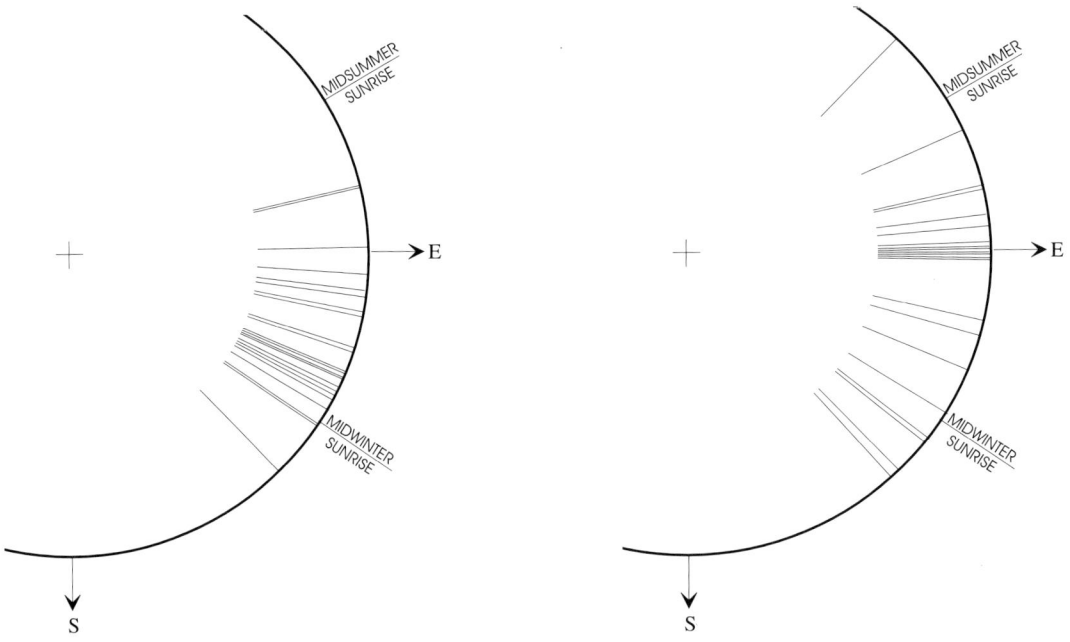

(*Left*) Orientations of 23 tombs of the Mondego Basin. (*Right*) Orientations of 21 tombs of the Vouga, Alto Pavia, Torto and Coa Basins.

Casa da Orca da Cunha Baixa, Mangualde, one of the tombs of the Mondego Basin.

the second, the Moinhos de Vento/Ameal culture, the chambered tombs are similar in construction to the antas of Alentejo, with each stone of the chamber leaning on its predecessor, except that the number of stones forming the chamber is nine rather than seven. The tombs have long corridors, with up to nine orthostats on each side. The culture flourished in the second half of the fourth millennium and during most of the third, and many of the tombs were reused during the Early/Middle Bronze Age (c. 2300–1300 BC).

We measured forty tombs of the region (and visited three others) in September 1994 and June 1995, in collaboration with João Carlos de Senna-Martinez of the University of Lisbon,[18] and in 1997 José Manuel Quintã Ventura and I measured a further eight. The results are listed in Table 6.5. As usual, all the tombs faced the eastern half of the horizon, but Pedralta is anomalous in facing northeast, well north of the range of sunrise, and three others in facing south of the range. Of the tombs, therefore, 44 (91·7%) were SR, while three of the remaining four were SC.

Tombs of the coastal region of north-central Portugal

This area lies between the basin of the Douro river to the north and the Mondego river in the south, and extends inland from the coast as far as the Paiva river and the Montemuro, Gralheira and Caramulo mountain ranges. Only recently has it received serious attention from archaeologists, and carbon-14 dates are still lacking, so that the likely chronology derives from what is known from neighbouring regions. This suggests that the earliest monuments appeared late in the fifth millennium or early in the fourth, and that tomb-building continued until late in the second millennium.

Hundreds of tumuli from the region are known. Their interior structures are of four main types:

(a) Megalithic chambers with a single capstone, two or three orthostats to each side, and a well-defined entrance. They were built around the beginning of the fourth millennium and were in use until the middle of the millennium and beyond.

(b) Similar monuments but with a closed chamber and therefore no clear orientation.

(c) Megalithic passage graves such as are familiar from the Mondego Plateau, though relatively rare in this region. These passage graves are in all cases late additions to existing necropolises, and date perhaps from the second half of the fourth millennium.

(d) The so-called 'sub-megalithic constructions' in which a funerary pit replaced the central megalithic chamber. This type of monument is the most common, but it has of course no clear orientation. The tumuli are small, and in some cases are composed exclusively of stones (and so better termed 'cairns'). These constructions belong to the Bronze Age of the region, that is, the second millennium BC.

In 1997 José Ventura and I measured eight tombs from this region (Table 5.6). As usual all faced the eastern horizon but, unusually, five of the eight faced south of midwinter sunrise. Indeed one, a seven-stone anta, faced 174°, exceptionally far south for a Portugese tomb and especially for an anta. The custom here, therefore, may be characterized as SR/SC.

Tombs on the north bank of the Douro Basin

The megalithic monuments in the region immediately north of the Douro have been under investigation for the past quarter-century, and a clear picture is emerging. Construction began around the end of the fifth millennium or the beginning of the fourth. Most of the monuments had a closed stone structure beneath a tumulus, and so were without a clear orientation, while others had megalithic open chambers. The passage graves with polygonal chambers familiar from the Beiras and the Alentejo are rare. Then, around the end of the third millennium and the beginning of the second, we find monuments within the megalithic tradition but with smaller tumuli and either a small chamber of the cist type or simply a 'funerary pit'; these have of course no clear orientation.

Ten of these monuments (see Table 5.7) were measured at different times by Luis Tirapicos of Porto, and by José Ventura and me. One faced a most anomalous 10°, but the other nine faced within the narrow range of 81°–107°, sunrise in the spring and autumn.

Orientations of 30 Portugese tombs north of the Douro.

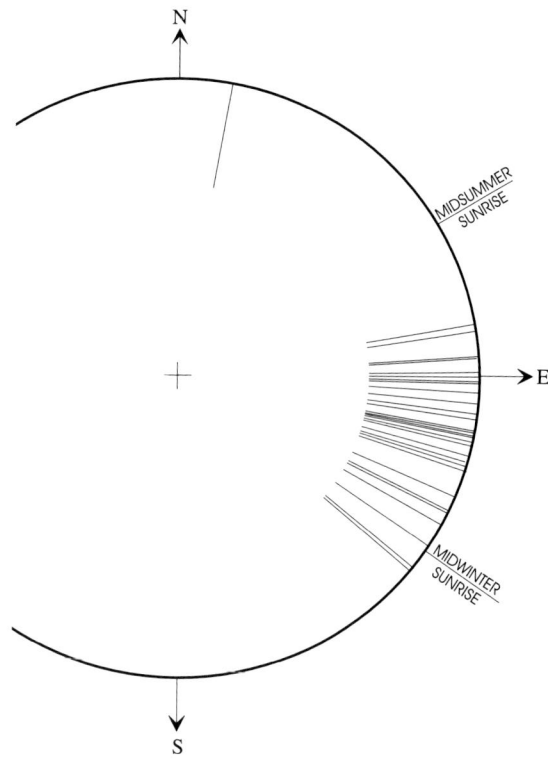

Tombs of the Miranda Plateau and Trás-os-Montes

The northeast of Portugal, from the Douro to the borders with Spain, corresponds to the old administrative region of Trás-os-Montes. Geologically, it is in part a continuation of the Spanish *meseta*. The monuments there are of two types, tumuli that cover a central burial pit, and 'classical monuments' with a megalithic chamber and passage. In the latter the chamber is usually polygonal, with a backstone, three stones to each side of the backstone, and either one or two capstones. The passage consists of a short corridor with either one or two stones to each side. The fragmentary evidence as to date suggests that the monuments of the first type belong to the first half of the fourth millennium, while those of the second appear around the middle of the millennium.

Luis Tirapicos measured seven of these at various times (Table 5.8). All faced within the range 101°–130°: sunrise in the winter months (or marginally further south).

Tombs of the Minho

The Minho occupies an area of nearly 5,000 square kilometres of northwest Portugal. It is located in the ancient Iberic massif which, with its deep valleys separated by mountains and areas of plateau, was ideal for early human settlement. The building of megalithic monuments in the form of simple sepulchres under tumuli is thought to have begun here around the beginning of the fourth millennium BC, but information so far published concerning tombs at Alto da Portela

(*Above*) Fonte Coberta, Chã de Alijó, in the Miranda Plateau. (*Below*) Mamoa de Lamas, Braga, in the Minho. (Photographs courtesy of Luis Tirapicos.)

do Pau at Castro Laboreiro suggests the second half of the fifth millennium as their possible construction date. In the first half of the third millennium, it seems, there appeared, alongside the simple sepulchres, tombs with an entrance or with a short but well-differentiated corridor; and in the second half of the third millennium we encounter substantial dolmenic structures with undifferentiated corridors.

It was during the later colonization of the coastal plains, in contrast to the previous custom of settling in the high lands of the interior, that tombs were distributed around the landscape and apparently used as markers for the territorial borders. It is possible that to this period also belong the tumuli without dolmenic structures, and monuments with small chambers and undifferentiated and relatively long corridors.

In 1997 Nuno Miguel Soares and I measured eight tombs in the Minho, and Soares and Tirapicos measured a further four in 2000. Their orientations are listed in Table 5.9. All are SR.

A pattern confirmed

In south Iberia we find that the tombs overwhelmingly faced the eastern horizon and south of midsummer sunrise, and that while in some places nearly all the orientations were within the range of sunrise (SR), elsewhere some tombs faced sunrise while others faced the sun when it was climbing in the sky or even around culmination (SR/SC).

In west Iberia (as understood in this chapter), the emphasis on sunrise is even stronger. We noted that every single one of the 177 antas was SR, and one can say the same of the overwhelming majority of the other tombs of the region. Of the 335 tombs of all types for which we have quantitative orientations, plus the 11 that faced in 'typical' directions, every one faced easterly. Only two (0·6%) faced north of midsummer sunrise, and only one (0·3%) faced south of 146°. Indeed, only eight (2·3%) faced south of 130°, so that of the 346 tombs, no fewer than 336 (97·1%) faced within the range 60°–130°; that is, sunrise or marginally further south.

Further reading

A guide to the megalithic monuments of the Evora region (Câmara Municipal de Évora, Evora, 1992).

P. Bueno Ramírez, *Los dólmenes de Valencia de Alcántara* (Madrid, 1988).

M. Hoskin and colleagues, "Studies in Iberian archaeoastronomy: (5) Orientations of megalithic tombs of northern and western Iberia", *AA*, no. 23 (1998), S39–87.

M. Hoskin and C. Sauch i Aparicio, "Studies in Iberian archaeoastronomy: (6) Orientations of megalithic tombs of Badajoz and neighbouring Portugal", *AA*, no. 24 (1999), S35–40.

F. Jordá Cerdá *et al.*, *Historia de España*, i: *Prehistoria* (Madrid, 1986).

J. Oliveira, *Sepulturas megalíticas del término municipal de Cedillo* (Cedillo, 1995).

Notes and references

1 For further details see Hoskin and colleagues, "Studies (5)", Section M. For an introduction to the central Alentejo written in English, see *A guide to the megalithic monuments of the Evora region*.

2 For further details see Hoskin and Sauch, "Studies (6)".

3 See Hoskin and colleagues, "Studies (5)", Section L.

4 See Hoskin and Sauch, "Studies (6)".

5 Bueno, *Los dólmenes de Valencia de Alcántara*.

6 See Hoskin and Sauch, "Studies (6)"; Hoskin and

colleagues, "Studies (5)", Section K; J. A. Belmonte and J. R. Belmonte, "Astronomía, cultura y religión en la prehistoria de la Península Ibérica: Los dólmenes de Valencia de Alcántara", *Tribuna de astronomía*, no. 116/117 (July/August 1995), 18–25 and 72.

7 Hoskin and colleagues, "Studies (5)", Section J.

8 See Chapters 8 and 9.

9 Belmonte and Belmonte, *op. cit.*

10 Strabo, *Geography*, transl. by H. L. Jones, ii (London 1960), 3.4.16 (cited by Belmonte and Belmonte, *op. cit.*, 24).

11 For more information on the Cáceres tombs, see Oliveira, *Sepulturas megalíticas del término municipal de Cedillo*.

12 P. Bueno Ramirez, "La Necrópolis de Santiago de Alcántara (Cáceres): Una hipótesis de interpretación para los sepulcros de pequeño tamaño del megalitismo occidental", *Boletín del Seminario de Estudios de Arte y Arqueología*, lx (1994), 25–100.

13 For further details see Hoskin and colleagues, "Studies (5)", Section J.

14 For further details see Hoskin and colleagues, "Studies (5)", Section H.

15 For a detailed discussion, with bibliography, see M. Socorro López Plaza, "Revisión de las orientaciones de los sepulcros megalíticos de Salamanca", *Actas del IV Congreso de la SEAC "Astronomía en la cultura"*, ed. by C. Jaschek and F. Atrio Baradela (Salamanca, 1997), 209–15.

16 See Hoskin and colleagues, "Studies (5)", Section H.

17 For more on this see J. C. de Senna-Martinez, M. Socorro López Plaza and M. A. Hoskin, "Territorio, ideología y cultura material en el megalitismo de la Plataforma del Mondego (centro de Portugal)", *O neolítico atlántico e as orixes do megalitismo*, ed. by A. Rodríguez Casal (Santiago de Compostela, 1997), 657–76.

18 See Hoskin and colleagues, "Studies (5)", Section G.

19 *Ibid.*, S63.

Easterly-facing Tombs (III): North Iberia and Neighbouring France

In our clockwise progress around Iberia we now cross the northern border of Portugal and enter Spain once more. We find ourselves in Galicia, where there are inumerable tumuli but the megalithic tombs are well scattered. Then, as we turn eastwards across the north of Spain, we pass through Asturias and Cantabria, where most of the monuments are again in the form of tumuli without orientations, until we come once more to megalithic tombs in the province of Burgos. From there to the French frontier, through the Spanish Basque Country (País Vasco) and adjacent regions of Navarra, tombs are relatively numerous, though in the mountainous areas they are often small and in poor condition. We then cross the frontier into the French Basque Country (Pays Basque), where the tombs have much in common with their Spanish counterparts. To end our circuit of the peninsula we study the tombs on either side of the central Pyrenees, stopping short of the northeastern corner of Cataluña and the adjacent region of France where (as we shall see in Chapter 10) different customs prevailed.

The province of Burgos remains in the memory because of one of a number of incidents that befell us over the years as we were required to take a small saloon car along unmade country roads, many of them in very poor condition. One day our fieldwork took us to a village on high ground some kilometres north of the city, where we enquired of a local man as to the

The autonomous regions (*communidades autónomas*) of northern Spain.

A Mina de Parxubeira (A Coruña), a typical Galician *anta de corredor*.

whereabouts of the tombs. Some while later, as we drove across the fields, the car became bogged down in mud and refused to move. Setting off to the village to ask for help, by good fortune I met a tractor driven by the very man from whom we had earlier asked directions. He was in fact the owner of the tombs, which were his pride and joy — his tractor was plastered with photographs of them. Neighbouring farmers were totally indifferent to his monuments, and so he had been delighted (and vindicated) to encounter foreigners making a pilgrimage to study them. He was more than happy to help, but the only tow-point on our car was in the front, and this would have taken us still further into trouble. It happened that the car, remarkably, had an external spare tyre, and to frustrate thieves this tyre was secured to the car by a padlock and chain. Our rescuer put a hawser around this simple chain, and with great delicacy eased the car free of the mud.

Galicia

Galicia is the autonomous region of Spain that occupies the northwest corner of Iberia, being bounded by Portugal to the south and by sea to the west and north. Its most celebrated city is Santiago de Compostela, whose cathedral houses the reputed tomb of the apostle St James and has long been a centre of pilgrimage. Galicia is rich in Neolithic and Bronze Age remains, belonging to cultures that are related to those of neighbouring Asturias and, more especially, northern

Portugal.[1] Tumuli, or *mamoas*, are extraordinarily abundant: the catalogue for the province of Lugo lists no fewer than 748, while the inventory for the province of Pontevedra contains an astonishing two thousand.

By contrast, the stone communal tombs that are currently accessible to the investigator are thinly scattered. These *antas* (the local language shares with Portugese this general term for 'dolmen') are megalithic: tholos tombs are unknown, and the use of dry-stone walling is rare. The tombs are varied in location, size and structure, and there is no agreed classification, but they fall into three main types (all different from the antas of the Alentejo with their leaning sidestones):

(a) *Antas simples*, with a small chamber, completely closed (and so without orientation) and usually with a single capstone. The chamber is typically polygonal or near-circular, and of less than 2m in diameter.

(b) *Antas de corredor*, the most impressive monuments, and the ones with which we are concerned. Here the polygonal chamber, which may be up to 4m or 5m in diameter, has an entrance, and therefore an orientation. Often there is a seven-stone chamber (backstone plus three true ortho-stats to each side). In some cases the entrance leads to a corridor which may have its own capstone(s), but in other cases the corridor may not be clearly differentiated from the chamber, the sidestones of the chamber simply converging at the entrance. Lengthy corridors are unknown; overall, the chamber and corridor may measure up to 7m. Radiocarbon studies suggest that con-struction of the tombs began soon after 4000 BC, reached a peak around 3000 BC, and continued until late in the third millennium.[2]

(c) *Arcas megalíticas*, simple tombs with a single, carefully worked capstone and a rectangular chamber. These were a prelude to the cists for individual inhumation that become common in the early Bronze Age.

In July 1995 Antón Rodríguez Casal of the University of Santiago de Compostela and I measured 32 *antas de corredor*, and in November of that year a further four. Accurate measurement is fre-quently made difficult when the tomb, despite its type-name, in fact has no corridor; and when present the corridor may not be aligned with the backstone. At Mamoa de Caída, for example, the corridor is aligned some 20° to the south of the direction faced by the backstone, while at neighbouring Mamoa del Pecado the corridor is aligned well to the north of the backstone. As a result, the measured azimuths are subject to considerable uncertainty.

Furthermore, the variety of location, size and structure and the poor condition of some of the monuments make interpretation difficult. Three of the tombs, Pedro da Xesta 1–3, near the Portugese border, are tiny. Two others, Casota de Frean and A Fornella, were neighbouring monu-ments, unusual in having rectangular chambers with only a single, massive stone at each side. The remainder were sizeable *antas de corredor* with more complex chambers.

Despite these obstacles to interpretation, the results (Table 7.1) demonstrate that the builders did not orientate their tombs at random but were following a custom; and that the custom was similar throughout Galicia, and therefore was probably rooted in astronomy. Tombs faced towards

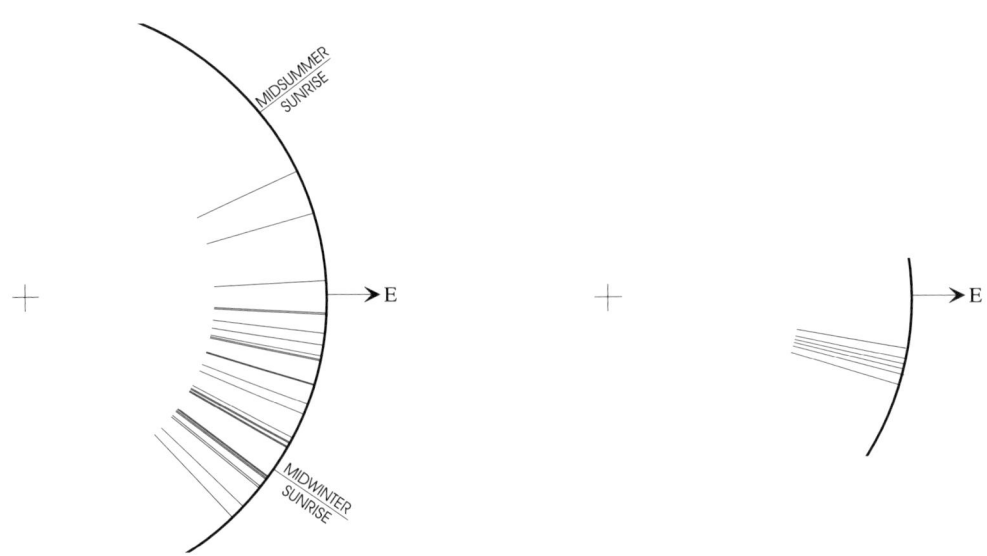

(*Left*) Orientations of 27 *antas de corredor* of the Galician provinces of A Coruña, Lugo and Pontevedra. (*Right*) Orientations of six *antas de corredor* near the Portugese border with Galicia.

the eastern half of the horizon, and all are SR or SC, the most northerly-facing tomb, Mamoa do Rei, having azimuth 64°. The location of the major tomb of Pedra Cuberta is particularly signifi-cant: the large stones of which it is constructed were dragged several hundred metres down the eastern slope of a valley, across the valley floor, and half-way up the western slope, apparently in order that the tomb might look easterly (and towards an acceptably low horizon).

It is a moot point, whether all the tombs were oriented on sunrise (SR). The only tombs that may have faced too far south for sunrise are: *A Fornella*, whose unusual three-stone chamber has already been mentioned; *Pedro da Xesta 2*, a tiny tomb also with a rectangular chamber; *Pedro da Xesta 3*, whose chamber has an area of only 1 square metre; and *Dolmen de Bravos*, a small, hill-top tomb, with a complete seven-stone chamber. Dolmen de Bravos is therefore the only typical *anta de corredor* to face too far south for sunrise, which it does by some 12°. It seems preferable to regard this tomb as a minor anomaly, and to conclude that the Galician tombs were, like their Portuguese neighbours to the south, oriented on sunrise.

Interestingly, the six tombs we measured along the frontier with Portugal in the far south of Galicia, not only are SR but have orientations within the narrow range 100°–107°.

Scattered tombs of north-central Spain

Before we turn to the concentrations of tombs in the mountains of the Spanish Basque Country, we mention the handful of dolmens that occur, often in little groups, at intervals across a vast area of north-central Spain, and often at a considerable distance inland. They are distinguished by their size; by their long, and sometimes very long, corridors; and (with one exception) by their faithful observance of the easterly orientation customs.[3]

(i) *Province of Burgos*

The province of Burgos is in the northeast of Castilla y León. In the region around the hamlet of Sedano, some 40km north of Burgos city, we located six scattered sepulchres with corridor, one of which has a corridor an extraordinary 14 metres long. All are on high ground if not actually on a hilltop. Details of the orientations are given in Table 7.2, where it will be seen that all six tombs face in azimuth between 101° and 126°, four of the orientations falling within a range of only 5° that includes the direction of midwinter sunrise.

22km north-northeast of Burgos is the hamlet of Ruyales del Paramo, and in a hollow on elevated ground outside the village are two tombs. One is in ruinous condition and yielded no orientation. The other, some 200m away, is substantial in size: its chamber is 5m in diameter, and the ruined corridor is over 9m long. Its orientation of 214° is wholly exceptional, though the presence of the lengthy corridor leaves no doubt that this is one of the rare Iberian tombs (outside the far northeast of Cataluña and the southern tip of Cádiz) that unequivocally faces the western half of the horizon.

On lowish ground near the hamlet of Quintanilla de las Viñas, 30km south-southeast of Burgos, is the sepulchre of Cubillejo de Lara de Los Infantes. Its corridor extends to 10m. It was oriented just south of midwinter sunrise.[4]

Cubillejo de Lara, with the subcircular chamber and long corridor typical of Burgos tombs. In this case the corridor is 10 metres in length.

Sorginetxe, southeast of Vitoria. In this isolated tomb each successive sidestone leans against its predecessor, as in a Portugese anta.

(ii) *Province of Alava*

One of the provinces that border Burgos on the east is Alava, southernmost of the three that make up the Spanish Basque Country.[5]

Near the border with Burgos, and some 30km southwest of the town of Vitoria, is the little hamlet of Molinilla, and near the road to Salcedo lies the dolmen of La Mina. It is a sepulchre that is unusual in having an additional structure on the south side of the corridor. It too faced just south of midwinter sunrise.

At Anda-Catadiano, on a plain in the valley of Cuartango 15km west of Vitoria, are the remains of a cluster of four tombs, all now in poor condition. Two have surviving stones of a corridor or gallery. Gurpide Sur, best classified as a galleried tomb, has orientation 108° while facing a mountainous skyline with altitude 10°. San Sebastián Sur is probably a megalithic sepulchre; it faces approximately 94° with altitude 6°. Both are therefore SR.

To the east of Vitoria, and now prominent in a valley site alongside the main road to Pamplona, is the massive tomb of Aitzkomendi. It was discovered more than a century and a half ago, and its corridor fell victim to the early excavators. Each side is formed by a single massive orthostat.

Its orientation is about 100° and so it is SR. Some 6km to the southwest of Aitzkomendi is the equally fine dolmen of Sorginetxe. There is no record of the dolmen having a corridor, and its sidestones are not orthostats but lean against adjacent stones in the manner of a Portugese anta. It faces 131°, but the skyline altitude is no less than 8° and it too is SR.

To the north of the medieval hilltop town of Laguardia in the south of Alava, the impressive mountains of the Cordillera de Cantabria run in an east–west direction. On the south side of the mountain range, where the steep slopes give way to a gentler incline, lies a line of seven widely-scattered tombs. Six of these clearly have corridors and are megalithic sepulchres in our terminology, and the seventh, Alto de la Huesera, also has the vestiges of a corridor.[6] The chambers vary in length from 5m to little more than 2m. All the tombs (see Table 7.2) faced the sun long after it had risen and was climbing in the sky, and so we have here a custom that was strictly SC (and not SR/SC).

(iii) *Province of Soria*

Well to the south of Alava is the province of Soria, and 20km northeast of the town of that name is the isolated sepulchre of El Alto de la Tejera. It is sited on the top of a hill outside the modern village of Castilfrío de la Sierra, and is in poor condition, with a ruined corridor some 7m in length. It faces 135° and is SC.

Chabola de la Hechicera, one of the sepulchres with corridor near Laguardia.

La Mina de Farangortea, with its
shaped entrance stone.

(iv) *Province of Guadalajara*

A further 100km to the south, and therefore well to the interior of the peninsula, is the hamlet
of Aguilar de Anguita, in the province of Guadalajara. Nearby is the sepulchre of Portillo de las
Cortes. The chamber is a modest 3m in width, but the corridor is again long, measuring some
9½m. It faced 115° and so is SR.

Three other 'sepulchres' in the area were excavated long ago. Local enquiries suggest that no
trace now remains of two of these, at Alcolea del Pina and Anguita. At Garbajosa, however, we
were taken by proud locals to the "dolmen", which disappointingly proved to be formed of natural
rocks of unusual shapes, beneath which tradition has it that there were prehistoric burials.

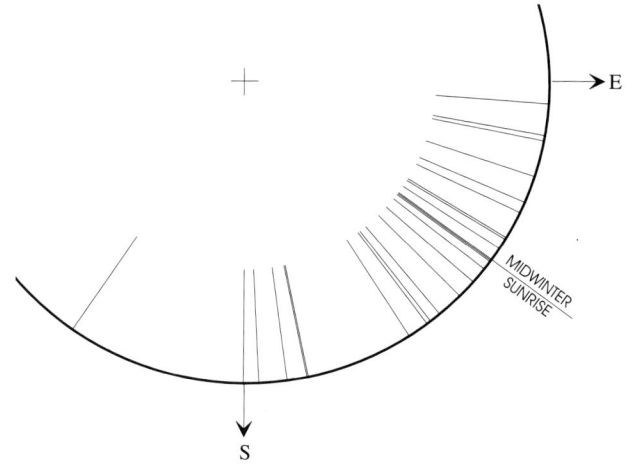

Orientations of the 25 scattered tombs of north-central Spain. The tomb with orientation 214°, Ruyales del Paramo, is one of the rare Iberian tombs outside Cataluña and Cádiz to face the western half of the horizon.

(v) *Province of Navarra*

To the east of the Spanish Basque Country is the province (and autonomous region) of Navarra. The part of the province that borders the Basque Country will be discussed in the next section, but here we mention two isolated pairs of tombs located elsewhere. One pair, Portillo de Enériz and La Mina de Farangortea, lie on elevated ground some 20km south-southwest of Pamplona. They are of almost identical construction. In each the lower portion of the entrance stone to the chamber survives; it has a shaped opening, which is unusual in this area. The corridors are short but made of substantial orthostats. Although the tombs are perhaps 1km apart, they have identical orientations of 168° (and so are SC).

The other pair lie close to the French border, near Isaba, high in the Roncal Valley. One, Arrako, is a galleried tomb; we located it only on our second attempt. The first attempt took place in a blizzard, and we enquired after the tomb from traffic police who were preoccupied with discouraging cars from attempting to cross the frontier in the appalling conditions prevailing. We were nearly arrested for being insane. Our second attempt was made in good weather, and we found that the tomb faces well within the range of sunrise. The other, Sakulo, we did not locate, but its reported orientation is south-southeast, which would be well south of the range of sunrise.

These tombs, some of which have corridors of lengths unknown in most other parts of Iberia, are scattered over a vast area that measures 250km from east to west and 200km from north to south. Nevertheless, with the exception of Ruyales del Paramo, they all face within the southeast quadrant, and so are either SR or SC. It is remarkable to visit the most isolated of these tombs, often many tens of kilometres from its nearest known neighbour, and to find that it too faces in one of the customary directions.

Guipúzcoa and the neighbouring region of Navarra

Numerous tombs and other prehistoric monuments are to be found in the mountainous Basque province of Guipúzcoa (and in the region of Navarra immediately adjoining it to the east).[7] The majority are at elevations ranging from 500 to 1200 metres. They are found on mountain ridges dividing two watersheds, on gently sloping hillsides, and to the sides of paths leading from one pasture to another.[8]

The tombs take many forms, and most are small and today in poor if not ruinous condition (though even a small tomb may be the focus of a tumulus of impressive size). Unfortunately, the present condition of many of these tombs is often so poor that its type is uncertain.

The sites we visited fell into four groups: the Sierra de Urquilla, the ridge of which forms the border between the provinces of Guipúzcoa and Alava; the Sierra de Aralar; the region of Uharte-Arakil in neighbouring Navarra; and the northeast corner of Guipúzcoa, not far from San Sebastián. We accumulated a total of 26 orientations (Table 7.3, and histogram on p. 122).

Two comments should be made. First, within the predominantly SR custom there are notable differences between the different areas. On the Sierra de Aralar the orientations of the seven tombs are scattered over the unusually wide range of 70°, and two faced close to midwinter sunrise while two more face still further south and are clearly SC. By contrast, the nineteen other orientations lie within a strictly SR range of only 37° and most of the tombs faced sunrise in the spring and autumn.

Second, while the tombs whose orientations we have listed in this section are overwhelmingly SR, the published inventory of Guipúzcoa monuments[9] suggests that we should hesitate before characterizing the custom of the region as such. It is true that the inventory assigns certain orientations that we found to be seriously in error. Nevertheless, the inventory does imply that a sizeable minority of tombs *not* measured by us are SC rather than SR, and if this is true then our sample cannot be wholly representative.

The dolmenic chambers of the Pays Basque of France

The formidable mountains of the Pyrenees, which divide modern Spain from France, have proved no barrier to cultures past or present. Today at the Mediterranean end of the chain the Catalan culture flourishes on both the French and the Spanish side of the divide, while near the Bay of Biscay the same is true of the Basque culture. And so it was in prehistoric times: the mountains that resist the passage of the modern car and train no doubt offered welcome pasture in the dry summers to peoples from the lower ground to both north and south.

The 110 dolmenic chambers in the French Basque Country belong in the present chapter because of their cultural links with the Spanish Basque tombs we have just discussed. Fortunately, Yves Chevalier, the French archaeologist whose tragically early death was recounted in Chapter 1, had studied the French Basque tombs and indeed had been able to prepare a list of orientations for me during his last illness. What follows is based on this list and on the article he published.[10]

The general term 'dolmenic chambers' seems appropriate because many of the monuments are so insignificant that to refer to them all as 'dolmens' might be misleading. This word is best reserved for the tombs built with true megaliths, whereas the tiny chambers lined with little slabs are better thought of as 'dolmenic cists'. We might speak of a dolmen when the monument exceeds some 2m × 1m × 1m in size. If so, then there are some twenty dolmens in the Basque Country, the rest being dolmenic cists.

The dolmens properly so called had trapezoidal chambers, and the backstone was almost always located in between sidestones. The tomb was surrounded by a tumulus some 8m to 12m in diameter. In most dolmens each of the sides had a single slab. The chamber varied in length between 2 and 3 metres, and in width between 1 and 1½ metres. Often the chamber was wider at the backstone than at the entrance, and the backstone was sometimes at an angle to the axis of the chamber.

Those dolmens with other than a single stone to each side took two forms: in some, either one or both sides were formed by two (or more) stones in a line, while at the entrance of others an additional stone to each side lay askew the axis and served to narrow the entrance.

Dolmenic cists account for some three-quarters of the region's monuments of the dolmenic tradition. In plan they are miniatures of the dolmens properly so-called, being on average 1½m long, ¾m wide, and ½m high.

Great uncertainty surrounds the dating of these various types of dolmenic monuments. It is probable that the dolmens belong to the Neolithic, but it is not clear whether the cists preceded or succeeded them, though it is likely that the tradition of cist construction survived for many centuries.

There is a striking parallel between the customs observed by the tomb-builders in the Spanish

Gastenya at Mendive (Basse-Navarre), one of the few sizeable tombs of the French Basque Country (photograph courtesy of M. J. Blot).

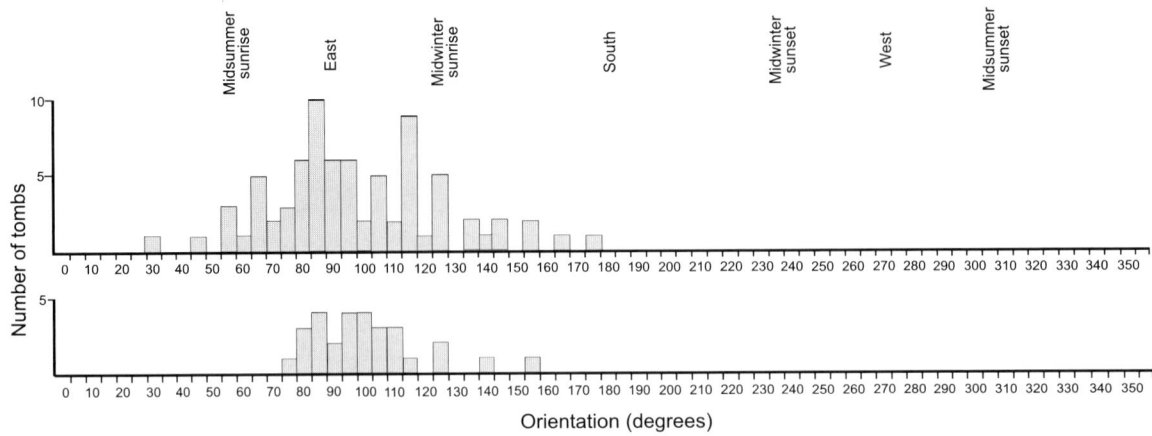

(*Above*) Histogram showing the orientations of 77 dolmens and dolmenic cists of the French Basque Country. (*Below*) Histogram showing the orientations of 26 megalithic tombs of Guipúzcoa and neighbouring Navarra, in the Spanish Basque Country.

Basque Country and those observed by their French counterparts. Not only are the layouts of the monuments very similar, but so are the orientation customs. Of the 26 Spanish tombs, 24 (92·3%) faced sunrise, while just two (7·7%) faced too far south. The orientations of 77 dolmens and dolmenic cists from the French Basque Country are listed in Table 7.4. Of these, 66 (85·7%) faced sunrise, nine (11·7%) faced too far south, while the remaining two (2·6%) are reported as facing too far north. The match is remarkable.

Ariège and west Cataluña

As we proceed from the Basque Country eastwards along the Pyrenees towards the Mediterranean, dolmens are scarce — though in a lovely location high in the mountains near the frontier north of Ainsa in Aragon is the charming dolmen of Piedra del Vasar. It faces 110° and is SR (see Table 7.5).

Midway along the mountain range, on the French side, is the *département* of Ariège. There a mere 16 dolmens have been identified, but most of these are in ruins, and only a handful have measurable orientations. They are 'simple dolmens', built of just four slabs (one at the back, one to each side, and one on top), but on a massive scale. Three of the four that we located in May 1999 were on high ground not far from the town of Mas d'Azil; one faces 77° and two 106°. The fourth, by strange contrast, was in a little valley, beside a stream and facing a steep slope; it has azimuth 86°. We also located a fifth tomb, Genat, near Larège, on high, indeed precipitous ground; this however was a 'paradolmen', in which the builders made use of natural rock for part of the structure. All four dolmens, and the paradolmen, faced sunrise.

A little further east, and high in the mountains just beyond the principality of Andorra, is Cerdagne, a region that straddles the border between Cataluña in Spain and Pyrénées-Orientales

(*Above*) Piedra del Vasar, an isolated tomb in the high Pyrenees.

(*Below*) Cap del Pouech, above Mas d'Azil in Ariège.

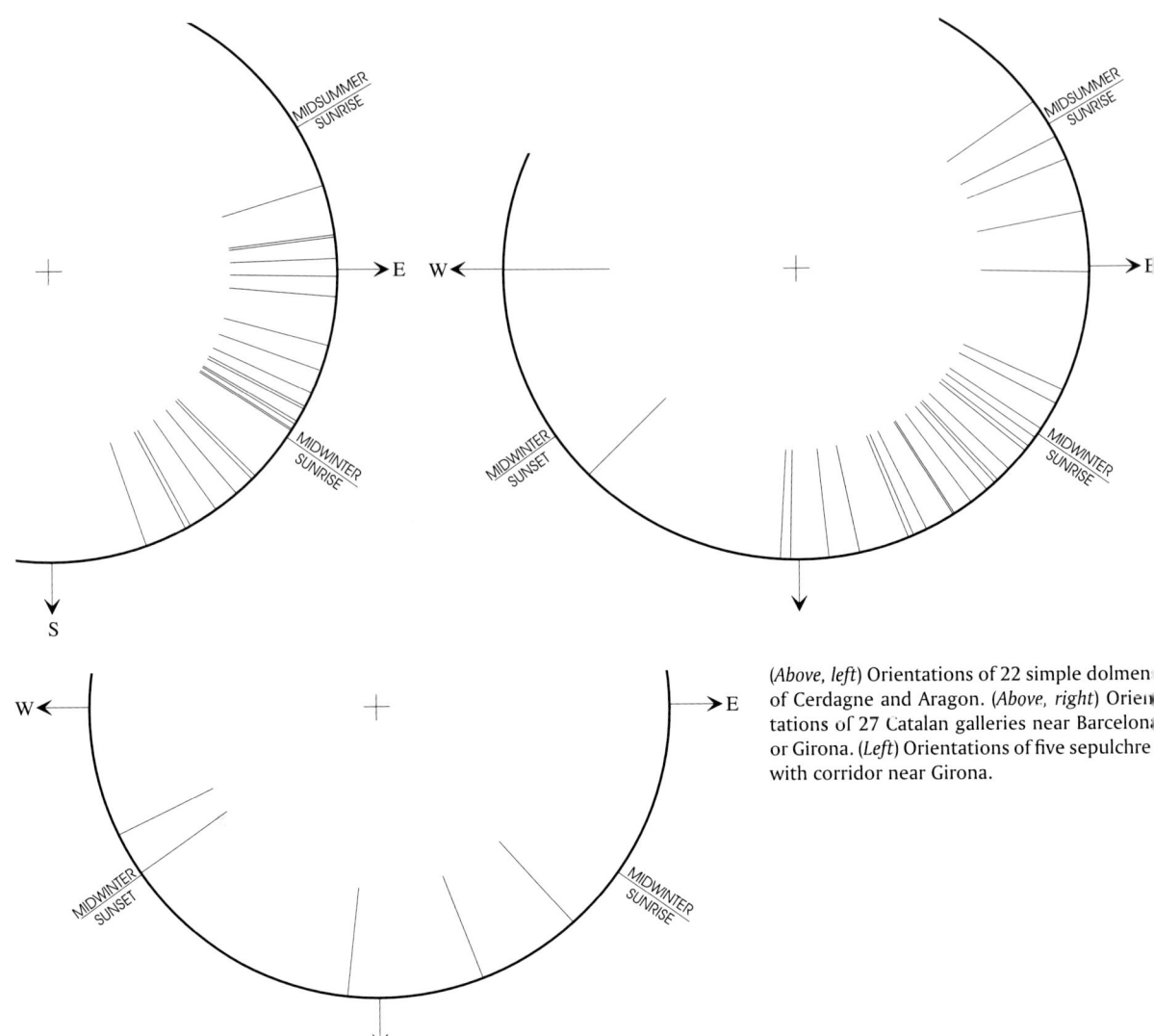

(*Above, left*) Orientations of 22 simple dolmen of Cerdagne and Aragon. (*Above, right*) Orientations of 27 Catalan galleries near Barcelona or Girona. (*Left*) Orientations of five sepulchres with corridor near Girona.

in France. Cerdagne has a significant number of megalithic tombs. The earliest were small, rectangular 'Neolithic cists', containing a single burial, or occasionally two. These are dated to the late fourth and early third millennia. Communal tombs then appear in the form of 'Catalan galleries', in which the chamber has a corridor that is of similar width; these are assigned to the middle of the third millennium. From the later third millennium we have 'megalithic cists', which are closed chambers with a tumulus, access to the chamber being obtained by raising the cover stone; paradolmens; and 'paramegalithic crypts', adapted from natural caves and hollows.

Towards the close of the third millennium there developed the simple dolmen, but with a stone of reduced height across the entrance, the space or 'window' immediately above it allowing access to the chamber. They were constructed around the period 2200–2000 BC, and continued in use for nearly a thousand years, during the early-middle Bronze Age. A variant of the form had a removable door-stone.

For the most part the simple dolmens were well scattered, in terrain that is hilly and even mountainous. In September 1997, with the help of Oriol Mercadal i Fernàndez, Sara Aliaga i Rodrigo, and Albert Villaró, we visited sixteen of these dolmens on the Spanish side of the frontier and three more in France.[11] In addition, the orientations of two further Catalan dolmens were among measures that were published long ago and which we found to be reliable.[12] The results are listed in Table 7.6. Fourteen faced directions in which the sun rose at some time of year (SR), but seven faced directions in which the sun had always risen and was climbing in the sky (SC). The orientations of the simple dolmens of Cerdagne, therefore, are SR/SC.

South of the mountains, in the plains of west Cataluña, megalithic tombs are few and very far between, but we measured seven Catalan galleries at various distances to the north and northwest of Barcelona, and three near Mataró, some 25km northeast of Barcelona in the direction of the frontier between Spain and France (Table 7.7). The seven are oriented in the southeast quadrant, so they too are SR/SC. But while one Mataró gallery faces 140°, another, whose front had been destroyed to make a road, appears to face west, and there is no doubt that the third faces 225°, in the direction of sunset close to the winter solstice.

If we proceed parallel to the coast, towards the frontier, then when we are near Girona, we find a remarkable concentration of tombs (Table 7.8), most of them Catalan galleries. We have measurements for seventeen galleries, and all face within the range 55°–183° and so are without exception SR/SC. But of five sepulchres with corridor, one faces close to south, two to the east of south, and two to the west of south.

These encounters with westerly-facing tombs hint at what awaits us in the tiny region of northeast Spain that lies within twenty or so kilometres of the frontier: an area thickly sewn with tombs, a substantial number of which face westerly. To make sense of this confusion of orientations we need to take a different route, approaching Mediterranean France from the north of that country (Chapter 8), investigating the dolmens of Provence and east Languedoc (Chapter 9), and only late in Chapter 10 making our way once more back across the mountains into Cataluña.

We therefore leave the remaining Catalan dolmens until Chapter 10, and (since Murcia and Valencia are almost empty of tombs) terminate here our circuit of the Iberian peninsula.

A pattern established

In the present chapter we have determined the orientations of a further 220 tombs, plus one whose orientation is 'typical'. Of these, just 5 (2·3%) face in the range 0°–60°, north of midsummer sunrise, while 211 (95·5%) are SR/SC. Only 5 (2·3%) face in the range 190°–360°, and all but one of these are in Cataluña, near the region where westerly-facing tombs are in fact common.

In the course of our circuit we have measured some 850 megalithic and tholos tombs in Spain and Portugal, and a further 85 across the Pyrenees in France. Of the 935, only 17 (1·8%) faced easterly and north of midsummer sunrise, and the same number faced westerly in the range 190°–360°; the remaining 901 (96·4%) were SR/SC, facing in the range 60°–190°.

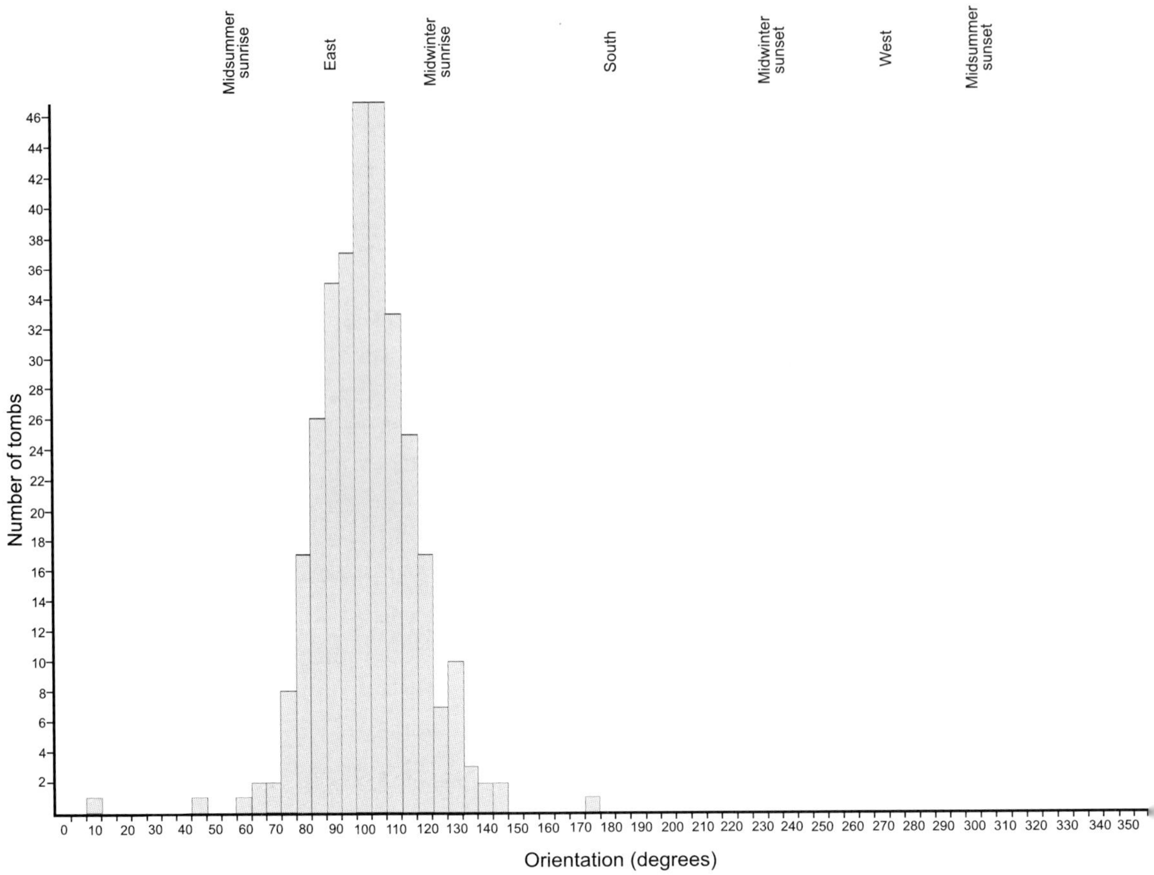

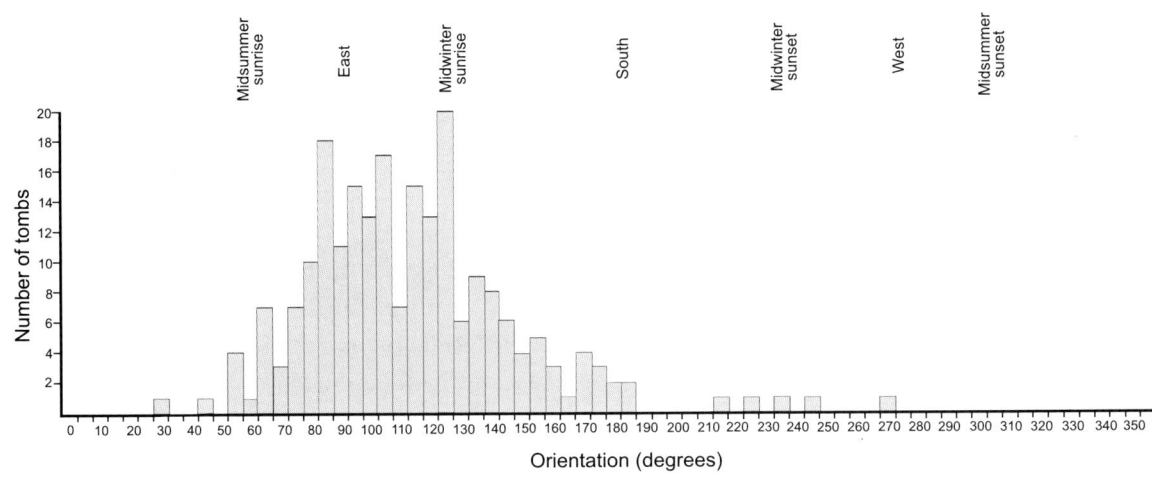

Histogram showing the orientations of 324 tombs of west Iberia.

Histogram showing the orientations of 221 tombs of north Iberia and neighbouring France.

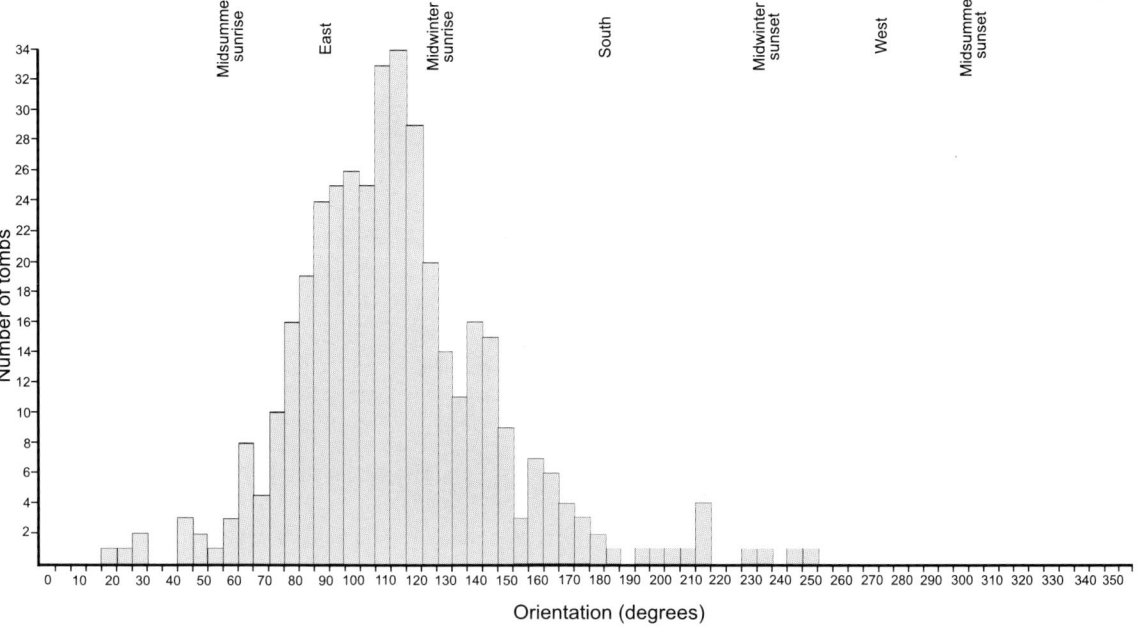

Histogram showing the orientations of 390 tombs of south Iberia.

The breakdown by region is significant: in the south of the peninsula 94·4% of the tombs were SR/SC; in the north, 95·5%; and in the west, an astonishing 99·4%. Most striking of all, in the west 96·9% faced in the range 60°–130° (less than one-fifth of a circle), and so were SR or almost so.

This suggests the following scenario:

(i) in the west of Iberia tombs were oriented in the range of sunrise (or moonrise) because custom required that they face the rising of one or other of these luminaries;

(ii) the preponderance of these orientations to the south of east (rather than to the north of east) makes it likely that tombs were laid out, like Christian churches, to face sunrise on the very day when construction began, for in most places the autumn or early winter would be the time when the harvest was in and men had leisure to commence such projects; and

(iii) this SR custom originated in west Iberia, but spread to the rest of the peninsula where in many places it became attenuated with distance and time, and became SR/SC.

We must now see whether similar customs prevailed across the Pyrenees, in the south of France.

Further reading

Gipuzkoa. Carta arqueologica, I: Megalitos (Sociedad de Ciencias Aranzadi, San Sebastian, 1990).

M. Hoskin and colleagues, "Studies in Iberian archaeoastronomy: (5) Orientations of megalithic tombs of northern and western Iberia", *AA*, no. 23 (1998), S39–87.

F. Jordá Cerdá *et al.*, *Historia de España*, i: *Prehistoria* (Madrid, 1986).

A. A. Rodríguez Casal, "Le mégalithisme en Galice", in *Mégalithismes de l'Atlantique à l'Ethiopie*, ed. by J. Guilaine (Paris, 1999), 91–106.

A. A. Rodríguez Casal, *O megalitismo: A primeira arquitectura monumental de Galicia* (Santiago de Compostela, 1990; in Gallego).

J. I. Vegas Arambaru, *Dolmenes en Alava: Guía para su visita* (2nd edn, Argitalpen Saila, 1983).

Notes and references

1 For an introduction to megalithism in Galicia, see A. A. Rodríguez Casal, "Le mégalithisme en Galice"; and (in Gallego) his "Neolitización e megalitismo en Galicia", in *O neolítico atlántico e as orixes do megalitismo*, ed. by Rodríguez Casal (Santiago de Compostela, 1997), 447–62. For further information, his *O megalitismo*. The present account is based on Section D of Hoskin and colleagues, "Studies (5)".

2 F. A. Matthías and J. Mª Bello Diéguez, "Cronología y periodización del fenómeno megalítico en Galicia a la luz de las dataciones por carbono 14", in Rodríguez Casal (ed.), *O neolítico atlántico*, 507–20.

3 For further details see Hoskin and colleagues, "Studies (5)", Section B.

4 A further tomb is reported at Atapuerca some 15km to the east of Burgos; but of this only a ruined tumulus is now to be seen.

5 A guide to the tombs of Alava is Vegas Arambaru, *Dolmenes en Alava*.

6 *Ibid.*, 11.

7 A magnificent inventory of the megalithic tombs of Guipúzcoa is *Gipuzkoa. Carta arqueologica, I: Megalitos*. It is a shame that the monuments are not more worthy of the attention lavished on them.

8 For further details see Hoskin and colleagues, "Studies (5)", Section C.

9 *Gipuzkoa. Carta arqueologica, I: Megalitos*.

10 Y. Chevalier, "A propos des monuments dolmeniques du Pays Basque: Étude préliminaire", *Archives des Pyrénées Occidentales*, vii (1987), 142–8.

11 For further details see Hoskin and colleagues, "Studies (5)", Section A.

12 J. P. O'Reilly, "On the orientation of certain dolmens recently discovered in Catalonia", *Proceedings of the Royal Irish Academy*, 3rd ser., iii (1893–96), 573–9. Dolmen de la Cabana de la Mosquera has been 'reconstructed' and now faces west of south; La Casa Encantada de la Serra de Pinyana we were unable to visit.

8

Easterly-facing Tombs (IV): The French Causses

The region from the French Mediterranean coast, northwards through the Garrigues (so-named from a word for 'oak'[1]) into the high plateaux known as the Causses, is exceptionally rich in dolmens. Much of the area is limestone, where the caves hollowed out by the action of rainwater offered early settlers not only attractive shelter but also places where they could deposit their dead. The early Neolithic population flourished there, expanded, and established themselves in the landscape; and around 3500 BC the practice of individual burial, or of multiple burials in caves or hypogea (*hypogeum*, 'below ground', an artificial cavity excavated out of the bedrock), gave way to the construction of megalithic dolmens, some three thousand of which are known from the area.

As my Iberian jigsaw approached completion, the problem of central and southern France began to loom. Without the investigation of an area so rich in megalithic monuments, this work would be grievously incomplete, not least because it appeared that some of the tombs faced east and others west. Yet most of the dolmens were known to be small in scale — 'simple dolmens' in both the technical and the popular senses of 'simple' — and situated mostly in the remote and well-forested highlands of the Causses. To locate and measure a representative sample, at the rate of perhaps three or four a day, would be prohibitively expensive in both time and money.

I have recounted earlier how I found a glimmer of hope in the wide-ranging thesis published in 1984 by Yves Chevalier.[2] It was clear from his brief discussions of orientations that he had in fact measured several hundred tombs. Perhaps the measures were not as carefully made as a specialist would wish, and the author doubtless had taken no account of the angular altitude of the skyline; but since his data embraced great numbers of orientations the errors would tend to cancel out, and if the skyline was supposed always to have an altitude of (say) 2°, the overall picture of any given region that resulted would be broadly correct, however imperfect in detail.

The sudden death of M. Chevalier, when he had agreed to my request that he publish his measured orientations, was a grievous blow, but with the kind cooperation of his family I was allowed to visit the family home in Brittany, remove his papers to my hotel room, and work on them undisturbed for a week. Chevalier had been meticulous in the extreme, writing in an immaculate, tiny hand, and taking immense pains when drawing site plans and pie-charts. I found that, except for the tombs in the French Basque Country (see Chapter 7), of which he had prepared me a list, I would have to rely on these pie-charts, which I measured with a protractor. Clearly, the error in his original compass measure was being augmented by the error when he drew the representation of this measure on the pie-chart, and by the error I made in using the protractor; these errors accumulate (and so may well improperly extend the authentic ranges of orientations), and I wished it were otherwise. Fortunately, the numbers of tombs involved were great and so the basic patterns could be relied upon.[3]

For the *département* of Lot, Chevalier had on occasion availed himself of the magnificent inventory published by Jean Clottes.[4] This inventory includes an orientation for each dolmen, clearly measured with care and in the knowledge that magnetic variation changes with time and therefore the date of any compass measure should be recorded. This taught me an important lesson: French archaeologists, unlike their Iberian colleagues, have long been conscious that valuable insights can be obtained from orientations. It also taught me a second lesson: few French archaeologists have more than the vaguest idea of how to handle (and interpret) these orientations. Thus M. Clottes is careful to give not only the year but the month of each compass measure, although the direction of magnetic north alters by only a few *minutes* each *year*, and so only after a decade or more does the change become significant for our purposes. Likewise, I find it is common for French archaeologists to suppose that any southwesterly-oriented tomb faced sunset on the day that construction began, even if the orientation is in fact as much as 20° or even 30° south of midwinter sunset. But these limitations are of minor importance; the availability of great quantities of dolmen orientations measured with serious intent is invaluable, and a later inventory by Clottes and Cl. Maurand[5] enabled me to increase the number of orientations in the article[6] I ghost-wrote for Chevalier to nearly a thousand.

The *départements* of the centre-west of France. Causse-type dolmens are concentrated in Lot and Aveyron, but are also to be found in Vienne, Charente, Haute-Vienne, Creuse, Dordogne, Corrèze, Tarn-et-Garonne, Tarn, Lozère, Ardèche and Gard.

A typical Causse-type dolmen: Les Géantes B, Bourg-St-Andéol (Ardèche).

In a recent book[7] Jean Guilaine expresses the current consensus as to the periodization of dolmen construction in southern France. In the second half of the fifth millennium BC and the first half of the fourth, there is evidence that certain individuals were thought to merit burial in stone tombs, and these tombs were sometimes enclosed in mounds that gave them greater dignity. Around 3500 BC, and until 2800 or so (the Late Neolithic), this developed into the custom of building communal tombs of stones, impressive, permanent, and no doubt serving as symbols of the ancestors and perhaps territorial markers. Between 2800 and 2400, when copper became widely known, dolmen building continued but with diminished enthusiasm; and there followed some three centuries when building had stopped, although the tombs continued in use despite the revival of the custom of individual burial. Then, between 2100 and 1500 (the Early Bronze Age), while some dolmens continued in use, other customs came to predominate, and the practice of dolmenic burial declined and eventually ceased.

One archaeologist writing recently on the communal tombs of the region known as the Quercy agrees with Guilaine's chronology and dates the earliest to the second half of the fourth millennium,[8] while two others, discussing those in the Midi-Pyrénées, place their construction slightly later, after 3000 BC.[9]

The 'Causse-type dolmens' (hereafter: C-dolmens) with which we are concerned in this chapter are very numerous, totalling some two thousand, and they are spread over a vast area.[10] In limited numbers they are to be found away to the northwest, towards the Atlantic coast, in the *départements* of Corrèze, Haute-Vienne, Creuse, Dordogne, Charente and even Vienne (Table 8.1). Their heartland is in the interior *départements* of Lot (Table 8.2) and Aveyron (Table 8.3), with smaller numbers in adjoining Tarn-et-Garonne (Table 8.4) and Tarn (Table 8.5). Further south they are to be found in Lozère (Table 8.6), and on both sides of the border between Ardèche and Gard (Table 8.7). But although C-dolmens are found within a few kilometres of the Rhône, there is none across the river in Provence, nor are any to be found in the south of Gard, near the Mediterranean coast.

A typical C-dolmen was 'simple'. Its trapezoidal chamber was constructed of just four megaliths: a backstone, one stone to each side, and a capstone that frequently overlapped the chamber. The sidestones rested against the backstone and often extended beyond it. The average length of the chamber was some 2½m, with 5m as the maximum, and the ratio of length to width varied from 1.3 to 3.6.

There were normally no entrance stones, pierced or otherwise, and no corridor; but occasionally there was a small vestibule formed of a single stone to either side, or a 'coudé' (that is, 'elbow-shaped' or 'angled') corridor, similarly formed. The vestibule might be 1m in length, but a coudé corridor could be twice as long. Another variant occurs in Lot, where a second chamber was sometimes added to the first, to form what Jean Clottes terms a 'double dolmen' (Table 8.8).

The orientation of a simple dolmen, or of a simple dolmen with vestibule, is well-defined, whereas double dolmens and dolmens with coudé corridors have dual orientation, the differences between the two values being minor in the case of the former and substantial in the latter.

We see from Table 8.8 that all the eleven double dolmens there listed faced easterly, nine of them within the range of sunrise, one too far north and one too far south; as we shall find, this matches the pattern of the simple dolmens. In the great majority of surviving tombs with coudé corridors (see Table 8.9), the chamber faced easterly and for some reason the corridor was angled sharply right, to the south-southeast or even south.

Dolmen de Gouziac S, Hures (Lozère), a Causse-type dolmen with coudé corridor (plan by D. and Y. Chevalier).

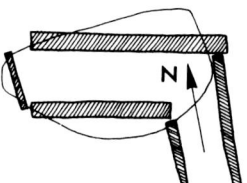

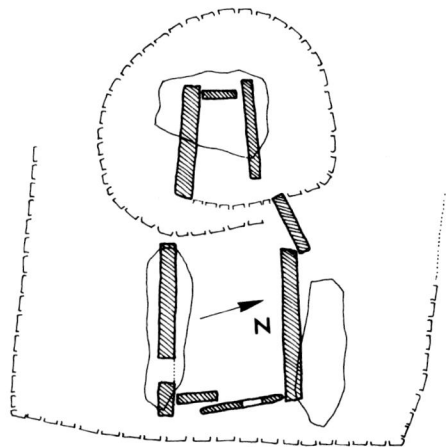

Dolmen du Pech de Grammont, Gramat (Lot), a 'double' Causse-type dolmen (plan by D. and Y. Chevalier).

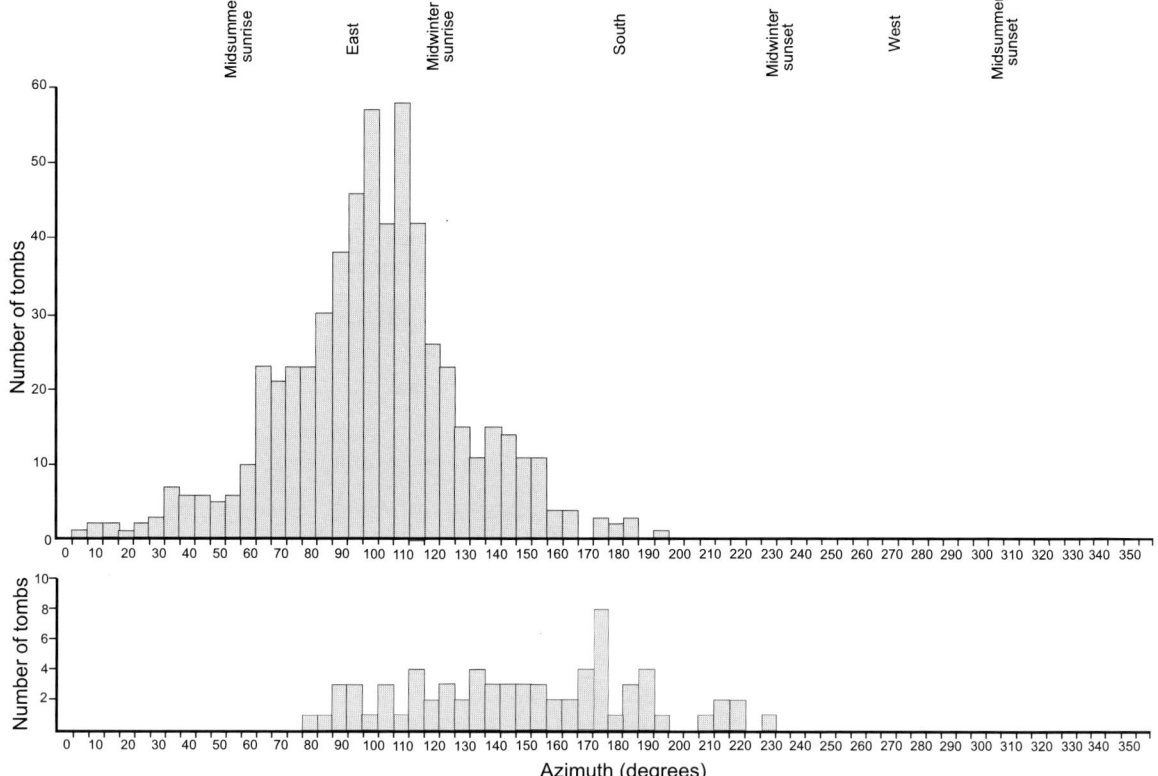

(Above) Histogram of the orientations of 543 simple Causse-type dolmens and 54 Causse-type dolmens with vestibule in *départements* other than Ardèche and Gard; *(below)* histogram of the orientations of 67 simple Causse-type dolmens and 5 Causse-type dolmens with vestibule in Ardèche and Gard.

Because the orientations of double dolmens and of dolmens with coudé corridors are ambivalent, in what follows we shall restrict ourselves to the simple dolmens, with or without vestibule; and we shall deal first with dolmens in *départements* other than Ardèche and Gard. I rely entirely on the data published by Clottes and on the measures I made from Chevalier's pie-charts.

The orientations listed in Tables 8.1–8.6 can, I think, fairly be described as astonishing: of the 597 tombs scattered across a wide area of France (and measured by three different archaeologists), we find that almost every one faced the eastern half of the horizon. The great majority faced within the range of sunrise, but it appears — if the reported orientations are accurate — that some 37 (6·2%) faced too far north and 89 or so (14·9%) too far south. Only nine (1·5%) faced south of 166° (and therefore around culmination). The conclusion is that C-dolmens outside Ardèche and Gard faced easterly: most of them in directions of sunrise (SR dolmens), though a handful faced north of midsummer sunrise and rather more south of midwinter sunrise, in directions where the sun was risen and climbing in the sky (SC) but was still some way short of culmination.

In Ardèche and Gard (Table 8.7), however, the orientations, though easterly for the most part,

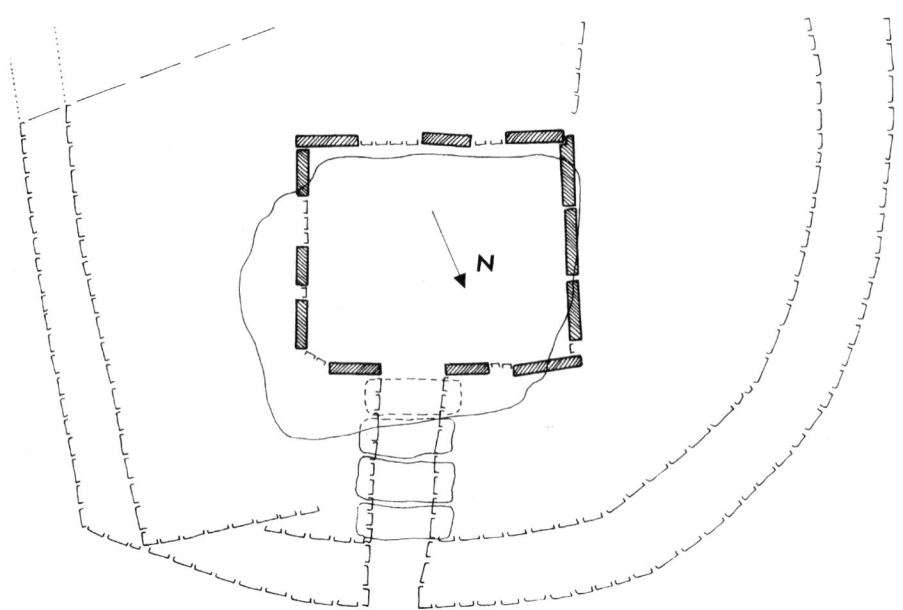

Dolmen F de Bougon (Deux-Sèvres), an Angoumois-type dolmen (after J. P. Mohen).

are strikingly different: not a single one of the 72 C-dolmens faced north of 80°, while no fewer than 26 (36.1%) faced south of 166°, directions almost unknown among the 597 C-dolmens further to the northwest. In the next chapter we shall ask whether the presence in Gard and Ardèche of dolmens of quite different structure and orientation offers an explanation for this apparent anomaly.

Appendix: The Angoumois-type Dolmens

Chevalier also studied a group of dolmens from the area of France north of Bordeaux, and although these tombs are geographically peripheral to our study, they do extend our coverage of central France to the Atlantic Ocean.[11]

The heart of the area of these 'Angoumois-type corridor dolmens' (hereafter: A-dolmens) is the middle valley of the River Charente. But the area extends widely, towards the coast of Charente-Maritime and into the southern part of the *départements* of Vienne and Deux-Sèvres, while there are a handful of A-dolmens in Dordogne, Vendée and Haute-Vienne.

The A-dolmen is a passage tomb with a trapezoidal chamber that is wider than it is long in three-quarters of the examples. An opening, generally offset to the right as viewed from the exterior, and sometimes formed by a pierced slab, gave access to the chamber, which had sides of several orthostats perfectly shaped and joined. The covering was normally by means of a single fitted capstone, though some chambers lined with more modest orthostats seem to have been originally covered by a corbelled vault that has long since disappeared. The A-dolmen was typically

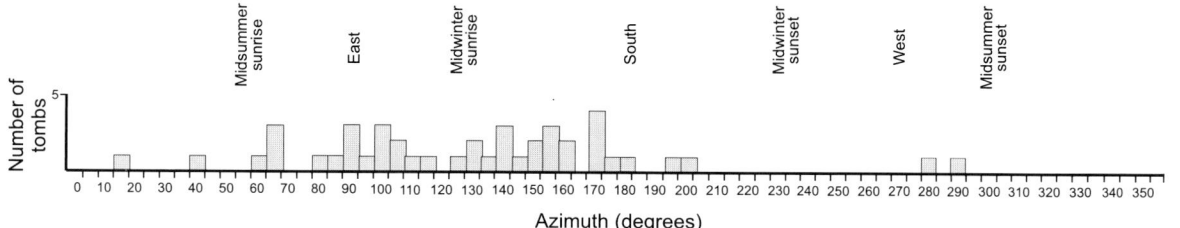

Histogram showing the orientations of 44 Angoumois-type dolmens.

3½m wide, and some 2m in both length and height.

The corridor seems usually to have been made partly of slabs and partly dry-stone, except in the north of the region where it was often entirely dry-stone. It was usually covered by more than one capstone, and was typically some 5m in length, ¾m in width and 1m in height.

A tumulus could contain one, two, three or even four dolmens. When it contained just one dolmen, it was circular with a diameter typically approaching 20m, and a height of 1½m or 2m. On the other hand, if it contained more than one dolmen, it was elongated, with a maximum length of 40m or even 50m; in such tumuli the corridors were parallel to each other and opened on the same side of the mound. In the valley of the Charente the monuments were often grouped in necropolises of from three to six tombs, while in Charente-Maritime they are to be found in twos and threes. Elsewhere they are usually isolated.

According to Chevalier, the contents of the tombs suggest that they were constructed by people who were in the region from around 2900 BC, but those of corbelled construction may have been a little earlier. However, these were by no means the first communal tombs to be built in the area: they were preceded by circular tombs of false cupola construction, which a recent writer dates to the middle of the fifth millennium.[12] For some reason, not only in Charente but along the Atlantic coast, circular construction was replaced by trapezoidal around the end of the fourth millennium.

The orientations of 44 A-tombs are listed in Table 8.10. Two faced north of midsummer sunrise and two face westerly, but the remaining 40 are SR or SC, in similar numbers.

Further reading

Y. Chevalier, *L'architecture des dolmens entre Languedoc et centre-ouest de France* (Bonn, 1984).

Y. Chevalier, "Orientations of 935 dolmens of southern France", *AA*, no. 24 (1999), S47–82.

J. Clottes, "Inventaire des mégalithes de France: Lot", supplement 1/5 (1977) to *Gallia préhistoire*.

J. Clottes and Cl. Maurand, "Inventaire des mégalithes de France: Aveyron. L'Ouest aveyronnais: Causses de Limo-gne et de Villeneuve", supplement 1/7 (1983) to *Gallia préhistoire*.

J. Guilaine, *Au temps des dolmens* (Paris, 1998).

B. Pajot, "Les dolmens du Quercy", in *Mégalithismes de l'Atlantique à l'Ethiopie*, ed. by J. Guilaine (Paris, 1999), 141–72.

P. Soulier (ed.), *La France des dolmens et des sépultures collectives* (Paris, 1998).

Notes and references

1. B. Marc, *Dolmens et menhirs en Languedoc et Roussillon* (Montpellier, 1999), 73.

2. Chevalier, *L'architecture des dolmens*.

3. It so happens that in revising for the present book his tables as compiled and published by me in Chevalier, "Orientations", I realized that he had duplicated four tombs under different headings, having changed his mind about their classification: Caporie 1 at Méjannes-le-Clap; Le Ranc d'Aven 1 at Chandolas; Les Géantes 1 at Bourg-St-Andéol (all three in Tables 1 and 3(i) of the article); and Les Géantes 3 (Table 3(i), both with and without vestibule). My pairs of independent measures differed by 2°, 3°, 6° and 11° respectively.

4. Clottes, "Inventaire: Lot".

5. Clottes and Maurand, "Inventaire: Aveyron".

6. Chevalier, "Orientations".

7. Guilaine, *Au temps des dolmens*, 19–20.

8. Pajot, "Les dolmens du Quercy", 169.

9. J. Jaubert and M. Leduc, "Les sépultures mégalithiques en Midi-Pyrénées", in *La France des dolmens*, ed. by Soulier, 197–216, p. 197.

10. For further information on what follows, see Chevalier, *L'architecture des dolmens* and "Orientations".

11. See Chevalier, *L'architecture des dolmens* and "Orientations".

12. Xavier Gutherz, "Le mégalithisme en Poitou-Charente", in *La France des dolmens*, ed. by Soulier, 283–90, p. 283.

9

Westerly-facing Tombs (I): Provence and East Languedoc

Chevalier had not attempted to deal with the dolmens of southwest France, but neither had he been able to deal adequately with Provence, the southeast region of France bordered by the sea and the Italian frontier. Following a visit in the spring of 1999, I wrote to Gérard Sauzade of Aix-en-Provence asking if he would be interested to collaborate in fieldwork. This produced an astonishing response: a complete list of the surviving Provençal dolmens with the orientation of each. Although the orientation was often measured to an accuracy of only 5°, and sometimes even 10°, and although information on skyline altitudes was lacking, I found myself supplied with data from which the general pattern of orientations could be extracted with complete confidence.[1] As a result, in my second visit I could concentrate on the Mediterranean *départements* further to the west.

This reconnaissance made clear to me the complexity of the intermingling there of orientation customs, but was otherwise uneventful. Happily so. On more than one occasion we found ourselves literally in the firing line, for in the hills are numerous wild boar; these animals, themselves not noted for their amiable character, attract hunters who do not hesitate to shoot anything that moves. The hunters themselves wear bright clothing for identification, and it behoves archaeoastronomers plunging through bushes where no sane person could be expected to go, to demonstrate their human status by maintaining a raucous conversation.

The dolmens across the south of France from Spain to Italy can be divided into two geographical areas. The first and smaller consists of the *départements* of Pyrénées-Orientales (which borders Spain) and neighbouring Aude, together with west Hérault. I shall argue in the next chapter that a custom favouring easterly orientations spread into this area across the Pyrenees from Spanish Cataluña, extending eastwards as far as Lodève and the Causse du Larzac in central Hérault, and generating confusion as it encountered customs of building westerly-facing tombs spreading in the opposite direction.

We were able to confirm that the easterly-facing custom extended almost to the Causse du Larzac when we visited Octon, only a few kilometres southwest of Lodève. A generation ago there were eleven dolmens on the high plateau above the little town, and we are told they all faced between 140° and 176°;[2] another study[3] agrees that they faced within a range of 40°. Today six dolmens remain. Of these we located and measured three and found them to face 151°, 165° and 173°, so confirming the earlier accounts.

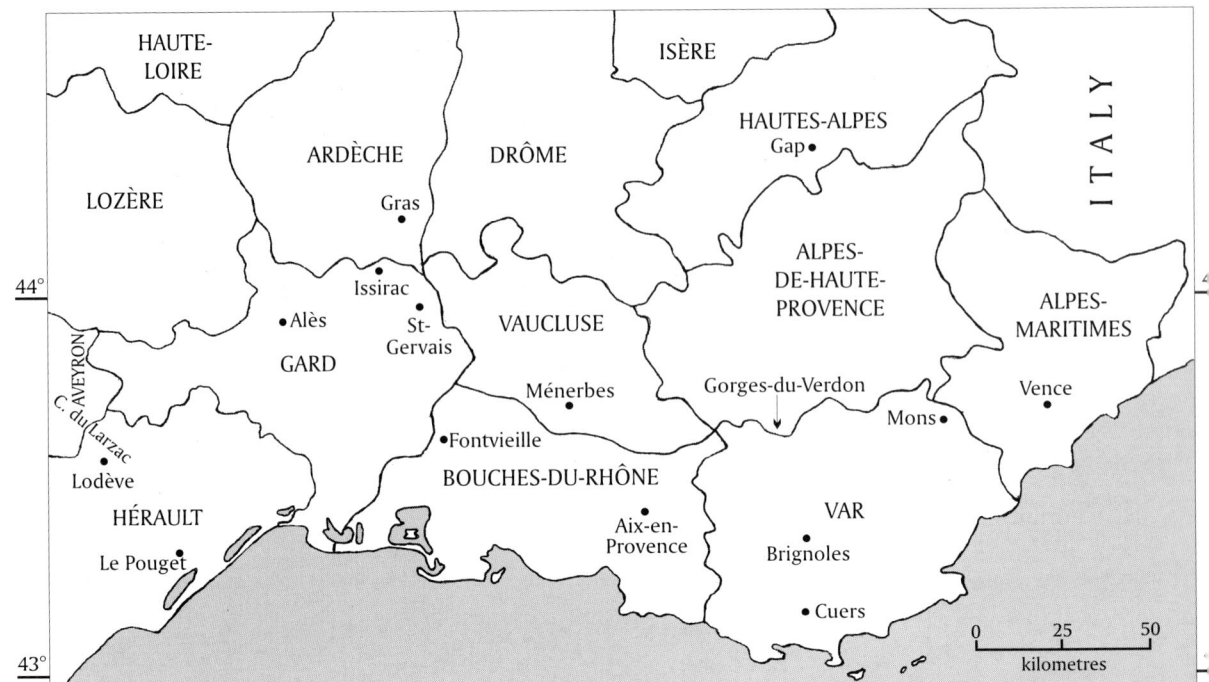

Provence (Bouches-du-Rhône, Vaucluse, Var and the Alpine *départements*) and east Languedoc. Bas-Rhône-type dolmens (BR-dolmens), westerly-facing and with dry-stone as a component of the construction of the chamber, appear to have originated at Fontvieille and to have spread from there as far as Vence in the east, Le Pouget and nearby St Pargoire in the west, and Gras in the north. Those nearest to Fontvieille had elongated chambers, faced sunset, and had side-walls entirely of dry-stone, while those further afield often had square chambers, sometimes faced south of midwinter sunset, and (in Provence) included orthostats in their side-walls. Languedoc-type dolmens (L-dolmens), also westerly-facing but with megalithic chambers, are concentrated in Hérault to the east of the Causse du Larzac, but are found in Gard as far as Alès, with a scattering in Aveyron and Lozère. Causse-type dolmens (C-dolmens, see Chapter 8), likewise megalithic but easterly-facing, are found not only in Aveyron and Lozère but in Ardèche and the very north of Gard. In the south of Ardèche, where BR-dolmens and C-dolmens occur in close proximity, the BR-dolmens mostly face around south — orientations unknown elsewhere — while several C-dolmens face southwest, unlike any of the 597 C-dolmens discussed in Chapter 8. This seems to suggest a *rapprochement* between the opposing customs invariably followed elsewhere by the builders of these dolmens.

The second and larger geographical area extends from the Causse du Larzac eastwards to the Italian frontier. It therefore includes most of the *départements* of east Languedoc and, across the Rhône, the whole of Provence. Well inland, in the far north of Gard and in Ardèche, we again encounter the Causse-type dolmens (C-dolmens) discussed in the last chapter, but in the coastal *départements* the dolmens are of two main types, both westerly-facing. Their structures have much in common with each other and with the C-dolmens, but archaeologists are not agreed as to which of these three types (if any) was the earliest, or in which direction any influence passed. We shall use orientations to suggest an answer.

The Languedoc-type dolmens (hereafter: L-dolmens) are found mainly in east Hérault and west Gard, between the Causse du Larzac in Hérault and just south of Alès in Gard, with a scattering further north, across the borders into Aveyron and Lozère.

The Bas-Rhône-type dolmens (hereafter: BR-dolmens) are found in Provence, but they are also

138

present in numbers in Languedoc, in an area that is very similar to that of the L-dolmens but which extends further to the northeast: namely, up through Gard and into south Ardèche, where C-dolmens are numerous. As we saw in the last chapter, the builders of C-dolmens normally observed an easterly custom, and the interaction (or so it seems to me) of the contrasting customs in south Ardèche has interesting consequences.

Bas-Rhône-type dolmens

In Languedoc the construction of a BR-dolmen normally differs strikingly from that of neighbouring C- or L-dolmens, in that its chamber has sides that are not megalithic but made entirely of dry-stone construction. As a result, the only megaliths its builders required were for the back-stone, the capstone, and the two entrance pillars that led to the centrally-placed corridor (which was almost always short and sometimes merely token). No doubt to protect the ends of the dry-stone sides, the backstone and the entrance pillars projected out beyond the sides — in contrast to the normal C- or L-dolmen, where the side orthostats leant against the backstone.

A spectacular example of a Languedocian BR-dolmen is Le Pas de Gallardet at Le Pouget in Hérault. The enlightened farmer who owns the land has collaborated with archaeologists in a restoration that is a model of its kind. A displayed notice has detailed drawings of the site both

The chamber and entrance of the reconstructed BR-dolmen at Le Pouget.

before and after reconstruction, and in the monument itself the restorers have been careful to distinguish the original stones from the modern replacements. Dry-stone walls, being vulnerable, are rarely intact after the passage of millennia, and it is not easy to obtain a clear picture of their original state; but at Le Pouget one can see how the sides were lightly corbelled before capstones were lowered into place.

Because his experience of BR-dolmens was largely limited to Languedoc, Chevalier took dry-stone side-walls to be their defining characteristic. In Provence, however, there is less uniformity, and although dry-stone is normally a component of the construction, it is the projection of the backstone and pillars beyond the sides that Sauzade sees as the identifying trait of a BR-dolmen.[4] Granted this, Provence has only BR-dolmens.

The Provençal data that Sauzade supplied also included orientations (Table 9.1) of hypogea at Fontvieille, near Arles in west Provence. In Menorca and elsewhere there are a number of crudely-shaped burial chambers excavated below ground in the bedrock and reached by a ramp leading down from the surface, and the orientation of such a hypogeum is normally ill-defined. I therefore ignored these Fontvieille monuments, until Sauzade sent me publications that brought home to me their central importance for the understanding of west Mediterranean archaeoastronomy.[5]

This called for a further visit to the region. To my dismay, I found that the landowner of three of the four hypogea has recently seen fit to set up lofty fences intended to deny access to these great monuments that form part of the heritage of France, access that public and archaeologists alike have enjoyed (with the full encouragement of previous owners) for generations and even centuries. It is perhaps not surprising that determined visitors have already made breaches in the fences. In any case, the fourth hypogeum is beyond his control.

The term 'hypogeum' is something of a misnomer for these magnificent tombs, for were it not for its half-dozen or so capstones, each chamber would be completely open to the sky for the whole of its considerable length. The tombs are, rather, deep trenches excavated in the bedrock, roofed with megaliths, and accessed at one end via a ramp leading down from ground level. But these are no ordinary trenches, for the workmanship of the chambers is astonishing in quality. In shape the sides and the back are almost perfect planes, as are the internal surfaces of the rectangular roof slabs, which fit together with immaculate precision (though left unfinished on the outside). As Guilaine remarks, "Par la qualité de leur architecture, ces tombs sont uniques dans tout le sud de la France".[6]

In both horizontal and vertical cross-sections the chambers are trapezoidal, with a floor that widens in the direction of the entrance, and sides that slope inwards and upwards. At Le Castellet, for example, the chamber has a height of 2.3m throughout, but at floor level it widens from 1.6m at the back to 2.1m at the entrance, and at roof level from 1.3m to 1.8m.

Three of the tombs approach 20m in overall length, but the fourth (which has a central chamber 4m in height and two side-chambers) reaches a staggering 42½m, making it "le plus impressionant monument préhistorique de France".[7]

Because the dolmenic capstones make these monuments very different from the true hypogea found elsewhere, we may term them 'dolmenic hypogea'. They lie within a few hundred metres

(Left) The ramp leading down to the dolmenic hypogeum of La Source, Fontvieille. The capstones are carefully shaped on the lower ~~ce~~ but left in their natural state above ground. (*Right*) The interior of the dolmenic hypogeum of Le Castellet, Fontvieille. The floor, ~~de~~-walls, entrance and ramp in the photograph have been excavated out of the bedrock, but the roof is formed of slabs. Note the ~~traordinary~~ care with which the various components have been shaped, and the near-perfect fit between adjacent roof slabs.

of each other, and in their midst is another tomb, Dolmen de Coutignargues; this is one of three such in the area, and all are exceptionally long by the standards of Provençal dolmens, ranging from 8m to over 10m. They are perhaps 'hypogeic dolmens', for they too are set in deep trenches. Sauzade persuasively sees them as variants of the dolmenic hypogea, for they are found in places where the bedrock was of inferior quality, so that the excavated chamber had to be supplied with dry-stone sides to define its shape and support the capstones. He emphasises the similarities between the two types of monument:

> The dolmens of Fontvieille are the close copy of the hypogea: similar dimensions, the same trapezoidal shape, a tomb that is largely underground.... It is the same basic plan realized in the different materials. A different technical solution has been adopted because the rock did not permit the excavation of an artificial grotto.[8]

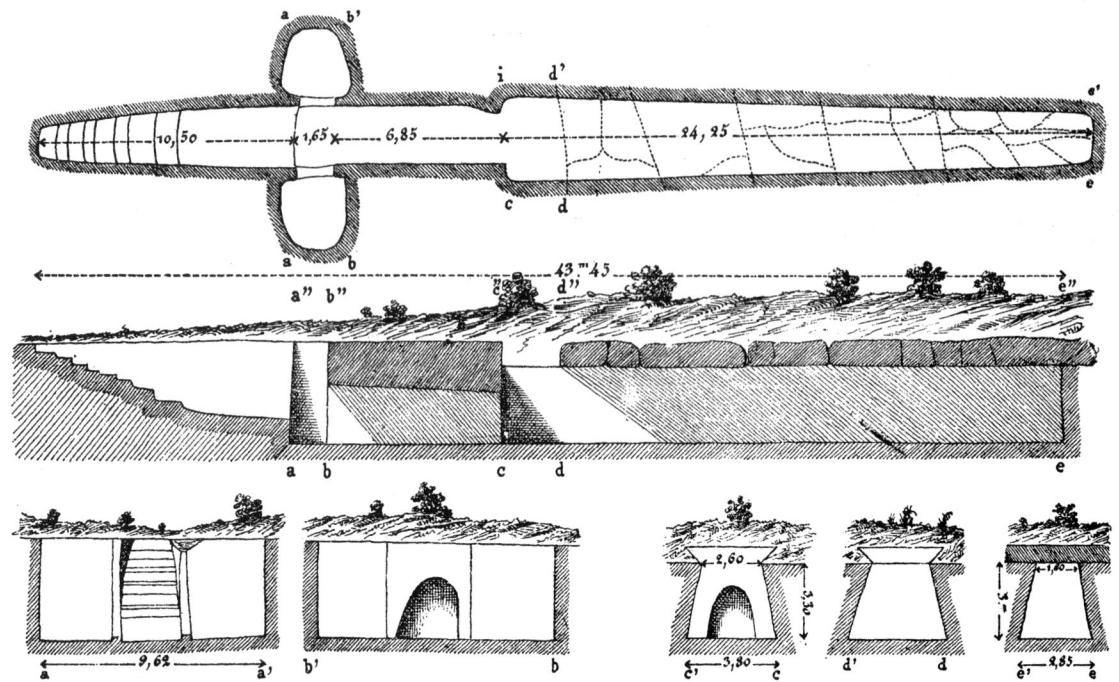

Plan of Épée-de-Roland, the largest of the dolmenic hypogea at Fontvieille (after Cazalis de Fondouce).

A generation ago, Glyn Daniel remarked that "The problem of the chronology and interpretation of the Arles-Fontvieille tombs is a most crucial one — indeed, perhaps the most crucial one — in any analysis of the French megalithic tombs", adding that "It is reasonable to suppose that the builders of the Arles-Fontvieille tombs would have expanded outside [this region], and we argue that one area of expansion was to the west to build the tombs between Béziers and Carcassonne. They may well have spread into other areas of southern France...".[9]

Sauzade likewise sees the Fontvieille tombs as "à l'origine"[10] of the dolmenic customs of the region, and he shows how this hypothesis helps explain the variations in the structure of the dolmens that are scattered throughout Provence: with increasing distance from Fontvieille, the customs exemplified at Fontvieille are less and less rigidly observed, as we might expect if Fontvieille were in fact their place of origin. We follow his analysis, extend it westwards into Languedoc, and consider the implications of the hypothesis for archaeoastronomy.

The Fontvieille dolmens are within a few kilometres of the Rhône, which is the border with Languedoc, and so are the most westerly of all Provençal dolmens. As we have seen, (i) they are set in deep trenches cut in the bedrock; (ii) they have greatly elongated chambers; and (iii) their side-walls are exclusively dry-stone.

It is very rare for dolmens to be built in deep trenches in this way, and those at Fontvieille may indeed be the result of unsatisfactory attempts to build hypogea. Elongated chambers, however,

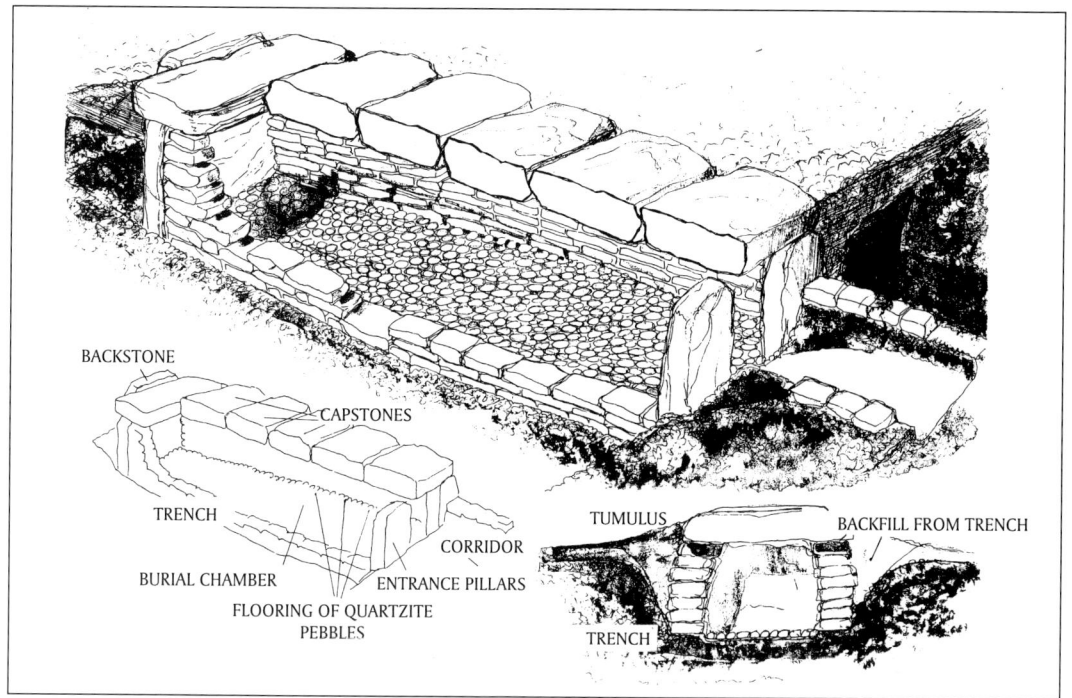

An axonometric drawing showing the characteristics of a Fontvieille BR-dolmen (based on Dolmen de Coutignargues). Note the considerable length of the chamber, the side-walls entirely of dry-stone, and the unusual positioning of the dolmen in an excavated trench, so that the capstones are almost at ground level. (After the drawing by J.-M. Gassend.)

are found in all the dolmens in the west of Provence, sixteen in all, and Sauzade makes this the characteristic of the first of the three classes into which he divides the Provençal tombs; those of the other two classes, which have small chambers that are nearly square, are found further to the east, at distances from Fontvieille of 140km or more. Exclusively dry-stone walling is found at Fontvieille and in the four other Provençal dolmens that lie within 60km of Fontvieille; but beyond that distance we routinely find side-walls that include orthostats in their construction, or are made mainly (though not exclusively) of orthostats.

No fewer than 67 of the Provençal dolmens belong to Sauzade's second class. They are found in the east of Provence, in an area that extends from Brignoles in Var, as far as Vence (Alpes-Maritimes), some 40km from the Italian frontier; and from the Gorges-du-Verdon in Alpes-de-Haute-Provence, south to the Mediterranean coast. Whereas the Fontvieille tombs belong to the late fourth millennium, many tombs of the second class date from the middle of the third.[11] We should note that there are large areas — notably the north of Vaucluse, Var, Alpes-de-Haute-Provence and Alpes-Maritimes — that are dolmen-free even though the materials for their construction were abundant: Provençal dolmens are thin on the ground.

A typical dolmen of the second class has a modest square chamber measuring less than 2m in each direction, with two pillars forming a narrow entrance that is usually furnished with a

Dolmen de Maurely at St-Antonin-sur-Bayon, a BR-dolmen of the first class. As with the Fontvieille dolmens, the chamber is elongated and the orientation within the range of sunset, but the side-walls are no longer purely dry-stone.

threshold slab. The use of dry-stone in some aspect of the construction is common. Dolmens often have chambers with matching sides that alternate orthostats with dry-stone walling, and this is sometimes repeated in the corridor. In Alpes-Maritimes one also finds dolmens whose sides are formed of horizontal slabs surmounted by dry-stone walling. Elsewhere dry-stone is sometimes used to plug any gaps left by the orthostats, though in Var a number of tombs have sides that are entirely dry-stone. Nevertheless, although the custom of having sides that are purely dry-stone had been relaxed, dolmen builders continued to observe the BR-custom (the identifying custom, in Sauzade's view) of having backstones and entrance pillars that project beyond the sides: a custom that is most appropriate to tombs constructed (as at Fontvieille) with purely dry-stone walls, where the projecting megaliths would have protected the vulnerable extremities of the dry-stone.

Finally, dolmens of a small, geographically-isolated third class are (or, more usually, were) to be found away in Hautes-Alpes, in the area not far from the town of Gap. These 'Alpine dolmens' are some 140km north of the most northerly of the square-chambered dolmens, whose form they resemble, although their sides usually have two orthostats rather than one, and the corridor is as wide as the chamber.

Of seven dolmens reported there, four are certainly authentic, but only one of these, the Dolmen du Villard at Lauzet-Ubaye in the north of Alpes-de-Haute-Provence, survives. The chamber,

Dolmen des Riens, a BR-dolmen of the second class, at Mons in east Provence. Note the entrance pillars, the small, square chamber, and the reduced use of dry-stone in the side-walls.

which is about 1¾m in length and a little over 1m in width, is roughly rectangular, and has six orthostats and a capstone. At the west end, two pillars enclose a narrow, low entrance in which a threshold stone supports a vertical slab intended to close the entrance. In front of the entrance is the corridor, each side of which is formed of three orthostats aligned with the sides of the chamber. No materials earlier than the Late Copper Age have been recovered from this remote group of Alpine dolmens, which confirms that the custom of megalithic building reached this area last of all, in the mid-third millennium,[12] and that these tombs represent the furthest extension to the southeast of west European megalithism.

We have seen that elongated chambers are a feature of the Fontvieille tombs and of all other Provençal dolmens within 140km of Fontvieille; and that the exclusive use of dry-stone side-walling extends eastwards for a radius of 60km from Fontvieille. But what of the orientations? There is a striking consistency in the orientations of the seven Fontvieille tombs (Tables 9.1 and 9.2[13]): six of the seven face marginally south of due west, within a range of only 11°, while the seventh, La Mérindole, faces 287°, north of west: all the Fontvieille tombs faced well within the range of sunset (and so were 'SS' in our terminology). Furthermore, one has to travel 130km east from Fontvieille, to beyond Toulon, before one finds dolmens (of the first class) that faced westerly but south of the range of sunset. All the 17 Provençal tombs at or near to Fontvieille faced within the range of sunset, with declinations ranging from $-13\frac{1}{2}°$ to $+20°$.

Remarkably, every single one of the 84 Provençal dolmens faced westerly (see Table 9.2). But at distances from Fontvieille of more than 130km, orientations as much as 25° or more south of midwinter sunset were acceptable, though none faced so far south as to be around culmination. More specifically, 15 square-chambered dolmens faced between 206° and 230°, between south-southwest and midwinter sunset, where the sun was descending (and so we term these dolmens 'SD'). It seems that the strict, sunset custom that prevailed around Fontvieille was relaxed further east, just like the custom of having elongated chambers, and the custom of building with dry-stone sides.

North and west of Fontvieille, across the Rhône in Languedoc, data are lacking on any BR-dolmens at less than 50km or so from the hypogea; and as we travel further afield the situation becomes more complex, as we begin to encounter C-dolmens in the north and L-dolmens in the west. In Gard, some 50km north of Fontvieille, at Saint-Gervais-les-Bagnols, the BR-dolmen of Coste-Rigaude has an elongated chamber, as has Dolmen de Concouvèze at Saint-Laurent-la-Vernède not far away; but further north, at Issirac in north Gard and Gras in south Ardèche, the BR-dolmens have chambers that are roughly square. It may well be, therefore, that what we found to happen in Provence — the relaxation with increasing distance from Fontvieille of the custom of elongated chambers — is repeated in Languedoc.

The data on orientations (see Table 9.3), sparse though they are, suggest that in Languedoc as

The most famous of the L-dolmens: Coste-Rouge, in the grounds of the priory of St-Michel-de-Grandmont, near Lodève.

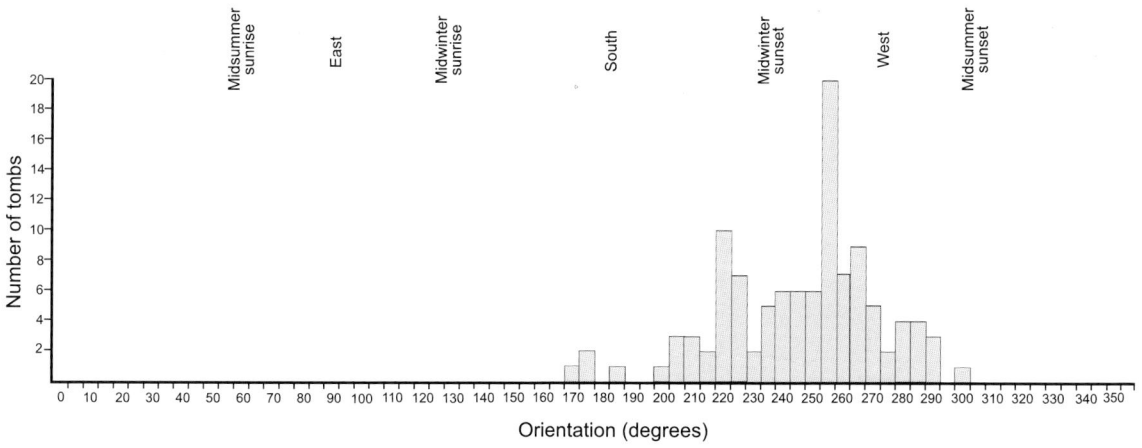

Histogram showing the orientations of 110 BR-dolmens of Provence and east Languedoc. The five tombs with azimuths closest to due south are all in Ardèche.

in Provence, the strict SS custom was likewise relaxed with increasing distance from Fontvieille. Coste-Rigaude and Concouvèze are among five Languedocian BR-dolmens that lie between 50km and 70km to the north or west of Fontvieille, and all faced sunset. But beyond this distance a number of the BR-dolmens faced a little south of midwinter sunset, as did the square-chambered BR-dolmens of east Provence.

The evidence from the BR-dolmens to the north and west of Fontvieille therefore suggests that (as in Provence) two of the Fontvieille customs — of building chambers that were both elongated and facing sunset — were relaxed with increasing distance. This evidence is therefore consistent with such dolmens having their origins in Fontvieille. But the paucity of tombs that both lie in those directions and are close to Fontvieille prevents us from insisting on this to the extent that seems justified from the Provençal dolmens to the east, where the data are complete, there are other tombs close to Fontvieille itself, and only BR-dolmens (as defined by Sauzade) are to be found.

The table lists six BR-dolmens far enough north of Fontvieille to be in Ardèche, where they are among C-dolmens. More of these in a moment; for the present we simply note that the first five entries in this table — which are the dolmens facing closest to south — are from among these six. The sixth and the twenty remaining BR-dolmens in east Languedoc all face between 209° and 301°, a range virtually identical with that of the BR-dolmens in Provence. We may therefore say that, unless among C-dolmens in Ardèche, BR-dolmens, whether in Languedoc or Provence, faced between south-southwest and midsummer sunset.

Languedoc-type dolmens

This brings us to L-dolmens, whose territory is similar to that of the BR-dolmens in Languedoc except that it stops well short of the Gard/Ardèche frontier where C-dolmens begin.[14]

The structure of an L-dolmen is similar to that of the C-dolmens of the last chapter, but is more

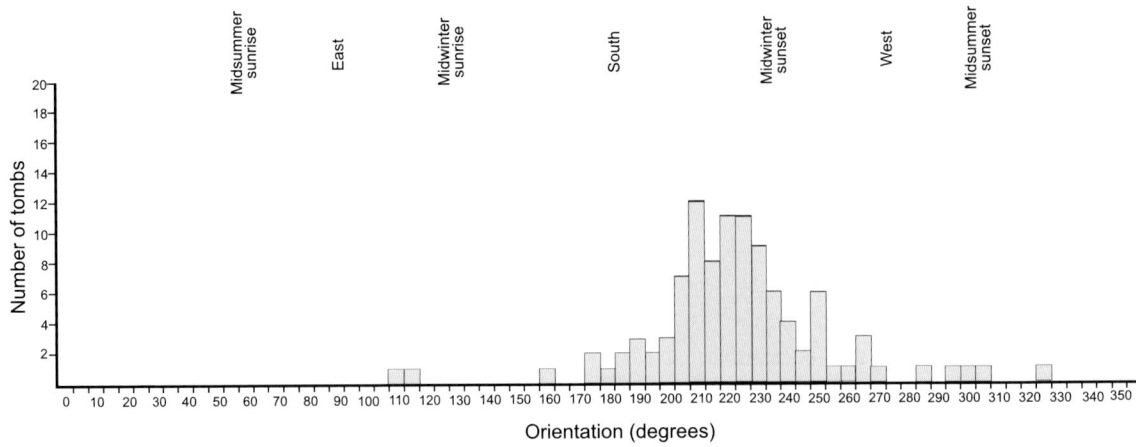

Histogram showing the orientations of 103 L-dolmens of east Languedoc.

elaborate. Again, each side was formed of a single orthostat that leant against the backstone and, again, the trapezoidal chamber was longer than it was wide (though the difference in the two dimensions was less pronounced). At the entrance, however, the L-dolmen had either one or two pillars, internal to the side-stones and leading to a corridor. If there were two pillars the corridor was centrally placed; but sometimes the builders made do with a single entrance pillar, in which case the corridor was set to one side and aligned with the absent pillar (and so the plan of the tomb had the form of a 'p' or a 'q'). The corridor usually extended to the edge of the tumulus, and so could be up to 8m in length; and sometimes it was made of dry-stone rather than orthostats.

L-dolmens are strongly concentrated in east Hérault, an area that attracted much attention from archaeologists a generation ago, and having tested samples I have confidence in the general reliability of measures published by J. Arnal[15] or by G. Combarnous.[16] When these are added to orientations taken by Chevalier or by myself, we have a total of 103 L-dolmens (Table 9.4). Three clearly faced the eastern horizon while one by contrast faced well north of midsummer sunset; but the remaining 99 (96·1%) faced between 176° and 306°: towards the sun around culmination or while descending (that is, SD), or within the range of sunset or thereabouts (SS). Of these, the vast majority faced between south-southwest and midsummer sunset, the range of the BR-dolmens. We conclude that the L-dolmens faced within a range very similar to that of the BR-dolmens, except that directions around culmination were also permissible.

Origins and interactions

Was there interaction between the customs embodied in these west-facing BR- and L-dolmens and those observed by the builders of the east-facing C-dolmens, the discussion of whose presence in Ardèche and north Gard we postponed from the last chapter? Which if any of the three types was the first to develop?

Radiocarbon dates for the construction (as opposed to the use) of a tomb are notoriously difficult to obtain, especially when nearly every tomb has been pillaged over the millennia and its fabric disturbed. Chevalier, working when radiocarbon dating was in its infancy, thought there was evidence that the C-dolmens were later than the L-dolmens, and that the C-dolmens in the Causses of the northwest were later than those in the southeast. He therefore saw the form of a C-dolmen as a simplification of that of an L-dolmen; and he thought that the L-dolmen developed in east Languedoc, and then gave rise to the C-dolmen, first in Gard and Ardèche, and then further and further away to the northwest, in the direction of the Bay of Biscay. He knew of course that L-dolmens faced west and that C-dolmens normally faced east; but he rightly pointed out that in Gard and Ardèche there were C-dolmens that faced to the west of due south.

But this seems unsatisfactory. If the earliest C-dolmens — supposedly those in Gard and Ardèche — were simplified L-dolmens in structure and some of them mimicked the westerly orientation custom of the L-dolmens, how did the 597 C-dolmens to the northwest of Gard and Ardèche come to face exclusively in easterly directions, as we saw in the last chapter — directions where the sun rose or was climbing in the sky (SR/SC), with orientations around culmination excessively rare and westerly ones unknown?

It has indeed been customary to see L-dolmens as first on the scene, and therefore earlier than the BR-dolmens. But then why should the L-dolmens face west in the first place?

We now turn again to Ardèche and the lands along its southerly border with Gard. This region contains the southeastern end of the great swathe of C-dolmens that began away to the northwest, not far from the Bay of Biscay. The territory of the L-dolmens has its northeastern limit in Gard, but I believe this limit lies some way short of the border. However, the territory of the BR-dolmens extends up through Gard beyond that of the L-dolmens, and continues across the border of Gard and into Ardèche, as far as Gras. In south Ardèche six of them (see Table 9.3) are to be found amidst numerous C-dolmens, and their orientations are remarkable when we remember that elsewhere every single one of the 104 BR-dolmens (84 in Provence and 20 in east Languedoc) faced westerly of south-southwest. Here in Ardèche five of the six faced southerly of south-southwest, with azimuths 168°, 174°, 176°, 184° and 201°, none (one might say) in flagrant violation of the westerly custom, but outside the normal range, and in such a way as to be less in conflict with the normal (easterly) orientation of a C-dolmen. In construction, too, these BR-dolmens are unusual, for they have their side-walls exterior to the backstone, as in a C-dolmen.[17]

But equally the orientation custom observed by the builders of BR-dolmens seems to have had a reverse influence on the orientations chosen for neighbouring C-dolmens. In *départements* other than Gard and Ardèche, as we saw in the last chapter, only nine C-dolmens out of 597 (1·5%) faced south of 166°, while no fewer than 128 (21·4%) faced north of 80°. In Gard and Ardèche (Table 8.7; see histogram on p. 133), by contrast, not a single one of the 72 C-dolmens faced north of 80°, while no fewer than 26 (36·1%) faced south of 166°. Indeed, we even find among them orientations well west of south: 211°, 215°, 217°, 221°, 222° and 229° — directions wholly alien to the C-dolmens in other *départements*.

In Gard and Ardèche, therefore — where contrasting customs of both construction and east/

west orientation were to be found in neighbouring BR- and C-dolmens — we find that the westerly range of orientations of BR-dolmens was shifted anticlockwise by some tens of degrees as compared with what happens elsewhere, while the easterly range of the C-dolmens was shifted clockwise by a similar amount. This suggests that construction of the two types was going on at the same time, and that constructors who were following one set of customs were nevertheless influenced by the different set of customs embodied in tombs elsewhere in the area.

A coherent picture of the dolmens of southern France now begins to emerge. First, within the context of southwest-European megalithism, the C-dolmens of the Causses are thoroughly orthodox: 'simple' tombs built of just four megaliths, and facing the eastern horizon, with concentration in the range of sunrise. But the BR-dolmens in the Mediterranean coastal region are wholly unorthodox: many are not truly megalithic but have dry-stone side-walls, and all faced the western horizon with concentration in the range of sunset.

Westerly orientations were almost unknown in the vast areas of Portugal, Spain and France that we discussed in the last four chapters. The very occasional west-facing tomb from among the many hundreds measured remains in the memory: the sepulchre north of Burgos where our car got stuck in mud, the quasi-anta at the petrol station west of Lisbon, the pair of tholoi at Los Millares in Almería, the little group at La Janda in Cádiz. The BR-dolmens, then, are wholly exceptional in orientation as in construction, and this suggests that the customs they embody were not the result of outside influence but originated in Provence or Languedoc — more specifically, in the minds of whoever controlled the workforce that built the hypogea and dolmens at Fontvieille; and that in Gard and Ardèche the unorthodox customs embodied in the BR-dolmens, as they spread northwards, encountered the orthodox C-dolmen customs as they spread southeast, with influence both ways. This two-way influence, seemingly an inescapable inference from our data on Ardèche, implies that construction of the two types of dolmen went on there simultaneously.

The L-dolmens occupy limited territory similar to that of the BR-dolmens of Languedoc, but without the extension north into Ardèche. Rather than being the first on the scene in the Midi, they now seem to represent a later compromise between the unorthodoxy of the BR-dolmens found in the same region and the orthodoxy of the C-dolmens found immediately to the north. As with a C-dolmen, the chamber of an L-dolmen has a single orthostat to each side, and a backstone set between them. As with a BR-dolmen, the L-dolmen has an entrance with (either one or two) pillars, and a corridor; and it faces westerly.

To sum up the picture that seems to have emerged: (i) The custom of building elongated west-facing dolmens with dry-stone sides — and (therefore) backstones and entrance pillars that extended beyond the sides — originated at Fontvieille, probably as a development from the hypogea. This custom spread westwards to Lodève, northwards into Ardèche, and eastwards towards the Italian frontier, though there the use of megaliths was increasingly tolerated. (ii) Simple dolmens of familiar shape and orientation spread down through the Causses and into Ardèche and north Gard. (iii) There was something of a *rapprochement* between the Fontvieille custom of facing west and the Causse custom of facing east. (iv) Finally, in east Hérault there developed dolmens whose form imitated that of the simple dolmen in backstone and sides,[18] but which followed the

Fontvieille customs in entrance, corridor and orientation.

In the next chapter we shall suggest that the westerly-facing custom spread from Hérault towards the Pyrenees, and into Spanish Cataluña.

Further reading

Y. Chevalier, *L'architecture des dolmens entre Languedoc et centre-ouest de France* (Bonn, 1984).

Y. Chevalier, "Orientations of 935 dolmens of southern France", *AA*, no. 24 (1999), S47–82.

J. Guilaine, *Au temps des dolmens* (Paris, 1998).

B. Marc, *Dolmens et menhirs en Languedoc et Roussillon* (Montpellier, 1999).

G. Sauzade, "Des dolmens en Provence", in *Mégalithismes de l'Atlantique à l'Ethiopie*, ed. by J. Guilaine (Paris, 1999), 123–40.

G. Sauzade, "Les dolmens de Provence occidentale et la place des tombes de Fontvieille dans l'architecture mégalithique méridionale", in *Autour de Jean Arnal*, ed. by J. Guilaine and X. Gutherz (Montpellier, 1990), 305–34.

G. Sauzade, "Orientations of the Provençal dolmens", *AA*, no. 25 (2000), S1–10.

P. Soulier (ed.), *La France des dolmens et des sépultures collectives* (Paris, 1998).

Notes and references

1 Sauzade, "Orientations of the Provençal dolmens".

2 G. Combarnous, "Un pays de dolmens au coeur du Bas-Languedoc", *Cahiers ligures de préhistoire et d'archéologie*, ix (1960), 3–93, p. 74.

3 Groupe Archéologique Lodévois, "Les mégalithes du Lodévois", *ibid.*, x/1 (1961), 21–99, p. 60.

4 G. Sauzade, "Les sépultures collectives provençales", in *La France des dolmens*, ed. by Soulier, 293–328 (with full bibliography); "Des dolmens en Provence"; and "Les dolmens de Provence occidentale".

5 Notably Sauzade, "Les dolmens de Provence occidentale".

6 Guilaine, *Au temps des dolmens*, 60.

7 *Ibid.*, 61.

8 Sauzade, "Les dolmens de Provence occidentale", 311.

9 Glyn Daniel, *The prehistoric chamber tombs of France* (London, 1960), 161.

10 Sauzade, "Les sépultures collectives provençales", 295.

11 *Cf.* Guilaine, *Au temps des dolmens*, 55; Sauzade, "Des dolmens en Provence", 133, and "Les sépultures collectives provençales", 303.

12 Guilaine, *Au temps des dolmens*, 56.

13 Reproduced from Sauzade, "Orientations of the Provençal dolmens", with the addition of one tomb measured by Chevalier before it was destroyed.

14 Chevalier, "Orientations", Table 1 (L-dolmens), appears to place two L-dolmens in Ardèche. But Le Ranc d'Aven 1 is shown on Plate 30 of his *L'architecture des dolmens* and described as merely "related" ("*apparenté*") to L-dolmens; in my opinion it is better classed as a C-dolmen. Les Géantes 1 at Bourg-St-Andéol was also duplicated by Chevalier in Table 3(i) of "Orientations" as a C-dolmen, but in my opinion it is a BR-dolmen (see Chevalier, *L'architecture des dolmens*, Plate 50). Of the Gard dolmens listed in Table 1 of "Orientations", the nearest to Ardèche is Le Serre du Bouquet at Seynes, but, as Chevalier recognizes in his caption to Plate 50, its two entrance pillars project beyond the sides and so in my opinion it is a BR-dolmen. This being so, the southernmost C-dolmen in Gard is Caporie 1 at Méjannes-le-Clap and the nearest L-dolmens listed are at Tornac nearly 40km away.

15 J. Arnal, *Les dolmens du Département de l'Hérault* (= *Préhistoire*, xv; Paris, 1963).

16 Cambarnous, "Un pays de dolmens".

17 Chevalier, *L'architecture des dolmens*, Plate 33/2 (La Tour, Géantes); 34/1 (Les Clausasses 3, Gras); 35 (Les Clausasses 1 and 2, Gras); and 50/1 (Géantes 1).

18 I find that influence from the northwest, and the development of simple dolmens into L-dolmens, is the opinion of Marc Bordreuil writing in *La France des dolmens*, 135–58, on "Recherches sur le monumentalisme funéraire et les sépultures mégalithiques en Languedoc oriental": "[Les dolmens simples] reçoivent ensuite un vestibule qui s'allonge en couloir d'abord en dalles puis mixte ou en murets de pierre sèche. Les influences viennent de Bretagne par ou autour du Massif central" (p. 150).

chamber that is cut into the ground in the form of a trench. It is a miserable tomb compared to the great dolmenic hypogea of Fontvieille (Chapter 9), but, like them, it faced within the range of sunset, having orientation 242°.

A feature of the territory along the border between Hérault and Aude is the great *allées couvertes* that dwarf the other megalithic tombs of the region. These have segmented chambers, and long, parallel sides whose orthostats reduce somewhat in height towards the entrance. According to Guilaine they were built around 3000 BC,[3] though he sees Aude megalithism as spanning the third millennium, and, if so, the beginning of the millennium is an early date for such mature monuments. Casulha at Lauriol has yet to be excavated, but St-Eugène at Rieux-Minervois is 14m in length, Jappeloup at Paulignan is on a similar scale, while Morrel das Fadas at Siran is a staggering 24m, which makes it the largest true dolmen in the whole of the south of France. These four extraordinary monuments face 178°, 150°, 174° and 143° respectively, and so are SC.

In addition to Bois-de-Monsieur and no. 8 at Bois Bas, there are several other tombs in the area that have sides with multiple orthostats, like the *allées couvertes* but altogether smaller. The orientations of these galleries (see Table 10.1(c)) range between 111° and 194°. Three of the eleven face a little west of south, though one has a corridor that swings left so that it ends up facing 176°; with a little licence we may class these galleries as SR/SC.

Ten of the eleven simple dolmens listed in Table 10.1(d) are either at Octon, or at Bois Bas and nearby Lacs, and in a population for statistical analysis this is not ideal. At least two of the eleven unequivocally face westerly and two more face west of due south. Other tombs of the region that appear to be simple dolmens may in fact have lost their corridors; these, and other tombs too ruined to classify, or of exceptional form, are listed as 'miscellaneous' (Table 10.1(e)). Half face easterly and half westerly.

The orientations may be mixed, but they are not random. Aside from the BR-dolmen Bois Bas 4 that turns its back on its twin, none of the 36 dolmens that we measured faced northerly, between midsummer sunset and midsummer sunrise: evidence that, despite the variety of structure and orientation verging on confusion, the skies were once more involved in the local customs of orientation.

If we disregard the (sometimes debatable) classifications and simply consider the overall pattern of orientations, we find that in west Hérault and north Aude exactly two-thirds of the 36 tombs face easterly and one-third westerly. This is in remarkable contrast to east Hérault, where easterly orientations are very rare: for some reason, there were very different customs to either side of the Causse du Larzac. Does the situation further to the southwest shed any light on this?

South Aude and the east Pyrenees

The river Aude flows through the medieval town of Carcassonne and then follows an easterly course towards the sea. South of the river is the heart of the *département* of Aude, which is largely depopulated today and was seemingly so in prehistoric times also, for dolmens there are scarce. But near the southern borders of Aude, and in the Catalan region spanning both sides of the Pyrenees that divide France from Spain, tombs become numerous once more. We discussed in Chapter 7 the tombs further inland from the Mediterranean — in the high mountains near Andorra, in the *département* of Ariège, and in the centre of Spanish Cataluña — as well as those that lie between Barcelona and the region of Girona, nearer to the coast. Now we must investigate the tombs of south Aude and of the coastal section of Pyrénées-Orientales, together with the tiny corner of Spain that lies within some twenty kilometres of both the sea and the frontier with France.

Dolmens south of the mountains

Josep Tarrús, the authority on the dolmens of Cataluña, was sufficiently intrigued by my interest in the customs of orientations to revisit all the known tombs in this corner of Spain (together with the culturally-related ones just across the border, on the northern slopes of the mountains), so as to remeasure their orientations and classify them afresh.[4] His data form the basis of Table 10.2.

Tarrús had already found good evidence of surprisingly early construction dates of 4200 and 3900 BC for two of the dolmens of what we shall term 'the Tarrús region';[5] it therefore seems that dolmenic construction began in Cataluña centuries earlier than in Languedoc and Provence. These dates, and the presence of even earlier cists and other pre-dolmenic structures, allow him to argue that the custom of megalithic tomb building developed locally, rather than by influence from further east. Given the geographical isolation of the Catalan dolmens from those in the rest of Iberia, this seems very possible. According to Tarrús in his most recent formulation,[6] in a scheme whose tidyness is consoling after the confusion of west Hérault and north Aude, megalithic tomb-building began on the Spanish side of the frontier in the fifth millennium, with little closed cists covered by tumuli. These were sometimes below ground, sometimes partly buried; but sometimes they were on the surface, in locations of some prominence.

At the end of the fifth millennium, and more especially in the first half of the fourth, the first communal tombs appeared, with subcircular chambers, and corridors; these of course include the two for which we have dates. In the second half of the millennium the subcircular chambers developed into chambers of trapezoidal shape. Then, in the first half of the third millennium, the trapezoidal chambers became rectangular, and the corridors widened, in some cases being — at least at their inner extremity — as wide as the chamber itself (in which case the tomb is a 'Catalan gallery'). In the second half of the third millennium, the rectangular chambers with corridor evolved into simple dolmens; in some, the chamber could be accessed over a 'septal' slab positioned at the front, or via a movable stone located above a kerbstone, or through a porch reached from overhead. Dolmens were re-used in the second millennium, which is why they yield grave-goods from the Bronze Age, but the custom of building communal tombs declined and then was abandoned.

This simplicity of this scheme is not matched by a corresponding simplicity in the customs of orientation, for both easterly- and westerly-facing tombs are present, sometimes in close

(*Above*) Vinyes Mortes II, a Catalan dolmen with trapezoidal chamber.

(*Below*) Coll de Madas I, a 'Catalan gallery', in the light of the setting sun.

proximity. In his re-examination of the dolmens of his region, therefore, Tarrús paid special atten-tion to the customs of orientation. Unfortunately the difference between one type of tomb and another is not great, and so it is not always evident to which class a given tomb should be assigned, especially if the corridor has disappeared. Indeed, Tarrús makes no bones about having changed his opinion in a not-inconsiderable number of instances,[7] and the situation is not helped when in my view he was right the first time; in addition, there are a dozen tombs (included in Table 10.2) which he cannot categorize with confidence and which we therefore omit from the following discussion. Nevertheless, he seems to me to have taken an important step towards solv-ing the mystery of the mixture of orientation customs on the Spanish side of the mountains.

In what follows, we ignore orientations between 175° and 185° inclusive, because these cannot with confidence be said to be directed to the eastern or the western horizon. These aside, the orientations (Table 10.2) divide as follows:

	easterly	westerly
subcircular chambers and corridors	7	2
trapezoidal chambers and corridors	21	25
rectangular chambers and wide corridors/galleries	15	3
simple dolmens	5	1

We see that only a minority of tombs had westerly orientations, except among those with tra-pezoidal chambers, where rather over half the orientations were westerly. We remember that megalithic trapezoidal chambers and corridors (and westerly orientations) are characteristics of the L-dolmens of east Languedoc; furthermore, pottery typical of east Languedoc at the end of the Neolithic and the beginning of the Copper Age has been found in two dolmens (and a cave) in Cataluña.[8] Tarrús therefore suggests that towards the end of the fourth millennium there was contact between the megalithic groups of east Languedoc and northeast Cataluña. His opinion is that, while the constructors of the earliest Catalan dolmens mostly followed the local, easterly customs, as did those of the latest, in the intervening period some peoples of the region may have followed an alternative, westerly custom emanating from Languedoc. "Perhaps in this way we may explain this brief taste in the Catalan region for orientations to the southwest, a custom that scarcely existed there previously and which was later to disappear."[9]

For this to be possible, of course, the L-dolmens must predate the similar tombs of Cataluña. Guilaine takes 3500 BC as the time when megalithism first began to enjoy a widespread vogue in parts of southern France, and for him the period known as the final Neolithic — during which the Fontvieille hypogea and the neighbouring BR-dolmens were built — lasted from 3500 to 2900 or thereabouts.[10] If so, then there is indeed time, if only just, for the westerly custom of Fontvieille to extend to the L-dolmens and thence to some of the trapezoidal dolmens of Cataluña.

Dolmens north of the mountains

Richard Iund, who lives in the dolmenic heart of Pyrénées-Orientales and who had collaborated with me in the field, was kind enough to address the parallel problem in his area.[11] He accepts the typology and chronology of Tarrús, but the patterns of tomb orientations on the French side

La Siureda, a 'simple dolmen' on the northern slopes of the Pyrenees.

of the mountains are less clear, not to say baffling. This is partly because we are dealing with a region where megalithism developed later than in neighbouring regions, and did so in response to influences from opposite directions, from Languedoc to the north (where there is confusion enough already) and Cataluña to the south. Furthermore, the period of dolmen construction was relatively brief, being concentrated in the third millennium.[12] The situation is further complicated when authorities differ as to the correct classification of an unexcavated tomb; and north of the mountains most tombs still await the archaeologist's trowel.

The tombs of Cataluña that Tarrús assigns to the fourth millennium — those with subcircular or trapezoidal chambers — have few counterparts north of the mountains (except, of course, among the handful of dolmens just across the frontier and close to the sea, and so in the Tarrús region). In the first half of the third millennium, however, we find in the Iund region tombs of two different types, one familiar from Cataluña, the other not. The familar type consists of what further south would be considered a Catalan gallery, where the side-walls of the rectangular chamber are continued by the orthostats of the corridor; such tombs in the Iund region may well reflect an influence from across the mountains to the south. In tombs of the other type, there is a corridor that throughout its length is markedly narrower than the chamber, as in an L-dolmen.

Two rivers, the Agly and the Têt, cross Pyrénées-Orientales from west to east, and in attempt to clarify the different influences on the dolmens of his region Iund subdivided it into three zones:

north of the Agly; between the Agly and the Têt; and south of the Têt. Of the tombs dated to the first half of the third millennium, those with narrow corridors, which are not numerous, are mostly in the northern and central zones — as one might expect if the form originated further north. In Table 10.3 there are nine, of which six face easterly (between 90° and 128°), one close to south (183°), and two westerly (205° and 293°).

Galleries are more plentiful. In the central and southern zones only one gallery faces westerly (236°), while all the other nine face easterly (between 111° and 153°); this pattern is not very different from that of the 19 tombs of this general type across the mountains in the Tarrús region. In the northern zone, however, nine of the eleven galleries face southerly, between 169° and 209°, while just one faces easterly (135°) and one westerly (267°); but this statistic may be misleading, for four of the nine are in one little necropolis whose tombs have similar (southerly) orientations.

In the Iund region as in that of Tarrús, the tombs constructed in the second half of the third millennium were simple dolmens (with or without some more developed method of access). The problem, as we have already remarked, is to distinguish a true simple dolmen from a dolmen that has lost its corridor or whose corridor will be revealed only by excavation. And authorities differ

Corbatura, a restored 'simple dolmen' at Corneilla-du-Conflent, south of the Têt.

even on the present evidence. Dolmen de la Cova de l'Alarb, just inside the frontier with Spain, is for Tarrús an early dolmen with a trapezoidal chamber and corridor; but for Françoise Claustre, head of the local museum at Céret, it is a (rectangular) simple dolmen.[13]

Iund's northern zone has only seven simple dolmens. These have orientations between 40° and 185°, but three of the seven are at one site and have almost identical orientations, so again we have an unsatisfactory sample. Only in Iund's central and southern zones do we have a promising database, of 33 simple dolmens (though qualified as usual by doubts as to the correctness of the classifications). Of these, thirteen face easterly (between 38° and 148°), eleven southerly (between 158° and 203°) and nine westerly (between 227° and 289°): a dispiriting picture.

A riddle wrapped in mystery inside an enigma

Winston Churchill's famous characterization of Soviet Russia can be applied to the understanding of the orientations discussed in this chapter. The most basic picture is clear enough: if we disregard the (sometimes debatable) typology and periodization and limit ourselves to the location and orientation of each tomb, we find that, of the ones listed in Tables 10.1, 10.2 and 10.3, those facing the western horizon constitute respectively 33.3%, 38.0% and 37.5% of the totals. This is in stark contrast to the monuments of the rest of Iberia, the rest of southern France (and, for that matter, the various Mediterranean islands, as we shall see), where almost none or almost all of the tombs of a given region faced westerly.

It seems a reasonable generalization (and one that the following chapters will confirm) to regard easterly customs as the norm and westerly customs almost as an aberration. In periodization, tombs of the Tarrús region span the fourth and third millennia; those of east Languedoc (Chapter 9) the second half of the fourth together with the third; and those of Aude and Pyrénées-Orientales the third. Tarrús has argued — I think, convincingly — that his tombs at first followed a normal, easterly custom, and that they were then subject to influences from east Languedoc in the late fourth millennium. In the Iund region, the (third-millennium) galleries and perhaps the simple dolmens reflect influence from Cataluña, while the trapezoidal chambers with corridors seem Languedocian; westerly customs (along with easterly) could have come from either direction.

One would like to understand the origin of the easterly custom we find as far east as in the simple dolmens at Octon, near the Causse du Larzac beyond which westerly orientations are the norm. Did the custom arise locally? Does it reflect influence all the way from Cataluña, in which case the Octon tombs are presumably late? Or are the tombs associated with the Causse-type dolmens further to the north, in which case they may be earlier? Grave goods might have supplied the answer, but of the Octon tombs, "Plusieurs sont entièrement vides, hélas".[14]

As we have already mentioned in passing, the one consistent feature in all the regions covered in this chapter is the orientations of the galleries and *allées couvertes*. Of the 55 listed, 40 (72·7%) face the southeast quadrant, and 52 (94·5%) have orientations within the range 90°–210°. Only three face further west (238°, 256° and 267°). Why this should be so, and how more generally to understand the mingling of customs that occurs in west Languedoc and the east Pyrenees, must await the measurement of additional tombs and, more especially, confirmation of the typology and dating of those already measured.

Further reading

M. Bordreuil, "Recherches sur le monomentalisme funéraire et les sepultures mégalithiques en Languedoc oriental", in *La France des dolmens et des sépultures collectives*, ed. by Philippe Soulier (Paris, 1998), 135–58.

F. Claustre, "Monuments mégalithiques et grottes sepulcrales en Roussillon", *ibid.*, 159–74.

C. and J. Guilaine, "Les dolmens de l'Aude", *ibid.*, 175–6.

J. Guilaine, *Au temps des dolmens* (Paris, 1998).

M. Hoskin and T. Palmo i Pérez, "Studies in Iberian archaeoastronomy: (4) The orientations of megalithic tombs of eastern Catalunya", *JHA*, xxix (1998), 63–79; *idem*, "The orientations of megalithic tombs of eastern Catalunya: Addendum", *AA*, no. 24 (1999), S89–90.

R. Iund, "Orientations of dolmens north of the eastern Pyrenees", *AA*, no. 26 (2001), in press.

J. Tarrús, "Réflexions sur le mégalithisme en Catalogne", in *Mégalithismes de l'Atlantique à l'Ethiopie*, ed. by J. Guilaine (Paris, 1999), 107–21.

J. Tarrús, contribution to Y. Chevalier, "Orientations of 935 dolmens of southern France", *AA*, no. 24 (1999), S47–82, pp. S75–78.

J. Tarrús and J. Chinchilla, *Els monuments megalítics* (Girona, 1992); J. Tarrús *et al.*, *Dòlmens i menhirs: 111 monuments megalítics de l'Alt Empordà i Vallespir oriental* (Figueres, 1988), and *Dòlmens i menhirs: 48 monuments megalítics del Baix Empordà, el Gironès i la Selva* (Figueres, 1990) (all in Catalan).

References

1 Groupe Archéologique Lodévois, "Les mégalithes du Lodévois", *Cahiers ligures de préhistoire et d'archéologie*, x/1 (1961), 21–99, p. 60, suggest that all the Octon tombs may have been galleries, but the tumuli of those we examined hardly leave room for this. Bordreuil ("Recherches", 138) thinks some were simple dolmens and some galleries.

2 Guilaine and Guilaine, "Les dolmens de l'Aude", 176.

3 *Ibid.*

4 Tarrús, contribution to Chevalier, "Orientations".

5 Guilaine, *Au temps des dolmens*, 57; Tarrús, "Réflexions", 118. Details are given in Tarrús and Chinchilla, *Els monuments megalítics*, 79. The radiocarbon dates are confirmed by those derived by other techniques.

6 Tarrús, contribution to Chevalier, "Orientations".

7 *Ibid.*, S76.

8 Josep Tarrús, "Consideracions sobre el Neolític Final–Calcolític a Catalunya (2500 a.C.)", *Cypsela* (Girona), v (1985), 45–57.

9 Tarrús, contribution to Chevalier, "Orientations", S78.

10 Guilaine, *Au temps des dolmens*, 19.

11 Iund, "Orientations".

12 Guilaine and Guilaine, "Les dolmens de l'Aude", 176.

13 Claustre, "Monuments mégalithiques", 162.

14 Bordreuil, "Recherches", 138.

11

Westerly-facing Tombs (II):
The Balearic Islands

Today we think of the Balearic Islands as comprising four major islands (plus a number of tiny islets). But in ancient historic times the Balearics consisted only of Menorca and Mallorca, while Ibiza and the much smaller Formentera formed the Pityusae. The Carthaginians settled Ibiza in 654 BC, but apart from a minor presence on Mallorca they were content merely to trade with the Balearics.

This division reflects the situation that existed in the two millennia before the Carthaginians arrived. Apart from a single megalithic sepulchre on Formentera, there is little sign of prehistoric occupation of the Pityusae. On the Balearic Islands, by contrast, we find in the third millennium BC a variety of signs of human occupation, leading to the erection of small but carefully-constructed megalithic sepulchres. The second and first millennia saw the development of the sophisticated tombs of the 'talayotic' Bronze Age culture, whose sanctuaries we studied in Chapter 4 and which survived after a fashion until the Roman occupation of the islands in 123 BC.

The megalithic sepulchre of Ses Roques Llises.

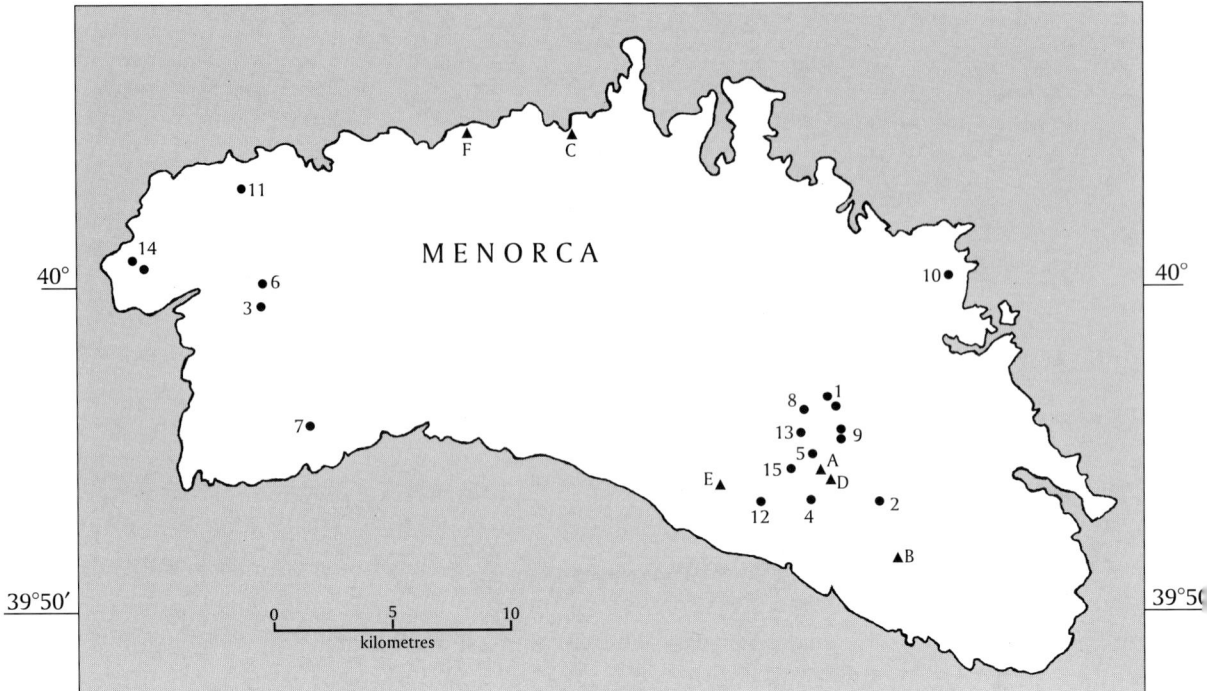

The megalithic sepulchres (triangles) and navetas (circles) of Menorca.

A Alcaidús	2 Binimaimut	9 Rafal Rubí S, N
B Binidalinet	3 Binipati Nou	10 Sa Torreta
C Ferragut Nou	4 Cotaina de C'an Rabassó	11 Son Morell
D Momplé	5 Cotaina d'En Carreras	12 Torralbene Nou
E Ses Roques Llises	6 Es Tudons	13 Torralbet d'Es Caragol
F Son Ermita	7 La Cova	14 Torre del Ram E, W
1 Biniac-L'Argentina E, W	8 Llumena d'En Montanyes	15 Torre Llisa Vell

The Balearic megalithic sepulchres

Of the early megalithic sepulchres,[1] only six were known when I first studied them: four in south-eastern Menorca, just one on Mallorca, and the one on Formentera already mentioned. The best preserved is Ses Roques Llises, near Alaior on Menorca. It has a rectangular chamber measuring some 2m × 4m consisting of (i) a backstone located in between the sidestones; (ii) sides each of two orthostats; and (iii) an entrance stone located in between the sidestones, with a circular 'porthole' for access; and there is (iv) a small corridor (or porch) that is narrower than the chamber. There are no surviving capstones, but we see clear signs of a tumulus.

The sepulchre at Binidalinet at San Lluís on Menorca is less complete, but we again find (i)–(iii) clearly present. And the Menorcan sepulchres at Momplé (in Maó) and Alcaidús (Alaior), which are only a stone's throw apart, display between them all four characteristics.

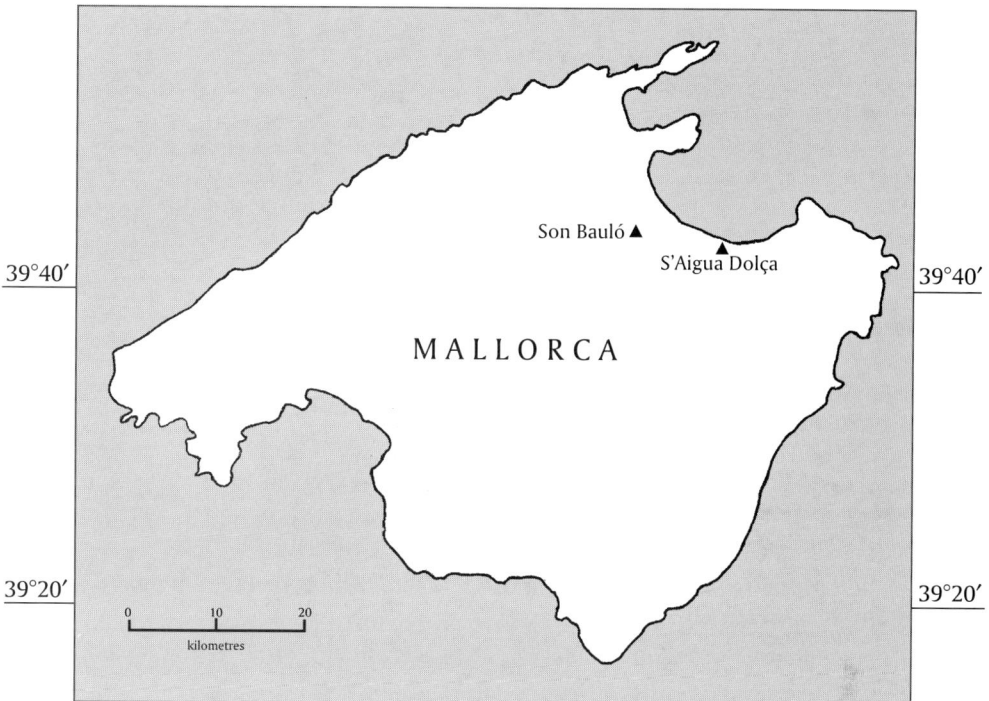

The two megalithic sepulchres of Mallorca.

The sepulchre on Mallorca, at Son Bauló de Dalt, has a single orthostat to each side, and a well-defined porch. That on Formentera, at Ca Na Costa, has by contrast a near-circular chamber formed of eight orthostats, one of which is perforated to form the entrance, and the corridor is more substantial, being formed of two orthostats on each side. Its tumulus is reinforced by slabs; each of these is located near the exterior of the tumulus, along one of twenty or so axial lines that we can imagine radiating out from the chamber.

All these six Balearic sepulchres (Table 11.1) face between 220° and 278°. It is the best-preserved of all, Ses Roques Llises, that has the extreme southerly direction of 220°. The well-defined orientation of this rectangular tomb, which is located on flat ground with a view in all directions, corresponds to declination –36°, and this is well south of the range of both sunset and moonset.

After I published these six orientations, three more sepulchres were discovered, two on Menorca and one on Mallorca.[2] I had by this time come to realize that westerly orientations were almost unknown on the Iberian mainland; yet the orientations of these three island tombs (Table 11.1) all lay between southwest and west, in confirmation of the pattern I had already announced for the Balearics. The two Menorcan sepulchres are located near the north coast, and so are distant from the four previously known; they are very incomplete but may well conform to the same structural pattern. The sepulchre on Mallorca is in better state, and this time each side of the chamber has three orthostats in the form of an arc, so providing something of a compromise

167

The orientations of the nine Balearic sepulchres currently known.

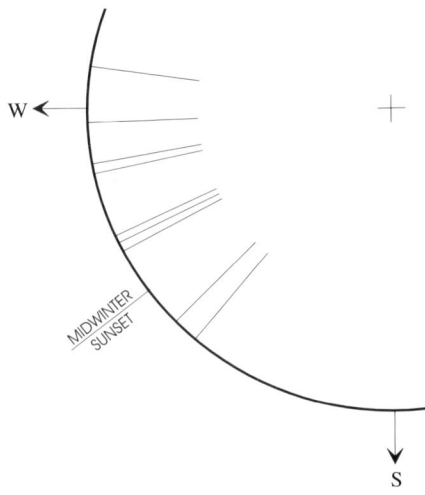

between the rectangles of Menorca and the circle of Ca Na Costa.

We see then that the structures of the tombs on Mallorca and Formentera display minor variations on the Menorcan theme, but four of those on Menorca (and probably all six) shared the characteristics (i)–(iv). William Waldren, who has pioneered the prehistory of the Balearics, speaks of "an arc of immediate influence [on the islands] extending from the region of Almeria in the south, along the Valencia coast and northward into Catalonia and the Pyrenees, reaching into the Languedoc and Provence of France".[3] Yves Chevalier, for his part, was in no doubt that the Balearic tombs were simply expatriate Languedoc dolmens (though an erroneous site-plan had misled him into thinking that the entrance of Ses Roques Llises resembled that of Coste-Rouge near Lodève in Languedoc[4]). How then do the characteristics of the Balearic sepulchre compare with those of the typical (and likewise westerly-facing) dolmen of eastern Languedoc, which we discussed in Chapter 9?

The forms are very similar, but not quite identical. In Languedoc, as on Menorca, the chamber was rectangular, longer than it was wide but without a sharp contrast between the two dimensions; and the backstone was likewise located between the sidestones. However, in Languedoc the sides were formed each of a single slab, whereas on Menorca there are at least two orthostats to each side (though we note that at Son Bauló de Dalt on Mallorca there was only one). Further, in Languedoc the entrance — located between the sidestones as on the Balearics — consisted of either two pillars (leading to a centrally placed corridor) or one (leading to a corridor that was consequently set to one side of the axis): the porthole typical of Menorcan sepulchres is unknown in Languedoc, although some Languedoc tombs have shaped pillars, and Coste-Rouge (see page 146) has a single entrance stone with a semicircular oven-style hole cut into its lower edge.

Alternatively, how do the Balearic sepulchres compare with the westerly-facing dolmens of Cataluña, which of course is geographically close to the Balearics? We saw in the last chapter that the majority of the Catalan tombs are 'sepulchres with corridor with trapezoidal chambers', which Tarrús dates to the second half of the fourth millennium, though a handful have rectangular

A typical 'porthole' entrance to a
Balearic sepulchre: Alcaidús.

chambers, and these he dates to the first half of the third millennium. On grounds both of date
and of shape of chamber, it is the latter that are closer to the Balearic sepulchres. Nevertheless,
it is unusual in Cataluña for a dolmen of this or any type to have a well-defined entrance stone
(or stones), such as we meet routinely in the Balearic sepulchres. More usually in Cataluña, either
the sides converge, or on one or both sides an orthostat is set askew to the axis, and the width
of the chamber is thereby reduced to that of the corridor. Thus we find one orthostat askew the
axis at Ruines and the same at nearby La Talaia, these being two of the three sepulchres that have
rectangular chambers and westerly orientations. On the other side of the hill on which these two
are located is the last of the three, Mas de la Mata. The site plan shows some sort of entrance
stones, but these may well have been mere thresholds (though because one orthostat from each
side has fallen inwards, visual inspection of the entrance is impracticable). This tomb is unusual
in that, in order to face west, it had to look uphill.

One of the very few Catalan dolmens with an unequivocal entrance is the magnificent Creu
d'en Cobertella, whose chamber Tarrús regards as trapezoidal; but here there are two tall entrance
pillars at right angles to the sides, quite unlike the porthole entrances of the Balearic sepulchres.

In Cataluña therefore, not only is a sculptured entrance, mandatory in the Balearics, apparently unknown, but well-defined entrances of any kind are rare. Waldren, writing without regard
to tomb orientations, sees influence on the early Balearic culture from both Cataluña and Languedoc; Chevalier, whose experience of Cataluña was admittedly limited, favoured Languedoc. The
conclusion from our comparison of the structures of the tombs of the three regions must be that
the origin of the Balearic sepulchres is much more likely to be found in eastern Hérault than in
Cataluña. Although the Languedoc tombs have only a single orthostat forming each side, and

although they normally have an entrance pillar or pillars while a single entrance stone with sculptured aperture is rare, a Languedoc tomb, like a Balearic sepulchre, routinely had a rectangular chamber with a well-defined entrance at right angles to the chamber, leading to a narrower porch or corridor.

The navetas of Menorca

During the second millennium the people who erected the sepulchres were replaced by, or developed into, the talayot builders who inhabited the limestone southern half of Menorca and occupied, though less intensely, the northern half of the island along with neighbouring Mallorca. As we saw in Chapter 4, the culture is named for the truncated conical towers or talayots built of rough megaliths that became a feature of many of the settlements on both islands. Apart from the talayots, the largest structures built by the talayotic (or late pre-talayotic) people were the Menorcan 'navetas', impressive communal tombs peculiar to the island, which were given this name because of the striking resemblance of the magnificent tomb of Es Tudons to an upturned boat.[5] Others are similarly elongated, but others again are oval-shaped on the exterior. Interestingly, no (burial) navetas have been identified elsewhere in the Balearics.

According to Luis Plantalamor, director of the Museum of Menorca,[6] the oval navetas are the oldest, and belong to the period 1800–1600 BC. Next in age are the elongated navetas of the eastern half of the island, which he dates to 1600–1400. Latest are the elongated navetas in the

The naveta of Es Tudons.

170

west, dated to the period 1400–1000 and hence clearly talayotic. As we shall see, this latter division of elongated navetas into two classes, 'oval' and 'elongated', though made without regard to the question of orientation, is supported by subtle differences in the orientations of the two classes.

Whether a naveta is oval or elongated in external shape, its interior chamber is always in the form of an extended rectangle, with the entrance at the middle of one of the shorter sides. Therefore, although navetas are built to an altogether larger scale, they resemble the earlier megalithic sepulchres in their basic design, for both have an entrance passage (or porch) that gives access to the rectangular chamber. But there the similarity ends, for the modest orthostats of the sepulchres are replaced in navetas by numerous courses of massive dry-stone blocks similar to those we find in the talayots, and the chambers of navetas are far grander.

Navetas also have some similarity to what archaeologists term 'naviforms' (or 'habitation navetas'), boat-shaped dwellings assigned to pre-talayotic times. A naviform was of course part of a settlement (and two naviforms sometimes shared a common wall), whereas a (burial) naveta was always isolated and at some distance from the nearest settlement. Nevertheless, structurally they have enough in common to give rise to debate in particular instances.

Even before restoration, Es Tudons was the best preserved of the navetas. In overall length it measures nearly 10m. From the exterior, a short low entrance passage gives access to a chimney, at which point one can choose between clambering to the upper floor, or continuing so as to enter the lower (and principal) chamber. Navetas normally possessed such an entrance passage, and many though not all were divided into two floors.

There is no doubt that Es Tudons and the other navetas were used for burial. Although some were cleared and reused, at Es Tudons the remains of some one hundred individuals were found; and at Cotaina d'en Carreras, which has not been excavated, human bones are still present in great quantity. But for all their scale, navetas were by no means the only funerary monuments. In the southeast of the island there is the greatest concentration of navetas; but, as we saw in Chapter 4, in the cliffs at Calas Covas over one hundred natural limestone caves were enlarged during the first millennium BC (and some supplied with formal entrances) and used for burials, creating a vast necropolis sufficient for the dead from innumerable settlements. Perhaps the navetas were reserved for prestige burials.

Each naveta has an entrance and an axis of symmetry, and therefore a well-defined orientation, even though some of the entrance passages are set off at a slight angle. In 1989 I made preliminary measures of seven navetas, and found them to face in the quadrant between west-southwest and south-southeast. The following year, in company with Juan José Morales Núñez, a local archaeologist, I measured all the eighteen identified navetas, and found confirmation of this pattern: all faced within the range from 159° to 254° (Table 11.2).

Two of the monuments lie within sight of each other: the impressive navetas at Rafal Rubí, which are twin structures (almost indistinguishable on photographs), literally a stone's throw apart. Yet one has orientation 192° and the other 245°. Although the builders were constrained by custom (the odds against the eleven new measures falling within the quadrant defined by the

The orientations of the eighteen Menorcan burial navetas, with broken lines for those in the west of the island.

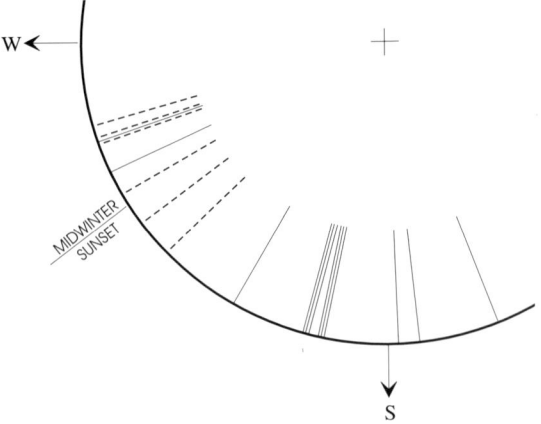

first seven purely by chance being untold millions to one), when they built the later naveta at Rafal Rubí they were perfectly content to set it at an angle of over 50° to the existing one. Furthermore, there was no requirement that the naveta have a clear view to the southern horizon, as there was with the taula sanctuaries, for these two navetas face rising ground.

It happens that the eighteen navetas are distributed equally between the three categories we mentioned earlier. The six navetas said to be earliest have oval exteriors and are located in the east of the island, near four of the earlier megalithic sepulchres. They face between 174° and 251°, an anti-clockwise shift and a broadening of the range when compared with the six sepulchres (range 220°–278°).

Four of the six elongated navetas in the east face 195° or thereabouts, and one at Rafal Rubí faces 245°, but Cotaina d'en Carreras faces 159°. It is the only naveta that faces significantly east of due south, and there was no topographical obstacle to its being oriented more southerly.

Curiously, the six navetas in the west of the island — supposedly the latest and so further from the six sepulchres in time as well as in space — face between 226° and 254°, within the range of the sepulchres and significantly more westerly on average than the navetas in the east.

To explain these variations on the southwesterly theme is not easy. The navetas in the west of Menorca do indeed face Mallorca, so a purely terrestrial motive for their orientation is to hand; but this will not do for the ones in the east, for the nearest land to the south is Africa, and it seems that we must look instead to the sky. Granted the overwhelming importance of the sun, and despite the Cotaina naveta's orientation 21° east of due south, it may well be that the sepulchres faced the sun while it was setting or descending, and the navetas while it was setting, descending, or around culmination.

As we saw in Chapter 2, attempts have been made in the past to place the origin of the talayotic culture in Nuraghic Sardinia, whence navigators are supposed to have arrived with a determination to build on Menorca in accordance with the customs they had been taught back home. But while questions of similarities of structure may be thought a matter of judgement, there is no doubt that the customs of orientation are totally opposed: navetas face westerly and (as we shall

The navetas of Rafal Rubí North (*above*) and South (*below*). Although they are in adjacent fields, their orientations differ by 53°, while still conforming to the overall pattern.

see in the next chapter) *tombe di giganti* face easterly. It seems much more likely that the talayotic culture developed out of the modest culture that built the megalithic sepulchres; or, at the very least, that the talayotic people took over from the earlier inhabitants the custom of orienting tombs westerly.

Further reading

Enciclopèdia de Menorca: Arqueologia (Mahón, 1982–).

M. Hoskin, "The talayotic culture of Menorca: A first recon- naissance", *AA*, no. 9 (1985), S133–51.

M. Hoskin and J. J. Morales Núñez, "The orientations of

the burial monuments of Menorca", *AA*, no. 16 (1991), S15–42).

C. Veny Meliá, "Las navetas", in *Prehistoria de Menorca*, ed. by J. Mascaró Pasarius (Mahón, 1982), 177–312.

Notes and references

1   A full bibliography down to 1991 is in Hoskin and Morales, "Orientations".

2   S. Gornés Hachero *et al.*, "Nous monuments funeraris del món pretalaiòtic de Menorca", in *X jornades d'estudis històrics locals: La prehistòria de les illes de la Mediter- rànea occidental*, ed. by G. Rosselló Bordoy (Palma de Mallorca, 1992), 419–41; M. Calvo Trias *et al.*, "El dolmen de S'Aigua Dolça", *Revista de arqueología*, no. 191 (March 1997), 18–29.

3   W. Waldren, *Early prehistoric settlement in the Balearic Islands* (Deiá, 1982); *cf*. his "The prehistoric sanctuary

of Son Mas", *Complutum extra*, vi (1996), 191–215, Fig. 1.

4   Y. Chevalier, *L'architecture des dolmens entre Languedoc et centre-ouest de la France* (Bonn, 1984), Plate 26. In manu- scripts Chevalier simply includes Balearic sepulchres among his Languedoc-type dolmens.

5   A full bibliography down to 1991 is again in Hoskin and Morales, "Orientations".

6   Private communication. See also *Enciclopèdia de Menorca: Arqueologia*.

Easterly-facing Tombs (V):
Corsica and Sardinia

I owe my introduction to the beautiful island of Sardinia with its extraordinary wealth of antiquities to Edoardo Proverbio of Cagliari University, who in 1989 invited me to join him in measuring the orientations of *tombe di giganti*, the communal tombs of the Nuraghic culture known by their folk name of 'tombs of giants'. I was to revisit the island many times, relying at first on shepherds and goatherds to help in the location of tombs of various kinds that were discussed in published articles. Gradually we developed a *modus operandi*: we would arrive in a town where we knew there to be tombs, and would ask around for guidance; and such is the unfailing generosity of the Sardinian people that we were soon locating tombs in some numbers. A member of staff of a *municipio* (townhall), approached without warning, would not infrequently rise from his desk to spend hours with us in the field. On one occasion when we were in search of a tiny temple, the municipal Landrover was pressed into service to guide our car to a remote hill, where the location of the monument was pointed out to us. Climbing the hill, we found ourselves unable to identify the tiny ruined temple amidst all the natural stone, so we descended and enquired of a cowherd in the valley. Leaving his herd, he led us back up the hill. My companion expressed to me her concern at this abandonment of his animals, at which the cowherd turned and said in English, "Cows OK!"

An insuperable obstacle was occasionally presented by dogs guarding a flock of sheep. Instead of assisting the shepherds, such dogs are in round-the-clock control of the sheep, except when the shepherds turn up in vehicles morning and evening to milk the flock. For the rest of the time the dogs rule the sheep with rods of iron, and put to flight any humans who approach. Explaining that you are an archaeologist interested only in the stones cuts no ice at all.

Problems of a more welcome kind were presented by farmers on whose land we suspected tombs to be. On arriving at a farmhouse and making enquiries, we would receive no immediate answer but would be invited in, sat down, and made to partake of cheese and wine. Only then would it transpire that they had no tombs. The same ritual would be repeated at the next farmhouse, and the next, by which time interest in tombs was losing its urgency.

I later made the acquaintance of Mauro Peppino Zedda, who grows vegetables in the summer and measures monuments in the winter. He turned up in Cambridge looking for me, and displaying all the symptoms of the lunatic fringe. Nothing could have been further from the truth, and before long I was working with him intensively all over the island. On our arrival in a town, he would ask "Where are the old men?", and soon would be engaging a group of these senior

Sardinian shepherds plying passing archaeologists with home-made food and, more especially, drink.

citizens in conversation; within minutes one of the more able-bodied would be in our car, *en route* for a tomb. On one occasion Zedda and I walked into a *municipio* unannounced, and in a few minutes were heading for the hills in the municipal Landrover in company with an archaeologist and two foresters. Anyone whose faith in human nature is in need of restoration should visit Sardinia.

One cannot say the same of the Corsicans, whose monuments are fortunately few, though important for our purpose. And it is with these that we begin.

The dolmens of Corsica

The island of Corsica is mountainous and densely forested. Herds of wild pigs feast off the chestnuts, and some of them may well be familiar with prehistoric remains that are unknown to archaeologists. The monuments that are known are mostly in the south and southwest of the island, and they include closed cists, menhirs carved with the outline of a human form, alignments of stones, and a small number of dolmens.[1] Next to nothing remains of the occupants of the dolmens or of any grave goods.

A recent survey of Corsican prehistory[2] suggests that cists were known from around 3000 BC and that they evolved into dolmens in the Copper Age, at the beginning of the second millennium; but this seems too late if the parallel history of Sardinia is taken into account. Giovanni Lilliu, the distinguished archaeologist of Sardinia, proposed a quarter of a century ago that there was a culture common to southern Corsica and northern Sardinia,[3] despite the turbulence of the narrow stretch of water that separates them; and his view has won widespread acceptance. The late third millennium seems a more likely period for the development of dolmens on both islands.

Corsican dolmens are of two types: those that are constructed on the surface, of which the finest and best-known is Dolmen de Fontanaccia (sometimes called Dolmen de Stazzona); and those that are built partly into the ground and surrounded by a ring of substantial stones that are the remains of the retaining kerb of a tumulus, the chief example being Dolmen de Settiva. The latter are seen as transitional between the coffers and the surface dolmens.

The chamber of a dolmen is nearly always rectangular, with sides formed of one or more orthostats together with a single backstone and a single capstone. The side opposite the backstone is (today) usually open, but occasionally it has two vertical stones that define the entrance.

Unlike Sardinia, Corsica has few shepherds, and fewer local residents with the helpful disposition of their neighbours to the south: the tomb-hunter must fend for himself. An article on Corsican dolmens published in 1985 by Joseph Cesari[4] identified a total of ten dolmens that might have been of interest to us, but two of these could be eliminated. One, Dolmen de Tremeca in Casaglione in the west-centre of the island, opens to the southeast, but Cesari's photograph and plan show that it has no quantifiable orientation. Of the Dolmen d'Eccica-Suarella, which is inland from Ajaccio, Cesaru says nothing beyond giving its name; as it was located in an inaccessible

Dolmen de Fontanaccia.

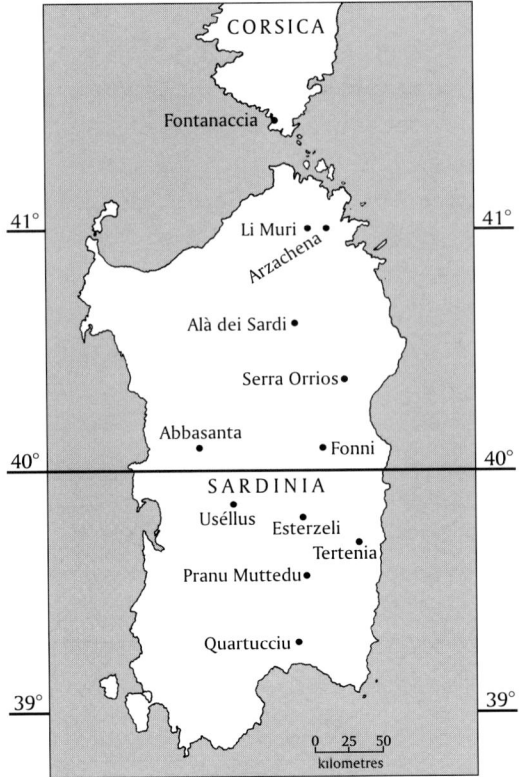

Sardinia and south Corsica, with the locations of sites mentioned in the text.

area, and the chances of reaching the area and then finding the dolmen were nil, we felt justified in neglecting it.

This left a total of eight, all in the southwest of the island. Some are easy to find, others verge on the impossible. But fortune smiled on us during our visits to the island in 1994 and 1995, and we located and measured all eight. Their orientations are given in Table 12.1.

Settiva, as already mentioned, is set into the ground rather than erected on the surface. It is surrounded by substantial stones, the remains of a tumulus that was perhaps 8 metres in diameter. Interestingly, although the dolmen is located in a flat area and the builders were free of any topographical constraints, they built the dolmen to face directly towards a nearby mountain, so high that its summit has an angular altitude from the tomb of no less than 16°.

Arghjola is the smallest of the eight, with a chamber measuring a mere 1–2m. It is very unusual in having been cut horizontally backwards into a slope, so that the front of the chamber is on the surface whereas the rear is half buried. Also, although the slope continues downwards for a few tens of metres, the ground very quickly rises again.

The remaining six were all erected on the surface, and all are prominent. Five are on elevations, and look down an extended slope; the extreme example is Belvedère, which looks over a

Dolmen de Vaccil-Vecchiu. A menhir in front of the entrance to the tomb is likewise to be found at Dolmen de Settiva, and also in the much later *tomba di giganti*, Sa Domu 'e s'Orcu at Quartucciu near the south coast of Sardinia, some 250km away (see p. 187).

precipitous descent, and ultimately out to sea. The sixth, Cardaccia, is on a high plateau.

In most of the dolmens, the chambers are formed of carefully fashioned orthostats, and so the tombs have well-defined orientations. Six face between 117½° and 165°, little more than an octant of a circle; a seventh, Vaccil-Vecchiu, faces almost due south (181½°), while Arghjola faces 217°, well to the west of south.

Even if we include Arghjola, we find that all the dolmens face within a range of 100°, and so it is clear that the constructors were following a custom. But the little dolmen of Arghjola is the only one that clearly faces the western half of the horizon, and its exceptional orientation seems in keeping with its anomalous location and construction: the tomb fits into neither of the two recognized types of Corsican dolmens. It therefore seems best to regard its orientation as anomalous. The other seven face between about east-southeast and south; and a recently published plan of a further dolmen, La Casa di l'Orcu at Monte Revincu (Santo-Pietro-di-Tenda) in the far north of the island, indicates that it too faces east-southeast.[5] It therefore appears that the orientation custom followed by the Corsican dolmen-builders required that their tombs faced within the southeast quadrant, and that most faced south of the range of sunrise (SC in our terminology).

We next explore the customs followed by their contemporaries to the south of the Straits of Bonifacio.

(*Above*) The second of the Li Muri sepulchres (looking north). In the background to the right is visible a sidestone of no. 1; part of the kerb of no. 4 is seen at the extreme left, and no. 3 is in the centre background. (*Below*) Tomb 2 at Pranu Muttedu, with a most unusual square entrance hollowed out of a single stone.

Early non-dolmenic tombs of Sardinia

Before we examine the comparable dolmens of Sardinia we must mention two clusters of early tombs were likewise free-standing monuments but appear to be independent of the mainstream dolmenic tradition. The first is at Li Muri near Arzachena in the far north of the island, where there is a celebrated group of five small rectangular megalithic sepulchres. Each is built of little orthostats, and is surrounded by the remains of a little tumulus. The tombs, which are so tightly packed that the ovals of the tumuli touch one another, are said to belong to the third millennium BC or even the fourth.[6] Each tomb apparently contained a single body. The orientations are shown in Table 12.2. There is no clear custom of orientation, although we note that three (and possibly four) faced within 20° of south.

The second group is at Pranu Muttedu near Goni, well to the south of the island (latitude 39.6°) and so, as we shall see, outside the region of the dolmenic culture. On the site are six free-standing tombs, together with stone circles, tombs of Domus de Janas form (cave-like structures excavated in the rocks), and an impressive number of menhirs (including a long row oriented roughly east–west). These tombs, which date from the early third millennium, are altogether more sophisticated in form than either the megalithic sepulchres of Li Muri or the dolmens of the north of the island. As the site appears to be unique and our concern is with more general patterns of orientation, we shall limit ourselves to listing in Table 12.3 the orientations of the five tombs that

The dolmen Sa Coveccada at Mores, considered by some to be the most beautiful of Mediterranean dolmens. Its similarity to the dolmen Coste-Rouge in east Languedoc (p. 146) is remarkable.

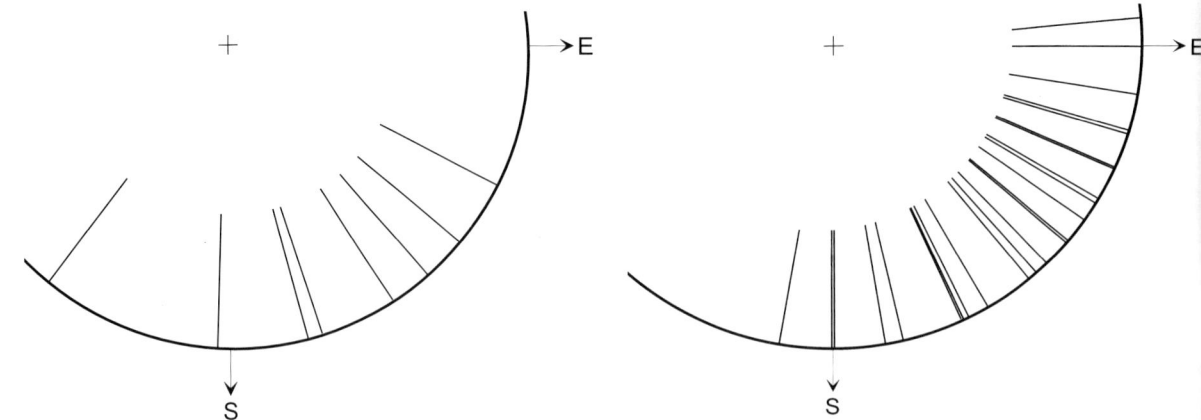

Orientations of 8 Corsican dolmens.   Orientations of 24 Sardinian dolmens.

faced in a defined direction, the sixth (after reconstruction) appearing to have no clear entrance. We note that while one of the five has orientation 100°, the others face within ten or so degrees of south. All five face within the southeast quadrant, give or take a very few degrees.

The dolmens of Sardinia

There are many 'paradolmens' in Sardinia, in which the builders reduced the work involved by availing themselves of a conveniently shaped natural rock (or rocks). To do this they may well have tolerated orientations outside their customary range, and so we rejected them and accepted only true (free-standing) dolmens, which in this early period are tombs with a rectangular (or trapezoidal) chamber whose back and sides are each formed of a single orthostat and a single massive capstone. An exceptionally fine example is Sa Coveccada at Mores.

We measured 24 dolmens that we regard as authentic, and these are listed in Table 12.4. All are in the northern half of the island (north of latitude 40°). We see that every dolmen faced within the southeast quadrant or almost so. Our conclusion is that the dolmens of northern Sardinia and those of southern Corsica had similar structures and had orientations within similar SR/SC ranges: the southeast quadrant (plus an extension of a few degrees west of due south, but before the sun had clearly begun its descent).

The *corridoi dolmenici* of Sardinia

Between the period of dolmenic construction and the later development of the sophisticated Nuraghic culture, tomb-building in Sardinia took the form of the *corridoi dolmenici*, the extended rectangular tombs with open entrances of a form similar to the *allée couverte* and the 'Catalan gallery' and which in Sardinia evolved into the *tomba di giganti*.

We located and measured twenty *corridoi dolmenici*, and the results are given in Table 12.5. In

The *corridoio dolmenico* of Corti Noa at Laconi.

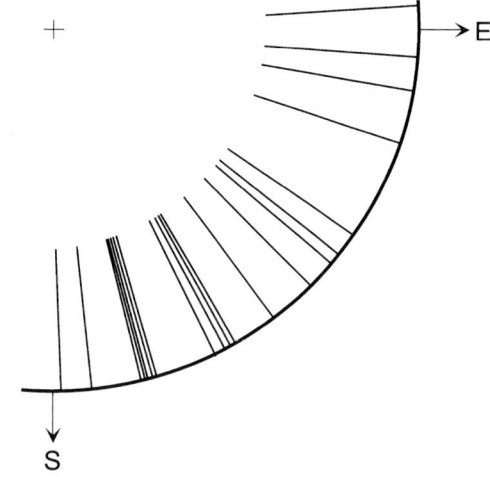

Orientations of 20 Sardinian *corridoi dolmenici*.

the case of one tomb that was open at both ends we took it upon ourselves to assume the orientation was normal. This being so, every one of the twenty faced the southeast quadrant or almost so, in continuation of the dolmenic tradition.

Although this total is relatively small, we note that those *corridoi dolmenici* that lie to the south of latitude 40° without exception faced nearer to south than to east, within the southeast–south octant. This suggests that even in the pre-Nuraghic period there was already something of a north–south divide as regards customs of tomb orientation, and this division will become significant in our discussion of *tombe di giganti*. We remember that most of the Pranu Muttedu tombs, which are from the southern half of the island, likewise faced close to south.

The *tombe di giganti*

The building of megalithic tombs in Sardinia began with the dolmens and continued with the *corridoi dolmenici*, both forms very familiar elsewhere in western Europe. The island then developed a rich culture that is to be found nowhere else. It takes its name from the towers or 'nuraghi', sophisticated and often complex truncated cones of false-cupola construction, whose purpose

A modest example of the many thousands of surviving nuraghi.

remains a mystery. More than seven thousand survive to this day, and the original total is esti-mated at twenty thousand.

Disagreement over the purpose of nuraghi has extended to their dating, the earliest having been assigned to the eighteenth century BC or later, and many attributed to Punic times. Recent work, however, appears to extend their origins back to the early centuries of the third millennium BC, and dates the end of the culture to near the beginning of the first millennium. If this is correct, then the dolmens of Sardinia, and presumably those of Corsica, must indeed predate the second millennium.

The Nuraghic people also developed a unique structure for their communal tombs, the so-called *tombe di giganti*. Although there are the considerable variations to be expected on so large an island, a *tomba di giganti* is a substantial monument. It has a long, narrow rectangular chamber, with an entrance at one end often marked with a tall stele with an access hole below and decora-tion above. To left and right of the stele, the tomb extends in a broad arc, the two arms ('exedra') defining a sacred space in front of the tomb. In its mature form, a *tomba di giganti* belongs to the height of the Nuraghic culture, the second half of the second millennium BC and the beginning of the first.

By 1990 Proverbio and colleagues (including myself) had accumulated measurements of the orientations of 48 *tombe di giganti*. All the tombs studied so far had belonged to the concentrations in the centre of the island, and without exception faced the eastern half of the horizon. It was important to extend the investigation to other parts of the island, and this I did in 1992 and 1993. This resulted in a further 30 tombs, mostly scattered across the north and centre. Of the total of 78 orientations, 73 faced in azimuth between 66½° and 173½°, and a further three faced close to south.

In 1994 I began my long and fruitful collaboration with Zedda, whose home in Isili is particularly

The central chamber of the nuraghe Is Paras, near Isili. In Santu Antine near Torralba, three such chambers are constructed at different levels, one above the other, an extraordinary achievement in dry-stone construction.

The *tomba di giganti* Thomes, near Dorgali. The remains of the exedra are seen to either side of the central stele, and the roof of the extensive central chamber can be glimpsed on the right.

convenient for the investigation of the southern half of the island. Zedda is an unrelenting task-master, and in 1994, 1995 and 1996 we were able to more than treble the total, from 78 to 252 — fifty times the number of tombs covered in the first publication on the subject. Although estimates vary of the number of *tombe di giganti* of which traces remain (in 1988 Lilliu[7] put the number at a minimum of 321), there is little doubt that most of the surviving tombs have at last been measured. Furthermore, our results are representative and cover the entire island. It seems therefore that further surveys of orientations cannot be expected to add anything of significance to the data.

Examination of these data on the 252 tombs (see Table 12.6), distributed over every part of the island, reveals a significant variation on the earlier east–south theme. A small but non-negligible number of tombs face outside the range previously found, and even beyond the limits of SR/SC orientations: some transgress the limits in the anti-clockwise direction and faced to the north of midsummer sunrise, while others do the same in the clockwise direction, facing well to the west of due south. Two tombs, indeed, face only a few degrees from due north, and orientations that face northerly are truly anomalous anywhere in the central or western Mediterranean, collectors' items indeed.

The *tomba di giganti* Selene 1, at Lanusei. The loss of both the central stele and the roof of the chamber allows the visitor to see the care with which the rectangular chamber was constructed. In front is the sacred space defined by the exedra.

The magnificent *tomba di giganti* Is Concias near the south coast, a rare example of a Mediterranean communal tomb that faces close to north. The entrance, in shadow, is to the right of the menhir.

The latitudes listed in Table 12.6 help clarify the situation. Eight of the twelve tombs with exceptionally northerly azimuths, between 0° and 64°, lie south of latitude 40°. Similarly, all the twenty tombs with azimuth between 192° and 360° lie south of latitude 40°. That is, of the 158 *tombe di giganti* in the northern half of the island (which includes the large concentrations of tombs around Fonni and Abbasanta), no fewer than 154 (97·5%) faced in azimuth between 65° and 192° — an enlargement of the southeast quadrant we found among the earlier dolmens and *corridoi dolmenici*, but nevertheless SR/SC (midsummer sunrise having azimuth around 63°, depending on latitude and skyline altitude). But among the 94 tombs in the south of the island, the same pattern, although generally observed, was violated by no fewer than 28 tombs, or 29·8% of the total: 8 (8·5%) faced north of azimuth 65°, and 20 (21·3%) faced west of azimuth 192°.[8]

It is interesting to note that the dolmens of both islands and the Sardinian *corridoi dolmenici* are also SR/SC, but with ranges that were more restricted than that of the (northern) *tombe di giganti*: it seems that as time passed and this new type of tomb was developed, the old customs of orientations were maintained, but in a more relaxed form. This seems in accordance with human nature: once a custom has been developed and is firmly established, it then tends with time to be observed with increasing 'permissiveness'.

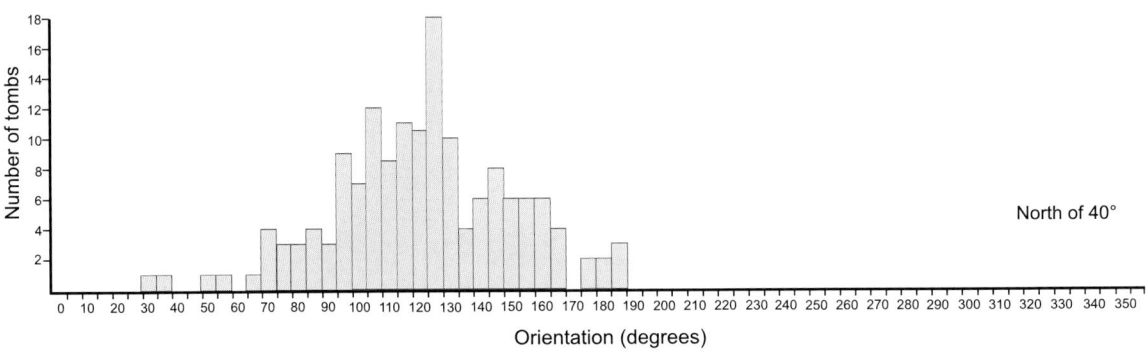

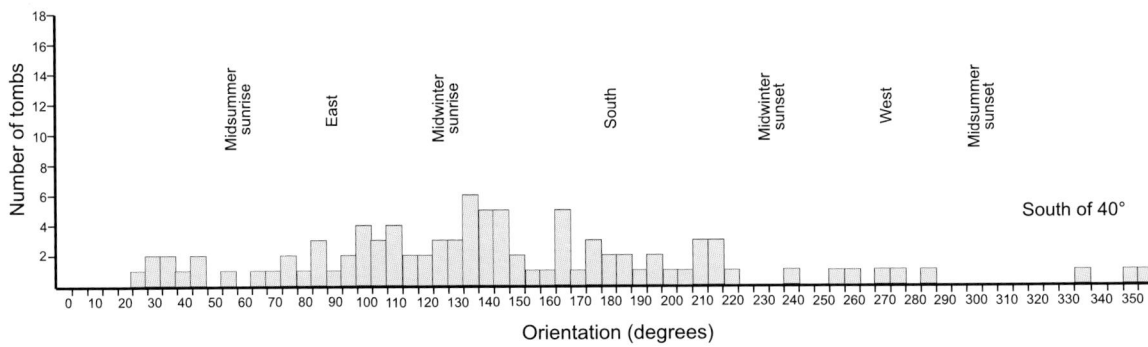

Histograms of 158 *tombe di giganti* of northern Sardinia and of 94 of southern Sardinia.

188

A corner of the Nuraghic temple at Esterzili. The end wall is to the right, while to the left the sidewall projects to make this of 'megaron' design.

The Nuraghic temples

Among the sacred places of the Nuraghe were a small number of free-standing temples; and the choice of temple orientation is a further clue to the religious beliefs of the builders — even though the example of Menorca shows that it is perfectly possible for a culture to orientate its temples and its tombs according to very different customs.

Five such temples are known, all in the eastern half of the island and four of them north of the 40° parallel. Four are rectangular, and known as 'megaron' because their sides extend beyond the front or back wall in the manner of Greek megaron temples, while the fifth (and most northerly) is elliptical in form. Their construction dates are a matter of debate. Some see actual Greek influence in their design, and if so they are to be dated as late as the middle of the first millennium BC. Lilliu has come to reject this supposed influence and now dates them much earlier.[10] Be that as it may, in 1992 we located these five temples, and measured the orientation of a side-wall of each of the rectangular temples and the approximate axis of the elliptical one.

The most southerly of the five is in the mountains above the little town of Esterzili, at a height of nearly 1000m. The massive structure has overall dimensions of 22½m by 7½m, and is situated on level ground that allowed the builders to select any orientation they wished. Because of its size and shape, its orientation is well defined: 167°.

The second and third lie to one edge of the well-preserved settlement at Serra Orrios, north-west of Dorgali. Here the low-lying ground is flat in all directions so again the builders were free in their choice of orientation. The smaller of the two has overall dimensions of 8m by 4m, and the orientation is well defined: 98°. The larger measures 10½m by 4½m overall, and again the orientation is well defined: 158°.

Why there were two temples on the site is anybody's guess. One suggestion is that the smaller was used on a daily basis by the local community, while the larger, with its spacious precinct, was used on special occasions by the whole population of the region. What is significant for our purposes is that both faced within the southeast quadrant; but that despite their proximity they nevertheless faced in very different directions.

The fourth and last of the rectangular temples is a tiny structure on a remote hillside to the northwest of Alà dei Sardi, at an elevation of about 1000m. Internally it measures a mere 4m by 2m, but its orientation is again well defined: 94°.

The fifth, and quite different temple, is Tempietto di Malchittu, a kilometre of so from the northern town of Arzachena. Elliptical in outline, it is perched on a saddle-shaped patch of ground in a little pass between two rocky eminences; it formed part of a settlement one of whose features was a fortification on one of the eminences. The external dimensions of the major and minor 'axes' are some 12m and 6m respectively. The orientation is partly dictated by the confined space available, and because of the shape of the building it is ill-defined: very approximately, 120°.

The data on the five temples are given in Table 12.7. All five face within the southeast quadrant — like the dolmens, the *corridoi dolmenici*, and most of the *tombe di giganti*.

The unique elliptical temple at Malchittu, near Arzachena.

190

Implications

The frequency with which the various tombs and temples of Corsica and northern Sardinia were oriented within the SR/SC range (from about 60° to about 190°) is remarkable.

(i) Of the 8 dolmens of Corsica, 7 were oriented within the range.

(ii) Of the 24 dolmens of (northern) Sardinia, all 24 were oriented within the range.

(iii) Of the 20 *corridoi dolmenici* of (northern) Sardinia, all 20 were oriented within the range.

(iv) Of the 158 *tombe di giganti* of northern Sardinia, 154 (97·5%) were oriented within the range.

(v) Of the 4 temples of northern Sardinia, all 4 were oriented within the range.

That is, of these 214 tombs and temples of Corsica and the northern half of Sardinia, widely spaced both geographically and in time, no fewer than 209 (97·7%) faced within the SC/SR range familiar from Iberia and France: in directions where the sun sometimes rose, or where the sun was to be seen climbing in the sky or around culmination.

Of course, a tomb that at times faced sunrise, also faced moonrise on frequent occasions. However, there is not a single monument of the 214 that faced too far north for sunrise but in a direction of moonrise.

In the south of Sardinia, however, we found no pre-Nuraghic monuments to measure, other than the handful of curious tombs at Pranu Muttedu. It must therefore have been an area to which the customs of construction and orientation spread from the north in Nuraghic times. Yet in the south some 30% of the *tombe di giganti* failed to conform.

This, we think, was due to outside influence. In the south the farming was good, and the area is one of the richest in minerals in the Mediterranean — obsidian from Monte Arci has been found in Neolithic and Copper Age sites in Spain, France and Italy. It is therefore probable that outsiders arrived at intervals from both east and west;[11] and the great variety of orientations that we encounter in the south of the island suggests that there the indigenous culture was less secure, and that other customs were occasionally allowed to take precedence.

The anomalous orientations usually occur in areas especially open to outside influence. Close to the south coast is Sa Domu 'e S'Orcu (see page 187), at Quartucciu, not far from Cagliari, which faces a most exceptional 353½°. On the southeast coast is Tertenia, a region that is isolated from the rest of the island by mountains; there both the surviving tombs are anomalous, facing 28° and 43½° respectively. A little further inland are the mountains of Esterzili, where there are tombs facing 24½°, 211½°, 224½°, 285½° and (at nearby Nurri) 335°. Across to the west, and not far from the deposits of obsidian, is Uséllus, where the tomb known as Motroxu 'e Bois has orientation 350°.

It may be significant that the Nurri tomb is perched on a rocky crag; its exedra is little more than token, and there is no room for a ceremonial space in front of the tomb. Similarly, Motroxu 'e Bois has no exedra and departs in other ways from the normal form of a *tomba di giganti*, although here there is no restriction of space. Sa Domu 'e S'Orcu, however, is unquestionably authentic, built on a magnificent scale, and still in excellent condition; which makes its northerly orientation all the more extraordinary.

Our conclusion therefore is that, in the period of the dolmenic culture of southern Corsica and northern Sardinia, the custom was established whereby tombs faced sunrise or the sun when climbing in the sky. In Sardinia this custom continued into the pre-Nuraghic period of the *corridoi dolmenici*, and thence into the Nuraghic period of the temples and the *tombe di giganti*, by which time it had spread throughout the island. The custom continued to be faithfully observed in the northern half of the island, where the culture was conservative and much of the land unattractive; but its spread into the southern half was to some extent corrupted by influences from outside.

Further reading

J. Cesari, *Corse des origines* (Paris, 1994).

J. Cesari, "Les dolmens de la Corse", *Archéologia*, no. 205 (September 1985), 32–45.

A. d'Anna *et al.*, "Les mégalithes de Corse: Un état de la question", in *La France des dolmens et des sépultures collectives*, ed. by Philippe Soulier (Paris, 1998), 90–105.

M. Hoskin *et al.*, "Orientations of Corsican dolmens", *JHA*, xxv (1994), 313–17, and "Further orientations of Corsican dolmens", *JHA*, xxvi (1995), 247–52.

M. Hoskin *et al.*, "The *tombe di giganti* and temples of Nur- aghic Sardinia", *AA*, no. 18 (1993), S1–26; M. Zedda *et al.*, "Orientations of 230 Sardinian *tombe di giganti*", *AA*, no. 21 (1996), S33–54; and Zedda and Hoskin, "Orientations of Sardinian Dolmens", *AA*, no. 22 (1997), S1–16.

G. Lilliu, *La civiltà dei Sardi: Dal neolitico all'età dei nuraghi* (Turin, 1967; 2nd edn, 1975).

G. Lilliu, *La civiltà dei Sardi dal paleolitico all'età dei nuraghi* (Rome, 1988).

G. Lilliu, *La civiltà nuragica* (Sassari, 1982).

Notes and references

1 An introduction to the prehistory of Corsica is Cesari, *Corse des origines*. For a survey with full bibliography see A. d'Anna *et al.*, "Les mégalithes de Corse".

2 Cesari, *Corse des origines*, 56.

3 Lilliu, *La civiltà dei Sardi*, 30ff.

4 Cesari, "Les dolmens de la Corse".

5 Fig. 4, p. 93, in A. d'Anna *et al.*, "Les mégalithes de Corse".

6 Lilliu, *La civiltà dei Sardi dal paleolitico*, 68.

7 Lilliu (*ibid.*, 517) speaks of there being 321 extant *tombe di giganti*, but we believe the number to be at least 400.

8 We explore the geographical distribution of *tombe di giganti* with various ranges of orientation in Zedda *et al.*, "Orientations of 230 Sardinian *tombe di giganti*".

9 Lilliu, *La civiltà nuragica*, 12, 106–11. Lilliu now suggests that the megaron temples may be fourteenth or thirteenth century.

10 Lilliu, *La civiltà dei Sardi dal paleolitico*, 27–114 and *passim*.

13

Malta, Sicily and Pantelleria

The Mediterranean is divided down the middle by the long peninsula of Italy and the island of Sicily. Separated by only a narrow straight, they provide our chosen area of study, the west Mediterranean, with a natural land frontier to the east.

Surprisingly, throughout the length and breadth of Italy dolmens are rare. The only region where they are present in any quantity is Puglia, which includes the 'heel' of Italy; this is the easternmost tip of the peninsula, and so the Puglia dolmens lie outside our area. And while Sicily has tombs of various kinds, which we shall briefly discuss, it seems — today, at least — to be wholly bereft of true dolmens.

Between the western tip of Sicily, and Tunisia on the African mainland, is a channel a mere 150km wide, and in this channel lies the tiny island of Pantelleria. Pantelleria has tombs but they are not truly megalithic, being made of piles of small boulders, with (in most cases) multiple chambers within. To the southeast of Pantelleria, and within sight of the southern tip of Sicily, are Malta and Gozo. Here there are dolmens — at least, that is the majority opinion — and so it is with these that we begin.

The dolmens of Malta and Gozo

In contrast to the magnificent temples that we discussed in Chapter 3, the dolmens of the Maltese islands have been described by two archaeoastronomers, Emília Pásztor and Curt Roslund, as "trivial and insignificant" in appearance.[1] They write:

> They consist of roughly-shaped capstones of local limestone measuring up to 4 metres in length, supported by a few uprights. Seen from a distance, they easily merge with the background of the landscape, as they seldom reach a height of one metre above the ground. Some sixteen dolmens have been recorded on the islands, most of them in a ruinous condition.

The monuments are known as dolmens partly because of their structural similarity to funerary monuments in other countries whose purpose is not in question, but Pásztor and Roslund argue that there is no compelling evidence that they are indeed true dolmens. They remark that there is no record of human bones having ever been found inside them, and in the case of the smaller ones the tiny space beneath the capstone makes it unlikely that they were used for repeated burials. David Trump, who was Curator of Archaeology at the National Museum of Malta and

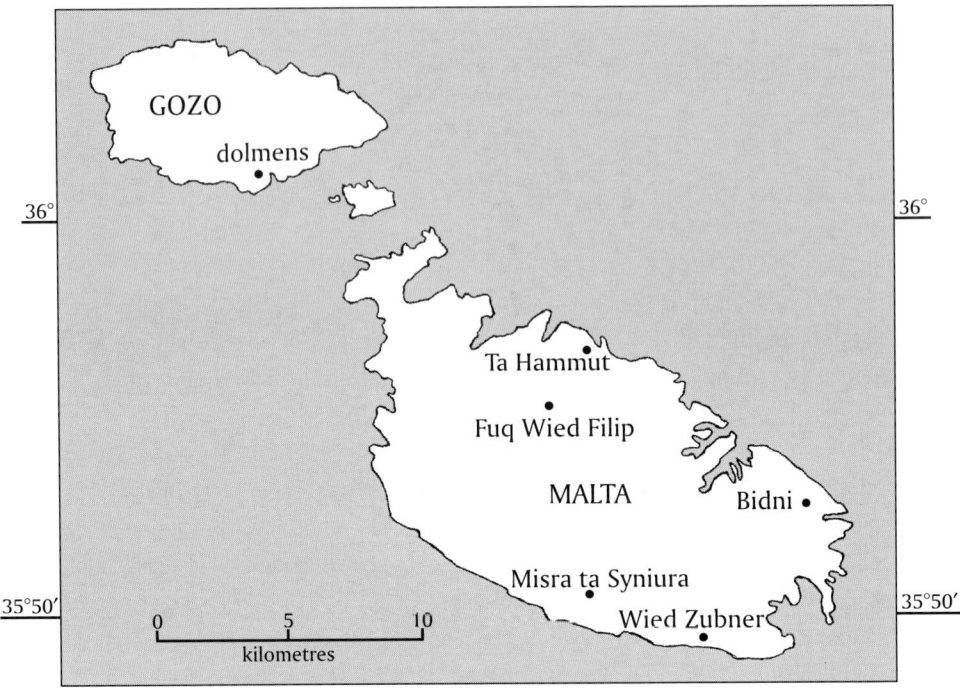

Locations of dolmens of Malta and Gozo.

knows the islands intimately, speaks of one as having "a slab of rock so low to the ground that only a scoop in the rock beneath it gave the space for even cremation burials".[2] But he is satisfied that they were for the dead: of the dolmen of Wied Znuber he writes, "It is a burial chamber thought to belong to the Early Bronze Age, a little after 2500 BC, and consists of a flat slab of rock some 1.0 metres across, supported horizontally above the ground on smaller rocks".[3] This date implies that the dolmen was erected after the collapse of the complex social structure that facilitated the building of the great temples, and presumably the tomb served the needs of no more than an extended family. There is, it seems, no correlation between the locations of the dolmens and those of the temples, and only in a couple of instances are dolmens and temples within walking distance of each other.

Pásztor and Roslund, who studied just seven of these structures, tell us that the majority of their monuments were found on the tops of ridges and that they commanded panoramic vistas of the valley below. "This may indicate that the dolmens were deliberately positioned as territorial markers by the local communities in an attempt to express their authority and domination over the land seen from the dolmens" — though this can be said of many funerary dolmens elsewhere, most of which are far more conspicuous in the landscape.

Pásztor and Roslund's measures of orientation did not lend themselves to any easy astronomical interpretation, and they opted for a topographical explanation:

(*Above*) Ta Hammut 2.

(*Below*) Gozo Dolmen 1. (Photographs courtesy of Giorgia Foderà Serio.)

An entirely different picture emerges when a relationship between the long axes and dominant landscape features is considered. With only one exception, all dolmens studied follow closely the landscape contours at the sites.... The same correspondence is seen for the valley stream below the dolmens.... To build on level ground along a height contour would of course have been in the interest of the builders, but most Maltese dolmens are located on flat land. Only the Ta Hammut dolmen is built on a gentle slope. Remembering that dolmens are often placed near ridge edges, the contours instead mark the course of valleys and the flow of streams on the valley floors. It is here suggested that the erection, placement and orientation of the Maltese dolmens might have been part of a water cult to fertility of the valleys.

The authors are to be applauded for their refusal to force an astronomical interpretation onto their measures. However, their acquaintance with so very few dolmens — less than half of the tiny handful surviving — left the question open. Accordingly, in 1999 Giorgia Foderà Serio and Juan Antonio Belmonte revisited the islands and examined fifteen dolmens, most if not all of those surviving.

In their opinion, the close similarity of the Maltese monuments to confirmed dolmens elsewhere corroborates Trump's verdict that these structures had a funerary purpose. As to their orientations, Foderà and Belmonte accept that since the monuments are crude and the supporting stones are separated by gaps, in some cases the intended entrance is ambiguous; their measures (generously supplied for publication in Table 13.1, where they appear for the first time) therefore include 'best guesses'. Nevertheless, at least 80% of the orientations lie in the southeast quadrant, and this proportion seems much too high to have arisen by chance or for reasons of topography.

The most likely conclusion, therefore, is that the Maltese structures were indeed dolmens and that they followed the SR/SC pattern so widespread elsewhere.

Sicily

It has been hard to believe that there were no dolmens in the vast island of Sicily, located as it is between the dolmen-rich lands of Sardinia and Tunisia. The matter has at last been investigated, by Giorgia Foderà in collaboration with Sebastiano Tusa, a leading Sicilian archaeologist, and they have kindly made their conclusions available in advance of publication: that although tombs of various kinds are found in scattered locations, only in very limited areas of the island are they to be found in quantity. Furthermore, all these tombs are either true hypogea, dolmenic hypogea, or paradolmens that incorporate natural features: so far as is known, no true Sicilian dolmen exists.[4]

Not far from the western tip of the island, at Roccazzo, is an extensive group of graves dating from the late Neolithic (fourth/third millennia BC). There are some two hundred in all, concentrated into fourteen hectares of an elevated plateau that commands a fine view in every direction. The constructors cut a circular shaft some 80cm in diameter vertically downwards into the limestone bedrock, to a depth of around a metre. They then struck sideways from this shaft, in

A typical hypogeic grave at Roccazzo.

a direction of their own choosing, and cut out an oval chamber large enough to contain a single body. The entrance was then closed with a near-vertical slab and the chamber sealed by filling the shaft to perhaps half its height with limestone dust mixed with water.

Although these little hypogeic graves are very different from the communal stone tombs to which this book is dedicated, each does have a freely-chosen orientation. At Roccazzo, 34 tombs could be measured, and except for one that faced 12°, all the orientations lay within the semicircle from 38° to 218°, the majority being SR/SC. At Tranchina, however, a site not far away, 28 of the 30 tombs had measurable directions, and of these no fewer than 26 (92·9%) faced between 69° and 182°, the two exceptions having orientation 240° and 250° respectively. The Tranchina range is classic SR/SC — indeed, it is normal today for the sun as it climbs in the sky actually to shine into the chamber of an excavated tomb — and it is remarkable to find so familiar an orientation pattern, in tombs very different from those we have studied elsewhere.

There is a third such necropolis, that of Ciachea at Capaci near Palermo. This is later in date, belonging to the second half of the third millennium, and the tombs have multiple chambers leading off each shaft. In consequence the orientations are widely scattered: it seems the earlier focus on the sun as it climbed in the sky had all but disappeared.

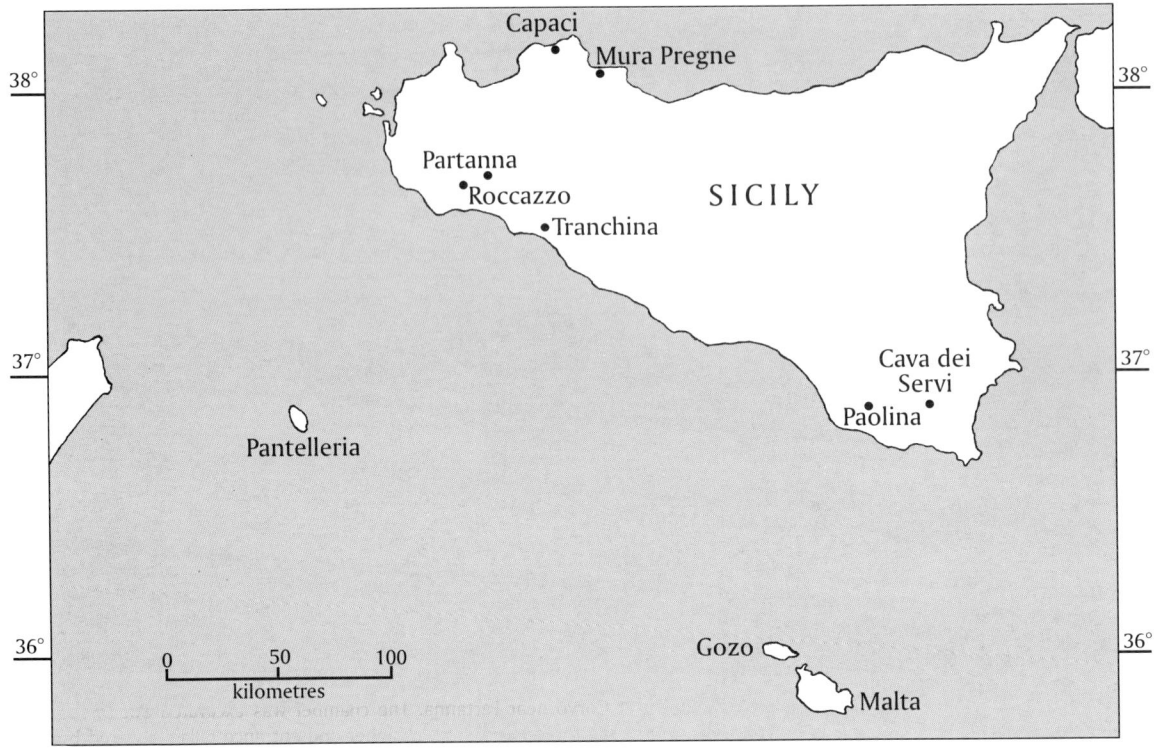

Malta and Gozo, Pantelleria, and Sicily, with the locations of the Sicilian sites discussed in the text.

The beginning of the Bronze Age at the end of the third millennium saw the development of tombs that were still hypogeic in character but were communal and beginning to incorporate megaliths in their structure. There are four of these at Paolina, on the southern tip of the island, from where Malta can be seen. In each a short dromos leads to an artificial cave, and the orientations are 163°, 169°, 169° and 179° respectively. Although the number of tombs is very small, the orientations are SC and their uniformity is striking.

The beginning of the second millennium saw a further evolution away from hypogea and towards structures that incorporated megaliths. In the west of the island, around Partanna, are over a dozen sizeable communal tombs in which the chamber is again excavated out of the bedrock. But whereas the roof of the chamber itself is sometimes bedrock, it is more usually a megalithic slab. The entrance is sometimes formed of two orthostatic pillars, sometimes of bedrock whose shape resembles orthostats; and there is a long dromos, which may be excavated in the bedrock but may also be lined with orthostats. One has the anomalous orientation of 329°, but three faced sunrise (orientations 101°, 114° and 114° respectively), while ten face between 126° and 224°. Tombs of similar construction are to be found in Sardinia.

Finally, there are three surviving tombs that appear at first sight to be dolmens, but are in fact paradolmens, incorporating natural features that helped dictate the orientation. Two survive at

(*Above*) The dolmenic hypogeum of Pizzo dell'Aquila, at Corvo near Partanna. The chamber was excavated out of the bedrock, entrance pillars placed in position (as seen in the foreground), and chamber and entrance pillars covered by an immense capstone. To the bottom left is the beginning of the dromos. (*Below*) The paradolmen of Mura Pregne. The 'sidestone' seen centre-left, which is a metre in width, has been adapted from a natural rock.

A typical sese, with one of the entrances.

Cava dei Servi near Modica towards the southern tip (orientations 59° and 64°), though others there are known to have been destroyed by forestation. A third, Dolmen di Mura Pregne, is on the north coast, to the southeast of Palermo; a natural block has been adapted to form one sidestone, and the tomb faces 171° (or just possibly 351°, though in that case it would face uphill).

The sesi of Pantelleria

The small volcanic island of Pantelleria lies to the southwest of Sicily, and is only 70km from the African coast. On the western tip of the island, a little over 2km south of the modern town of Pantelleria, is a major settlement of the early Bronze Age, dating from 1800–1600 BC. The settlement lies beside the sea on a low cliff, and a considerable section of the defensive wall that guarded it on the land side still survives. The dwellings of the settlement, which is estimated to have contained perhaps two thousand inhabitants, are sited on the lava flow of an extinct volcano — presumably so as not to encroach on the fertile agricultural land that lies close by, beyond the edge of the flow.

The cliff on which the settlement is situated runs south-southeast–north-northwest, with the sea to the west. To the east the land rises steadily up the lava flow. On this slope, outside the walls of the settlement, are to be found the remains of over fifty communal tombs known as 'sesi'. The sesi are roughly constructed of rocks of lava, and are oval in shape, though without any pronounced axis. They are some 4 to 15 metres in diameter, except for one, the Sese Grande, which is about 20 metres across and was evidently used for prestigious burials. Each sese has one or (usually) more passages constructed at ground level, and at the end of each passage is a small chamber. The Sese Grande has no fewer than twelve passages, each leading to its own chamber deep inside the monument; two of the twelve share the same external entrance and separate within the monument. It will be clear to the reader that the parallels that have been drawn between these monuments and the nuraghi of Sardinia, or the navetas of Menorca, are fanciful.

The sesi were last studied a century ago,[5] and so it seemed desirable to re-examine the monuments to establish whether — despite the unpromising indications of the published plans — the orientations of the entrances to the passages were in any way non-random. Accordingly, in June 1991 I visited the island with Giorgia Foderà and Sebastiano Tusa.[6] We located and examined 42 sesi, and we believe that only a handful eluded us. Many of the sesi are partly ruined, and the whole area is deep in vegetation that makes investigation hazardous. I discovered this the hard way, when I took a tumble on a sese and brought down several of the small boulders on top of me, to find myself ignominiously pinned to the ground until rescued. Because of the vegetation we were able to identify only a small proportion of the passages that must originally have been present. However, our sample is probably representative, and we think there is no point in pursuing the question of orientations further until the time comes when the area is cleared of

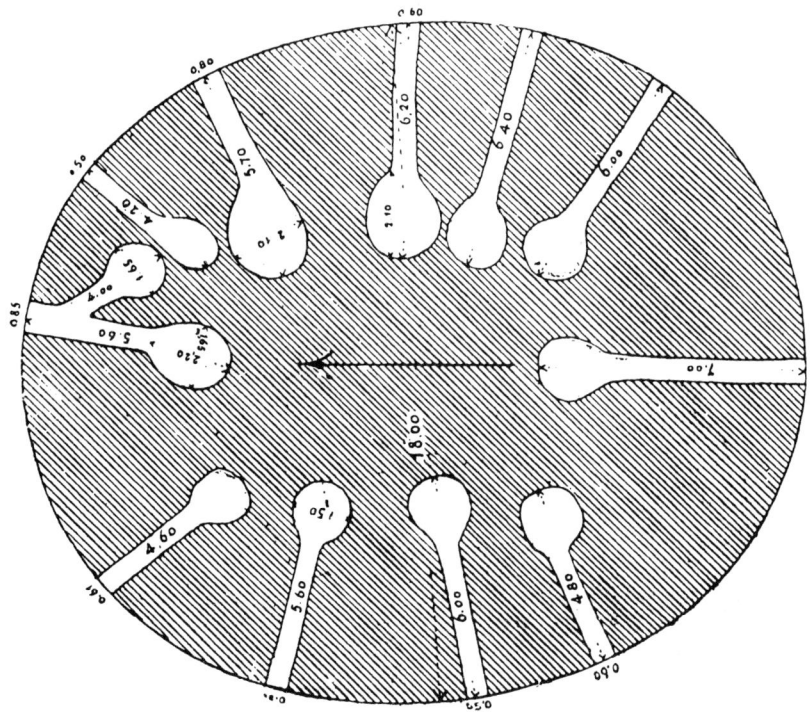

The ground plan of the Sese Grande (from Orsi, "Pantelleria", Fig. 39).

vegetation and archaeological excavation begins.

As will already be evident, the orientations of the passages (most of which have collapsed) are crudely defined, and allowance also has to be made for the possibility that our compass measures were affected by magnetic anomaly due to the lava. As a check on our method we remeasured the Sese Grande at the end of our visit, and we concluded that our results can be relied upon to some 5°. The orientations are given in Table 13.2. We see that two-fifths of the orientations are concentrated in little more than the quadrant from east to south (20 of the 49 orientations lie in the range 88° to 182°), but this may be associated with the direction of the upward slope of the lava flow, which is somewhat south of east. There is no indication that the builders constructed the passages with astronomical directions in mind, or that certain orientations were excluded. This negative conclusion was expected in the light of the nineteenth-century investigation, and it supports the theory that these people came from Sicily where their tombs were cut into cliffs without regard to the orientations, and that this hiatus in their burial customs persisted when they settled on Pantelleria.

Further reading

J. D. Evans, *The prehistoric antiquities of the Maltese islands* (London, 1971).

J. D. Evans, "The dolmens of Malta and the origins of the Tarxien culture", *Proceedings of the Prehistoric Society*, xxii (1956), 85–101.

P. Orsi, "Pantelleria: Risultati di una missione archeologica", *Monumenti antichi* (R. Accademia dei Lincei), ix (1899), cols 193–284, espec. cols 218–39.

David Trump, "Megalithic architecture in Malta", in *Megalithic monuments of Western Europe*, ed. by Colin Renfrew (London, 1983), 64–77.

S. Tusa, G. Foderà Serio and M. Hoskin, "Orientations of the *sesi* of Pantelleria", *AA*, no. 17 (1992), S15–20.

Notes and references

1   Emília Pásztor and Curt Roslund, "Orientation of Maltese 'dolmens'", *Journal of European archaeology*, v (1997), 183–9.

2   D. H. Trump, *Malta: An archaeological guide* (2nd edn, Valetta, 1988), 133.

3   *Ibid.*, 92.

4   A monument discovered by two amateur archaeologists in 1983 but now destroyed may have been a true dolmen. The discovery was reported in "Le ruspe travolgono un pezioso dolmen", *La Domenica* (Syracuse), 25 Sept. 1983. According to the unpublished thesis of Salvatore Piccolo, "I dolmen nella Sicilia Sud-orientale", Palermo University, 1994/95, the monument was at Currigi, Solarino, and Rodolfo Striccoli of the University of Bari considered it a true dolmen and similar to ones found in Puglia.

5   Orsi, "Pantelleria".

6   Tusa, Foderà Serio and Hoskin, "Orientations of the *sesi*".

14

Tunisia, Algeria and Morocco

I viewed the African shores of the West Mediterranean from afar with something approaching trepidation, for there seemed no reason to doubt that this *terra ignota* would prove to contain large numbers of dolmens contemporary with those of Iberia and France on the opposite shores, and I felt ill-equipped to investigate them. Fortunately Juan Antonio Belmonte of Tenerife, whose work has featured more than once in these pages, was planning to work in the area as and when the political situation allowed, and was learning some Arabic for the purpose. In the event, he and colleagues paid a visit to Tunisia in 1997 and one to Morocco the following year (though the dictates of self-preservation forced them to postpone Algeria to what one hopes will be a more peaceful future).

Algeria therefore remains a gap in our survey, which we partially fill by using work published over a generation ago by French archaeologists. As to Morocco, we rely on Belmonte's investigations, which drew on previous surveys by Maria Antonia Perera, head of the Heritage Division for the Island of Lanzarote, and appear to be reasonably complete; if so, tombs relevant to our interests are few and very late.

Tunisia has more to offer. Belmonte and his colleagues visited a number of sites, though none was thought earlier than the first millennium BC. Their results were enough to whet the appetite, but they had worked without the *Atlas préhistorique de la Tunisie* (which divides the country into no fewer than 46 regions, and dedicates one fascicule to each region), and so had been unaware of many important sites. Giorgia Foderà and I therefore visited the country twice in 1998, on the second occasion with Sebastiano Tusa whose Arabic was to prove as valuable as his archaeology. As in Belmonte's visit, all the sites we investigated belonged — with one important exception — to the first millennium BC, or even the first millennium AD: the dolmens of Tunisia are far later than the European and island tombs we have studied in the previous chapters, and most are proto-historic rather then prehistoric. Nevertheless, they are often numerous and in good condition, and offer materials for interesting exercises in archaeotopography if not in archaeoastronomy.

Our visits were more eventful than we would have wished. On the first occasion we took a car by boat from Sicily, unaware of the length of the formalities awaiting us on entry into Tunis, where Tunisian drivers of cars loaded with goods they had purchased in Sicily were haggling with customs officials over the duty payable on each item. We were also unaware that lead-free petrol is unknown in the interior, and when we realized this we had only just enough in the tank to reach a frontier station that sold 'green' fuel.

An archaeoastronomer off duty. While near Makhtar we became guests of a Berber family who lived in a village surrounding the remains of a Roman temple. Here an elder of the village is instructing Giorgia Foderà in a game similar to draughts, played (presumably without a break since Roman times) on an incised stone in front of the temple.

During our second visit, an enthusiastic local insisted on taking us up a mountain to show us a monument known to him alone, and this despite our protests that the hour was late and darkness about to fall. Darkness did fall, before we reached the monument, and our guide then declared himself totally lost. Fortunately the bleat of a distant sheep revealed the presence of a shepherd, whose knowledge of the terrain enabled us to extricate ourselves from the prospect of a night in the open. On another occasion a village shopkeeper showed us the track to monuments that are fully described in the *Atlas préhistorique* and publicly accessible. Nevertheless, when we revisited his shop to make a purchase, we learned to our dismay that our benefactor had since been interrogated in hostile fashion by security police from a town many kilometres distant, who had been informed of our presence in the area.

Tunisia

Our fieldwork in Tunisia centred on the market town of Makhtar, well to the interior of the country. It has a vast Roman archaeological site, in addition to earlier remains. Our most remarkable discovery, however, was some 16km to the southeast of Makhtar, on the high plateau above the village of Kesra. Modern Kesra lies alongside the main road in the valley below; old Kesra clings to the hillside, which is dominated by a Byzantine castle. Dolmens had been reported on the hillside itself, but we found no trace of these and we think they were destroyed by road construction. However, we explored the plateau above, and found Roman and pre-Roman remains of various kinds amidst the scattered dwellings. On the highest ground (35°48′42″N, 9°22′25″E), greatly to our surprise, we came across the remains of what in France we would unhesitatingly have termed an *allée couverte*, with backstone (the centre of which had been carefully smoothed), three orthostats aligned to form one side and one surviving orthostat from the other, and a low threshhold to separate the rectangular chamber from the corridor. Nearby was an altar. Some 40 metres away was a second such tomb, less complete but with a capstone *in situ*, and Tusa

The best-preserved of the '*allées couvertes*' above Kesra. In the foreground are three aligned orthostats forming one side of the chamber and passage, and beyond them is the backstone with its smoothed centre. Two capstones have fallen and lie on the ground. To the left in the middle distance is another such tomb.

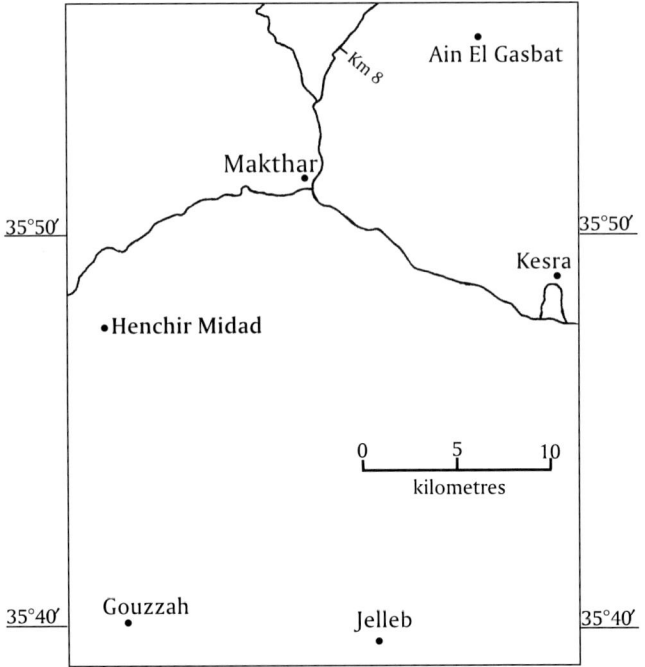

The area around Makthar with the sites mentioned in the text.

was able to identify two further galleried tombs nearby, in ruined condition. The orientations of these four tombs were, respectively, 82° (altitude 1°), 88° (1°), 96° (4°) and 71° (4°). In Europe, this would be a classic SR pattern for tombs at high elevations, in areas that offered pasture during the summer months. We have no evidence as to the date of these tombs beyond their structure, but the early or middle second millennium BC seems likely. It was by extraordinary luck that we came across them, deep in the interior of Tunisia, and if they do indeed have European associations there must surely be (or have been) similar monuments in areas nearer the coast.

We came across isolated dolmens of simple and crude construction in a number of places around Makthar, some being listed in the *Atlas* while others we found by chance. Northeast of Makthar is the settlement of Ain El Gasbat, where three modern Islamic graves (35°56′27″N, 9°18′34″E) had miniature symbolic dolmens placed in front of them, a charming example of the persistence of tradition. We found one dolmen near the settlement itself (35°56′23″N, 9°18′54″E), two on the plateau above (35°56′33″N, 9°19′12″E), and two more (35°55′15″N, 9°19′38″E; 35°55′06″N, 9°20′49″E) alongside the road to the nearby Roman town of Essfina. These had orientations 171°, 216°, 221°, 226° and 245°, respectively, with low skyline altitudes. Such measurements suggest a pattern. But two similar dolmens we discovered a few kilometres away (35°55′17″N, 9°13′36″E, above the main road from Makthar to Siliana and 8km from Makthar), faced 88° and 146°, while at Gouzzah, southwest of Makthar, there were dolmens (35°40′01″N, 9°06′01″E) facing 286°, 289°, and either 46° (if looking downhill) or 226° (uphill). Our growing

One of the better-preserved dolmens at Jelleb. Note that the ground rises behind the tomb, as usual at Jelleb.

doubts as to whether we were dealing with an astronomically-inspired pattern were confirmed at Jelleb, to the south of Makthar. Four tombs at the corners of a rectangular array there were difficult to interpret, but five simple dolmens nearby faced 59° (35°39'35"N, 9°14'27"E), 176°, 189°, 228° and 349° respectively. The reason for their orientations was unmistakable: every one faced downhill.

In the suburbs of Makthar itself, on either side of the road to Kesra, is a cluster of megalithic tombs of somewhat more complex construction. Belmonte and colleagues considered three to have orientations between 135½° and 169½°,[1] but on our first visit we thought the tombs no longer measurable, and by the time of our second visit a few weeks later they had been degraded even further.

Some 12km west-southwest of Makthar is the extraordinary site of Henchir Midad (35°47'N, 9°05'E). On the slopes above the water courses are the remains of a settlement of the Punic/ Roman period together with rows and rows of dolmens, some two hundred in total. The typical dolmen has a strictly rectangular chamber formed of five massive and carefully-shaped stones: a backstone, one stone to each side, one across the front with an access hole in a corner, and a capstone. Many of these dolmens are in excellent condition and have well-defined orientations; they line up on the slopes, side-by-side, in ranks one above another, and the view of the site as

A typical dolmen at Henchir Midad. It is formed of four orthostats, the one in front having a rectangular hole for access. This particular tomb has lost its capstone.

a whole is most remarkable. Curiously, however, it engenders little of the excitement that one experiences when exploring far less impressive sites in Europe or on the islands, for the orientation of one tomb is much the same as that of its neighbours to left and right (and above and below), and it seems evident at a glance that the tombs face downhill. True, the majority face southerly, but so does the site as a whole. In the southwest sector, where the slope is easterly or northerly, the tombs face easterly or northerly. We took some forty sample orientations — the tombs of one row, for example, faced 177°, 177°, 178°, 185°, 186°, 187°, 190°, 190°, 190°, 190°, 192° — but then decided that the topographical motivation for the orientations was so evident that our time would be better spent elsewhere.

Algeria

Because of the troubled political conditions prevailing in this former French colony, it would be folly to attempt archaeological fieldwork there at the present time. Fortunately, we do possess accounts from the mid-twentieth century of the important group of dolmens of Beni-Messous,[2] and in one of them the author, J.-P. Savary, pays special attention to their orientations.[3] Beni-Messous lies a dozen kilometres to the west of Algiers, and some two kilometres or so from the sea, which is visible from much of the area. Most of the dolmens surviving when the articles were written lay on an extensive plateau, but others lay on either side of a wadi and one on an adjacent plateau. There is little hard evidence as to their date, but Savary estimates 1000 BC.

The majority of the dolmens that survived in good condition resembled the 'simple dolmens' of the European mainland, with a rectangular chamber a little over 1m in width and from 1½m to 2m in length, formed of a backstone and, internal to the backstone, a single orthostat to each side; a capstone was *in situ* in a surprising number of cases. Dolmen II, however, had on each side two orthostats, of similar size, and a capstone that extended over all four sidestones. Two of the best-preserved tombs, Dolmens XIV and XV, displayed remains of a corridor equal in width to the chamber, and it is possible that such a corridor was present in all or most of them.

Because of the rectangular shape of the chambers, the orientations of these dolmens were often well defined, and Savary took great care over their measurement, citing even the very day when he measured the axis of the tomb relative to magnetic north. His 13 measures, corrected for magnetic variation and rounded to the nearest degree, are listed in Table 14.1. The tombs faced the eastern horizon, within an arc of one-fifth of a circle, between 86° and 158°. Nine faced within the range of sunrise, the interpretation uppermost in Savary's mind, for his orientation diagram includes a calendar of sunrise directions and he discusses the times of year when mortality was likely to be highest. But four faced south of sunrise, and so in our notation the tombs are SR/SC.

It may very well be that the rising or climbing sun did indeed provide the motivation that was in the minds of the builders, but it is scarcely possible from a single site to claim this with any conviction. We must suspend judgement until conditions permit the examination of parallel sites in the region, if such exist.

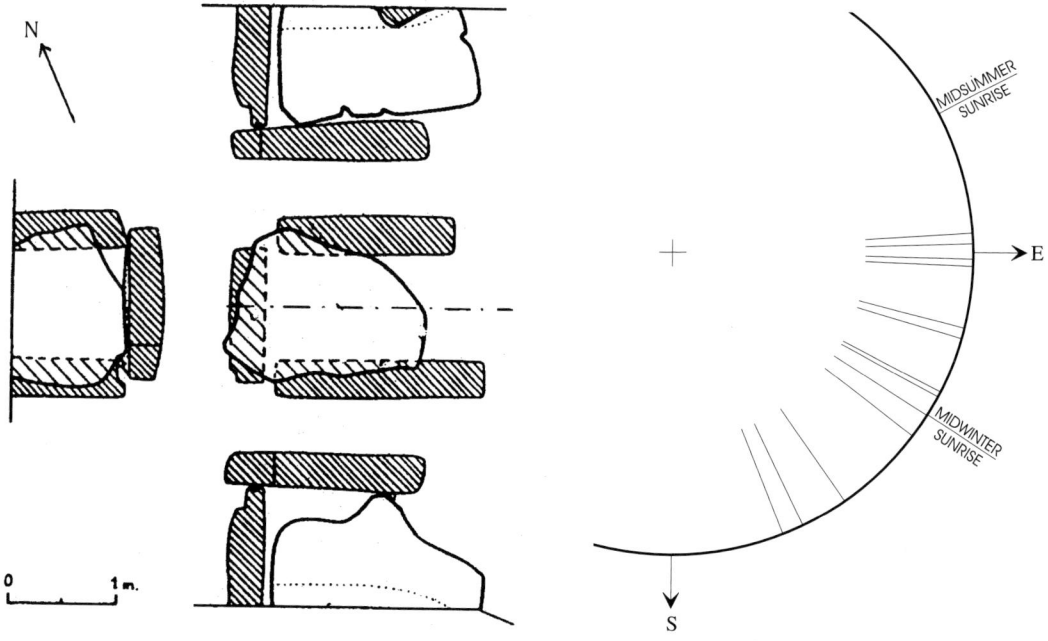

Dolmen I at Beni-Messous (after J.-P. Savery).   Orientations of 13 dolmens at Beni-Messous.

Morocco

Its geographical proximity makes Morocco of special interest to students of the prehistory of the Canary Islands, and we owe what little we know of the archaeotopography of the region to a group of scholars based in the Islands and led by Belmonte. They recently reported[4] on the orientations of 41 tumuli in two necropolises on the borders of the Sahara Desert, at Taouz al Qadim and Foum al Rjam (for location see map on page 4). They had intended to examine five such necropolises, on both sides of the frontier between Morocco and Algeria, but work on the two in Algeria had to be postponed until conditions in the country improve, and it transpired that the remaining one of the three in Morocco was largely destroyed.

Foum al Rjam is the name of a mountain pass near a bend in the Draa River, and many hundreds of tumuli are found on the eastern and western sides of the pass, on the crests and at the borders of the ravines to the east, and on the high plateau to the west. Most of the tumuli are simple cairns, but on the highest places — the crests to the east and the plateau to the west — there are more elaborate tumuli that clearly represent prestige burials. These tumuli, fewer than one in ten of the total, are known as 'skylight-tumuli' because they have a so-called skylight that is of unknown purpose; it is too small to give access to human beings, and sometimes it is closed by a large flat stone with a separate altar for offerings or holocausts. Belmonte and colleagues visited

No. 21 of the 'skylight-tumuli' at Foum al Rjam, and one of the best preserved of the eastern section of the necropolis (photograph courtesy of César Esteban).

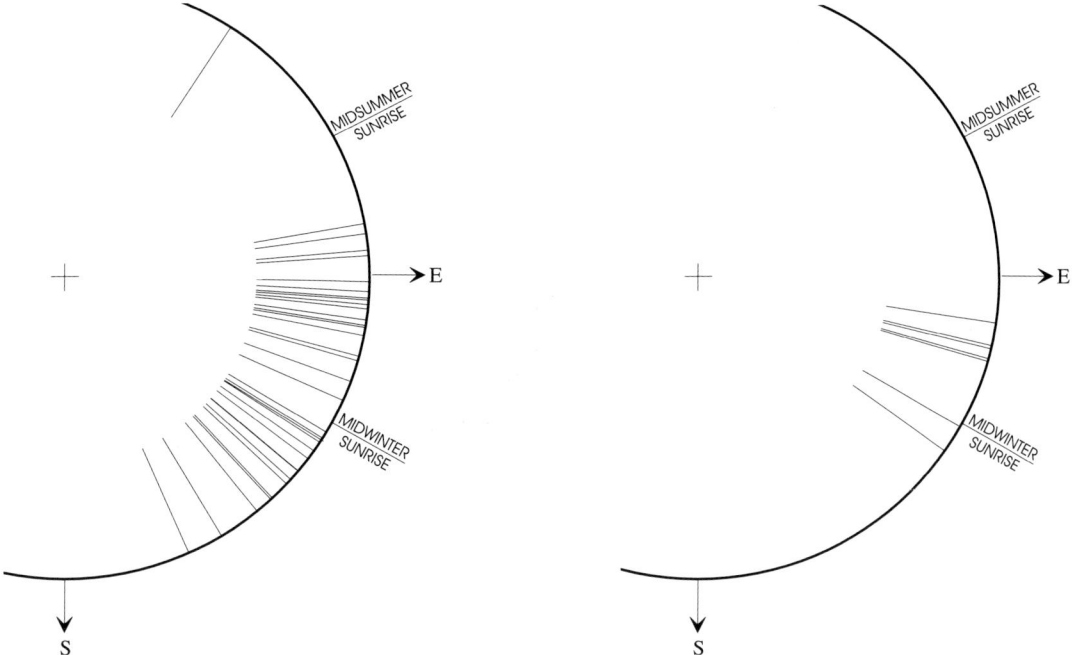

Orientations of 34 'skylight-tumuli' at Foum al Rjam.   Orientations of 7 'chapel-tumuli' at Taouz al Qadim.

some 300 tumuli, taking data for all the skylight-tumuli in the eastern section of the necropolis that were measurable, 23 in total, and for 11 of the 20 that were measurable in the western section; health problems prevented them from measuring the remaining nine.

Their measures for these 34 skylight-tumuli are shown in Table 14.2. All face the eastern horizon, and it is difficult not to be impressed with the remarkable similarity between their range and that of the Beni-Messous tombs in Algeria. One skylight-tumulus has a wholly anomalous orientation of 33°, but the remaining 33 all face between 82° and 156°, virtually identical with the 86°–158° of the thirteen tombs of Beni-Messous.

With two exceptions the measurable skylight-tumuli are located on crests and mountain tops, with a clear view of the eastern horizon, and this encourages an astronomical interpretation of the data. However, it could be argued that in the southeast one can see the Draa River after its change of direction, with associated palm-tree forests, and for a necropolis on the edge of the Sahara this might be incentive enough for the choice of orientation. On the other hand, the investigators find that the histogram of declinations (which of course take into account skyline altitudes) has peaks around 0° and –30°, the first being the direction of the equinox sunrise, and the second within a few degrees of midwinter sunrise and the extreme southerly moonrise. They are unable to explain these peaks on purely topographical grounds and therefore prefer an archaeoastronomical interpretation, while admitting that the evidence is far from conclusive.

The second necropolis, Taouz al Qadim, is on a rocky hill some 4km from the oasis of Taouz. In the judgement of Belmonte and colleagues, nearby alphabetical inscriptions combine with considerations of style to suggest construction dates between the third or second centuries BC and the arrival of Islam in the seventh century AD, though other investigators place the Taouz al Qadim necropolis no earlier than the first century AD.[5]

The necropolis consists of eleven large tumuli, four of which were cairns and so without orientation, while seven were 'chapel-tumuli'. The chapel-tumuli are those with so-called chapels to one side, and they appear to have been the tombs of prestigious chiefs or priests. The chapels (Table 14.3) may well have been places where the living slept so as to commune with the ancestor. They are always to the east or southeast of the tumulus, and all are prominently located with a view of the eastern horizon. Six of the seven faced sunrise in the winter months, while the seventh nominally faced too far south; but the poor condition of the monument makes this a doubtful exception to the rule that these monuments faced sunrise.

It seems, therefore, that both the Foum al Rjam and the Taouz al Qadim tombs face directions that might be described as easterly/southeasterly, and it is tempting to characterize them as SR/SC and SR respectively. But we are dealing with just two restricted sites; and as Belmonte and colleagues rightly remark, the orientations at Foum al Rjam may be directed to the Draa River, while the number of tombs at Taouz al Qadim is small. However, the similarity between the ranges at Foum al Rjam and at Beni-Messous in Algeria is remarkable, and suggests an SR/SC hypothesis to be tested in Algeria when conditions permit.

Further reading

Atlas préhistorique de la Tunisie, published in Rome in fascicules by École Française de Rome.

J. A. Belmonte et al., "Mediterranean archaeoastronomy and archaeotopography: Pre-Roman tombs of Africa Proconsularis", AA, no. 23 (1998), S7–24.

J. A. Belmonte et al., "Pre-Islamic burial monuments in northern and Saharan Morocco", AA, no. 24 (1999), S21–34.

G. Camps, Aux origines de la Berberie: Monuments et rites funéraires protohistoriques (Paris, 1961).

J.-P. Savary, "Monuments en pierres sèches de Fadnoun", Mémoires C. R. A. H. E. Algérie, vi (1966), 43–48.

J.-P. Savary, "L'architecture et l'orientation des dolmens de Beni Messous", Lybica, xvii (1969), 271–330.

Notes and references

1. Belmonte et al., "Mediterranean archaeoastronomy", Table 3.

2. Savary, "L'architecture"; G. Camps, "Les dolmens de Beni-Messous", Lybica, i (1953), 329–72; idem, "Des dolmens à vingt kilométres d'Alger", Algéria, n.s., no. 37 (1954), 5–10.

3. Savary, "L'architecture".

4. Belmonte et al., "Pre-Islamic burial monuments".

5. G. Camps, "Djorf Torba", Encyclopédie Berbère, xvi (1997), 2477–88.

15

Retrospect: Funerary Customs of Orientation in Mediterranean Prehistory

In the last ten chapters we have presented the orientations of over two-and-a-half thousand pre-historic communal tombs of the central and west Mediterranean. What picture has emerged?

Until the protohistoric period, in the last centuries before Christ, the tombs of the islands of Malta, Sicily and Pantelleria and of the north African coastal regions were few in number, and heterogeneous in type. Not always is there evidence that the builders were following any custom of orientation; and nowhere is it certain that the custom, if any, was astronomically motivated. This leaves us with three geographical areas, all rich in tombs whose orientations were demonstrably governed by the sky, for they display remarkable consistency over vast areas: the Iberian peninsula, southern France, and the islands of Corsica and Sardinia.

The Iberian Peninsula

As we noted at the end of our circuit of Iberia and the French Pyrenees (p. 127), 99·4% of the 324 tombs of west Iberia were SR/SC, and 96·9% were SR or almost so, mostly facing sunrise in the autumn/spring or winter. This is most easily explained on the hypothesis that tombs were laid out to face sunrise on the day that construction began.

In south and north Iberia (and neighbouring France), the orientations are SR/SC rather than specifically SR: 94·4% of the 390 tombs and 95·5% of the 221 tombs, respectively, faced either sunrise, or the sun while it was climbing in the sky or around culmination. As it is widely held that the west Iberian tombs include the oldest in the peninsula, it seems that the SR custom was relaxed as it spread, and became in many places SR/SC; this accords with our everyday experience, that customs are relaxed with the passage of time.

Southern France

In the French Causses outside of Ardèche and Gard, we reported measures of 597 simple dolmens and dolmens with vestibule, as well as 54 that are double or coudé and therefore have ambivalent orientations. Simple dolmens are modest tombs with a single stone to each side,

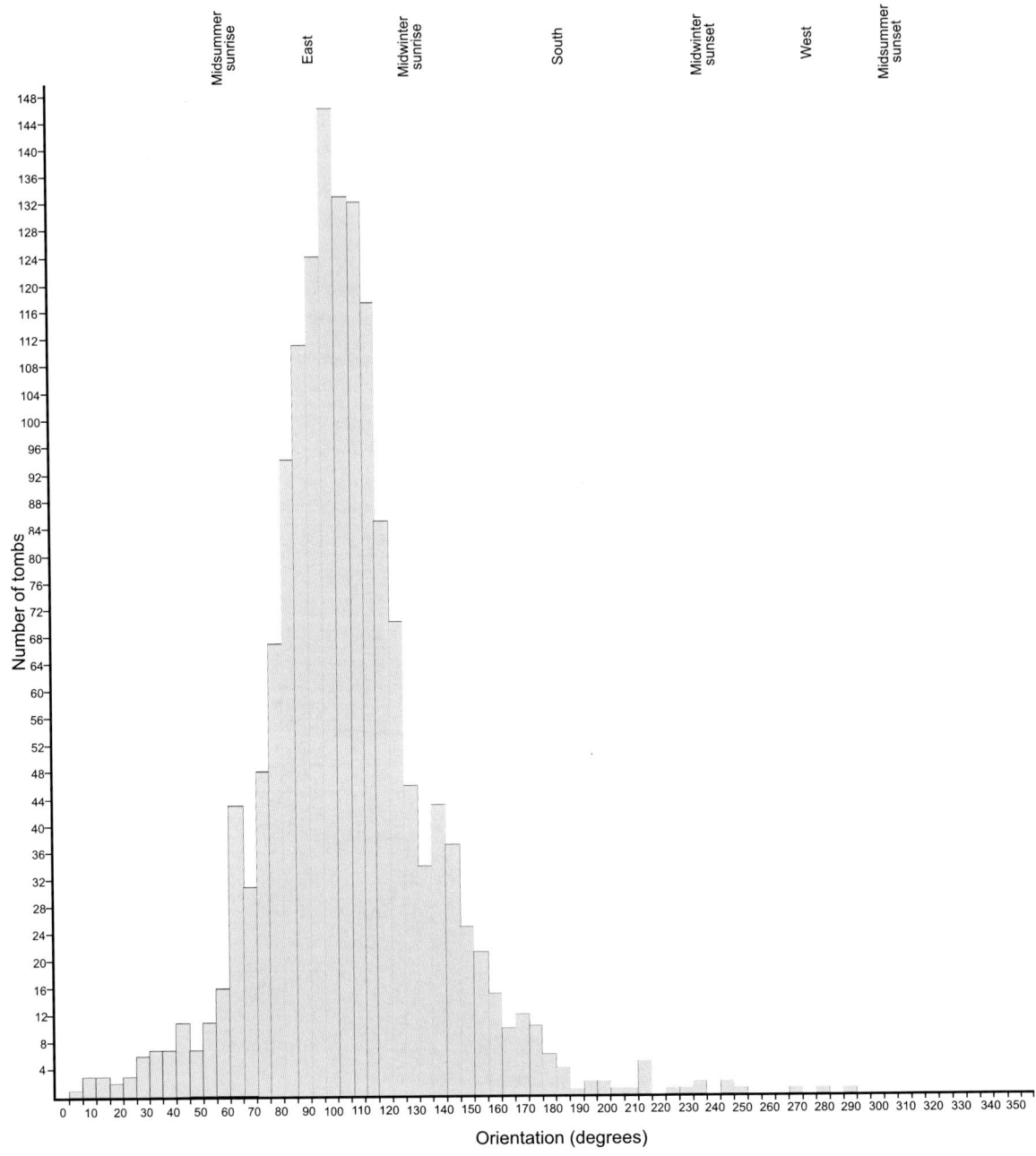

Histogram of the orientations of 1576 dolmens of Iberia and west-central France (Chapters 5–8, excluding Ardèche and Gard).

and disturbance of these sidestones over the millennia will lead to uncertainty in the measured orientations. Furthermore, the orientations listed are the work of archaeologists whose primary concerns lay elsewhere, and for some tombs I was reduced to measuring piecharts left by Yves

Chevalier. Nevertheless, 100% of the listed orientations lie in the range 0°–192°: westerly orientations are unknown. 37 tombs (6·2%) faced in the range 0°–60°, north of the range of sunrise; a mere 9 (1·5%) faced south of 166° and therefore around culmination. The remaining 551 (92·3%) faced in the range 60°–166°, towards sunrise or the sun when it was climbing in the sky.

In Provence and east Languedoc, in striking contrast, the tombs face westerly. We have orientations for 110 BR-dolmens and 103 L-dolmens. All the BR dolmens face in the range 168°–302°, virtually the mirror image of the SR/SC range of 60°–190° that we discussed above, and therefore to be characterized as SD/SS ('sun descending/sunset'). We followed Sauzade in arguing that a sunset custom was (for unknown reasons) adopted by the excavators of the great dolmenic hypogea and hypogeic dolmens at Fontvieille, and that their customs of both structure and orientation spread thence to east, north and west, becoming attenuated as they went, though most BR-dolmens continued to be SS rather than SD. We gave reasons for thinking that L-dolmens are later than BR-dolmens, and this is supported by their orientations; for just as in south and north Iberia the SR custom of west Iberia was relaxed to become SR/SC, so it seems the predominantly SS custom of the BR-dolmens was relaxed to become SD/SS among the L-dolmens.

In Gard and Ardèche, where the (normally east-facing) C-dolmens of the Causses shared territory with a handful of (normally west-facing) BR-dolmens, we found that the orientations of both became markedly southerly, and we interpreted this as arising from a *rapprochement* between the different customs.

More generally, in west Languedoc, Aude, Pyrénées-Orientales and across the mountains into east Cataluña, we found a mixture of orientations, over one-third of the tombs facing westerly and nearly two-thirds facing easterly. This confused situation seems the result of competing influences between the easterly customs that Cataluña shared with the rest of Iberia and the French Causses, and the westerly customs of Provence and east Languedoc. The offshore Balearic Islands, however, whose tombs face westerly, seem in this respect to have been subject to influence only from Mediterranean France.

Corsica and Sardinia

In southern Corsica and northern Sardinia we first encountered dolmens of classic construction, and then (in Sardinia) the counterparts of the *allées couvertes*. Almost all of them faced easterly, but with no apparent concern for sunrise as such. Instead, with one minor exception, the 32 dolmens and the 20 *corridoi dolmenici* all faced the southeast quadrant (give or take a degree or two). When the *corridoi* developed into *tombe di giganti*, it seems that the quadrant was extended to produce a classic SR/SC pattern: of the 158 *tombe* in the northern half of the island, 154 (97·5%) had orientations within the range 60°–190°, the remaining 4 facing further north. This suggests that the quadrant may have been a restricted form of the SR/SC range.

The 94 *tombe* in the south of the island are again mostly SR/SC but with frequent exceptions, and we gave reasons for thinking this was due to influences from outside the island, as peoples of other cultures were drawn there by the natural resources on offer.

Solarists and lunatics

With the possible exception of Matarrubilla and three other tombs of the far south of the Iberian peninsula, I have found no hint among our two-and-a-half thousand tomb orientations of alignment either on individual stars (nearly all of which are in any case invisible near the horizon) or on constellations. The overwhelming majority of the orientations are within the SR/SC range, between midsummer sunrise and around culmination — or, in Provence and regions influenced from there, the SD/SS range, from culmination to midsummer sunset.

There remains for me the difficulty that a tomb that faces sunrise *ipso facto* faces moonrise at some times of the lunar cycle, and respected colleagues argue in particular instances for lunar orientations. But I find a wholly negligible number of tombs that faced just north of midsummer sunrise, outside the range of sunrise but inside the range of moonrise. And I know of numerous piecharts and histograms — not least, the extraordinary histogram (p. 98) of the 177 antas of central Portugal — where the southern limit of the range coincides in striking fashion with the southern limit of sunrise.

In consequence I have emerged from this fieldwork a solarist as far as tombs of the west Mediterranean are concerned. But lunar orientations have a fundamental role to play elsewhere in archaeoastronomy, and in the eastern Mediterranean I know a site where an unusually convincing case can be made for lunar orientations. This is the subject of our Appendix.

APPENDIX

The Minoan Cemetery at Armenoi, Crete

The communal tombs of the central and western Mediterranean that we investigated in the preceding chapters were erected above ground and built of stone. In almost every instance the damage inflicted on this surface structure by the passage of the millennia has reduced the accuracy with which the modern investigator can measure the orientation; and in any case, in the shaping and positioning of large stones the abilities of the original constructors, however impressive, were restricted by the primitive technology at their disposal. The archaeoastronomer who is imperfectly reconciled to the struggle to interpret ruined structures dreams of encountering hundreds of tombs built with high precision to a uniform plan by a single culture.

Such good fortune befell Maria Papathanassiou of Athens University and myself in July 1991, when the authorities of the Cretan mountain village of Anogheia invited us to measure the orientations of their monuments, which included the Idean Cave, legendary birthplace of Zeus. It was an experience in itself to live in a tightly-knit community where the law of distant Athens was not always seen as having priority. A young man wishing to marry a girl in the face of opposition from her family will still carry her off to the hills, in the expectation that this will lead her family to reverse their attitude and now insist that they marry; and no discredit is seen as attaching to him. Ancient remedies continue in use: the guide assigned to us was unable to be of much help because of illness, caused, it later transpired, by an enemy having put the Evil Eye upon him; he was to develop a tolerable *modus vivendi* whereby when he felt unwell he took himself to the local Orthodox priest who would relieve the symptoms with the appropriate prayers.

Memories of the German occupation during the Second World War were still very much alive. Our village had resisted, and been burned to the ground for its pains. Other villages had collaborated, and in these we were not always welcome if it became known where our allegiance lay.

As to the Idean Cave, we did our best, but the Cave did not lend itself to well-defined measurements; nor did the other monuments, however impressive, prove numerous enough to offer the basis for a statistical investigation. These monuments included peak sanctuaries, a demanding subject for inquiry since to measure each sanctuary it was necessary to climb a mountain peak.

While we were measuring the Idean Cave, two tourists enquired what we were doing. When we explained the purpose of our measures, they told us of a cemetery they had visited where there were a great many tombs all of which faced east. We had only a very few days left of our

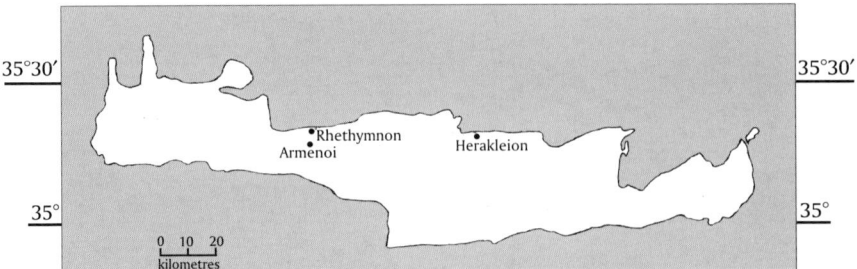

The island of Crete, with the location of Armenoi.

visit, but we drove to the cemetery and soon realized that here was an archaeoastronomical resource of exceptional quality.[1] It lies near the village of Armenoi, in a hilly region some ten kilometres south of the port of Rhethymnon on the north coast of the island. Not far away are areas where the Minoan civilization flourished, but it is not known where the people buried at Armenoi actually lived — surface surveys and test excavations have failed to locate what must have been a substantial settlement. It may therefore be that the people lived in a locality now obliterated by the modern buildings of Rhethymnon.

The cemetery, which extends over an area of 35 acres, consists of some three hundred tombs cut deep into the 'kouskouras' limestone bedrock of a little eminence. It now ranks as the greatest cemetery of the Late Minoan II–IIIB Period (1450–1190 BC). The earliest of the tombs so far dated is no. 200, which was in use during the second half of the fifteenth century BC, but this tomb is of different construction from the rest. The others are all chamber tombs cut into the bedrock, and date from the late fifteenth, and more especially from the fourteenth and thirteenth centuries. After the site was abandoned, leaves and soil filled the entrances to the tombs, and for three millennia the cemetery was lost to sight, its contents undisturbed, until its rediscovery in modern times. Excavation began in 1969, and over three-quarters of the tombs have now been examined.[2]

The Minoans carefully planned the site, which has paved paths and some levelling of the ground. Here and there the grain of the rock proved difficult to work, and a tomb was left unfinished. These unfinished tombs give clear evidence of the sequence of construction. First, the passage or 'dromos' (beginning with a ramp or steps) was cut into the rock, with carefully-fashioned sides that incline inwards a little as they rise from their base; these sides are usually straight and parallel and so the typical dromos has a very well defined orientation. When the dromos was complete, the outline of the entrance was incised into the rock-face at the end of the dromos, and the chamber (usually circular or horse-shoe in shape) cut away. A dromos is typically between 1m and 2½m in width and between 3½m and 7m in length (although some are longer — one prestige tomb has a dromos no less than 16 metres long). Occasionally a niche is built into a side-wall.

The tombs appear to have served for family burials, and in some the remains of as many as sixteen skeletons were found. When a new body was introduced, bones from previous burials were pushed to one side to make room. The remains from over five hundred skeletons at Armenoi demonstrate that the legend that the Minoans were of small stature is quite false. But their lifetime

(Left) Tomb 57, which the builders abandoned after outlining the entrance to the chamber and making a start on its excavation. (Right) Tomb 146, an example of a dromos quarried to a high level of geometrical precision.

was surprisingly brief: for those who survived childhood, the average age at death was 31 years for men and 28 for women.[3]

The precision with which the walls of the dromos were cut from the bedrock means that most of the orientations (defined as usual as the direction outwards from the chamber) are measurable with an accuracy of better than one degree. A mere handful of tombs that are in poor condition, or where construction is incomplete, have orientations of less accuracy. Only one tomb (no. 178) is anomalous and has no defined axis, though it too faces easterly.

By April 1994, when we made our fourth visit, Maria Papathanassiou and I had measured all the 224 tombs excavated up to that time. They occur in three zones. The first, which we term Zone A, consists of the land along the foot of the eastern slope of the eminence; all the tombs in Zone A lie close to the part of the boundary fence that extends to left and right of the entrance to the site (and indeed some lie just outside the fence). The majority of these 113 tombs are tightly-packed in an irregular double row that extends roughly from north to south, but with a 'kink' in the middle that runs briefly from northwest to southeast and encourages orientations further north of east than usual.

Zone B, which adjoins Zone A above and to the west, consists of the upper eastern slope and, more especially, the crest of the eminence. The 52 tombs here are much more scattered.

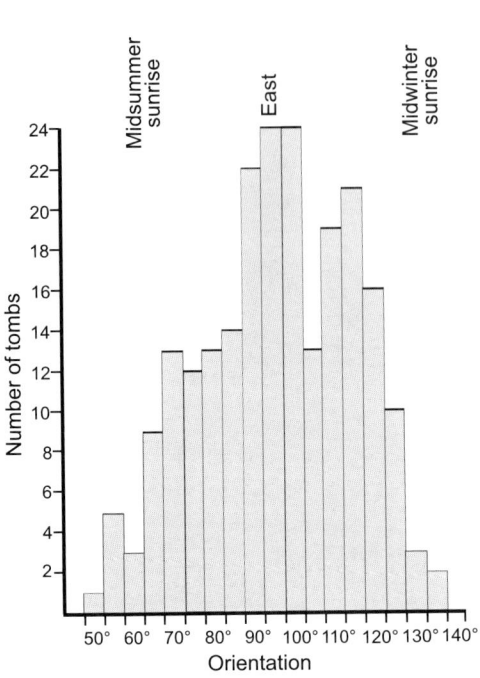
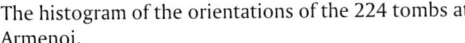

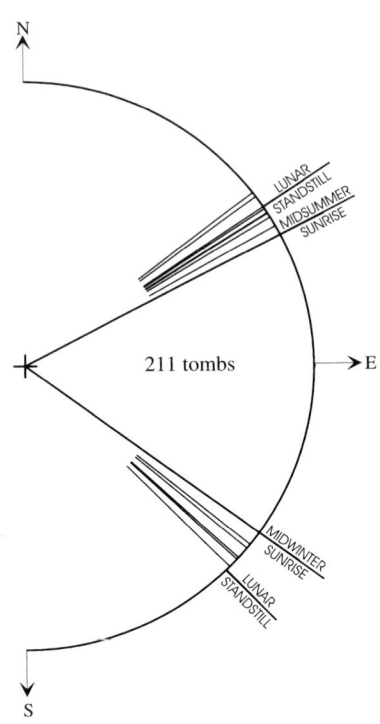

The histogram of the orientations of the 224 tombs at Armenoi.

The orientations of the 224 tombs at Armenoi, with those that faced beyond the range of sunrise individually shown.

Zone C lies a short distance away to the south, on the southern slope of the eminence. Here there is a cluster of 59 tombs.

The orientations (Table A.1) are exceptionally consistent. Every one of the 224 tombs faces easterly, between northeast and southeast. No fewer than 207 tombs faced the rising of the sun at some time during the year, while four more lay only marginally outside this range; the remaining 13 tombs faced either a few degrees south of midwinter sunrise, or a few degrees north of midsummer sunrise. With two minor exceptions (tombs that faced marginally north of the range of moonrise), every tomb faced moonrise at some time during the lunar cycle. That is, the range of orientations approximated (but only roughly) to the range of sunrise, and matched almost exactly the range of moonrise. It seems unlikely that this occurred by chance.

One possibility that suggested itself was that the tombs were constructed to face sunrise on the day work began. But if so, and if the commencement dates were scattered uniformly throughout the year, we would expect most tombs to face close to midsummer or midwinter sunrise, for these are the times of year when the position of sunrise changes little from one day to the next. But the histogram of orientations actually peaks around east, where the sun rises in spring and autumn. To account for the histogram in terms of sunrise we would therefore need an additional assumption, for example that for some reason construction frequently began in the spring and/or

The view of Mount Vrysinas from overhead the chamber of Tomb 165, whose dromos is aligned with the mountain peak.

autumn; or that sometimes the builders simply oriented their tomb in a direction they knew to be easterly.

Another possibility is that the tombs were constructed to face moonrise on the day work began. Moonrise may seem less plausible than sunrise, because of the rapid movement of the moon along the horizon from one night to the next, though this objection would lose its force if (say) the orientation was always to the full moon.

It is true that the histogram of orientations is, in principle, similarly unfavourable to the moonrise hypothesis, if tomb building began at arbitrary dates throughout the year. But whereas sunrise is visible except on the cloudiest of days, and even then is known to be occurring close to the position of sunrise the day before, the situation is otherwise with the moon. There are considerable periods every month when the moon on rising is lost in the glare of the sun, and so is invisible even when the weather is fine. If therefore we suppose that each tomb was to be laid out to face a direction within the range of moonrise, then the builders could have ensured this *either* by orienting the tomb to face moonrise on the day construction began, if moonrise was in fact visible, *or* by orienting the tomb roughly east if moonrise could not be seen. This could account for the shape of the histogram.

The argument in favour of moonrise is strengthened by the imposing presence, some 3km to the east of the cemetery, of Mount Vrysinas, on the summit of which there was in earlier times one of the most important of the Cretan peak sanctuaries (azimuth about 106° as seen from the cemetery). There is some reason to think that the sanctuary was dedicated to a lunar goddess,[4] and the earliest of the tombs so far excavated faces directly towards the peak. Yet the sanctuary itself was not the 'target', for the average orientation is some 10½° north of the mountain peak; significantly, this is also the average orientation of moonrise (and, indeed, sunrise). The location for the cemetery may therefore have been chosen for a less specific reason: because from its tombs the dead would at appropriate times 'see' the moon rising on a mountain sacred to the moon.

In this respect, the site is probably unique. (i) If the cemetery had been located further east and so was nearer the mountain, it would not have been possible to find a gradient sloping downwards towards the mountain, as required for the construction of a dromos. Instead, the land would have been flat or, on the lower slopes of Vrysinas, inclined upwards and so sloping away from the mountain. (ii) If the cemetery had been located further west, the mountain profile would have been smaller and the moon at its northernmost rising would have been seen, not on the mountain itself, but on flat ground to the north. (iii) The same would have been true had the cemetery been located further north. If, therefore, the people buried there had lived out their lives near modern Rhethymnon, to the north of Armenoi, the cemetery would have been uniquely defined as the nearest suitable site from which the dead would consistently see the moon rising on Vrysinas.

The range of orientations, therefore, suggests that the tombs were laid out to face roughly in a direction where sunrise, or moonrise, was known to occur. As the range of tomb orientation is greater than the range of sunrise but is almost identical with the range of moonrise, and as the tombs faced a mountain that may have been sacred to the moon (whose importance to the Minoans is well established), it seems most likely that the tombs were laid out to face moonrise.

Further reading

M. Papathanassiou, M. Hoskin and H. Papadopoulou, "Orientations of tombs at the Late-Minoan cemetery at Armenoi, Crete", *AA*, no. 17 (1992), S43–55.

M. Papathanassiou and M. Hoskin, "The Late-Minoan cemetery at Armenoi: A reappraisal", *JHA*, xxvii (1996), 53–59.

Notes and references

1   The site is discussed in detail, with plans, in the articles cited under "Further Reading".

2   For brief reports on some of these, see Iannis Tzedakis, "Armenoi (Rhethymnon)", *Archaiologikon Deltion*, Chronicles, xxv (1970), 476–7; xxvi (1971), 513–16; xxvii (1972), 639–44; xxix (1973–74), 917–21; and xxxi (1976), 368–72 (in Greek).

3   P. J. P. McGeorge, "New elements on the average duration of life in Minoan Crete", *Cretike Hestia*, Period D, i (1987), 9–13 (in Greek).

4   According to Paul Fauré, writing in *Bulletin de correspondance hellénique*, lxxxix (1965), 27–63, p. 51, the deity worshipped on Mount Vrysinas was Dictynna, "Mistress of the mountains", identified later with Artemis the huntress and rearer of children, who was associated with the moon in the west of Crete. It is by no means certain that the sanctuary *was* involved in the worship of a lunar goddess, but the association with Dictynna makes this a possibility.

Corpus Mensurarum

Unless otherwise stated in the relevant chapter, the azimuths in these tables were measured with a magnetic compass, and then corrected for the magnetic variation appropriate to the place and date, and for the known error in the construction of the compass. Where an azimuth is followed by the letter 'c' (for *circa*), this indicates a measure of low precision, usually because of the condition of the monument but occasionally because of the risk of magnetic anomaly in the rock.

The angular altitude of the skyline was normally measured with a handheld clinometer. In cases where the datum on altitude is unavailable (either because we were hampered by bad weather or restricted visibility, or because the orientation was measured by another investigator), a typical value has been assumed for the calculation of declination, and this is stated in the table.

Latitudes are given only to the nearest tenth of a degree, because this accuracy is more than sufficient for our purposes. Declinations have been calculated with the computer program kindly supplied by Clive Ruggles (see his Web site http://www.le.ac.uk/archaeology/rug/), and this resulted in a huge saving of labour and, no doubt, the avoidance of many arithmetical errors.

Chapter 3. The Temples of Malta and Gozo

3.1. Orientations of the principal axes of the temples of Malta and Gozo.

Az.°	Alt.°	Lat.°	Dec.°	Temple/Phase	Az.°	Alt.°	Lat.°	Dec.°	Temple/Phase
92.7	3.7	35.8	−0.1	Mnajdra I (Early Tarxien)	168.5	2.5	35.9	−50.4	Skorba II (Ggantija)
25.5	1.0	36.1	−27.6	Ggantija I (Ggantija)	168.5	0.6	35.9	−52.4	Tarxien IV (Ggantija)
29.0	−0.4	35.8	−31.4	Hagar Qim I (Ggantija)	186.0	−0.4	35.8	−54.8	Hagar Qim II (Tarxien)
31.0	3.4	35.9	−29.9	Ta' Hagrat (Ggantija)	193.5	1.3	36.0	−51.0	Bugibba (Tarxien)
34.5	1.0	36.1	−34.1	Ggantija II (Ggantija)	198.0	0.7	35.9	−50.2	Tarxien III (Early Tarxien)
38.0c	2.3	35.9	−35.5	Skorba I (Ggantija)	201.0	0.7	35.9	−48.9	Tarxien I (Early Tarxien)
38.5	−0.3	35.8	−38.1	Mnajdra II (Tarxien)	204.0	−0.3	35.8	−48.6	Mnajdra III (Ggantija)
49.6	0.7	35.9	−44.1	Kordin (Ggantija)					

Chapter 4. The Sanctuaries of Menorca and Mallorca

4.1. Orientations of 25 taula sanctuaries of Menorca.

Az.°	Alt.°	Lat.°	Dec.°	Sanctuary	Az.°	Alt.°	Lat.°	Dec.°	Sanctuary
Southern taulas					183	0	39.9	−50½	Binimaimut
110	0	39.9	−16	Torralba d'en Salort	184	0	39.9	−50½	Trepucó
143	0	40.0	−38½	Torre Trencada	184	0	39.9	−50½	Sonacasana (east)
155	0	39.9	−44½	Talati de Dalt	186c	0	39.9	−50½	Sonacasana (west)
164	0	40.0	−48	So N'Olivaret Nou	188	0	39.9	−50	Cotaina
165c	0	40.0	−48½	Es Tudons	190	0	39.9	−49½	Torralbec Vell
166	0	40.0	−48½	Bella Ventura	193c	0	40.0	−49	So N'Angladó
171	0	39.9	−50	Torre Llisa Vell	200	0	40.0	−46½	Son Catlar
173	0	40.0	−50	Torre Llafuda (west)	202	0	39.9	−46	Biniac
177	0	40.0	−50½	Binimassó	210c	0	39.9	−42	Torre d'en Gaumes
178	0	39.9	−50½	Binicodrell Nou					
180c	0	39.9	−50½	Binissafullet Nou	*Northern taulas*				
180c	0	40.0	−50½	Torre Llafuda (east)	125	0	40.0	−26½	Sa Torreta
180c	0	39.9	−50½	Son Rotger	176	1½	40.0	−48½	Algairens

4.2. Orientations of 15 talayotic sanctuaries of Mallorca.

Az.°	Alt.°	Lat.°	Dec.°	Sanctuary	Az.°	Alt.°	Lat.°	Dec.°	Sanctuary
121	*	39.7	−21½	Son Marí	168	*	39.4	−46	Capocorb d'en Jaquetó
147	−0½	39.4	−41½	Es Pedregar 1	168	*	39.5	−46	Es Fornets
148	*	39.4	−38½	Capocorb Vell	188	*	39.4	−47	Capocorb d'en Jaquetó
154	0	39.4	−44½	Capocorb d'en Jaquetó 2	195	*	39.8	−45½	Almallutx 2
158	*	39.4	−43	Capocorb d'en Jaquetó 1	198	*	39.8	−44½	Almallutx 1
158	*	39.4	−43	Capocorb d'en Jaquetó 3	213	*	39.4	−38	Tabaies de'n Clar
160	14	39.8	−33½	Son Mas	228	*	40.0	−29	Ses Arenes de Forment
163	*	39.3	−45	Ets Antigors					

*Horizon altitude not available; assumed to be 3° for calculation of declination.

Chapter 5. Tombs of South Iberia

5.1. Orientations of 48 tholoi and related tombs at Los Millares (lat. 37.0°).

Az. °	Alt. °	Dec. °	Tomb	Az. °	Alt. °	Dec. °	Tomb	Az. °	Alt. °	Dec. °	Tomb
62	1	+22½	36	95	2½	−2½	65	111	−0½	−17½	39
65	1	+20	68*	96	2	−4	8	111	0	−17	50
72c	2½	+15½	69	96	1½	−4	13*	112c	−0½	−18	51
76	4	+13½	11	96	1½	−4	34*	113	−0½	−19	22
82	4	+8½	10	98	1½	−5½	52	114c	−0½	−19½	15
83	4	+8	14	99	1½	−6½	28	114	−0½	−19½	26
86	3	+5	3	99	1½	−6½	41	116	−0½	−21½	7
87	3	+4	54	99c	1½	−6½	57	116	−0½	−21½	17
87c	3	+4	55	101	1	−8½	40	117	−0½	−22	27
89c	3	+2½	46	101	1	−8½	47	117	−0½	−22	29
89c	3	+2½	61	101	1	−8½	53	127c	−0½	−29½	9
89	3	+2½	71	104c	0½	−11	16	137	0	−36	48*
90	3	+1½	73	107	0	−14	25	146	0½	−41½	35*
92	2½	−0½	12	107	0	−14	67*	150	0½	−44	21*
94	2	−2	1	109c	0	−15½	60	212	4	−39½	30
95	2	−3	20	110c	−0½	−16½	62	216	4	−37	31

Tombs in too poor a state to be measured but with 'typical' orientations: 2, 4, 5, 6, 18, 19, 32, 42, 43, 49, 56, 66, 70, 72, 74, 75, 77, 78.
*Passage measured.
Numbers 1–56 according to M. Amalgro and A. Arribas, *El poblado y la necrópolis megalíticos de Los Millares* (*Bibliotheca Praehistorica Hispana*, iii; Madrid, 1963).

5.2. Orientations of 41 megalithic sepulchres at Alhama de Almería (lat. 37.0°), author's numbering.

Az. °	Alt. °	Dec. °	Tomb	Az. °	Alt. °	Dec. °	Tomb	Az. °	Alt. °	Dec. °	Tomb
Upper site				140	2	−36½	15	107	−0½	−14½	28
97	−0½	−6	1	140	2	−36½	16	107	−0½	−14½	29
104	−0½	−12	2	142c	2	−37½	17	110c	−0½	−16½	30
107	−0½	−14½	3	146	2	−40	18	111	−0½	−16½	31
109	−0½	−16	4	147c	2	−40½	19	114c	0	−19½	32
113	−0½	−19	5	150	2½	−42	20	117c	0	−21½	33
115/124	−0½/0	−20½/−27	6	152c	2	−43½	21	117c	0	−21½	34
116	−0½	−21	7	158	1½	−47	22	122/141	0/3	−25½/−36½	35
122	0	−25½	8					123	0	−26	36
122c	−0½	−26	9	*Lower site*				125	0½	−27½	37
125	0	−27½	10	76	3	+13	23	126	0½	−28	38
129	0	−30½	11	79	2½	+10	24	130	0½	−31	39
129	0	−30½	12	88	2	+2½	25	131c	0	−31	40
135	2½	−32½	13	95/121	0/0	−4½/−24½	26	132	0	−32½	41
139	1	−36½	14	99	−0½	−8	27				

Tombs 6, 26 and 35 have chambers whose sides are not orthogonal to the backstone but are slewed to the right (see text).

5.3. Orientations of 10 tholoi at Barranquete (lat. 36.8°).

Az. °	Alt. °	Dec. °	Tomb	Az. °	Alt. °	Dec. °	Tomb
95c	1½	−3½	7	127	0½	−28½	2
104	1	−11	9	128	0½	−29½	3
107	1	−13	4	130	1	−30½	11
117	0½	−21½	8	134c	1	−33½	6
124c	0½	−26½	1	147?	1½	−41	5

Numbers according to Ma. J. Amalgro Gorbea, *El poblado y la necrópolis de El Barranquete* (*Acta Arqueológica Hispánica*, vi; Madrid, 1973).

5.4. Orientations of 79 megalithic sepulchres near the Río Gor (lat. 37.5°), and of the related Dolmen de Bagil, Moratalla, Murcia (lat. 38.2°).

Az. °	Alt. °	Dec. °	Tomb	Az. °	Alt. °	Dec. °	Tomb	Az. °	Alt. °	Dec. °	Tomb
East edge of plateau				109	1½	−14½	158	*West slope of valley*			
119	3	−21	112	114	2½	−17½	58	67	1½	+19	69
120	3	−21½	110	115	2½	−18	55	81	2½	+8½	85
130	1½	−30	113	116	2½	−19	56	87	1	+3	20
135c	2	−33	104/5	116	2½	−19	29	87	2½	+3½	72
138	2	−35	111	116c	2½	−19	157	92	2½	0	73
147	1½	−41	102	120	2½	−22	31	95c	2	−21	78
147c	1½	−41	106	121	2½	−22½	82	97	5½	−2½	128
147	1½	−41	119	122	2½	−23½	33	101	2½	−7½	66
148	1½	−41½	114	122	3	−23	42	106	4½	−10	19
148	1½	−41½	117	122	2½	−23½	145	107c	2	−12½	74
155	1½	−45	109	124	2½	−25	22	110c	2	−14½	75
161	2	−47	108	126	2½	−26½	21	111	5	−13½	43
161	2	−47	120/1	126	2½	−26½	150	111	2	−15½	71
167	1½	−49½	116	135	1½	−33½	23	113c	2	−17	76
				135	1½	−33½	61	117	3	−19½	68
East slope of valley				135	1½	−33½	149	119c	2	−21½	16
140	13	−27	134	138	1½	−35½	146	121c	3½	−22	15
148	8½	−35	135	140	2	−36	27	123	8	−20	14
154	14	−33	138	140	1½	−36½	154	134	3	−31½	86
159c	10½	−38	140	141c	1½	−37	148	140	6	−33	17
165	4½	−46	132	142	1½	−38	32	140	6	−33	18
171	4	−48	137	143	2	−38	24	142	6½	−33½	129
171c	3	−49	141	143	1½	−38½	163	144	7½	−34	70
177	2	−50½	133	147c	1½	−41	159	147	3½	−39	65
177	18	−34½	142	150	2	−42	151	165	16½	−34½	130
				152c	2	−43	57	170	11	−40½	28
West edge of plateau				166c	1	−50	162				
81	0½	+7	161					*Moratalla, Murcia*			
94	1	−3	84					91	1	−0½	Bagil*

*Measure courtesy of Juan Antonio Belmonte.
Numbers according to M. García Sanchez and J.-C. Spahni, "Sepulcros megalíticos de la región de Gorafe (Granada)", *Archivo de prehistoria Levantina*, viii (1959), 43–111.

5.5. Orientations of 9 megalithic sepulchres at Baños de Alicún (lat. 37.5°).

Az.°	Alt.°	Dec.°	Tomb		Az.°	Alt.°	Dec.°	Tomb
120	6	−19½	10		165	3	−47½	8
123c	7½	−20½	12		175	8½	−44	6
129	30	−7½	4		184?	4	−48½?	3
145	6	−35½	7		204	1½	−45½	9
155	2½	−44	11					

Numbers according to García Sanchez and Spahni.

5.6. Orientations of 8 megalithic sepulchres at Fonelas (lat. 37.4°), alt. 1° assumed throughout, author's numbering.

Az.°	Dec.°	Tomb		Az.°	Dec.°	Tomb		Az.°	Dec.°	Tomb
93	−2	2		126	−27½	8		164c	−49	3
109	−14½	9		137c	−35	5		197/17	−49/+50	7
112	−17	10		144	−39½	6				

5.7. Orientations of 41 megalithic sepulchres at Montefrío (lat. 37.3°), author's numbering.

Az.°	Alt.°	Dec.°	Tomb		Az.°	Alt.°	Dec.°	Tomb		Az.°	Alt.°	Dec.°	Tomb
74	6?	+16½	1		102	5	−6½	15		117	8?	−16	29
82	4?	+8½	2		103	5½	−7	16		120	5½	−20	30
83	1	+6	3		104	5½	−8	17		120	6	−19½	31
85	6	+7½	4		106	5?	−9½	18		120	6½	−19	32
85	1?	+4½	5		107	6	−9½	19		122	6½	−20½	33
87	9	+8	6		108	1½	−13½	20		123	6½	−21½	34
90	1	+0½	7		110	5	−12½	21		124	6½	−22	35
90	3	+1½	8		111	6½	−12½	22		125	6½	−22½	36
90	3	+1½	9		111	6½	−12½	23		127	6½	−24	37
91	1	−0½	10		115	8	−14½	24		128	10?	−22	38
96	3	−3	11		114	5½	−15½	25		137	2½	−34	39
99	8	−2½	12		114	6½	−14½	26		138	7	−31	40
102	2	−8½	13		115	6	−16	27		159	3	−45½	41
102	3	−8	14		116	6½	−16	28					

5.8. Orientations of 7 megalithic sepulchres at El Pantano de los Bermejales (lat. 37.0°).

Az.°	Alt.°	Dec.°	Group		Az.°	Alt.°	Dec.°	Group
96	3	−3	3		120	2	−22½	6
96c	3	−3	5		125	2	−26	6
108	3	−12½	2		145	1	−40½	5
112	3	−15½	2					

Groups according to A. Arribas Palau and J. E. Ferrer Palma, "La necrópolis megalítica del Pantano de los Bermejales (Granada): Actuaciones arqueológicas", *Anuario arqueológico de Andalucía*, 1986, 307–10.

5.11. Orientations of 16 tombs in the province of Sevilla.

Az. °	Alt. °	Lat. °	Dec. °	Tomb
Megalithic (misc.)				
32c	8	37.9	+48½	Bradford, Almadén de la Plata
70	3	37.9	+17½	Palacio 5, Almadén de la Plata
79	1	37.9	+9	Cañalazarza, Almadén de la Plata
79c	1	37.3	+8½	La Casilla, El Gandul
80	2	37.9	+9	Palacio 1, Almadén de la Plata
82	1	37.9	+6½	La Dehesa, Almadén de la Plata
91	0	37.3	−1	Tumba del Pedrejón, El Gandul
95	0	37.9	−4½	Gabino, Almadén de la Plata
102	3	37.8	−7½	Palacio 4, Almadén de la Plata
128	0	37.9	−29½	Palacio 2, Almadén de la Plata
136	0	37.8	−35	Palacio 3, Almadén de la Plata
139	0	37.3	−37½	Las Canteras, El Gandul
Tholoi				
17¾	0	37.4	+48½	Matarrubilla, Valencina de la Concepción
77	0	37.3	+10	El Término, El Grandul
131	−0½	37.3	−32½	Cueva del Vaquero, El Gandul
242¾	2	37.4	−20¼	La Pastora, Valencina de la Concepción

5.12. Orientations of 6 megalithic sepulchres in the province of Cádiz.

Az. °	Alt. °	Lat. °	Dec. °	Tomb
32	1	36.3	+43½	Los Charcones, Benalup
214	1	36.2	−41½	Tomb 1E, La Laguna de la Janda
216	1	36.2	−40½	Tomb 3G, La Laguna de la Janda
231	1	36.2	−30	Tomb 2F, La Laguna de la Janda
234	0	36.2	−28½	Tomb C, La Laguna de la Janda
250	1	36.2	−15½	Tomb 4H, La Laguna de la Janda

Letters according to C. de Mergelina, "Los focos dolménicos de la Laguna de la Janda", *Memorias de la Sociedad Española de Antropología, Etnografía y Prehistoria*, iii (1924), 97–126; numbers as cited therein.

5.9. Orientations of 13 tombs in the province of Málaga.

Az. °	Alt. °	Lat. °	Dec. °	Tomb
Megalithic sepulchres				
81	3	36.8	+8½	Chaperas 1
97	4	36.9	−3	Tajillo del Moro
45c	0	37.0	+34	Menga
132	11	36.7	−24½	Encinas Borrachas 1
180c	8½	36.7	−45	Encinas Borrachas 2
72	3½	36.8	+16½	El Gigante
92	1	36.8	−1	La Giganta
77	1½	36.8	+11	La Angostura 1
109	5	36.8	−12	La Angostura 2
125	5	36.8	−24	La Angostura 3
76	0	36.8	+10½	El Moral
Galleried tomb				
96c	4	37.0	−2½	Viera
Tholos				
199	−5	37.0	−44½	El Romeral

5.10. Orientations of 15 tombs in the province of Córdoba.

Az. °	Alt. °	Lat. °	Dec. °	Tomb
Megalithic (misc.)				
61	0	38.3	+22	Doña Rama 1, Belmez
64	6	38.3	+24	Obaton 4, Fuente Obejuna
67	4	38.3	+20½	Sierrazuela, Villanueva de Córdoba
68	1	38.3	+17½	La Fuente de Corcho, Belmez
80	0	38.3	+7½	Torno, Belmez
90	2	38.3	+1	La Casa de D. Pedro, Belmez
91	0	37.8	−1	La Sierra Zuela de Posadas 1
92	0	38.3	−2	Navalcautivo Hormaco, V. de Córdoba
101	0	38.3	−9	El Gigante o Galegos, Fuente Obejuna
105	0	37.8	−12	La Sierra Zuela de Posadas 2
106	0	38.3	−13	La Horma, Fuente Obejuna
Tholoi				
74	1	38.3	+13	Delgados 3, Fuente Obejuna
79	0	38.3	+8	Delgados 1, Fuente Obejuna
87	1	38.2	+2½	Minguillo 4, Villanueva de Córdoba
122c	1	38.3	−24	Delgados 2, Fuente Obejuna

5.13. Orientations of 33 tombs in the province of Huelva.

Az. °	Alt. °	Lat. °	Dec. °	Tomb
Antas				
93	1	38.0	-2	Pasada del Abad, Rosal de la Frontera
96	4	37.9	-2½	Alcalaboza, Aroche
Megalithic (misc.)				
52	1	37.7	+29½	Puente de los Muertos, Zalamea la Real
66	2	37.5	+20	La Plazuela 1, Villanueva de los Castillejos
74	7	37.7	+17	La Cantina, El Campillo
75	0	37.6	+11½	Los Gabrieles 2, Valverde del Camino
75	0	37.5	+11½	El Labradillo, Beas
80	4	37.9	+10	Valdelinares, Zufre
82	1	37.6	+6½	El Pozuelo 5, Zalamea la Real
83	1	37.6	+6	Los Gabrieles 3, Valverde del Camino
83	0	37.4	+5	De Soto 1, Trigueros
85	3	37.6	+6	El Pozuelo 6, Zalamea la Real
85	1	37.6	+4½	Martin Gil, Zalamea la Real
86	0	37.6	+3	El Pozuelo 2, Zalamea la Real
90	0	37.6	-0½	Los Gabrieles 6, Valverde del Camino
91	5	37.6	+2	El Pozuelo 8, Zalamea la Real
91	2	37.6	0	El Pozuelo 7, Zalamea la Real
92	1	37.4	-1	De Soto 2, Trigueros
94	2	37.5	-2	La Plazuela 2, Villanueva de los Castillejos
98	0	37.6	-6½	Los Gabrieles 5, Valverde del Camino
100	0	37.6	-8½	El Pozuelo 4, Zalamea la Real
101	4	37.7	-6½	El Cañuelo, Zalamea la Real
104	0	37.6	-11½	Los Gabrieles 4, Valverde del Camino
116	3	37.6	-18½	La Mezquita, Zalamea la Real
117	2	37.6	-20	Mascotejo 1, Berrocal
118?	4	37.6	-19½	Mascotejo 2, Berrocal
120	3	37.6	-21½	El Pozuelo 1, Zalamea la Real
120	2	37.6	-22	El Pozuelo 3, Zalamea la Real
130	0	37.5	-31	Mesa de las Huecas 20, Niebla
Anomalous construction				
179	5	38.0	-47	La Balleza, Aroche
Tholoi				
85	2	37.8	+5	Charco del Toro, Santa Bárbara de Casa
161	4	37.8	-45	El Bizco, Santa Bárbara de Casa
170	-0½	37.8	-52½	El Morino, Santa Bárbara de Casa

5.14. Orientations of 10 tombs of southeast Badajoz.

Az. °	Alt. °	Lat. °	Dec. °	Tomb
Megalithic (misc.)				
26	1	38.1	+45½	La Dehesa del Hospital, Monesterio
43*	1	38.2	+35½	Juncoso 2, Llerena
44*	4	38.2	+37	Alquitones, Llerena
50	1	38.2	+31	[Road Ex202, Km 52]
65	4½	38.0	+22	La Cueva, Llerena
66*	2½	38.2	+20	Juncoso, Llerena
92	2	38.3	-0½	Valvengo 1, Jerez de los Caballeros
Anomalous construction				
87	0	38.9	+2	Magacela, Mérida
Tholoi				
61	0½	38.2	+22½	Veguilla 1, Llerena
86	3	38.3	+3	La Grania del Toriñuelo, Jerez de los Caballeros

*Measure possibly affected by magnetic anomaly.

5.15. *See following page.*

5.16. Orientations of 9 tombs north or west of Lisbon.

Az. °	Alt. °	Lat. °	Dec. °	Tomb
Antas				
98	0	38.8	-6½	Monte Abraão, Sintra
110	1	38.8	-15	El Carrascal, Agualua
111	2	38.9	-15	Carcavelos, Loures
Megalithic (misc.)				
80	-0½	38.8	+7	Bela Vista, Sintra
213	1½	38.8	-40	Estria, Sintra
Tholoi				
105	1	38.9	-11	Tituaria, Mafra
118	5	38.8	-18	S. Martinho 1, Sintra
152	-0½	38.8	-44½	Monge, Sintra
160	-0½	39.1	-47	Barro, Torres Vedras

Chapter 6. Tombs of West Iberia

5.15. Orientations of 24 tombs of southern Portugal.

Az. °	Alt. °	Lat. °	Dec. °	Tomb
Antas				
82	0	37.8	+6	Pedra d'Anta 1, Ourique
108	1	38.1	-13½	Pedra Branca, Santiago do Cacém
Megalithic (nine-stone chambers)				
108	1	37.4	-14	Curral da Castelhana, Alcoutim*
109	6	37.4	-11½	Cerro das Pedras Altas, Tavira*
115	0½	37.4	-19½	Cerro da Masmorra, Tavira*
Megalithic (misc.)				
70	0	37.6	+15½	Fernão Vaz 1, Ourique
73	0	37.6	+12½	Fernão Vaz 2, Ourique
81	0	37.8	+6½	Carborela, Ourique
100	2	38.1	-7	Palhota, Santiago do Cacém
107c	0½	37.6	-13½	Brejo, Ourique
108	0	37.2	-14	Alcalár 1, Portimão
116	-0½	37.1	-21	Pedra Escorregadia, Vila do Bispo
118	4	37.5	-19½	Lavajo, Alcoutim*
Tholoi				
54c	0	37.2	+27½	Alcalár 11, Portimão
65	0	37.7	+19	?, Ourique
99	0	37.2	-7½	Alcalár 7, Portimão
102c	0	37.2	-9	Alcalár 3, Portimão
103	0	37.6	-10½	Cerro de Gatão, Ourique
106c	0	37.6	-13	M. Velha, Ourique
112	0	37.4	-7½	Eira dos Palheiros, Alcoutim*
112	4	37.3	-15	Corte Cabreria, Aljezur
120	1	37.2	-23	Alcalár 4, Portimão
120c	0	37.2	-24	Alcalár 9, Portimão
127	2	37.6	-27½	Baranco de Nora Velha, Ourique

*Measures courtesy of Fernando Pimenta.

6.1. Orientations of 12 'small' tombs of central Alentejo and the Elvas region, and of 10 tombs of the central Alentejo of uncertain type.

Az. °	Alt. °	Lat. °	Dec. °	Tomb
'Small' tombs of central Alentejo				
73	1	38.8	+13½	Mijadouros, Estremoz
79	0½	39.3	+8½	Cabeço, Ponte de Sor
79	2	38.9	+9½	Monte das Olveiras 2, Mora
97	1	38.6	-5	Giões, Évora
99	0½	38.9	-7	Remendo 2 , Mora
113	0	38.9	-18	Gonçala 6, Mora
120	1	38.9	-22½	Monte dos Condes, Mora
129	0	38.6	-30	Anta Cist., Vale de Moura, Évora
'Small' tombs of the Elvas region				
71c	4	39.0	+17	Cegonha
93	0½	39.0	-2½	Torrão 3
101	1	39.0	-8	Cabeça Gorda
126	0½	38.9	-27	Pombal 4
Central Alentejo tombs of uncertain type				
78	0	38.4	+9	Poço de Gateira 1, Reguengos
85	1	38.6	+4½	Colmeeiro 2, Redondo
91	1	38.6	-0½	Godinha de Cima 2, Redondo
102	2	38.4	-8½	Poço de Gateira 2, Reguengos
103	0	38.4	-10½	Sta Margarida 1, Reguengos
109	0	38.7	-15	Lucas 1, Alandroal
113	0	38.6	-18	Godinha de Cima 1, Redondo
115	3	38.7	-17½	Cubo, Alandroal
typ	0	39.3	typ	Alminho 2, Ponte de Sor
typ	0	38.7	typ	Hortinas, Alandroal

typ: quantitative measure not possible, but tomb faced in a 'typical' direction.

5.16. *See preceding page.*

… seven stone antas of Portugal and neighbouring provinces of Spain. Towns are from the Alentejo region of Portugal unless otherwise specified.

Az. °	Alt. °	Lat. °	Dec. °	Tomb
61	1	38.3	+23	Dehesa Bollai 1, Jerez de los Caballeros (B)
64	1	39.0	+20½	Contada, Elvas
70	4	39.4	+18	Huerta de las Monjas, Valencia de Alcántara (C)
76	0	39.4	+10½	Lanchas 1, Valencia de Alcántara (C)
77	0½	38.9	+10	Gonçala 2, Mora
79	1	38.9	+9	Remendo 1, Mora
79	2½	39.5	+10	Pero d'Alba, Castelo de Vide
81	3½	39.3	+9	Datas 1, Valencia de Alcántara (C)
81	6½	39.4	+11	Sobral, Castelo de Vide
81	0½	39.4	+7	Coureilos 3, Castelo de Vide
82	0	37.8	+6	Pedra d'Anta 1, Ourique, S. Portugal*
82	0	38.9	+6	Caeira 3, Mora
82	2	39.4	+7½	Tapada del Anta, Valencia de Alcántara (C)
82	0	38.4	+6	Herdade do Duque, Reguengos
82	0	38.6	+6	Patalim, Évora
82	0	39.4	+6	Coureilos 2, Castelo de Vide
82c	–0½	39.0	+5½	Torrão 1, Elvas
83	0	39.4	+8	Coureilos 4, Castelo de Vide
83	0	38.9	+5	Caeira 4, Mora
83	0½	38.9	+5½	Cré 1, Mora
83	0	39.3	+5	Morera, Valencia de Alcántara (C)
84	3	39.0	+6½	Olival do Monte Velho, Elvas
84	0	38.6	+4½	Silval, Évora
84	0	39.4	+4½	Coureilos 1, Castelo de Vide
84	1	38.6	+5	Paredes, Évora
84c	0	38.8	+4½	Defesinhas 1, Elvas
85	0½	38.9	+4	Cré 2, Mora
85	0	38.6	+3½	Bota 1, Évora
86	2	38.5	+4	Camino de los Bombonas, Barcarrota (B)
86	2	38.5	+4	Hermosina, Barcarrota (B)
86	2½	39.5	+4½	Currais do Galhordas, Castelo de Vide
86	0	39.4	+2½	Zafra 2, Valencia de Alcántara (C)
86	5	39.4	+6	Tapias 2, Valencia de Alcántara (C)
86	1½	38.7	+4	Claros Montes 1, Arraiolos
87	1	39.1	+2½	Dehesa de la Muela, Mérida (B)
88	–0½	38.9	+1	Caeira 1, Mora
88	0½	39.4	+1½	Barca, Valencia de Alcántara (C)
88	1	38.6	+2	Pinheiro do Campo 1, Évora
89	0½	39.4	+1	Huerta Nueva, Valencia de Alcántara (C)
89	4	39.4	+3	Miera, Valencia de Alcántara (C)
89	0½	38.6	+1	Freixo de Cima 1, Évora
89	0	38.9	+0½	San Diniz, Mora
89	4	38.9	+3	Gonçala 6, Mora
90	1½	38.9	+0½	Figueirinha 2, Mora
90	0½	38.9	+0½	Portela, Mora
91	0	38.4	–1	Farisoa 4, Reguengos
91	0	38.9	–1	Cabeção, Mora
91	1½	38.8	0	Entreaguas, Estremoz
91	0	39.3	–1	Aldeia da Mata, Crato
91	0	39.2	–1	S. Lourenço 1, Crato
91	1	38.5	–0½	Rana, Barcarrota (B)
91	0	39.2	–1	Tapadôes, Crato
92	3	39.4	0	Pombal, Castelo de Vide
92	1	38.9	–1	Torre das Aguias 1, Mora
93	1	38.0	–2	Pasada del Abad, Rosal (H)*
93	1	38.6	–2	Herdade de Anta, Évora
93	1	38.9	–2	Cré 3, Mora
93	4	39.4	0	Zafra 3, Valencia de Alcántara (C)
93	–0½	39.0	–3	Monte dos Frades, Elvas
94	0½	38.6	–3	Aguiar, Évora
94	1½	38.9	–2½	Torre das Aguias 2, Mora
94	0	38.9	–3½	Adua 1, Mora
94	0½	38.9	–3	Caeira 2, Mora
94	0½	38.6	–3	Sauza 4, Évora
95	2½	38.5	–2½	Tajeño, Barcarrota (B)
95	2	39.0	–3	Serrinha, Crato
95	0	38.6	–4½	Vale d'Anta, Redondo
95	5	39.4	–1	Zafra 4, Valencia de Alcántara (C)
95	2	38.7	–3	Claros Montes 2, Arraiolos
95	0	38.4	–4½	Cebolinhos 3, Reguengos
95	0	38.9	–4½	Gonçala 1, Mora
95c	0	38.6	–4½	Bota 2, Évora
96	0½	38.6	–4½	Colmeeiro, Redondo
96	4	37.9	–2½	Alcalaboza, Aroche (H)*
96	2	38.5	–3½	San Blas, Barcarrota (B)
96	–0½	38.6	–5½	Cabeças, Évora
98	–0½	38.4	–7	Vale Carneiro 1, Reguengos
98	1	38.8	–6	Sardinha, Elvas
98	1	38.6	–6	Sauza 3, Évora
98	0½	38.6	–6	Paço 1, Redondo
98	0	38.8	–6½	Monte Abraão, Sintra (nr Lisbon)*
99	10½	39.5	0	Olheiros, Castelo de Vide
99	–0½	38.6	–8	Zambujalinho, Évora
100	5	39.4	–4½	Lanchas 2, Valencia de Alcántara (C)
100	0½	38.9	–8	Gonçala 4, Mora
100	1	38.6	–7½	Vale de Moura 1, Évora
100	0½	39.3	–7½	Cajirón 1, Valencia de Alcántara (C)
100	1	38.6	–7½	Silveira, Redondo
101	1½	38.5	–8	Lapita, Barcarrota (B)
101	0	38.6	–9	Paço das Vinhas 1, Évora
101	0½	38.6	–8½	Horta do Zambujeiro, Redondo
101	0	38.8	–9	Monte Ruivo, Elvas

Table 6.2 continued]

Az.°	Alt.°	Lat.°	Dec.°	Tomb
101	0	39.4	-9	Gáfete 1, Crato
101	5½	39.3	-5	Cajirón 2, Valencia de Alcántara (C)
101	6½	39.4	-4½	Zafra 1, Valencia de Alcántara (C)
101	0½	38.9	-8½	Anta Grande dos Antões, Mora
101	0	38.4	-9	Cebolinhos 2, Reguengos
102	4	38.7	-7	Pão Mole, Alandroal
102	1	38.6	-9	Candeeira, Redondo
102	-0½	38.9	-10	Torre das Arcas 1, Elvas
102	0	39.3	-9½	Marquesa, Valencia de Alcántara (C)
102	0	39.4	-9½	Gáfete 2, Crato
102	0	39.0	-9½	Lácara, Mérida (B)
103	2	38.8	-9	Casas do Canal, Estremoz
103	-0½	38.4	-11	Farisoa 1, Reguengos
103	1	38.6	-9½	Azaruja 2, Évora
103	0	38.6	-10½	Azaruja 1, Évora
103	0	38.4	-10½	Gorginos 3, Reguengos
103	0	38.6	-10½	Barrosinha 1, Évora
103	2½	38.4	-8½	Olival de Pega 2, Reguengos
104	0½	39.3	-11	Bernardo, Ponte de Sor
104	2½	39.3	-9½	Anta de Crato, Crato
104	0½	38.6	-11	Anta Grande de Zambujeiro, Évora
104	0	38.4	-11½	Monte Novo 2, Reguengos
104	3	38.4	-9	Anta Grande, Olival de Pega, Reguengos
104	0½	38.6	-11	Freixo de Cima 2, Évora
104	1	39.4	-10½	São Gens, Nisa
104	0	38.4	-11½	Farisoa 5, Reguengos
104c	2	39.0	-9½	Don Miguel, Elvas
105	3½	39.4	-9½	Fragoso, Valencia de Alcántara (C)
105	1	38.8	-11½	São Rafael 1, Elvas
105	0	38.4	-12	Farisoa 2, Reguengos
105	-0½	39.3	-12½	Matanga, Ponte de Sor
105	1	38.6	-11½	Sauza 1, Évora
105	6	38.5	-8	Milano, Barcarrota (B)
105	1	38.9	-11	Monte das Oliveiras, Mora
106	-0½	38.6	-13	Pau, Évora
106	0½	38.7	-12½	Santa Luzia, Alandroal
106	5½	39.3	-9	Datas 2, Valencia de Alcántara (C)
106	1½	38.9	-11½	Briços, Mora
106	0	38.4	-13	Cebolinhos 1, Reguengos
106	0	38.4	-13	Vidigueiras 2, Reguengos
107	2½	38.7	-11½	Galvães, Alandroal
107	0½	38.6	-13	Sauza 2, Évora
108	1	38.9	-13½	Gonçala 3, Mora
108	1	38.1	-13½	Pedra Branca, Santiago do Cacém, S. Portugal*
108	0	38.8	-14½	Defesinhas 2, Elvas
108	0	38.8	-14½	Sobral, Elvas
109	1	38.9	-14½	Pombal 5, Elvas
109	-0½	38.6	-15½	Azinheiras, Évora
109	1	38.4	-14½	Passo 1, Reguengos
109	0	38.9	-15	Pena Clara 1, Elvas
110	2	39.4	-14	Tapias 1, Valencia de Alcántara (C)
110	0	38.9	-16	Lapeira, Mora
110	1	38.9	-15	Gonçala 5, Mora
110	0	38.8	-15	Carrascal, Agualua, nr Lisbon*
110c	0	38.6	-16	Vale de Rodrigo 3, Évora
111	1½	38.8	-15½	Forte de Botas, Elvas
111	2	39.5	-15	Conto do Zé Godinho, Castelo de Vide
111	0	38.9	-16½	Quinta das Longas, Elvas
111	2	38.9	-15	Carcavelos, Loures, nr Lisbon*
112	0	38.9	-17½	Monte dos Negros, Elvas
112	4½	38.5	-14	Palacio, Barcarrota (B)
112	0	38.6	-17½	Vale de Moura 2, Évora
112c	0	38.6	-17½	Vale de Rodrigo 2, Évora
113	0½	38.6	-18	Hospital, Redondo
113	0	38.4	-18	Farisoa 7, Reguengos
113	0	38.4	-18	Gorginos 1, Reguengos
114	0	38.8	-19	São Rafael 2, Elvas
114	0½	39.4	-18½	Corchero, Valencia de Alcántara (C)
116	10	38.8	-13	Cortiçeira, Estremoz
116	0½	38.6	-20	Vidigueiras, Redondo
117	2	38.6	-19½	Casas Novas, Redondo
118	-0½	38.9	-22	Torre das Arcas 2, Elvas
118	1	38.8	-21	Valmor, Elvas
118	0	38.4	-22	Vidigueiras 1, Reguengos
121	2½	38.5	-22	Rocaamador, Barcarrota (B)
121	2½	39.4	-22	Melriça, Castelo de Vide
122	-0½	38.6	-25½	Barrosinha 2, Évora
122c		38.8	-25	Avessadas, Elvas
122c	0	38.6	-25	Pinheiro do Campo 2, Évora
128	9	39.6	-21½	La Tierra Caída 2, Cedillo (NW C)
129	10	39.6	-21½	La Tierra Caída 1, Cedillo (NW C)
typ	0	38.4	typ	Monte Novo 1, Reguengos
typ	0	38.4	typ	Monte Novo 4, Reguengos
typ	0	38.4	typ	Vale Carneiro 5, Reguengos
typ	0½	38.6	typ	Paço 2, Redondo

typ: quantitative measure not possible, but tomb faced in a 'typical' direction. C: Cáceres; B: Badajoz; H: Huelva. *Repeated here from a previous table.

6.3. Orientations of 33 schist tombs of NW Cáceres and the Portugese Upper Tejo.

Az. °	Alt. °	Lat. °	Dec. °	Tomb
Area of Rosmaninhal, Portugal				
88	0	39.8	+1	Amieiro 2
88	0	39.8	+1	Couto da Espanhola 2
93	0	39.8	−2½	Amieiro 3
99	0	39.7	−7½	Samarrudo 1
102	0	39.7	−9½	Mesas
104	0	39.7	−11	Cubieiras 2
104	0	39.7	−11	Zambujo 1
106	0	39.7	−12½	Tapada da Ordem 1
109	0	39.7	−15	Zambujo 3
111	0	39.7	−16½	Zambujo 2
111	0	39.8	−16½	Couto da Espanhola 6
114	0	39.7	−18½	Tapada da Ordem 2
143	0	39.7	−38½	Samarrudo 2
typ	0	39.8	typ	Amieiro 8
Area of Vila Velha de Ródão, Portugal				
76	1½	39.7	+11½	Santo Amaro 2
93	3	39.7	−0½	Santo Amaro 1
93	2	39.8	−1	Casa da Moura
95	7½	39.7	+1	Cabeço de Anta
95	0½	39.7	−4	Vale das Cobras
130	3½	39.8	−27	Silveirinha
Area of Nisa, Portugal				
92	1½	39.6	−1	Terra da Frágua
97	0	39.6	−6	Tapada do Muro
101	1	39.6	−8	Terra da Azinheira
102	0	39.6	−9½	Naves
104	0	39.6	−11	Tapada do Sobreirão
109	1½	39.6	−14	Oiro
Northwestern Cáceres, Spain				
86	0	39.6	+2½	Baldio Gitano 1, Santiago de Alcántara
92	0½	39.6	−1½	Cerro de la Caldera, Herrera de Alcántara
94	0	39.6	−3½	Joaninha, Cedillo
98	3	39.6	−4½	Valle Pepino 1, Santiago de Alcántara
98c	0½	39.6	−6	Fuente de la Sevillana, Cedillo
98	0	39.6	−6½	Valle Pepino 2, Santiago de Alcántara
99	3	39.6	−5	Baldio Morchon, Santiago de Alcántara
105	5½	39.6	−8	Era de la Laguna 2, Santiago de Alcántara
112c	0½	39.6	−17	Cuatro Lindones, Cedillo

The two seven-stone antas of northwestern Cáceres are listed in Table 6.2.
typ: quantitative measure not possible, but tomb faced in a 'typical' direction.

6.4. Orientations of 21 megalithic tombs of the province of Salamanca.

Az. °	Alt. °	Lat. °	Dec. °	Tomb/Type
84c	1	40.9	+5	Casa del Moro, Traguntia (a)
87c	0	40.7	+2	Castillos 1, Hurtada, Villar de Argañán (b)
93c	2½	40.5	−1	Torreón, Navamorales (a)
104c	3½	40.6	−8½	Piedras Hincadas, El Valle (b)
105c	2	40.6	−10	Prado Nuevo, Salvatierra de Tormes (a)
105c	1	40.8	−11	Torre, Vecinos (a)
109	2	40.6	−13	Teriñuelo, Aldeavieja de Tormes (a)
109	0	40.9	−14½	Eras, Fuenteliante (?)
110	0	41.0	−15½	Casa del Moro, Gejuelo del Barro (a)
111	1	41.0	−15½	Zafrón, Doñinos de Ledesma (a)
112	0	41.0	−17	Méson de Porqueriza, La Mata de Ledesma (a)
112	0½	41.0	−16½	Sahelicejos, Villar de Peralonso (a)
115	0	41.0	−19	Torrejón, Villarmayor (a)
116	2	40.6	−18½	Prado de la Nava, Salvatierra de Tormes (a)
117c	0½	40.9	−20	Navalito, Lumbrales (b)
117	0½	41.0	−20	Casa del Moro, Villasdardo (a)
119	1½	40.6	−21	Rábida 1, Ciudad Rodrigo (c)
121	1½	40.9	−22	Torrecilla, S. Benito de La Valmuza (a)
124	0½	40.0	−25½	Castillejo 1, Martín de Yeltes (a)
128c	6½	40.6	−23	Cista, El Valle (c)
133	7	40.6	−26	Rábida 2, Ciudad Rodrigo (a)

6.5. *See following page.*

6.6. Orientations of 8 tombs of the coastal region of north-central Portugal.

Az. °	Alt. °	Lat. °	Dec. °	Tomb
73	−0½	40.8	+12	Pedra da Moura 1, S. Jouga = Cerqueira 1, Cambra
79	3½	40.9	+10½	Arreçaio 2, Sta Eulália, Arouca
87	5	40.9	+5½	Portela da Anta, Albergaria da Serra, Arouca
126	−0½	40.8	−27½	Pedra da Moura 3, S. Jouga (?)
128	−0½	40.8	−28½	Coval 2, S. Jouga
141	1	40.9	−35½	Alijada 2, Sta Eulália, Arouca
146	1	40.9	−38½	Alijada 1, Sta Eulália, Arouca
174	−0½	40.8	−50	Juncal 1, Manhouce, S. Pedro do Sul

6.5. Orientations of 48 megalithic tombs of the Mondego Plateau.

Az. °	Alt. °	Lat. °	Dec. °	Tomb/Type
Mondego Basin				
77	7	40.4	+14½	Lapa da Recainha, Oliveira do Hospital (II)
77c	1	40.2	+10½	S. Pedro Dias, Vila Nova de Poiares (II)
89	0	40.5	+0½	Orca do Outeira do Rato, Lapa do Lobo (II)
94	3	40.5	–1	Orca do Carcalval de Louça, Paranhos, Seia (?)
97	2	40.7	–4	Orca de Corgas de Matança, Fornos de Alg. (II)
98	1½	40.5	–4½	Arquinha da Moura, Lageosa, Tondela (II)
101	1½	40.5	–7½	Sobreda, Oliveira do Hospital (II)
102	0	40.5	–9½	Orca de Pramelas, Canas de Senhorim, Nelas (I)
108	4	40.8	–11	Carapito 1, Aguiar da Beira (I)
109	2½	40.4	–13	Orca de Fiais da Telha, Carregal do Sal (II)
113	3	40.6	–15½	Casa da Orca da Cunha Baixa, Mangualde (II)
113c	2½	40.4	–16	Orca 2 do Ameal, Carregal do Sal (I)
114	0	40.7	–18½	Mamaltar de Vale de Fachas, Viseu (II)
114	5½	40.5	–14½	Orca de Rio Torto, Gouveia (II)
116c	3	40.5	–17½	Orca do Folhadal, Nelas, Viseu (I)
117c	3½	40.8	–18	Carapito 2, Aguiar da Beira (I)
118	1½	40.7	–20	Casa de Orca de Cortiço, Fornos de Alg. (II)
119	2½	40.5	–20½	Orca de Santo Tisco, Carregal do Sal (I/II)
121	2½	40.5	–21½	Orca de Vale Torto, Paranhos, Seia (?)
124c	1½	40.5	–24½	Mondegã, Lapa de Tourais (I/II)
124	1½	40.4	–24½	Seixo da Beira, Oliveira do Hospital (II)
126c	2½	40.5	–24½	Chaveiral 2, Pranhos, Seia (I)
136c	3½	40.5	–30½	Chaveiral 1, Pranhos, Seia (I)
typ	0	40.5	typ	Penela 1, Lageosa, Tondela (?)
typ	0	40.5	typ	Penela 2, Lageosa, Tondela (?)
typ	?	40.5	typ	Areal, Tondela (?)
Vouga Basin				
44	–0½	40.8	+32	Pedralta, Cota, Viseu (II)
66	1	40.7	+18½	Chão Redondo 1, Sever do Vouga (I)
90	0	40.7	–0½	Antelas, Oliveira de Frades (I)
91c	9	40.7	+5	Os Chascos, Ribeiradio, Oliveira de Frades (?)
106	5	40.7	–9	Lapa do Repilau, Couto de Cima, Viseu (II)
122	1½	40.7	–23½	Fojo 1, Couto de Cima, Viseu (?)
129	4	40.6	–25½	Espirito Santo d'Arca 2, Caramulo (?)
Alto Paiva Basin (South Douro)				
78	3½	40.8	+11½	Orca dos Juncais, Vila Nova de Paiva (II)
83	0½	41.0	+5½	Chã de Brinco 1, Cinfães (I)
89	4	41.1	+3½	Felgueiras 1, Serra de Montemuro, Resende (?)
113	–0½	40.8	–18½	Orca do Tanque, Vila Nova de Paiva (II)
103	5½	40.8	–6	Orca dos Castenairos, Vila Nova de Paiva (I/II)
136	1½	40.9	–31½	Lameira Travessa 2, Vila Nova de Paiva (II?)
138	2	40.8	–33	Orca de Pendilhe, Vila Nova de Paiva (II)

Table 6.5 continued]

Az. °	Alt. °	Lat. °	Dec. °	Tomb/Type
Torto Basin (South Douro)				
77	–0½	40.9	+9	Lameira de Cima 2, Antas, Penedono (II)
85	2½	41.0	+5	Dolmen de Areita, S. João da Pesqueira (I/II)
88	3	41.0	+3½	S. do M. 3, Penela da Beira, Penedono (II)
89	–0½	40.9	0	Lameira de Cima 1, Antas, Penedono (II)
90	4	41.0	+2½	S. do M. 5, Penela da Beira, Penedono (?)
128c	4	41.0	–25	S. do M. 1, Penela da Beira, Penedono (?)
typ	4	41.0	typ	S. do M. 2, Penela da Beira, Penedono (?)
Coa Basin				
91	6	40.6	+3	Pera do Moço, Guarda (II?)

typ: quantitative measure not possible, but tomb faced in a 'typical' direction.
S. do M.: Senhora do Monte; Alg.: Algodres

6.6. *See previous page.*

6.7. Orientations of 11 tombs on the north bank of the Douro Basin.

Az. °	Alt. °	Lat. °	Dec. °	Tomb
10	0	41.2	+47	Cabritos 2, Amarante
81	2	41.2	+7	Santa Marta, Penafiel
86	0	41.2	+2½	Outeiro de Ante 1, Baião
89	0	41.2	+0½	Chã de Parada 1, Baião
90	0½	41.2	+0½	Outeiro de Anta 2, Baião
93	0	41.2	–2½	Meninas de Castro, Baião
95	2½	41.2	–2½	Meninas do Crasto 2, Baião
98	0	41.2	–6½	Chã de Arcas 5, Baião
100	4	41.3	–5	Lamoso, Paços de Ferreira
103	–0½	41.2	–10½	Outeiro dos Gregos 3, Baião
107	1½	41.2	–12	Outeiro de Ante 3, Baião

6.8. Orientations of 7 tombs of the Miranda Plateau and Trás-os-Montes.

Az. °	Alt. °	Lat. °	Dec. °	Tomb
101	–0½	41.3	–9	Madorras 1, Sabrosa
106	2	41.3	–11	Zedes, Carrazeda de Ansiães
116	2	41.3	–18	Fonte Coberta, Chã de Alijó
119	2½	41.4	–19½	Dólmen de Arcã, Abreiro, Mirandela
124	2½	41.5	–23	Chã das Arcas 4, Vila Pouca de Aguiar
129	5½	41.2	–24	Pala da Moura, Vilarinho da Castanheira, Carrazeda de Ansiães
130	4	41.4	–26	Anta da Caravela, Caravelas, Mirandela

Az. °	Alt. °	Lat. °	Dec. °	Tomb
80	1	41.9	+8	Mezio 4, Arcos do Valdevez
86	0	41.6	+2½	Rápido 1, Esposende
91	5	41.8	+2½	Eireira, Afife, Viana do Castelo
91	0	42.1	–1	Alto da Portela do Pau 1, Castro Laboreiro, Melgaço
97	1½	41.6	–4½	Castelo de Neiva 1, Viana do Castelo
100	5	41.5	–4	Lamas, Braga

Az. °	Alt. °	Lat. °	Dec. °	Tomb
101	[2]	42.0	–7	Batateiro, Melgaço
102	3	41.9	–7	Mezio 3, Arcos do Valdevez
105	1½	41.8	–10½	Barrosa, Vila Praia de Âncora
108	0½	42.1	–13	Alto da Portela do Pau 2, Castro Laboreiro, Melgaço
113	0	41.6	–17½	Portalagem, Esposende
116	0½	41.5	–19	Cima de Vila 1, Esposende

Chapter 7. Tombs of North Iberia and Neighbouring France

7.1. Orientations of 34 antas de corredor of Galicia.

Az. °	Alt. °	Lat. °	Dec. °	Tomb
Province of A Coruña (NW Galicia)				
93	4	43.0	+0½	Arca da Piosa
93	2½	42.7	–0½	Casota do Fusiño
97	3	42.9	–3	Parxubeira
99	3½	42.6	–4½	Axeitos
101	5	43.0	–4½	Pedra Cuberta
102c	3	42.8	–7	Argalo
102	–0½	42.7	–9½	Pedro da Xesta 1
107	3½	43.1	–10	Casota de Freán
113	–0½	43.0	–17½	Casa dos Mouros
118	0	43.0	–20½	Forno dos Mouros
119	1½	43.0	–20	Dolmen de Monte Carneo
120	3½	42.7	–19	Arca de Barbanza
127	3	43.2	–24	Dombate
129	0½	43.1	–27½	A Fornella (Aprazadoiro)
129c	1	42.7	–27	Cavada 1
typ		42.7		Casoto do Paramo
Province of Pontevedra (SW Galicia)				
65	0½	42.3	+18	Mámoa do Rei, M. Cabeiro
87c	5	42.4	+5½	Mámoa do Rei, Morazzo
111	–0½	42.2	–16	Dolmen de Meixueiro
127	2	42.3	–25	Chan de Arquiña

Az. °	Alt. °	Lat. °	Dec. °	Tomb
Province of Lugo (NE Galicia)				
74	1	42.7	+12	Campo de Valentín
107	2½	42.7	–11	Santa Mariña 30
119	1	43.0	–20½	Veira 1 = D. de A. Moruxosa
120c	0	43.1	–22	Mámoa do Pecado
127	3	42.7	–24	Santa Mariña 19
127	1	43.1	–25½	Mámoa da Caída
134	3	42.7	–28½	Santa Mariña 11
137	1	43.1	–32	Dolmen de Bravos
Province of Ourense (SE Galicia)				
100	1½	41.9	–6½	Outeiro de Cavalcadre 5
102	–0½	42.1	–9½	Outeiro Ferro-Penagachi 11*
103	0	42.1	–10	Outeiro Ferro-Penagachi 16*
104	1½	41.9	–9½	Veiga de Maus de Salas
105	2	41.9	–10	Outeiro de Cavalcadre 1
107	–0½	42.1	–13½	Outeiro de Ferro-Penagachi 9*

*In Portugal

7.2. Orientations of 25 tombs of north-central Spain.

Az. °	Alt. °	Lat. °	Dec. °	Tomb
Province of Burgos				
101	0½	42.7	−8	Ciella, Sedano
113	1	42.7	−16½	Porquera de Butrón, Sedano
121	2	42.7	−21	La Cabaña, Sedano
121	0	42.7	−22½	San Quirce, Sedano
126	1	42.7	−25	Huidobro, Sedano
126	0	42.7	−26	Las Arnillas, Sedano
214	6	42.5	−32½	Ruyales del Paramo 1
126	1	42.1	−25½	Cubillejo de Lara, Mambrilla de Lara
Province of Alava				
128	1½	42.7	−26	La Mina, Molinilla
108	10	42.9	−6	Gurpide Sur, Catadiano
94c	6	42.9	+1	San Sebastian Sur, Catadiano
100	3	42.9	−5½	Aitzkomendi, Eguílaz
131	8	42.8	−22½	Sorginetxe, Arrizala
140c	0½	42.6	−34½	Alto de la Huesera, Laguardia
142	0	42.6	−36	El Encinal, Elvillar
143	0	42.6	−36½	Chabola de la Hechicera, Laguardia
147	1	42.6	−37½	Layaza, Laguardia
172	2	42.6	−45	San Martín, Laguardia
177c	1	42.6	−46½	La Cascaja, Peciña
180	0½	42.6	−47½	El Sotillo, Laguardia
Province of Soria				
135	0½	41.9	−31½	El Alto de la Tejera, Carrascosa de la Sierra
Province of Guadalajara				
115	1	41.4	−17½	Portillo de las Cortes, Aguilar de Anguita
Province of Navarra				
168	−0½	42.6	−47	Portillo de Enériz, Farangortea
168	−0½	42.6	−47	La Mina de Farangortea, Farangortea
123	11	42.9	−15	Arrako, Roncal

7.3. Orientations of 26 megalithic tombs in Guipúzcoa and neighbouring regions of Navarra.

Az. °	Alt. °	Lat. °	Dec. °	Tomb
Sierra de Aralar				
77c	13	43.0	+18	Uidui
95	2½	43.0	−2	Zearragoena
107	1½	43.0	−11½	Uelogoena Norte
125	5	43.0	−21	Arraztarangaña
126	2	43.0	−24	Uelogoena Sur
141	5	43.0	−30½	Jentillari
157	0½	43.0	−42½	Aranzadi
Sierra de Urquilla				
84	4	42.9	+7	Beotegi
85	0	42.9	+3½	Intxusburu
106	0½	42.9	−11½	Txarrigorri
109	4	42.9	−11	Muñaan
115	1	42.9	−17½	Igartza Mendebaidea (Trikiharria)
Uharte-Arrakil				
80	2	42.9	+8½	Aubia
82	5	42.9	+9	Pamplonagain
84	0	42.9	+4	Ipar Aubia
87	2	42.9	+3½	Ekialdeko Elurmenta
93	5	42.9	+1	Errengeneko Debata 3
97	7	42.9	−0½	Seakoin 1
101	1	42.9	−7½	Erbilerri
Northeast Guipúzcoa				
78	3½	43.2	+11	Ponzontorriko
91	6	43.3	+3½	Igoingo Lepua 1
92	2	43.2	−0½	Arritxieta
97	2	43.2	−4	Sagastietako Lepua 1
100	2	43.2	−6	Sagastietako Lepua 2
102	3	43.2	−7	Akolako Lepua 1
103	8½	43.2	−3½	Akolako Lepua 2

7.4. Orientations of 77 dolmenic chambers of the French Basque Country (lat. 43°N, alt. 2° assumed throughout).

Az.	Dec.	Tomb
30	+41	Larria 1N, Sare (L)
45	+32	Xarita 1, Sare (L)
55	+26	Baihuntza 2, St Ét. (BN)
55	+26	Abrakou, Banca (BN)
55	+26	Ibantelli E, Sare (L)
60	+23	Arguibele 1, Ascain (L)
65	+19	, Jarra ( )
65	+19	Dondenia 2, St Martin (BN)
65	+19	Ibantelli W, Sare (L)
65	+19	Xarita 2, Sare (L)
65	+19	Altxaan, Sare (L)
70	+16	Larria 2, Sare (L)
70	+16	Androla, Ascain (L)
75	+12	Arguibele S, Ascain (L)
75	+12	Gastenbakarre 2, Sare (L)
75	+12	Usatuita 1, Urrugne (L)
75	+12	Lezante 2, Urrugne (L)
80	+8	Iguski W, Itxassou (L)
80	+8	Larria 3, Sare (L)
80	+8	Lezante 1, Urrugne (L)
80	+8	Larria 1S, Sare (L)
80	+8	Arrokagaray, Itxassou (L)
85	+5	Zelaia 1, Ascain (L)
85	+5	Urbisi, Urgrne (L)
85	+5	Argainé 1, Sare (L)
85	+5	Osin, Biriatou (L)
85	+5	Xoldokozelai, Urrugne (L)
85	+5	Ameztia, Sare (L)
85	+5	Argainé 2, Sare (L)
85	+5	Arradoy, Ispoure (BN)
85	+5	Lapitzeta W, Sare (L)
85	+5	Galbario 3, Urrugne (L)
90	+1	Iuskadi, Itxassou (L)
90	+1	Arguibele N, Ascain (L)
90	+1	Usatuita 2, Urrugne (L)
90	+1	Bordeta, Barcus (S)
90	+1	Meatze, Itxassou (L)
90	+1	Buluntza, Ahaxe (BN)
95	-2	Xoldokorisko, Ascain (L)
95	-2	Xominen 2, Sare (L)
95	-2	Gastenbakarre 3, Sare (L)
95	-2	Ihicelhaya, Ascain (L)
95	-2	Urdoze, St Ét. (BN)
95	-2	Berdaritz, Aldudes (BN)
100	-6	Arrondo, Irouléguy (BN)
100	-6	Artxuita, Irouléguy (BN)
105	-10	Atermin, Sare (L)
105	-10	Caque 1, Arette (S)
105	-10	Ithé 2, Aussurucq (S)
105	-10	Arrixabale, Sare (L)
105	-10	Plateau Vert 1, Bidarray (BN)
110	-13	Onega, Urrugne (L)
110	-13	Baihuntza 1, St Ét. (BN)
115	-17	Gastenbakarre 1, Sare (L)
115	-17	Xeruen, Ascain (L)
115	-17	Petillare, Lecumberry (BN)
115	-17	Mugi 2, Urrugne (L)
115	-17	Gastenbakarre 1, Sare (L)
115	-17	Bagozabalaga, Larrau (S)
115	-17	Galbario 1, Urrugne (L)
115	-17	Tomba, Sare (L)
115	-17	Ithé 1, Aussurucq (S)
120	-20	Armiaga, Behorleguy (BN)
125	-24	Xominen 1, Sare (L)
125	-24	Erintsou, Urrugne (L)
125	-24	Mugi 1, Urrugne (L)
125	-24	Xuberraxain-Harria, Mendive (BN)
125	-24	Arxilondo, Lecumberry (BN)
135	-30	Gastenya, Mendive (BN)
135	-30	Mikelare, St Martin (BN)
140	-33	Zelaia 2, Ascain (L)
145	-35	Urrixka 1, Aldudes (BN)
145	-35	Iropile, Esterençuby (BN)
155	-40	Erdikoharria, Sare (L)
155	-40	Dondenia 3, St Martin (BN)
165	-43	Kutxaxarria, Urepel (BN)
175	-45	Mokua, Urrugne (L)

St Ét.: St Étienne-de-Baigorry; St Martin: St Martin-d'Arrossa; BN: province of Basse-Navarre; L: province of Labourd; S: province of Soule. Azimuths were measured by Yves Chevalier to the nearest 5°. To compensate for the magnetic variation at the time of the fieldwork (about 4°), 5° has been subtracted from each measure.

7.5. Orientations of 4 simple dolmens and 1 paradolmen of Ariège.

Az.	Alt.	Lat.	Dec.	Tomb
77	0	43.1	+9	Cap del Pouech, Mas d'Azil
86	16	42.9	+13½	Ayer
106	0	43.2	-12	Brillaud, Mas d'Azil
106	1	43.1	-11	Peyre, Mas d'Azil
Paradolmen				
126	5	42.8	-22	Genat, Larège

7.6. Orientations of 21 simple dolmens of Cerdagne and one of Aragon.

Az. °	Alt. °	Lat. °	Dec. °	Tomb
Cerdagne				
73	9	42.2	+18½	Pedracabana, Cabó
83	2½	42.4	+6½	La Barraca del Camp d'en Josepó, Bellver de Cerdanya
83	2½	42.2	+6½	Tarter del Serrat de Malpàs, Cabó
88	0	42.4	+1	Can' Orèn I, Prullans
91	0½	42.4	-0½	CM de les Agudes, Montferrer i Castellbò
95	1	42.4	-3½	CM de Coll de Pou, Montferrer i Castellbò
105	6	42.4	-7	CM de la Llosa, Les Valls de Valira
115	3	42.2	-16	CM de Coll de Jou, Montferrer i Castellbò
118	2	42.4	-19	CM de Turbiàs, Montferrer i Castellbò
118	10	42.5	-13	La Borda, Eina (France)
121	3	42.2	-20½	CM de l'Oliva, Cabó
122	[1]	42.3	-22	La Casa Encantada de la Serra de Pinyana, Senterada*
123	3	42.3	-21½	La Cabana de la Mosquera, Baix Pallars*
123	4	42.2	-21	CM de Colomera, Cabó
135	3	42.5	-29	La Cova del Camp de la Marunya, Enveig (France)
136	5	42.3	-28	La Cabaneta de Perauba, Baix Pallars
140	3	42.2	-32½	CM del Serrat de les Cobertrades, Cabó
145	10	42.4	-28½	CM de Bescaran, Les Valls de Valira
151	3	42.5	-37½	Èguet, Éguet (France)
152	13	42.4	-29	El Paborde, Alp
161	3	42.4	-41½	CM de Sarcèdol, Montferrer i Castellbò
Aragon				
110	6	42.6	-10½	Piedra del Vasar (Losa de la Campa), Tella

CM: Cabana del Moro. Tombs are in Spain unless otherwise stated.
*Taken from J. P. O'Reilly, "On the orientation of certain dolmens recently discovered in Catalonia", Proceedings of the Royal Irish Academy, 3rd ser., iii (1893–96), 573–9.

7.8. Orientations of 22 tombs near Girona.

Az. °	Alt. °	Lat. °	Dec. °	Tomb
Sepulchres with corridor				
138	-0½	41.9	-34½	Puig ses Forques, Calonge (129)
159	-0½	41.9	-45	Mas Bou-Serenys, S. Cristina d'Aro (139)
186	0	41.9	-48½	Can Mina dels Torrents, Llanfranc-Palafrugell (110)
235	1	41.9	-25	Llobinar, Fitor-Fonteta (124)
244	0	41.9	-19½	Serra Mitjana, Fitor-Fonteta (119)
Catalan galleries				
55	-0½	41.9	+24½	Puig d'Arques, Cruïlles (149)
63	*	41.9	+19	Carena Jonquet-Vidal, Torrent (113)
68	0	41.9	+16	Tres Peus, Fitor-Fonteta (116)
79	2	41.9	+9½	Roca de la Gla, Fitor-Fonteta (120)
126	-0½	42.1	-27	Turó de Sant Dalmau, Canet d'Adri (158)
129	-0½	41.9	-29	Mas Estanyet, Fitor-Fonteta (122)
128	*	41.9	-28	Revolts de Torrent, S. Climent de Peralta (112)
137	-0½	42.0	-34	Cementiri dels Moros, Torrent (111)
138	*	42.0	-34	Clot de la Tina. S. Pol-La Bispal (126)
144	0	41.9	-37½	Cova d'en Daina, Romanyà de la Selva (134)
148	0	41.9	-39½	Serra de Cals, Fitor-Fonteta (115)
148	*	41.9	-39½	Dr Pericot, Fitor-Fonteta (118)
154	-0½	41.9	-43	Montagut, Palamós (128)
158	*	41.9	-44½	Vinya Gran, Fitor-Fonteta (121)
168	*	41.9	-46½	En Botey, Fitor-Fonteta (123)
181	0	41.9	-48½	Tres Caires, Fitor-Fonteta (114)
183	*	41.9	-47½	Taula dels Tres Pagesos, Fitor-Fonteta (125)

*Alt. assumed to be +1° (az. measured by J. Tarrús).
Numbers according to J. Tarrús and J. Chinchilla, *Els monuments megalítics* (Girona, 1992).

7.7. Orientations of 10 Catalan galleries near Barcelona.

Az. °	Alt. °	Lat. °	Dec. °	Tomb
91	0	41.9	-1	Collet de Su, Riner
115	2	41.4	-17½	Mas Pla, Querol-Valldossera
118	-1	41.8	-22	Tomba dels Moros, Llanera
124	2	41.6	-23½	Les Maioles, Rubio, Anoia
131c	?	41.8	20	La Pera d'Ardèvol, Pinós
140	3	41.6	-32½	Can Gol, La Roca del Vallès/Mataró
157	1	42.0	-42½	Puig Ses Lloses, Folgaroles
174	2½	42.0	-45½	Puig Ses Pedres, Santa Marcia de Corcó
225	12	41.6	-22½	La Roca d'en Toni, St Geius de Vilassar/Mataró
270c	1	41.6	-0½	Pedra Arca, Llinars del Vallès/Mataró

Chapter 8. Tombs of the French Causses

Azimuths in Tables 8.1 to 8.10 were measured by Y. Chevalier ("Orientations of 935 dolmens of southern France", *AA*, no. 24 (1999), S47–82), J. Clottes ("Inventaire des mégalithes de France: Lot", supplement 1/5 (1977) to *Gallia préhistoire*), and J. Clottes and Cl. Maurand ("Inventaire des mégalithes de France: Aveyron. L'Ouest aveyronnais: Causses de Limogne et de Villeneuve", supplement 1/7 (1983) to *Gallia préhistoire*). For the calculation of declination an altitude of 2° has been assumed. Except for Ardèche and Gard, a single latitude has been adopted for all the tombs of a given *département*: 44° for Tarn, Tarn-et-Garonne and Vaucluse; 44½° for Aveyron, Lot and Lozère; 45° for Dordogne; 45½° for Charente, Charente-Maritime and Corrèze; 46° for Creuse and Haute-Vienne; and 46½° for Deux-Sèvres and Vienne.

8.1. Orientations of 18 simple C-dolmens, and 5 C-dolmens with vestibule, of western *départements*.

Az.°	Dec.°	Tomb	Az.°	Dec.°	Tomb
Simple dolmens			122	−20	La Chassagne, St-Cernin-de-Larche (Co)
74	+12	Combe-Fosse, Jugeals-Nazareth (Co)	128	−24	Brioux, Payré (V)
77	+10	La Ramière, Noailhac (Co)	129	−25	Chez Vinaigre, Ronsenac (Ch)
78	+10	Rochesseux, Aubazine (Co)	147	−35	La Route-Vieille, Noailles (Co)
80	+8	Fontourcy, Beynat (Co)	151	−36	Mourioux 1, Mourioux (Cr)
87	+3	La Borderie, Altillac (Co)	158	−38	La Reynex, La Croisille (HV)
87	+3	La Villedieu, Magnac-Bourg (HV)			
88	+3	Bonarme, St-Pardoux-et-Vielvic (D)	*Dolmens with vestibule*		
89	+2	La Côte, St-Laurent-sur-Gorre (HV)	12	+45	Vaure, Miallet (D)
93	−1	La Palein, St-Cernin-de-Larche (Co)	138	−30	L'Étang, Dignac (Ch)
101	−6	Ménardeix, Pionnat (Cr)	141	−32	Chantegrel, St-Chamassy (D)
112	−14	La Brande, Dirac (Ch)	144	−33	La Gélie, Édon (Ch)
119	−18	Le Busserais, La Bussière (V)	154	−38	La Jolinie, St-Jory-de-Chalais (D)

Ch: Charente; Co: Corrèze; Cr: Creuse; D: Dordogne; HV: Haute-Vienne; V: Vienne

8.2(a). Numbers of simple C-dolmens with given orientations, from among the 352 simple C-dolmens of Lot whose orientations are listed by Clottes in his inventory. Corresponding declinations are within brackets, while within parentheses are the numbers assigned to the dolmens in Clottes's inventory.

10° [+46°]: 1 (270)
14° [+45°]: 1 (81)
22° [+43°]: 1 (403)
25° [+42°]: 1 (511)
29° [+40°]: 1 (88)
35° [+37°]: 1 (36)
36° [+37°]: 1 (556)
40° [+35°]: 4 (77, 206, 366, 484)
41° [+34°]: 1 (243)
44° [+32°]: 1 (161)
45° [+32°]: 1 (294)
46° [+31°]: 1 (125)
47° [+30°]: 1 (490)
50° [+29°]: 1 (23)
51° [+28°]: 1 (344)
52° [+27°]: 1 (51)
53° [+27°]: 1 (504)
54° [+26°]: 1 (495)
55° [+25°]: 1 (459)
56° [+25°]: 1 (257)
58° [+23°]: 1 (217)
60° [+22°]: 1 (40)
61° [+21°]: 2 (444, 507)
62° [+21°]: 2 (308, 434)

63° [+20°]: 1 (506)
64° [+19°]: 8 (26, 62, 76, 80, 273, 280, 421, 500)
66° [+18°]: 2 (163, 279)
67° [+17°]: 4 (219, 287, 466, 563)
68° [+17°]: 3 (6, 248, 559)
69° [+16°]: 3 (57, 354, 548)
70° [+15°]: 1 (350)
71° [+15°]: 2 (32, 160)
72° [+14°]: 3 (213, 262, 407)
73° [+13°]: 2 (63, 187)
74° [+13°]: 4 (235, 310, 353, 565)
75° [+12°]: 1 (261)
76° [+11°]: 3 (317, 362, 529)
77° [+10°]: 1 (525)
78° [+9°]: 3 (35, 37, 113)
79° [+9°]: 2 (169, 250)
80° [+8°]: 1 (293)
81° [+8°]: 1 (553)
82° [+7°]: 2 (156, 234)
84° [+5°]: 5 (116, 227, 304, 379, 487)
85° [+5°]: 1 (241)
86° [+4°]: 2 (20, 64)
87° [+3°]: 1 (315)
88° [+3°]: 2 (66, 228)

Table 8.2(a) continued]

89° [+2°]: 5 (135, 190, 255, 417, 431)
90° [+1°]: 4 (202, 398, 415, 460)
91° [0°]: 2 (3, 327)
92° [0°]: 5 (53, 167, 197, 305, 316)
93° [−1°]: 3 (74, 208, 307)
94° [−2°]: 10 (25, 72, 168, 188, 309, 388, 400, 430, 481, 502)
95° [−2°]: 2 (285, 318)
96° [−3°]: 6 (13, 118, 230, 523, 539, 550)
97° [−4°]: 5 (4, 282, 340, 425, 569)
98° [−4°]: 4 (59, 251, 348, 438)
99° [−5°]: 15 (22, 46, 67, 73, 114, 249, 256, 263, 314, 347,
            351, 377, 385, 465, 478)
100° [−6°]: 6 (158, 198, 265, 352, 399, 469)
101° [−7°]: 6 (129, 236, 268, 345, 493, 522)
102° [−7°]: 8 (44, 127, 260, 295, 435, 436, 443, 561)
103° [−8°]: 4 (136, 275, 419, 440)
104° [−9°]: 12 (28, 55, 98, 200, 276, 306, 328, 346, 365,
            447, 501, 524)
105° [−9°]: 6 (175, 209, 290, 333, 424, 534)
106° [−10°]: 7 (139, 195, 301, 339, 396, 482, 527)
107° [−11°]: 4 (90, 99, 193, 225)
108° [−12°]: 2 (189, 269)
109° [−12°]: 13 (101, 117, 191, 194, 267, 274, 357, 441,
            449, 470, 477, 485, 544)
110° [−13°]: 9 (82, 96, 120, 210, 360, 381, 428, 471, 475)
111° [−14°]: 8 (27, 253, 325, 358, 414, 461, 532, 533)
112° [−14°]: 9 (111, 133, 157, 207, 303, 343, 361, 380, 519)
113° [−15°]: 1 (61)
114° [−16°]: 9 (17, 24, 150, 222, 224, 297, 323, 416, 458)
115° [−16°]: 8 (93, 119, 181, 258, 292, 397, 408, 476)
116° [−17°]: 4 (322, 373, 386, 468)
117° [−18°]: 6 (97, 146, 221, 289, 392, 395)
118° [−18°]: 3 (71, 108, 480)
119° [−19°]: 5 (48, 298, 467, 503, 537)
120° [−20°]: 1 (296)

121° [−20°]: 3 (165, 218, 423)
124° [−22°]: 6 (11, 105, 173, 300, 336, 420)
125° [−23°]: 3 (311, 437, 464)
127° [−24°]: 3 (33, 299, 384)
128° [−25°]: 1 (486)
129° [−25°]: 1 (530)
130° [−26°]: 3 (145, 445, 494)
131° [−27°]: 1 (406)
133° [−28°]: 2 (56, 363)
134° [−28°]: 6 (12, 16, 211, 331, 335, 359)
135° [−29°]: 1 (271)
136° [−29°]: 1 (85)
139° [−31°]: 5 (92, 164, 229, 233, 564)
140° [−32°]: 2 (128, 364)
142° [−33°]: 2 (278, 560)
144° [−34°]: 3 (172, 242, 247)
145° [−34°]: 1 (126)
146° [−35°]: 3 (50, 212, 245)
147° [−35°]: 1 (18)
148° [−36°]: 2 (95, 122)
149° [−36°]: 3 (246, 492, 520)
151° [−37°]: 2 (54, 91)
152° [−37°]: 1 (84)
154° [−38°]: 5 (1, 34, 103, 171, 284)
155° [−39°]: 2 (324, 332)
157° [−39°]: 1 (439)
160° [−40°]: 2 (185, 570)
163° [−41°]: 1 (159)
174° [−43°]: 1 (455)
177° [−44°]: 1 (94)
182° [−44°]: 1 (514)
183° [−44°]: 1 (491)
184° [−44°]: 1 (456)
192° [−43°]: 1 (131)

8.2(b). Orientations of 39 C-dolmens with vestibule of Lot.

Az. °	Dec. °	Tomb	Az. °	Dec. °	Tomb
4	+47	Touron, Lavercantière	84	+5	Lei Barto, Béduer
34	+38	Noutari 1, Carennac	90	+1	Gabaudet 1, Issendolus
36	+37	Marsigaillet 2, Laramière	93	−1	Barthès 2, Floirac
51	+28	Le Pech d'Arsou, Corn	94	−2	La Rue, Rocamadour
64	+19	Cloup de Coutze, Béduer	95*	−2	La Pélasse, Montvalent
70*	+15	Grézelade 3, Lanzac	99	−5	Les Escurettes, Padirac
72*	+14	Le Moulin 1, Reilhac	99	−5	Le Terrou, Gramat
74	+13	Pierre Levée de la Pannonie, Rocamadour	99	−5	Barrade, Montvalent
77	+10	La Borie du Bois 2, Laramière	102	−7	Le Pech de Tibouyé 3, Cabrerets
78	+10	Le Pech 1, Alvignac	102	−7	Le Pech de Goubières 1, Rocamadour
80*	+8	Bartassou, Serignac	104	−9	Le Pech de Molinié 2, Larroque-Toirac
81	+8	Cambajou 1, Montfaucon	108*	−12	Le Pech de la Barre, Cabrerets

Table 8.2(b) continued]

Az. °	Dec. °	Tomb	Az. °	Dec. °	Tomb
109	−12	Barthès 1, Floirac	124	−22	Barrières 3, Miers
109	−12	Pradines, Cadrieu	127	−24	La Baune, Les Junies
109	−12	Bougoulat, Padirac	131*	−27	Boygues Basse, Carlucet
111	−14	Le Puech Roussille, Béduer	131	−27	Pech Plumé, Loubressac
114*	−16	Butte-St-Simon, Belfort-du-Quercy	143	−33	Les Escabasses 2, Flaujac-Gare
120	−20	Le Pech 4, Alvignac	161	−41	Pourquayré, Marcilhac-sur-Célé
122	−21	Les Junies, Quetty	166	−42	Les Mazuquarts, Flaujac-Gare
124	−22	Le Pech de la Curado, Carayac			

*From the inventory by Clottes.

8.3. Orientations of 121 simple C-dolmens, and 8 dolmens with vestibule, of Aveyron.

Az. °	Dec. °	Tomb	Az. °	Dec. °	Tomb
Simple dolmens			84*	+5	Bois de Galtier, Martiel
27*	+41	Puech du Dougnou, Ols-et-Rinhodes	84	+5	?, Mostuéjouls
28*	+41	Devès des Gleyettes 2, Martiel	84	+5	Auriac, St-Rome-de-?
32*	+39	Puech Mort 1, Martiel	85*	+5	Les Places 3, Foissac
34*	+38	Puech Mort 2, Martiel	85*	+5	Puech de la Pruneyrie, Martiel
35	+37	Randelle, Verrières	86*	+4	Le Pet 2, Ambeyrac
35	+37	Le Bouissou, Agen d'Aveyron	86	+4	Larquinel, Verrières
40*	+35	Tombeau des Anglais, Causse-et-Diège	86	+4	Combe Croise, La Cavalerie
47*	+30	Le Causse, Villeneuve	87*	+3	Le Pet 3, Ambeyrac
47*	+30	Le Devès 3, Martiel	88*	+3	Tombe de l'Homme, Villeneuve
50*	+29	Tombeau des Anglais, Martiel	88	+3	La Plaine, St-André-de-Vézines
56*	+25	Glèbes, La Capelle-Balaguier	88	+3	La Borie Blanque, St-Rome-de-Tarn
56*	+25	Le Devès 1, Martiel	90*	+1	Barthas de Bouillac, Martiel
59*	+23	Pouzets, La Capelle-Balaguier	90*	+1	Le Rey, Villeneuve
60*	+22	Jonade 1, Foissac	90*	+1	Les Garrigues 1, Foissac
63	+20	Le Serre de Cabrié, St-André-de-Vézines	90*	+1	Tombeau des Géants, Villeneuve
63*	+20	Bois del Rey 2, Martiel	91*	0	Puech de Saint-Clair, Martiel
65*	+19	Les Rousiès 1, Martiel	92*	0	Les Garrigues 2, Foissac
66*	+18	Puech Youles 4, Ols-et-Rinhodes	92*	0	Puech Redon, Martiel
67*	+17	Les Aumières 1, Ambeyrac	93*	−1	Cap de Saint-Marty 1, Balaguier-d'Olt
67*	+17	Puech de la Guise, Ols-et-Rinhodes	93	−1	Bouygues 1, Saujac
68*	+17	Causse du Prunier, Martiel	94*	−2	Cloup de Rhines, Foissac
70*	+15	Jonade 2, Foissac	94*	−2	Souloumbradou, Martiel
71	+15	Surgères 3, Gaillac d'Aveyron	95*	−2	Le Trep, Ols-et-Rinhodes
71	+15	Tiergues, St-Affrique	95*	−2	Puech Youles 5, Ols-et-Rinhodes
72*	+14	La Viguerie, Salles-Courbaties	96*	−3	Puech Youles 6, Ols-et-Rinhodes
75*	+12	Champs Grands, Martiel	96	−3	Combets 1, Millau
75*	+12	Puech Youles 2, Ols-et-Rinhodes,	96	−3	Espeyroux 2, Muret-le-Château
75	+12	Caramel, Salles-la-Source	96	−3	Laumière, St-Rome-de-Cernon
77	+10	Crassous, St-Affrique	97	−4	Labro 3, St-Georges-de-Luzençon
77*	+10	Bois Barrat, Ols-et-Rinhodes	97	−4	Espeyroux 4, Muret-le-Château
79	+9	La Fabière, La Cavalerie	100*	−6	Truffières 1, Vailhourles
80*	+8	Puech d'Ols, Ols-et-Rinhodes	100	−6	Buzeins 1, Buzeins
81*	+8	Combemousseuse, La Capelle-Balaguier	101*	−7	Le Cayre, Ols-et-Rinhodes
82*	+7	Croufel, La Capelle-Balaguier	101*	−7	Puech Mauriol, Ambeyrac
83*	+6	Le Causse 2, Villeneuve	102*	−7	Igues, Saujac
83*	+6	Puech Youles 1, Ols-et-Rinhodes	102*	−7	Les Agars 1, Ols-et-Rinhodes

Table 8.3 continued]

Az.°	Dec.°	Tomb	Az.°	Dec.°	Tomb
102*	−7	Truffières 2, Vailhourles	120	−20	Bouygues, Saujac
102	−7	Boussac E, St-Affrique	120*	−20	La Bouissière, Balaguier d'Olt
102	−7	Labro 1, St-Georges-de-Luzençon	122	−21	Pérignagol, Balsac
105*	−9	Bois d'Alary, Balaguier d'Olt	122	−21	La Liquisse, Nant
105*	−9	Cap de Saint-Marty 2, Balaguier d'Olt	123	−22	Nissac Sud, Versols-et-Lapeyre
105*	−9	Estrabols, Saujac	124*	−22	Devès des Gleyettes 1, Martiel
105*	−9	Les Aumières 2, Ambeyrac	125	−23	Duéjouls, Millau
105*	−9	Pré Carré 2, Monteils	127	−24	Lavernhe, Lestrade-et-Thouels
107	−11	Le Puech Gros, Rodelle	131	−27	Montaubert 1, Salles-la-Source
108*	−12	Le Devès 2, Martiel	131	−27	Commune 3, Vimenet
109*	−12	Le Pet 1, Ambeyrac	132*	−27	Combe del Mas, Balaguier d'Olt
109*	−12	Marie-Gaillard, Martiel	140*	−32	L'Homme Mort, Montsalès
109	−12	St Antonin, Salles-la-Source	145	−34	Géonade Ouest, Foissac
110	−13	Boussac Ouest, St-Affrique	145*	−34	Les Places 1, Foissac
110*	−13	Le Couderc, Foissac	145*	−34	Mas de Rénailhac, Balaguier d'Olt
111	−14	Buzeins 2, Buzeins	149	−36	Montaubert 2, Salles-la-Source
113*	−15	Cloup de Coubèles, Salvagnac-Cajarc	153	−38	La Vayssière 4, Salles-la-Source
113*	−15	Puech Youles 3, Ols-et-Rinhodes	165	−42	La Glène, St Léons
113	−15	Puechamp 6, Salles-la-Source	180*	−44	Le Causse Blanc, Capdenac-Gare
113	−15	Espeyroux 5, Muret-le-Château			
113	−15	Mas Rouquous, Salles-Curan			*Dolmens with vestibule*
115	−16	Lissalinie 1, Valady	81	+8	Genévrier, Salles-la-Source
115*	−16	Bois del Rey 1, Martiel	81*	+6	Mas de Lavencat, Salvagnac-Cajarc
115*	−16	Les Agars 2, Old-et-Rinhodes	83	+6	St-Germain, Sales-la-Source
115*	−16	Rosier 1, Martiel	84	+5	Montaubert 3, Salles-la-Source
116	−17	La Borie Blanque, St-Rome-de-Tarn	90*	+1	Couaylles, Martiel
117*	−18	Pré Carré 1, Montiels	90*	+1	Puech d'Alès 1, Martiel
119	−19	Le Pech de la Guise, La Capelle-Balaguier	95*	−2	Rosier 2, Martiel
120	−20	Capdenaguet, Balsac	120*	−20	Pierre Levée, Naussac

*From the inventory of Clottes and Maurand.

8.4. Orientations of 16 simple C-dolmens of Tarn-et-Garonne.

Az.°	Dec.°	Tomb
61	+22	La Veyrie 2, St-Antonin-Noble-Val
70	+15	Le Bosc, St-Antonin-Noble-Val
79	+9	Crabole 1, St-Projet
79	+9	Crabole 2, St-Projet
85	+5	Charles, Septfonds
86	+4	Le Pech, Bruniquel
87	+3	Finelles 1, Septfonds
90	+1	Finelles 3, Septfonds
92	0	Pécoupet, St-Antonin-Noble-Val
93	−1	Le Pech 10, Bruniquel
108	−12	La Veyrie 1, St-Antonin-Noble-Val
110	−13	Bartalbenque Ouest, Septfonds
113	−15	Le Pech 3, Bruniquel
125	−23	Le Pech 2, Bruniquel
128	−25	Le Pech d'Ax, St-Antonin-Noble-Val
141	−33	?, Lauzerte

8.5. Orientations of 13 simple C-dolmens, and 1 C-dolmen with vestibule, of Tarn.

Az.°	Dec.°	Tomb
Simple dolmens		
17	+45	Nougayrol, Trévien
60	+22	Peyro-Lebado, Crespin
76	+11	Gouty, Valderiès
88	+3	Suquet, Penne
116	−17	St-Paul, Ste-Cécile-du-Cayrou
122	−21	La Farge, St-Beauzile
123	−22	Le Pech, Milhars
135	−29	Cabanes, St-Beauzile
140	−32	Peyralade, Vaour
152	−38	Peyro-Lebado, Le Verdier
164	−42	Plo de la Gante, Labastide-Rouairoux
175	−44	Rivet 2, Marnaves
185	−44	Rivet 1, Marnaves
Dolmen with vestibule		
108	−12	Cayrou de L'Empiri, Alos

8.6. Orientations of 23 simple C-dolmens, and 1 C-dolmen with vestibule, of Lozère.

Az.°	Dec.°	Tomb		Az.°	Dec.°	Tomb
Simple dolmens				102	−7	Valbelle, Florac
64	+19	La Condamine, Montbrun		104	−9	Combe-Lébrouze, Montbrun
68	+17	Téoulets, Ste-Énimie		106	−10	Recoules de l'Hom, Le Massegros
76	+11	Drigas 2, Hures-la-Parade		112	−14	Costeguison, Meyrueis
76	+11	Les Ayguières, Chanac		122	−21	Les Avens, Hures-la-Parade
82	+7	Aurès, Gabuizières		124	−22	Gd Dolmen Aurès, Gatuzières
84	+5	Le Frayssé, Salles-Prunet		126	−23	La Rouvière 3, Chanac
86	+4	Le Féron, Le Born		130	−26	Casteviel, Ste-Croix-Vallée-Française
88	+3	La Bastide, Florac		138	−31	La Pierre Plate, Florac
90	+1	Cerrières, Hures-la-Parade		156	−39	Les Bastides, St-Pierre-des-Tripiers
96	−3	Drigas 1, Hures-la-Parade				
96	−3	?, Chirac		*Dolmen with vestibule*		
100	−6	Royde, Chanac		120	−20	La Prade, Allenc
100	−6	La Galline, Banassac				

8.7. Orientations of 66 simple C–dolmens and 5 C–dolmens with vestibule, in Ardèche (A) and Gard (G).

Az.°	Lat.°	Dec.°	Tomb		Az.°	Lat.°	Dec.°	Tomb
Simple dolmens					146	44.4	−35	D— , Chandolas(?)-de-St-Alban (A)
81	44.3	+7½	Les Conchettes, St-Paul-le-Jeune (A)		147	44.3	−35½	Combe de Blanc 3, St-Paul-le-Jeune (A)
84	44.4	+5½	Brahic 1, Brahic (A)		149	44.4	−36½	Fontrouine 4, Grospierres (A)
88	44.5	+2½	Chapias 1, Rosières (A)		151	44.5	−37	Les Clausasses 4, Gras (A)
90	44.3	+1	Mas de Baume 2, St-André-de-Cruzières (A)		152	44.4	−37½	Grange de Chevallier 1, Grospierres (A)
92	44.3	0	La Gautière 2, Aiguèze (G)		154	44.3	−38½	Les Oeillantes 1, Barjac (G)
93	44.4	−1	Beauregard, St-Remèze (A)		156	44.6	−39	Les Faysses, Vesseaux (A)
95	44.3	−2½	Pin d'Ismaël 4, Courry (G)		157	44.9	−39	Échamps, Borée (A)
96	44.4	−3	L'Abeille 1, Labeaume (A)		158	44.5	−40	Le Queiré, Vinezac (A)
100	44.3	−6	Mas de Baume 1, St-André-de-Cruzières (A)		162	44.5	−41	Les Traverses 1, Chauzon (A)
103	44.5	−8	La Grange aux Pères, Lablachère (A)		163	44.3	−41½	La Calade 2, Barjac (G)
106	44.5	−10	Flandrin A, Lablachère (A)		167	44.3	−42½	Bois du Garn, Le Garn (G)
107	44.4	−11	Bourbouillet 2, St-Alban-sur-Sampzon (A)		168	44.4	−42½	Bourbouillet 3, St-Alban-sur-Sampzon (A)
111	44.3	−13½	Les Conchettes 2, St-Paul-le-Jeune (A)		171	44.3	−43½	Les Peyrolles 1, St-André-de-Cruzières (A)
114	44.3	−15½	Pin d'Ismaël 3, Courry (G)		172	44.5	−43½	Flandrin 10, Lablachére (A)
116	44.5	−17	Rieutort, Chauzon (A)		173	44.4	−43½	Les Granges 17, Berrias-et-Casteljau (A)
117	44.5	−17½	Les Molasses 2, Chauzon (A)		173	44.3	−43½	Les Peyrolles 2, St-André-de-Cruzières (A)
117	44.5	−17½	Les Molasses 4, Chauzon (A)		175	44.4	−43½	Champvermeil, Bidon (A)
121	45.0	−20	Le Chabot, Colombier-le-Jeune (A)		176	44.4	−44	Ranc d'Aven 2, Chandolas (A)
123	44.4	−21½	Grange de Chevallier 2, Grospierres (A)		176	44.5	−43½	Flandrin D, Lablachère (A)
124	44.4	−22	Gabiane, Labeaume (A)		176	44.5	−43½	La Piole, Lablachère (A)
126	44.5	−23½	Dolmen 2, Chauzon (A)		176	44.4	−44	?, Brahic (A)
132	44.4?	−27	Générarques, ?		176	44.5	−43½	Clos Lorion, Rosières (A)
133	44.4	−28	Gour de l'Estang, Chandolas (A)		179	44.4	−44	Les Géantes 2, Bourg-St-Andéol (A)
136	44.3	−29½	Les Bouissières, St-Paul-le-Jeune (A)		184	44.4	−44	Serre de Bernard, Chandolas (A)
136*	44.4	−31½	Les Géantes B, Bourg-St-Andéol (A)		186	44.4	−43½	Combe de Lèque, St-Alban-sur-Sampzon (A)
137	44.4?	−30	Balaizuc, ?		187	44.4	−43½	Ranc d'Aven 1, Chandolas (A)
138	44.5	−30½	Flandrin B, Lablachère (A)		189	44.4	−43	Grange de Boisson 2, Grospierres (A)
140	44.5	−31½	Flandrin 11, Lablachère (A)		191	44.5	−43	Flandrin C, Lablachère (A)
141	44.5	−32	Méandre de Gen, Ruoms (A)		192	44.3	−43	Gaytière, Le Garn (G)
143	44.3	−34	La Calade 3, Barjac (G)		196	44.3	−42	Les Oeillantes 2, Barjac (G)

Table 8.7 continued]

Az.°	Lat.°	Dec.°	Tomb
211	44.4	−36½	Combe de Bonne Fille, Grospierres (A)
217	44.4	−33½	Grange de Boisson 1, Grospierres (A)
221	44.3	−31½	Les Buissières 2, St-Paul-le-Jeune (A)
222*	44.4	−32½	Les Géantes A, Bourg-St-Andéol (A)
229	44.4	−26½	Bourbouillet 1, St-Alban-sur-Sampzon (A)

Dolmens with vestibule

120	44.2	−19½	La Caporie 1, Méjeannes-le-Clap (G)
132	44.3	−27½	La Bartre, Laval-St-Roman (G)
172	44.3	−43½	Les Chaumettes, St-André-de-Cruzières (A)
192*	44.4	−45	Les Géants 3, Bourg-St-Andéol (A)
215	44.3	−34½	La Devèze, Barjac (G)

*Alt. 0°; az. measured by author.

8.9. Orientations of 27 C-dolmens with coudé corridors. First col.: az. of corridor, as listed by Chevalier; second col: az. of chamber, as listed by Clottes or as measured from a site plan of Chevalier.

Az. (i)°	Az. (ii)°	Tomb
10	'east'	Champerboux, Ste-Énimie (Lz)
83	15	Cérès, Salles-la-Source (Av)
114		L'Aumède-Haut, Chanac (Lz)
136		Changefège 2, Balsièges (Lz)
138	83	Gd Dolmen de Rouvière, Chanac (Lz)
139	54	Les Cloups, Ginouillac (Lt)
144	64	Changefège 1, Balsièges (Lz)
146	83	La Marconnière 1, St Saturnin-de-Lucian (Lz)
147	62	Griffié, St-Jean-de-Laur (Lt)
150		Montplaisir, Chenon (Ch)
	91	Le Pech 6, Alvignac (Lt)
155	100	Séveyrac, Bozouls (Av)
156	92	Le Mt-Roubio, Ste Énimie (Lz)
157		Trinquiez, Salles-la-Source (Av)
158		Lanas C, Lanas (A)
163	89	Les Escabasses 1, Flaujac-Gare (Lt)
173	102	Pérignac 2, Salles-la-Source (Av)
176	104	Poujoulet 1, Montrodat (Lz)
176	109	Aumède-Bas 3, Chanac (Lz)
176	108	Gouziac S, Hures (Lz)
	109	Surges, Thedirac (Lt)
177	110	Les Crozes 1, La Loubière (Av)
181	90	Vézinies 3, Salles-la-Source (Av)
184		La Nogarède, Chanac (Lz)
184	104	Gd Dolmen du Chardonnet, Auxillac (Lz)
186	116	Rouvière 2, Chanac (Lz)
	134	Causse de Bullac 2, Boussac (Lt)

A: Ardèche; Av: Aveyron; Ch: Charente; Lt: Lot; Lz: Lozère.

8.8. *See following page.*

8.10. Orientations of 44 Angoumoisin-type dolmens.

Az.°	Dec.°	Tomb
16	+44	La Petite Pérotte, Fontenille (Ch)
39	+34	Dolmen F, Bougon (DS)
62	+20	La Pierre Pèse, Limalonges (DS)
63	+20	La Motte de la Garde, Luxé (Ch)
65	+18	La Maison de la Vieille, Luxé (Ch)
67	+17	Russel 2, Limalonges (DS)
81	+8	La Case du Loup, St-Léon-d'Issigeac (D)
85	+5	Les Lisières A, Pamproux (DS)
89	+2	La Combe, Champniers (Ch)
91	+1	Villaigue A, St-Martin-l'Ars (V)
92	0	Laverré, Aslonnes (V)
97	−4	La Pierre Fouqueurée, Ardillières (CM)
98	−4	La Folatière, Luxé (Ch)
100	−6	Dolmen A6, Chenon (Ch)
102	−7	La Bassetière, Sillars (V)
103	−8	La Pierre Mouilleron, Nieul-sur-l'Autize (Ve)
106	−10	La Grelaudière, Verteuil (Ch)
112	−14	Arlait B, Château-Larcher (V)
114	−15	La Boixe G, Vervant (Ch)
126	−23	Les Roches, Chenon (Ch)
130	−25	La Grosse Pérotte, Fontenille (Ch)
132	−27	La Graube 2, L'Éguille (CM)
134	−28	La Pierre Levée, St-Même-les-Carrières (Ch)
139	−31	La Pierre Levée, St-Fort-sur-le-Né (Ch)
140	−31	La Boixe B, Vervant (Ch)
142	−32	La Lombertie, Édon (Ch)
145	−34	Le Gros Dognon, Ligné (Ch)
150	−36	La Boucharderie, St-Estèphe (Ch)
152	−37	La Peyrelevade, Paussac-St-Vivien (D)
155	−38	Dolmen A, Fouqueure (Ch)
155	−38	Dolmen B, Fouqueure (Ch)
156	−38	La Pierre Levée, Ardillières (CM)
159	−39	La Saussaye 1, Soubise (CM)
160	−40	Montplaisir, Chenon (Ch)
171	−42	La Pierre Levée 1, Chenon (Ch)
171	−42	La Pierre Levée 2, Chenon (Ch)
172	−41	Puynard, Sommières (V)
172	−42	La Motte de la Jacquille, Fontenille (Ch)
173	−42	La Pierrefitte, St-Georges (Ch)
180	−43	Châteauroux, Tonnay-Charente (CM)
194	−41	La Saussaye 2, Soubise (CM)
198	−39	Dolmen A, Bougon (DS)
281	+9	Dolmen C, Bougon (DS)
289	+15	Le Blanc, Beaumont (D)

Ch: Charente; CM: Charente-Maritime; D: Dordogne; DS: Deux-Sèvres; V: Vienne; Ve: Vendée.

8.8. Orientations of 11 double C-dolmens of Lot.

Az. °	Tomb	Az. °	Tomb
35/27	Le Verdier 1, Cajarc	108	Les Claouzelles, Padirac
92	Les Combarols, Durbans	108/108	Escazals, Durbans
93	Champ de Palabre, Mas de Brézac, Boussac	117	Borie Grand, Durbans
98	Bois des Garroustes, Serignac	118	La Péchette, Montfaucon
104/104	Pech de Grammont, Gramat	142	Les Ignes de Magnagues, Carennac
108/113	Pech Plumé 2, Loubressac		

Chapter 9. Tombs of Provence and East Languedoc

9.1. Orientations of the 4 Fontvieille dolmenic hypogea (lat. 43.7°).

Az. °	Alt. °	Dec. °	Tomb	Az. °	Alt. °	Dec. °	Tomb
259	0	−8½	La Source	267	0	−2½	Bounias
262	0	−6	Le Castellet	270	0	−0½	Épée de Roland (Les Cordes)

9.2. Orientations of 84 BR-dolmens in Provence.

Long-chambered dolmens of western Provence

(i) The Alpilles Group (including Fontvieille)

Az. °	Alt. °	Lat. °	Dec. °	Tomb
246	*	43.8	−16	Les Gavots, Orgon (BR)
256	*	43.7	−9	Le Roucas de l'Eure, Aureille (BR)
266	0	43.7	−3½	Coutignargues, Fontvieille (BR)
268	0	43.7	−2	Mas d'Argard, Fontvieille (BR)
287	0	43.7	+12	La Mérindole, Fontvieille (BR)

(ii) The North Luberon Group

Az. °	Alt. °	Lat. °	Dec. °	Tomb
234	7	43.8	−20	La Pichone, Ménerbes (Vcl)
252	24	43.8	+4½	L'Ubac, Goult (Vcl)

(iii) The Bassin d'Aix Group

Az. °	Alt. °	Lat. °	Dec. °	Tomb
241	*	43.6	−19½	Cudières 2, Jouques (BR)
248	*	43.5	−13	La Blaque, Aix-en-Provence (BR)
250	*	43.6	−14½	Cudières 1, Jouques (BR)
259	*	43.5	−7	Château Blanc, Ventabren (BR)
268	*	43.6	−0½	La Plaine, Meyrargues (BR)
286	0	43.5	+11	Maurely, St-Antonin-sur-Bayon (BR)

(iv) The Maures Group

Az. °	Alt. °	Lat. °	Dec. °	Tomb
221	*	43.1	−33½	Gotteaubry, La-Londe-Les-Maures (V)
223	*	43.1	−32	Maubelle, La Crau d'Hyères (V)
256	*	43.2	−17½	Les Antiquailles, Cuers (V)

Table 9.2 continued]

Square-chambered dolmens of eastern Provence

Az. °	Alt. °	Lat. °	Dec. °	Tomb
206	*	43.9	−38½	Les Pierres Blanches, Castellane (AHP)
206	*	43.7	−39	La Brainée, Mons (V)
206	*	43.6	−39	Bassegat, Fox-Amphoux (V)
221	*	43.9	−31½	Villevieille, Demandolx (AHP)
221	*	43.7	−31½	Le Serre-Dinguille, St-Cézaire-sur-Siagne (AM)
221	*	43.7	−31½	Les Clapières St-Cézaire-sur-Siagne (AM)
221	*	43.7	−31½	Bernard, St-Cézaire-sur-Siagne (AM)
221	*	43.2	−32	La Briande, Ramatuelle (V)
221	*	43.7	−31½	Pomeiret et Clauds, Cabris (AM)
222	*	43.7	−31	Clamarquier, Le Rouret (AM)
224	*	43.7	−30	La Pignatelle, Comps (V)
226	*	43.7	−29	Les Peyraoutes, Roquefort-les-Pins (AM)
226	*	43.7	−29	Pierre Haute, Chateauneuf-Grasse (AM)
226	*	43.6	−29	La Colle, Ampus (V)
226	*	43.6	−29	Camptracier, Tourrettes (AM)
231	*	43.7	−25½	Le Degoutaï, St-Vallier-de-Thiey (AM)
233	*	43.7	−24½	Les Blaquières, Vence (AM)
236	*	43.7	−22½	Stramousse, Cabris (AM)
239	*	43.6	−20½	Maren, Ampus (V)
239	*	43.5	−20½	Peicervier, Lorgues (V)
239	*	43.4	−20½	Camdumy, Cabasse (V)
241	*	43.7	−19½	St-Marcellin, Mons (V)
246	*	43.4	−16	La Bouissière, Cabasse (V)
246	*	43.7	−16	Les Claps, Escragnolles (AM)
246	*	43.7	−16	La Colle, Mons (V)
251	*	43.6	−12½	L'Etang, Figanières (V)
251	*	43.4	−12½	Les Adrets 2, Brignoles (V)
254	1	43.7	−11	Les Riens (or St Pierre), Mons (V)
256	*	43.7	−9	Avaye, Mons (V)
256	*	43.7	−9	Le Colleton, Mons (V)
256	*	43.7	−9	Peygros, Mons (V)
256	*	43.4	−9	Les Adrets 1, Brignoles (V)
256	*	43.4	−9	Les Adrets 3, Brignoles (V)
256	*	43.4	−9	Les Adrets 4, Brignoles (V)
256	*	43.4	−9	L'Amarron, Brignoles (V)

Az. °	Alt. °	Lat. °	Dec. °	Tomb
256	*	43.6	−9	La Pierre de la Fée, Draguignan (V)
256	*	43.6	−9	La Verrerie Vieille, Tourrettes (V)
256	*	43.4	−9	La Gaillarde, Roquebrune-sur-Argens (V)
256	*	43.4	−9	Le Jas de Parette, Vidauban (V)
256	*	43.3	−9	St-Sébastien 2, Plan-de-la-Tour (V)
256	*	43.4	−9	Pont Neuf, Cabasse (V)
256	*	43.4	−9	La Gastée, Cabasse (V)
256	*	43.7	−9	Mauvans Sud, St-Cézaire-sur-Siagne (AM)
256	*	43.7	−9	Les Verdolines, St-Vallier-de-Thiey (AM)
256	*	43.7	−9	Les Puades, St-Cézaire-sur-Siagne (AM)
258	*	43.4	−7½	L'Agriotier, Roquebrune-sur-Argens (V)
259	*	43.6	−7	La Colle, Montmeyan (V)
259	*	43.5	−7	Beaumont, Entrecasteaux (V)
260	*	43.3	−6	La Haute-Suane, St-Maxime (V)
260	*	43.6	−6	San Vas 1, Figanières (V)
266	*	43.5	−1½	Roques d'Aille, Lorgues (V)
266	*	43.3	−1½	St-Sébastien 1, Plan-de-la-Tour (V)
266	*	43.7	−1½	Les Caillassoux, St-Vallier-de-Thiey (AM)
267	*	43.3	−1	Les Lions, Grimaud (V)
267	*	43.7	−1	L'Appara, St-Vallier-de-Thiey (AM)
269	*	43.7	+0½	Le Collaret, Baudinard (V)
272	0	43.7	+1	La Graou, St-Cézaire-sur-Siagne (AM)
276	*	43.7	+5½	Le Prignon, St-Cézaire-sur-Siagne (AM)
276	*	43.4	+5½	Les Muraires 1, Le Luc (V)
278	*	43.6	+7	La Colle de Roussel, Seillans (V)
278	*	43.3	+7	Montrouge, St-Raphael (V)
278	*	43.4	+7	Valescure, St-Raphael (V)
278	*	43.4	+7	La Valbonette, St-Raphael (V)
286	*	43.7	+12½	Colbas 1, St-Cézaire-sur-Siagne (AM)
286	*	43.7	+12½	Colbas 2, St-Cézaire-sur-Siagne (AM)
289	*	43.6	+15	La Cabre d'Or 1, Figanières (V)
289	*	43.7	+15	Le Deffens 1, Baudinard (V)

Alpine dolmen

Az. °	Alt. °	Lat. °	Dec. °	Tomb
267	*	44.4	−1	Le Villard, Le Lauzet-Ubaye (AHP)

*Az. supplied by Gérard Sauzade; alt. assumed to be 2° for the calculation of declination.
AHP: Alpes-de-Haute-Provence; AM: Alpes-Maritimes; BR: Bouches-du-Rhône; V: Var; Vcl: Vaucluse.

9.3. Orientations of 26 BR-dolmens in eastern Languedoc.

Az.°	Alt.°	Lat.°	Dec.°	Tomb
168	*	44.4	-42½	La Tour, Géantes, Bourg-St-Andéol (A)
174	*	44.4	-43½	Les Clausasses 2, Gras (A)
176	*	44.4	-44	Les Clausasses 3, Gras (A)
184	*	44.4	-44	Les Clausasses 1, Gras (A)
201	*	44.4	-40	Les Géantes 1, Bourg-St-Andéol (A)
209	*	43.8	-37½	Lecou, Causse-de-la-Selle (H)
211	*	44.2	-36½	Peyro-Blanco, St-Julien-les-Rosiers (G)
212	*	43.7	-36½	Bois de l'Olivier, Cazevieille (H)
216	*	44.4	-34	Les Arredons, St-Remèze (A)
216	*	43.9	-34	Le Ginestou, Moulès-Baucels (H)
221	*	44.2	-31½	Issirac 1, Issirac (G)
222	0	43.9	-33	Junction D113/D513, Blandas (G)
225	*	43.7	-29½	Sauzet 1, Cazevieille (H)
229	*	43.8	-27	La Matte 1, N.D.-de-Londres (H)
235	0	43.6	-25	Le Pas de Gallardet, Le Pouget (H)
236	*	43.7	-22½	La Limite 2, Mas-de-Londres (H)
240	*	43.9	-20	Le Puech Auroux, Claret (H)
244	*	43.9	-17	Le Mas Neuf 2, Claret (H)
247	*	43.7	-15	Soulas, Viols-le-Fort (H)
252	*	43.7	-11½	Conquette 1, St-Martin-de-Londres (H)
262	*	44.2	-4½	Issirac 2, Issirac (G)
266	*	44.1	-1½	Le Mas de Vialès, Cavillargues (G)
266	*	44.2	-1½	Coste-Rigaude, St-Gervais-les-Bagnols (G)
270	*	44.1	+1	Concouvèze, St-Laurent-la-Vernède (G)
288	*	43.5	+14	La Rouquette, St-Pargoire (H)
301	*	43.7	+23	Cambous, Viols-en-Laval (H)

*Az. as measured by Y. Chevalier; alt. assumed to be 2° for the calculation of declination.
A: Ardèche; G: Gard; H: Hérault.

9.4. The orientations of 103 L-dolmens in east Languedoc.

Az.°	Alt.°	Lat.°	Dec.°	Tomb
108	*	43.7	-11½	Le Pioch Redon 1, St-Privat-les-Salces (H)
116	*	43.9	-17	Le Sotch de Gardie, Rogues (G)
162	*	43.7	-42	Cantagril, Argelliers (H)
176	0	43.8	-46½	La Prunarède 1, St-Maurice-Navacelles (H)
176	*	43.7	-44½	Le Bois de la Sourde, Arboras (H)
180	*	43.9	-44½	Prévinquières, Cornus (Av)
183	*	43.8	-44½	Montsaloux, La Vacquerie (H)
184	*	44.0	-44	La Baume-Sauclières, Sauclières (Av)
189	*	43.7	-44	La Croix de l'Yeuse 1, Montpeyroux (H)
189	*	43.9	-43½	Le Serre-Plumat, La Couvertoirade (Av)
190	*	43.7	-43½	Fourille, Le Puech (H)
195	*	43.7	-42½	La Bruyère d'Usclas, St-Privat-les-Salces (H)
197	*	43.9	-42	Le Mont-Aymat, La Couvertoirade (Av)
198	*	44.0	-41½	La Lèque, Fressac (G)
199	*	43.6	-37½	Roudanergues, Pézènes-les-Mines (H)
202	*	43.8	-40½	Le Ranquet, St-Maurice-Navacelles (H)
203	*	43.9	-40	La Grailhe, Campestre-et-Luc (G)
205	*	44.1	-39	La Blachère, Lanuéjols (L)
206	*	43.7	-39	Les Isserts, St-Jean-de-la-Blaquière (H)
207	*	43.7	-38½	La Caisse des Morts 2, Murles (H)
207	*	43.8	-38½	Uglas 2, St-Martin-de-Londres (H)
207	*	43.8	-38½	Uglas 3, St-Martin-de-Londres (H)
207	*	43.8	-38½	Uglas 6, St-Martin-de-Londres (H)
208	*	43.6	-38	Mas Reinhart 3, Vailhauquès (H)
208	0	43.7	-40	Coste-Rouge, Usclas-du-Bosc (H)
208	0	43.7	-40	Belvédère de Grandmont, Usclas-du-Bosc (H)
212	*	43.8	-36	Le Frouzet 1, St-Martin-de-Londres (H)
212	*	43.4	-36½	Lacoste, Frontignan (H)
212	*	43.7	-36½	Montcalmès, Puéchabon (H)
212	*	43.7	-36½	Pouland 1, Puéchabon (H)
212	*	43.7	-36½	Fraysse 1, Puéchabon (H)
212	*	43.7	-36½	Carrière d'Espinasse, Puéchabon (H)
212	*	43.7	-36½	Le Mas de Perry, Murles (H)
212	*	43.8	-36	La Limite 1, Mas-de-Londres (H)
212	*	43.7	-36½	Le Pigeonnier de Sallèles, Le Bosc (H)
213	*	43.8	-36	Ferrusat-Esquirol 3, La Vacquerie (H)
214	*	43.7	-35½	Le Pioch Redon 2, St-Privat-les-Salces (H)

Table 9.4 continued

Az.°	Alt.°	Lat.°	Dec.°	Tomb
214	*	43.7	−35½	La Croix de l'Yeuse 2, Montpeyroux (H)
214	0	43.8	−37½	Coste-Caude 2, La Vacquerie (H)
217	*	43.8	−34	Taoula Chiesa 2, St-Martin-de-Londres (H)
217	*	43.7	−34	La Combe du Rat, Argelliers (H)
217	*	43.8	−34	La Liquisse (Alaquisse), Rouet (H)
217	*	43.7	−34	La Rigoule, St-Guilhem-du-Désert (H)
218	0	43.8	−35	Coste-Caude 1, La Vacquerie (H)
218	*	43.9	−33	Bouisset, Ferrières-les-Verreries (H)
219	*	44.1	−32½	Le Serre du Bouquet, Seynes (G)
219	*	43.8	−32½	Suquet, Pégairolles-de-l'Esalette (H)
221	*	43.7	−31½	Le Mas Cournon, Argelliers (H)
222	*	43.8	−31	Cayla, St-Martin-de-Londres (H)
222	*	44.2	−31	Le Devois de Villeneuve, Vébron (L)
222	*	43.7	−31	La Caisse des Morts 1, Murles (H)
222	*	43.8	−31	La Matte 2, N. D.-de-Londres (H)
222	*	43.8	−31	La Caumette, N. D.-de-Londres (H)
222	*	43.8	−31	Moustachou 3, Causse-de-la-Selle (H)
224	*	43.8	−30	Montlous 2, St-Martin-de-Londres (H)
225	*	43.9	−29½	La Massèle 2, St-Hippolyte-du-Fort (G)
226	*	43.8	−28½	Moustachou 2, Causse-de-la-Selle (H)
226	*	43.6	−29	Le Mas Reinhart, Vailhauquès (H)
227	*	43.8	−28	Taoula Chiesa 1, St-Martin-de-Londres (H)
227	*	43.8	−28	Marviel, Rouet (H)
227	*	43.8	−28	Lamalou, Rouet (H)
227	*	43.9	−28	Ferrières 1, Ferrières-les-Verreries (H)
227	*	43.8	−28	Camp, Rouet (H)
227	*	43.9	−23	La Baume, Ferrières-les-Verreries (H)
227	*	43.7	−28	Pouland 2, Puéchabon (H)
227	*	43.8	−28	Bergerie de Lamalou 1, Rouet (H)
227	*	44.0	−27½	Le Col de l'Aubert, Monoblet (G)
228	*	43.9	−27½	Ayrolles, Alzon (G)
228	*	43.7	−27	Argelliers 1, Argelliers (H)
230	*	43.8	−26½	Vialaret, La Vacquerie (H)
230	*	43.8	−26½	Roubiac 2, Cazevieille (H)
231	*	43.7	−25½	Les Peyres-Carnes, Viols-en-Laval (H)
232	*	43.8	−25	Montlous 1, St-Martin-de-Londres (H)
232	*	43.9	−25	Roucayrol 2, Brissac (H)
232	*	43.7	−25	Fraysse 2, Puéchabon (H)
234	*	43.8	−24	La Maline-Séranne, St-André-de-Buèges (H)
234	*	43.9	−23½	Le Mas-Neuf 3, Claret (H)
236	*	43.9	−22½	Les Arques (Landres), Blandas (G)
236	*	43.8	−22½	Le Grand-Juyan de Roubiac, Cazevieille (H)
237	*	43.7	−22	Pouland 4, Puéchabon (H)
238	*	44.3	−21	Le Chamblon, Ste-Enimie (L)
238	*	44.0	−21	Les Aspères 2, Tornac (G)
239	3	43.8	−19½	Ferrusat-Esquirol 1, La Vacquerie (H)
240	*	43.9	−20	Banèle, St-Hippolyte-du-Fort (G)
246	3	43.8	−15	Ferrusat-Esquirol 2, La Vacquerie (H)
246	*	43.9	−16	Le Mas-Neuf 1, Claret (H)
248	*	43.7	−14½	Roquecombarde, St-Saturnin-de-Lucian (H)
248	*	43.9	−14½	Galabert, St-Hipplyte-du-Fort (G)
249	*	43.7	−14	La Rigoule-Lavagnes, St-Guilhem-du-Désert (H)
251	*	43.9	−12½	Les Chênes-Verts, Claret (H)
252	*	43.7	−11½	Boscorre, Argelliers (H)
252	*	43.8	−11½	Feuilles, Rouet (H)
253	*	44.0	−11	Vialamontel, Lapanouse-de-Cernon (Av)
258	*	43.9	−7½	Le Capucin, Claret (H)
263	*	43.8	−4	Le Grand-Juyan de la Figarède, Cazevieille (H)
263	*	43.7	−4	Roquecourbe, Montpeyroux (H)
266	*	44.0	−1½	Les Aspères 1 , Tornac (G)
271	*	44.0	+2	Balmaresse, St-Jean-du-Bruel (Av)
286	*	44.3	+12½	L'Aumède-Bas 1, Chanac (L)
296	*	43.9	+19½	La Gruelle, Cornus (Av)
300	*	43.8	+22½	Soulagets 1, St-Maurice-Navacelles (H)
306	*	43.8	+26½	Le Bosc-Gros, St-Maurice-Navacelles (H)
326	*	44.0	+38	La Grand Pallière, Anduze (G)

*Az. as measured by Y. Chevalier, G. Combarnous or J. Arnal; alt. assumed to be 2° for the calculation of declination.
Av: Aveyron; G: Gard; H: Hérault; L: Lozère.

Chapter 10. Tombs of West Languedoc and the East Pyrenees

10.1. Orientations of 36 tombs of west Hérault and north Aude.

Az.°	Alt.°	Lat.°	Dec.°	Tomb
BR–dolmens				
20	4	43.4	+46½	Bois Bas 4, Minerve (H)
236		43.4	−24½	Bois Bas 5, Minerve (H)
Major allées couvertes				
143	0	43.3	−36	D. des Fados, Siran (Au)
150	0	43.3	−39½	St-Eugène, Rieux-Minervois (Au)
174	0	43.3	−47	Jappeloup, Trausse (Au)
178	−0½	43.3	−48	Casulha (Lauriol 1), Siran (H)
Lesser galleries				
111	−0½	43.3	−16	Boun-Marcou, Mailhac (Au)
111	1	43.4	−14½	Bois Bas 1, Minerve (H)
112	0	43.2	−16½	Rougeats, Monze (Au)
133c	2	43.2	−28½	Peirières, Villedubert (Au)
156	−0½	43.4	−42½	Bois Bas 8, Minerve (H)
158	0	43.4	−43	Lacs 3, Minerve (H)
169	−0½	43.3	−47	Mousse 1, Siran (H)
172	0	43.3	−46½	Cigalière, Cesseras (H)
190	1	43.4	−45	Bois-de-Monsieur, Assignan (H)
192	0	43.4	−46	Lacs 1, Minerve (H)
194	3	43.4	−42	Cuégnos, Villespassans (H)
Simple dolmens				
65	0	43.4	+17½	Bois Bas 12, Minerve (H)
71	1	43.4	+14	Bois Bas 6, Minerve (H)
140	0	43.4	−34½	Lacs 2, Minerve (H)
151	0	43.7	−39½	Lacade 1, Toucou, Octon (H)
156	−0½	43.4	−42½	Bois Bas 7, Minerve (H)
165	0	43.7	−45	Lacade 3, Toucou, Octon (H)
173	0	43.7	−46½	Lacade 2, Toucou, Octon (H)
196	0	43.4	−45	Bois Bas 3, Minerve (H)
197	0	43.4	−44½	Ventajous, Cupserviès (Au)
228	0	43.4	−29½	Bois Bas 10, Minerve (H)
250	0	43.4	−15	Bois Bas 11, Minerve (H)
Miscellaneous				
108	0	43.6	−13½	La Caissende 1, Combes (H)
145	−0½	43.6	−37½	La Caissende 3, Combes (H)
145	−0½	43.3	−37½	Palet de Roland, Pépieux (Au)
153	−0½	43.4	−41½	Bois Bas 14, Minerve (H)
208	0	43.4	−40½	Pierre Plantée, Fournes-Cabardès (Au)
230	2	43.4	−26½	Mousse 3, Siran (H)
242	0	43.3	−20½	Roque Traoucado, Pépieux (Au)
249	3	43.4	−13	Mousse 2, Siran (H)

Au: Aude; H: Hérault.

10.2. Orientations of 90 tombs of the extreme northeast of Cataluña and 10 frontier tombs of Pyrénées-Orientales.

Az.°	Alt.°	Lat.°	Dec.°	Tomb
Tombs with subcircular chamber and corridor				
132	0	42.5	−30	49 = Font del Roure, Espolla (AS)
139	5	42.4	−30	50 = Arreganyats, Espolla (AS)
140	0	42.4	−35	13 = Mas Puig de Caneres, Darnius (AS)
163	−0½	42.4	−46	44 = Tires Llargues, S. Climent Sescebes (AS)
165	0	42.3	−46	81 = Mas Bofill, Palau-saverdera (SR)
165	0	42.4	−46½	43 = Gutina, S. Climent Sescebes (AS)
170	−0½	42.4	−48	62 = Puig Esquers I, Llança (AS)
178	*	42.4	−47	64 = Pla dels Capallans, Colera (AS)
214	0	42.3	−38½	75 = Barraca d'en Rabert, Pau (SR)
262	0	42.4	−6½	24 = Estanys II, La Jonquera (AS)

Table 10.2 continued]

Tombs with trapezoidal chamber and corridor

Az. °	Alt. °	Lat. °	Dec. °	Tomb
48	*	42.3	+30	100 = Mas Godo, Port de la Selva (CC)
114	10	42.5	-10½	28 = Coll de Madas II, La Jonquera (AS)
118	*	42.5	-20	5 = Cova de l'Alarb de Valmy, Argelès-sur-Mer (AN)
124	0	42.3	-25	94 = Mores Altes II, Port de la Selva (SR)
128	*	42.5	-26½	Coll de la Creu, Banyuls (AN)
138	*	42.4	-33	Prat Tancat, S. Climent Sescebes (AS)
142	2	42.3	-34	87 = Febrosa, Palau-saverdera (SR)
146	0	42.3	-38½	82 = Devesa, Palau-saverdera (SR)
148	*	42.4	-39	29 = Mesclants, La Jonquera (AS)
148	*	42.5	-38	7 = Cova de l'Alarb de Rimbau, Collioure (AN)
153	1	42.3	-41	93 = Mores Altes I, Port de la Selva (SR)
153	3	42.3	-39	77 = Coll del Bosc de la Margalla, Pau (SR)
153	-0½	42.4	-42	58 = Coma de Felis, Rabós d'Empordà (AS)
158	5	42.3	-39	83 = Muntanya d'en Caselles, Palau-saverdera (SR)
161	-0½	42.4	-45½	46 = Cabana Arqueta, S. Climent Sescebes (AS)
165	0	42.4	-46	52 = Barranc, Espolla (AS)
166	4	42.3	-42	106 = Creu d'en Cobertella, Roses (CC)
166	5	42.3	-41	Fontasia II, Pau (SR)
168	*	42.3	-46	97 = Pla d'Estar/Quindals, La Selva de Mar (SR)
168	*	42.5	-45½	Collet de Baix, Cantallops (AS)
170	-0½	42.4	-48	57 = Solar d'en Gibert, Rabós d'Empordà (AS)
175	15	42.4	-32½	51 = Les Morelles, Espolla (AS)
179	4	42.3	-44	95 = Taula dels Lladres, La Selva de Mar (SR)
182	1	42.4	-47	65 = Mas Patiràs, Colera (AS)
183	9	42.3	-39	92 = La Pallera, Port de la Selva (SR)
184	5	42.3	-42½	96 = La Mora, La Selva de Mar (SR)
188	*	42.5	-46½	8 = Coll del Brau, Banyuls (AN)
189	7	42.3	-40	73 = Vinya del Rei, Vilajuïga (SR)
193	-0½	42.3	-47½	67 = Caigut I, Vilajuïga (SR)
196	-0½	42.4	-46½	55 = Puig Balaguer, Espolla (AS)
198	*	42.4	-44	63 = Puig d'Esquers II, Colera (AS)
206	6	42.4	-36½	56 = Comes Llobes de Pils, Rabós d'Empordà (AS)
209	-0½	42.3	-41½	70 = Ruïnes, Vilajuïga (SR)
218	20	42.3	-19	90 = Riera Pujolar II, Port de la Selva (SR)
219	-0½	42.5	-36	32 = Coma de Gall, Cantallops (AS)
224	-0½	42.4	-33	53 = Girarols I, Espolla (AS)
227	3	42.3	-28	72 = Garrollar, Vilajuïga (SR)
228	*	42.3	-29	Roca Miralles, Port de la Selva (SR)
228	*	42.5	-29	Coll de Madas III, La Jonquera (AS)
228	*	42.3	-29	9 = Coll de les Portes, Cerbère (AN)
233	0	42.3	-26½	80 = Vinyes Mortes II, Pau (SR)
234	-0½	42.3	-26½	69 = Carena, Vilajuïga (SR)

Az. °	Alt. °	Lat. °	Dec. °	Tomb
240	0	42.3	-22	84 = Sureda I, Palau-saverdera (SR)
240	0	42.4	-22	61 = Passatge, Llança (AS)
244	-0½	42.3	-20	71 = Talaia, Vilajuïga (SR)
248	*	42.4	-15½	66 = Coll de Farella, Portbou (AS)
248	*	42.4	-15½	Verneda, Capmany (AS)
260	-0½	42.3	-8	109 = Turó de l'Home, Roses (CC)
263	*	42.3	-5	99 = La Cendrera, Port de la Selva (CC)
270	8	42.3	+5½	89 = Riera Pujolar I, Port de la Selva (SR)
304	0	42.3	+24	108 = Llit de la Generala, Roses (CC)

Tombs with indeterminate chamber and corridor

Az. °	Alt. °	Lat. °	Dec. °	Tomb
68	*	42.4	+16½	Cantons/Llipoters, Espolla (AS)
88	*	42.3	+2	107 = Casa Cremada, Roses (CC)
103	*	42.4	-9	Coll de Dofines, Rabós d'Empordà (AS)
128	*	42.4	-26½	30 = Pedreguers, La Jonquera (AS)
128	*	42.4	-26½	Puig Tifell, Llançà (AS)
150	9	42.3	-32	Fontasia I, Pau (SR)
160	-0½	42.3	-45	76 = Creu Blanca, Pau (SR)
168	*	42.3	-46	98 = Puig Saquera, Roses (SR)
198	*	42.3	-44	Barranc de Vilajuïga (SR)
207	-0½	42.3	-42½	68 = Caigut II, Vilajuïga (SR)
218	*	42.4	-35	Puig de Llop, Llançà (AS)
248	*	42.3	-15½	86 = Sureda II, Palau-saverdera (SR)

Tombs with square chamber and wide corridor / Catalan galleries

Az. °	Alt. °	Lat. °	Dec. °	Tomb
90c	4	42.4	+2½	54 = Girarols II, Espolla (AS)
98	*	42.5	-5½	6 = Collets de Cotlliure, Argelès-sur-Mer (AN)
118	*	42.4	-20	15 = Rocalba, Agullana (AS)
125	3	42.5	-23½	3 = Na Christiana, L'Albère (AN)
135	17	42.5	-18	4 = Balma del Moro, Laroque-des-Albères (AN)
140	1	42.4	-34	18 = Barraca del Lladre, L'Estrada/Agullana (AS)
148	*	42.4	-38½	Mas dels Buencs, La Jonquera (AS)
149	-0½	42.5	-40	31 = Coll de Madàs I, Cantallops (AS)
150	4	42.4	-36½	17 = Jaça d'en Torrent, L'Estrada/Agullana (AS)
152	0	42.4	-41	33 = Quer Afumat, Capmany (AS)
158	3	42.3	-42½	Taballera, Port de la Selva (SR)
164	0	42.4	-46	47 = Puig del Pal, Espolla (AS)
168	*	42.5	-45½	St Pere de Forquets, Argelès-sur-Mer (AN)
172	1	42.3	-46½	79 = Vinyes Mortes I, Pau (SR)
173	3	42.4	-44½	40 = Fontanilles, S. Climent Sescebes (AS)
179	0	42.4	-48	35 = Mirgoler, Capmany (AS)
202	13	42.3	-31	91 = Mas de la Mata, Port de la Selva (SR)
208	*	42.5	-40	Puig Gros, Cantallops (AS)
256	0	42.3	-11	78 = Puig Margall, Pau (SR)

table 10.2 continued]

Simple dolmens

Az.°	Alt.°	Lat.°	Dec.°	Tomb
132	0½	42.4	−29½	41 = Salt d'en Peió, Sant Climent Sescebes (AS)
134	−0½	42.4	−32	21 = Mas Baleta II, La Jonquera (AS)
147	−0½	42.4	−39	20 = Mas Baleta I, La Jonquera (AS)
148	5	42.5	−34	2 = Siureda, Maureillas (AN)

Az.°	Alt.°	Lat.°	Dec.°	Tomb
165	−0½	42.4	−46½	19 = Canadal, La Jonquera (AS)
175	0	42.4	−48	38 = Les Closes, Sant Climent Sescebes (AS)
178	*	42.4	−47	36 = Vinya Monera, Capmany (AS)
224	0	42.4	−32½	23 = Estanys I, La Jonquera (AS)

AN: L'Albera Nord (France); AS: L'Albera Sud; SR: La Serra de Rodes; CC: El Cap de Creus.
* Measurement by J. Tarrús; altitude assumed to be 1° for the calculation of declination.
Numbers according to J. Tarrús and J. Chinchilla, *Els monuments megalítics* (Girona, 1992).

10.3. Orientations of 72 dolmens of Pyrénées-Orientales and south Aude.

Az.°	Alt.°	Lat.°	Dec.°	Tomb
Subcircular dolmens				
258	*	42.9	−7	La Clape 8, Laroque-de-Fa (N)
161	*	42.7	−41½	Caladroy 1, Bélesta-de-la-Frontière (C)
Dolmens with narrow corridors				
110	*	42.9	−12½	Tres Peyros, Massac (N)
183	*	42.9	−44½	La Clape 7, Laroque-de-Fa (N)
293	*	42.9	+18½	La Gouma, Montgaillard (N)
103	0	42.6	−10	Prat Clos, Ria-Sirach (C)
109	0	42.7	−14	La Barraca, Tarerach (C)
126	*	42.7	−23½	Pla de l'Arca, Molitg-les-Bains (C)
205	*	42.7	−39	Mas Llussane, Tarerach (C)
90	0	42.6	−0½	Coll de la Llosa, St-Michel-de-Llotes (S)
128	9	42.5	−20	Plan d'Arques 1, Fuilla (S)
Galleries				
135	*	43.0	−29	Clot de l'Oste, Bouisse (N)
169	*	42.9	−43½	La Clape 6, Laroque-de-Fa (N)
176	*	43.0	−44	Bellongue, Fontjoncouse (N)
185	4	42.9	−43	La Clape 4, Laroque-de-Fa (N)
187	4	42.9	−43	La Clape 5, Laroque-de-Fa (N)
194	*	42.9	−42½	Paza 3, Rouffiac-des-Corbières (N)
197	7	42.9	−38	La Clape 1, Laroque-de-Fa (N)
203	*	42.9	−40	Table des Maures, Massac (N)
205	*	42.9	−39	Arco del Pech, Cubières-sur-Cinoble (N)
209	*	43.0	−37½	La Serre, Monthoumet (N)

Az.°	Alt.°	Lat.°	Dec.°	Tomb
267	*	42.9	−0½	Cabane des Maures, Rouffiac-des-Corbières (N)
111	*	42.7	−13½	Caouno del Moro, Feilluns (C)
145	*	42.8	−34½	Espandiols, St-Paul-de-Fenouillet (C)
153	0	42.7	−41½	Molí de Vent, Bélesta-de-la-Frontière (C)
236	*	42.7	−22	Saint-Martin, Latour-de-France (C)
113	0	42.6	−17	Serrat d'en Jacques, St-Michel-de-Llotes (S)
119	0	42.6	−21½	Poste de Tir, St-Michel-de-Llotes (S)
126	3	42.5	−23½	Balma de Na Christiana, S.-Jean-de-l'Albère (S)
136	17	42.5	−18	Balma del Moro, Laroque-des-Albères (S)
137	*	42.5	−30½	Serrat de les Fonts 1, St-Marsal (S)
147	11	42.6	−28½	Serrat d'en Parot, Corneilla-du-Conflent (S)
Simple dolmens				
40	*	42.9	+36½	Prat d'en Mourges, Camps-sur-Agly (N)
137	*	42.9	−30	Paza 1, Rouffiac-des-Corbières (N)
137	*	43.0	−30	Dolmen 1, Salza-Vignevieille (N)
138	*	43.0	−30½	Dolmen 3, Salza-Vignevieille (N)
144	*	43.0	−34	Dolmen 2, Salza-Vignevieille (N)
166	*	43.0	−42½	Coume-Jonquière, Davejean (N)
185	4	42.9	−43	La Clape 2, Laroque-de-Fa (N)
38	*	42.7	+37½	Peyralade, Mosset (C)
113	0	42.8	−17	Le Roc de l'Arca, Feilluns (C)
117	1	42.6	−19	Le Homme Mort 1, Ria-Sirach (C)
132	*	42.7	−27½	San Ponci, Molitg-les-Bains (C)
143	*	42.7	−33½	La Mort de l'Eygassier, Trevillach (C)
148	*	42.7	−36	Coll del Tribe, Molitg-les-Bains (C)

Table 10.3 continued]

Az.	Alt.	Lat.	Dec.	Tomb
°	°	°	°	
158	0	42.7	-43½	Cova del Misser, Campoussy (C)
164	5	42.6	-40½	Montsec, Ria-Sirach (C)
167	1	42.7	-45	Font de l'Orry, Eus (C)
175	*	42.7	-44½	Camp del Prat, Trilla (C)
179	*	42.8	-44½	Olivià d'en David, Salses-le-Château (C)
183	*	42.7	-44½	Taupels, Trilla (C)
202	0	42.6	-43½	Arca de Calahon 1, Molitg-les-Bains (C)
231	5	42.6	-24	Serrat d'en Gely, Castelnou (C)
235	1	42.6	-24½	Arca de Calahon 3, Molitg-les-Bains (C)
240	0	42.8	-22	La Rouvre, Ansignan (C)
289	*	42.6	+16	Camp de la Coma, Conat (C)
90c	9	42.6	+6	Corbatura, Corneilla-du-Conflent (S)
109	*	42.6	-12	La Lloseta, Clara-Villerach (S)
114	*	42.5	-15½	Serrat de les Fonts 2, St-Marsal (S)
118	1	42.6	-20	Cabana del Moro, Llauro (S)

Az.	Alt.	Lat.	Dec.	Tomb
°	°	°	°	
146	*	42.6	-35	Mas d'en Payrot, St-Michel-de-Llotes (S)
166	*	42.6	-43	Las Jasses, St-Michel-de-Llotes (S)
176	*	42.6	-44½	Valltorta, St-Michel-de-Llotes (S)
201	*	42.6	-41	Los Masos, St-Michel-de-Llotes (S)
227	*	42.6	-28	Serra 1, Fuilla (S)
232	*	42.6	-25	Raméra 1, Caixas (S)
238	*	42.6	-21	Serra 2, Fuilla (S)
249	5	42.5	-12	Serrat del Coll de les Arques, Taillet (S)
273	*	42.6	+4	Moragas, Boule d'Amont (S)
Simple dolmens with vestibule etc.				
133	0	42.6	-30½	Creu de la Falibe, St-Michel-de-Llotes (S)
147	5	42.5	-34	La Siureda, Maureillas-Las-Illas (S)
181	*	42.5	-44½	Caixa de Rotlan, Arles-sur-Tech (S)

(N): in northern part of region (Corbières/Aude, north of the Agly).
(C): in central part of region (between the Agly and the Têt).
(S): in southern part of region (Conflent, Aspres, Vallespir; south of the Têt).
*Az. as measured by R. lund, or as listed by J.-P. Bocquenet in his doctoral thesis, "Monuments et nécropoles mégalithiques dans les Corbières méridionales", Toulouse University, c. 1994; alt. assumed to be 3° for the calculation of declination.

Chapter 11. Tombs of the Balearic Islands

11.1. Orientations of 9 megalithic sepulchres of the Balearic Islands.

Az.	Alt.	Lat.	Dec.	Tomb
°	°	°	°	
220	0	39.9	-36	Ses Roques Llises (Menorca)
225	3	40.1	-30½	Ferragut Nou (Menorca)
242	0	39.8	-21	Son Bauló de Dalt (Mallorca)
244	*	39.9	-19	S'Aigua Dolça (Mallorca)
245	3	40.1	-17	So'n Ermita (Menorca)
258	1	39.9	-8½	Alcaidús (Menorca)
260	0	39.9	-7½	Binidalinet (Menorca)
268	0	39.7	-1½	Ca Na Costa (Formentera)
278	5	39.9	+9½	Momplé (Menorca)

*Altitude assumed to be 1° for the calculation of declination.

11.2. Orientations of 18 burial navetas of Menorca.

Az.°	Alt.°	Lat.°	Dec.°	Tomb	Az.°	Alt.°	Lat.°	Dec.°	Tomb
159	0½	39.9	−45½	Cotaina d'en Carreras (ee)	210	0½	39.9	−41	Torralbet d'es Caragol (oe)
174	0½	39.9	−49	Biniac-L'Argentina W (oe)	226	0	40.0	−32	Torre del Ram W (ew)
178	0	39.9	−50	Cotaina de C'an Rabassó (oe)	233	0	40.0	−27½	Torre del Ram E (ew)
192	1	39.9	−47½	Biniac-L'Argentina E (oe)	240	0	40.0	−22½	Binipati Nou (ew)
192	0	39.9	−48½	Llumena d'en Montanyes (oe)	245	3	39.9	−17	Rafal Rubí S
192	2½	39.9	−46½	Rafal Rubí N (ee)	251	1½	39.9	−13½	Torre Llisa Vell (oe)
195	0	40.0	−48	Sa Torreta (ee)	251	1½	40.0	−13½	Es Tudons (ew)
195c	0	39.9	−48	Torralbenc Nou (ee)	252	0	40.0	−13½	Son Morell (ew)
195	0½	39.9	−47	Binimaimut (ee)	254	0	40.0	−12	La Cova (ew)

ee: elongated, eastern region; ew: elongated, western region; oe: oval, eastern region.

Chapter 12. Tombs of Corsica and Sardinia

12.1. Orientations of 8 dolmens in southwest Corsica.

Az.°	Alt.°	Lat.°	Dec.°	Tomb
117½	4½	41.7	−17	Tola di u Tormentu
130	3	41.5	−26½	Fontanaccia
139	16	41.8	−21	Settiva
147c	0	41.7	−39	Figala-Sarra
162	−0½	41.6	−46½	Belvedère
165	0	41.6	−47	Cardiccia
181½	1	41.6	−48	Vaccil-Vecchiu
217	3	41.6	−34½	Arghjola

12.2. Orientations of the sepulchres at Li Muri (lat. 41.1°).

Az.°	Alt.°	Dec.°	No.
95/275	–	−4/+3½c	5
162	5	−41½	1
180	1	−48½	2
200	2½	−43	3

12.3. Orientations of tombs at Pranu Muttedu, Goni (lat. 39.6°).

Az.°	Alt.°	Dec.°	No.
100	1	−7½	6
169	1	−48½	2
184	1	−49½	3
185	1	−49½	1
185	1½	−49	5

12.4. Orientations of 24 dolmens in northern Sardinia.

Az.°	Alt.°	Lat.°	Dec.°	Tomb
84½	1	40.3	+4½	Nela, Sindia
90	3	40.3	+2	Cucche, Dorgali
99	1	40.1	−6½	Mesu Enas, Abasanta
106	0½	40.2	−12	Muttiano, Borore
106½	0½	40.2	−12½	Arghentu, Borore
113½	0½	40.3	−17½	Arbu 2, Birori
113½	0	40.1	−18	Su Nurazzolu, Abbasanta
120	1	40.2	−22	Mura Fratta, Aidomaggiore
121	4	40.5	−20½	Sa Coveccada, Mores
125	1	40.3	−25½	Noazza, Birori
130	2½	40.9	−27½	Ciuledda, Lúras
130½	6	41.1	−25	Balaiana Luriareddu, Luogosanto
136	1	40.2	−33	Sa Perda 'e s'Altare, Macomer
138½	1	40.2	−34½	Funtana Biu, Aidomaggiore
140½	3	40.3	−34	Punta Sa Femmina, Orani
150	3	40.9	−38½	Alzaledda, Lúras
154	−1	40.3	−45	Monte Longu, Dorgali
155	0	40.2	−44½	Su Succhiau, Aidomaggiore
155½	0	40.2	−44½	Scrallotza, Aidomaggiore
167	0	40.1	−48½	Mura de Putzu, Abbasanta
170½	0	40.6	−49	Cianna Su Laccu, Buddusò
180	2	40.3	−48	Motorra, Dorgali
180	4½	40.9	−47	Ladas, Lúras
190	1	40.1	−48½	Domusnovas Canales, Norbello

12.5. Orientations of 20 Sardinian *corridoi dolmenici*.

Az.°	Alt.°	Lat.°	Dec.°	Tomb	Az.°	Alt.°	Lat.°	Dec.°	Tomb
86	*	40.8	+3½	Su Lioni, Perfugas	152	0	41.1	−42	Lu Muntiuchiu di Lu Paladin Luogosanto
94½	1	40.3	−3	Sa Murtava, Oliena	154	1	39.6	−43½	Genna de Accas, Goni
99½	1	40.0	−7	Sa Perda Longa, Austis	164	*	40.7	−46	Su Cobesciu Basciu 2, Chiaramonti
108	1	40.1	−13½	Domusnovus Canales, Norbello	164	*	40.6	−46½	Montiju Coronas 2, Ozieri
124	*	40.7	−24½	Su Cobesciu Altu 1, Chiaramonti	165	*	40.7	−46½	Sa Turturina, Chiaramonti
128	*	40.7	−27½	Su Cobesciu Altu 2, Chiaramonti	165	*	40.8	−46½	Concas, Perfugas
130	*	40.6	−29	Montiju Coronas 1, Ozieri	166	−0½	40.2	−49½	Pedra in Cuccuru, Borore
135	*	40.7	−32	Su Cobesciu Basciu 1, Chiaramonti	174	0½	39.9	−49½	Corti Noa, Laconi
143	3	39.7	−35½	Frumini, Isili	178	*	39.7	−49½	Domu Beccia 3, Uras
150	7	39.7	−41½	Pranu Tres Literas, Isili					
151	0	39.8	−42½	S'Arcu Is Crabiolus, Seui					

*Altitude assumed to be 1° for the calculation of declination.

12.6. Orientations of 252 Sardinian *tombe di giganti*.

Az.°	Alt.°	Lat.°	Dec.°	Tomb	Az.°	Alt.°	Lat.°	Dec.°	Tomb
24½	8	39.8	+51½	Genna 'e Cussa 2, Esterzili	89	*	40.2	+ 1	Colombos, Sedilo
28½	0½	39.7	+42½	Su Prettu, Tertenia	89½	1	40.3	+ 1	Biristeddi, Dorgali
31½	1½	40.2	+41½	Orbezzari, Sedilo	91½	*	40.8	−0½	Contracalza, Perfugas
35	*	39.8	+39½	Fragori, Barisardo	92½	0½	39.4	−2	Monte Su Crobu 1, Muravera
35½	11	40.4	+47	Forghe, Loculi	93	*	40.2	−2	Erghighine 1, Sedilo
37½	13	39.4	+47½	Su Ingurtossu, Donori	93½	9	40.0	+3	Talei, S. Mauro, Sórgono
42	*	39.9	+35	Pala Niedda, Tortolí	93½	3½	40.1	−0½	Mastala, Fonni
44	5½	39.7	+37½	Barisoni, Tertenia	94½	0	40.3	−4	Zanchia, Silanus
44	*	39.1	+34½	Perda 'e Sali, Sarroch	94½	*	40.2	−3	Figu, Borore
51½	7½	40.4	+33½	Su Facchile de Othieri, Irgoli	94½	1½	41.0	−2½	Coddu Vecciu, Arzachena
53	2	39.7	+29	Mesedas, Las Plazzas	95½	1	40.3	−4	Biristeddi 2, Dorgali
54½	6	40.3	+30½	Intremontes, Oliena	96½	*	40.2	−4½	Orzanghere, Sedilo
65	*	39.7	+19½	Bingia 'e Monti, Gonnostramatza	97	1	40.3	−5	Perdas Doladas 3, Silanus
66½	0½	41.1	+17½	Albucciu/Malchittu, Arzachena	97½	1	39.6	−5½	Bruncu Ladu, Guasíla
68½	0½	40.3	+16	Santa Sabina 2, Silanus	97½	−0½	39.8	−6½	Corti Eccia 3, Esterzili
69½	1½	40.3	+16½	S'Iscra de Lottani, Dorgali	98	*	40.5	−5½	Sa Perda Covecada, Torra
69½	1	40.2	+16	Sos Ozastros (S 1), Aidomaggiore	98	*	40.6	−5½	Conca Nicollitta 4, Ozieri
70½	*	40.8	+15	Puzzu Canu 2, Perfugas	98½	−0½	39.8	−7½	Corti Eccia 2, Esterzili
72½	1	39.8	+13½	Genna 'e Cussa 3, Esterzili	99	*	39.9	−6½	Niddai, Arzana
74½	0½	40.3	+12	Santa Sabina 1, Silanus	99	3	41.1	−5	Li Mizzani, Palau
74½	2	39.7	+13	Perda Bianca 1, Seui (Orboredu)	100	*	39.9	−7½	Texere, Ilbono
75	6	39.8	+15½	Ardassai, Seui	100	*	39.9	−7½	Paule Luturru, Samugheo
77	*	40.5	+10	Sagarà, Nule	101	*	40.3	−8	Puttu Oes, Macomer
77	0	40.2	+9½	Sos Ozastros (S 2), Aidomaggiore	101	*	40.2	−8	Cubas 2, Dualchi
78½	3	40.0	+10½	Trodolossai, Sorgono	101	1	40.1	−8	Tanca Carboni, San Michele, Fonni
81½	0½	40.2	+6½	Nuscadore, Borore	102½	−0½	40.1	−10½	Goronna 2, Paulilatino
82	*	39.9	+ 6½	S. Salvatore, Tortolí	103	*	40.2	−9½	Santu Bainzu, Borore
82	0	40.3	+ 5½	Palatu, Birori	103	*	40.5	−9½	Sa Perda Longa, Torralba
83	*	39.9	+ 5½	Santa Maria 2, Samugheo	103½	1	40.2	−10	Tanca Gregu, Piemonte, Fonni
83	*	39.6	+ 6	Sedda Sa Caudeba 2, Collinas					
84	1½	40.2	+ 5½	Battos 1, Sedilo	105	*	40.3	−11	Sa Perda 'e S'Altare, Birori [2km south of Lodine],
86½	2	40.1	+ 4	Aiodda, Nurallao	105	2	40.1	−10½	Gavoi
87	3½	40.3	+ 4½	Thomes, Dorgali					
87½	−0½	40.1	+ 1	Goronna 1, Paulilatino					
87½	7½	39.9	+ 6½	Perda Longa (north), Tortolí					

Table 12.6 continued]

Az.°	Alt.°	Lat.°	Dec.°	Tomb
105	2	40.1	−10½	Tanca Angheleddu, N.S. del Monte, Fonni
105	0	39.6	−12	Sa Ruina de Su Procu, Mandas
105½	0½	40.1	−12	Rio Cispiri, Bonárcado
105½	1	40.1	−11½	—, Nurallao
105½	1	40.3	−11½	Perdas Doladas 2, Silanus
106	*	40.5	−11½	Isporo, Nule
106½	3½	39.0	−10½	Su Niu 'e Su Crobu, Sant'Antioco
106½	1½	40.3	−11½	Perdas Doladas 1, Silanus
106½	3	39.3	−11	Tasonis 1, Sinnai
107	1	40.1	−12½	Perdu Cossu 1, Norbello
108½	1	40.2	−13½	Santa Filiriga, Aidomaggiore
109	*	40.8	−14	Nuraghe Urigu, Perfugas
109½	3	39.8	−13	Lappidesas 2, Gonnosno'
110	0	40.2	−15½	Sos Ozastros (north), Aidomaggiore
110	2	40.5	−14	[field east of SS131], Torralba
110½	0	40.0	−16	Santu Luisu, Sorgono
110½	0½	41.1	−15½	Li Lolghi, Arzachena
110½	0	39.4	−16	Monte Su Crobu 3, Muravera
111	*	39.4	−15½	Bruncu Perdarba, Villaputzu
111	*	39.1	−16	Antigori 1, Sarroch
111½	0	40.2	−16½	Imbertighe, Borore
112	*	40.2	−16	Erghighine 3, Sedilo
112	5½	40.2	−13	Cualbu Cundenna, Praru Ebbas, Fonni
113	*	40.7	−17	Su Cobesciu Altu, Chiaramonti
113½	0	39.8	−18	Corti Eccia 1, Esterzili
113½	0½	40.1	−17½	Su Pranu 2, Abbasanta
114	*	40.6	−17½	Conca Nicollitta 3, Ozieri
114½	1½	40.2	−17½	Santu Antine 2, Sedilo
114½	2	40.0	−17½	Serra Tsargiu, S. Mauro, Sórgono
115	*	40.9	−18	Coas, Bortigiadas
115	1	40.1	−18½	Perdu Cossu 2, Norbello
115½	7½	40.3	−14	Oddo Caccara, Orani
116	1	39.9	−19	Pala de sa Cresia, Allai
116	1½	40.2	−19	Santu Antine 1, Sedilo
116½	1½	40.3	−19	Bolude, Silanus
117	1½	40.2	−19½	Battos 2, Sedilo
118½	*	40.1	−21	Muraguada, Paulilatino
119	*	40.8	−21	Campu d'Ulimu, Perfugas
119	*	40.8	−21	Pubuliosa, Perfugas
119	1	40.6	−21	Malacaruca, Alà dei Sardi
120	*	40.8	−22	Puzzu Canu 1, Perfugas
120	*	40.3	−22	Tamuli 1, Macomer
120	*	39.6	−22	Sedda Sa Caudeba 1, Collinas
120	3	40.2	−20½	Bidistili, Fonni
121	*	40.2	−22½	Uore, Borore
121½	0	39.4	−24	Monte Su Crobu 4, Muravera
121½	0	40.3	−24	Saperca 'e Noarza, Birori
122	*	40.3	−23½	Miuddu, Birori
122½	3½	40.3	−22	Scano di Montiferro
123	0	39.7	−25	Ollasta Entosu, Seui (Orboredu)
123	*	40.3	−24	Sa Perda 'e s'Altare, Birori
123	*	39.9	−24½	Coxina, Arzana
124	2	40.3	−24	Pischine 'e Ainos, Tresnuraghes
124	*	40.1	−25	Bena Sinis, Bonarcado
124	*	40.3	−25	Sarbogadas, Birori
124	0½	40.1	−25½	Su Pranu 1, Abbasanta
124½	1	40.3	−25	Corbos, Silanus
124½	1	40.5	−25	Prunaiola, Torralba
125	*	39.9	−25½	Selene 1, Lanusei
125	0	40.6	−26	Loelle south, Budussò
125	6	40.1	−22	Madau 4, Fonni
125½	1½	40.0	−25½	Sa Carcaredda A, Villagrande
125½	0½	40.3	−26½	Zóddoro, Silanus
126	*	40.3	−26	Lassia, Birori
126½	0	40.2	−27½	San Antonio, Macomer
126½	1	40.0	−26½	Sa Carcaredda B, Villagrande
127	*	40.3	−27	Perda Lassia, Birori
127	*	40.6	−27	Conca Nicollitta 2, Ozieri
127½	2	40.2	−26½	Bolossene, Aidomaggiore
127½	*	40.3	−27	Tamuli 2, Macomer
128	1	40.3	−27½	Solomo, Sindia
128	0½	40.1	−28	Noeddos, Paulilatino
129	*	40.8	−28	Sas Luzzanas, Perfugas
129	*	39.9	−28½	Selene 2, Lanusei
129	*	40.2	−28½	Filigorri, Sedilo
130	1½	40.2	−28½	Melas, Sedilo
130½	4	40.4	−27	Ter. di Corrias, Sorrotha, Lula
131	*	39.9	−30	Santa Maria 1, Samugheo
131	2	40.2	−29	Busoro, Sedilo
132	1	39.8	−30½	Bruncu S'Enna S'Omini, Seui
132	3	40.1	−28½	Madau 5, Fonni
132½	*	40.2	−30½	Erghighine 2, Sedilo
132½	10	40.5	−23	Laccaneddu (E of Alghero)
134	6	39.8	−27½	Lappidedas 1, Gonnosno'
134	*	40.2	−31½	Cubas 1, Dualchi
134½	6½	39.7	−27½	Is Pranus, Isili
134½	0½	40.4	−32	Sas Mulathas, Irgoli
134½	6	39.7	−28	Cranaxolu, Orroli
134½	6½	39.8	−27½	Lappidedas 3, Gonnosno'
136	1	39.8	−33	Troddolai, Seui
136	1	40.9	−32½	Su Monte de S'Ape, Olbia
136½	2½	39.7	−32	Scusorgiu, Gesturi
137	*	40.6	−33½	Conca Nicollitta 1, Ozieri
138	−0½	39.7	−36	Domu S'Orcu, Siddi
138½	0½	40.4	−35	Monte Su Crobu 2, Irgoli
138½	0½	39.3	−35½	Baioca, Sinnai

Table 12.6 continued]

Az. °	Alt. °	Lat. °	Dec. °	Tomb	Az. °	Alt. °	Lat. °	Dec. °	Tomb
138½	1½	39.6	−34½	Sa Mandara 1, Guasíla	165½	1	39.6	−47½	Sa Mandara 2, Guasíla
138½	4	40.1	−32	Madau 3, Fonni	167	*	39.1	−48½	Antigori 2, Sarroch
140	3	39.8	−34	Cuccuru de Pardu, Seui	169	1	39.8	−48½	Genna 'e Cussa 1, Esterzili
140	*	40.3	−35½	Noazza 1, Birori	173	*	40.1	−49	Pradu Maiore, Santu Lussurgiu
140	−0½	39.7	−37	Pitzu Ungronis, Nurri					
140½	*	40.3	−35½	Castigadu s'Altare, Macomer	173½	2½	40.2	−47	Iloi 1, Sedilo
141	1½	40.6	−35	Padentes, Alà dei Sardi	175½	9	39.5	−41½	San Cosimo 1, Gonnosfanadiga
141½	1	40.3	−36	S'Abbaía, Silanus					
143½	0½	39.1	−38½	Tracasi, Tratalias	175½	4½	39.8	−45½	Is Piluncchedas, Genoni
143½	6	39.5	−33½	S. Cosimo 2, Gonnosfanadiga	176½	1½	39.4	−49½	Is Carrubas de Brannau, Muravera
145	0½	40.2	−38½	Sa Matta 'e So Bide, Borore					
145	0½	39.7	−39	Domu Becchia 2, Uras	179	*	40.0	−49½	Osono, Triei
145	2	39.7	−37½	Calafrixidadda, Isili	181	*	40.1	−49½	Campu Dare' 1, Narbolia
145	2½	40.4	−36½	Ter. di Guiso, Sorrotha, Lula	181	−0½	39.3	−52½	Pirrei, Sinnai
145½	0	39.3	−40	Serucci, Gonnesa	182	*	39.1	−50½	Monte Mereu, Sarroch
145½	0	40.6	−39	Loelle north, Budussò	183½	−0½	39.1	−52	Creminalana, S. Giov. Suergiu
145½	2	40.4	−37½	Ter. di Porcu, Sorrotha, Lula					
146	1½	40.0	−38½	Muru Longu, Carcara, Villagrande	184½	0	40.1	−50½	[3km SE of town], Séneghe
					185	2	40.3	−48	Su Forrighesu, Sindia
146½	*	40.2	−39	Scano di Montiferro	187	0	39.9	−50	Pranu Lisa, Allai
146½	2½	40.0	−38	Trocculu, Villagrande	187	3½	40.0	−46	S'Ebregargiu, S. Mauro, Sórgono
147	1	40.2	−39½	Uras 2, Aidomaggiore					
148	*	40.3	−40	Tamuli 3, Macomer	189	*	39.7	−49	Buraxedu, Nurri
149	*	40.8	−40	Su Paladinu, Perfugas	189½	2½	40.3	−46½	Gonnigori, Oliena
149	0	39.3	−42	Tasonis 2, Sinnai	191½	0?	40.4	−49	Sant' Efis 2, Orune
149½	4	40.1	−38	Madau 2, Fonni	193½	6½	39.6	−42½	Linus Arbus, Gesico
150	−0½	39.4	−43	Cuili Loddo, Muravera	194½	1	39.4	−48	Basoru, San Vito
150½	0½	40.0	−42	Su Serragheddu, Villagrande	198	1½	39.7	−46	Domu Beccia 1, Uras
151	1	40.2	−41½	Maschiola, Aidomaggiore	204	−0½	39.3	−46½	Santa Itroxa, Sinnai
152½	3½	40.1	−40	Tanca Mele, S. Michele, Fonni	208½	4	39.1	−39½	Terra 'e Soli, Santadi
153½	1½	40.3	−42	Mura Ruja, Silanus	209½	1½	39.3	−41½	Sa Perda Lada, Decimoputzu
154	*	40.8	−42½	Crabiles, Bulzi					
155½	0	39.7	−45	Su Pranu, Orroli	211½	7	39.8	−35	Sa Cea de Is Molas, Esterzili
156	*	40.1	−44	Campu Dare' 1, Narbolia					
156½	3	40.1	−42	Madau 1, Fonni	214½	1½	39.7	−38½	Ollastedu, Gesturi
157	1	40.1	−44	Serra 'e Lizzos 2, Séneghe	215	*	39.9	−38½	Perda Carcina, Ilbono
157½	1	40.2	−44½	Iscrallotze, Aidomaggiore	215½	3	39.7	−36½	Su Cuaddu Nixias, Lunamatrona
158	0	40.0	−46	Su Cungiau de Tore, Sorgono					
158½	3	39.8	−43	Lappidedas 4, Gonnosno'	222½	2	39.8	−33	Sa Ucca de Is Canis, Esterzili
159	1	40.2	−45	Sa Tanca 'e su Crecu, Aidomaggiore					
					240½	3	39.7	−20½	Perda Bianca 2, Seui (Orboredu)
161½	1	40.0	−46	Ruina Chesos, Sorgono					
162	0	40.2	−47	Uras 1, Aidomaggiore	257½	−0½	39.4	−10½	Mitza 'e Fidi, Donori
162	3½	40.8	−43	Giagone, Erula	260	−0½	39.3	−9	Sa Murta Sterria, Maracalagonis
162	0½	40.0	−46½	Porcu Abbas, Villagrande					
163	*	39.9	−46½	Monte Forru, Ilbono	270	2	39.8	+1	Tacchesinu, Seui
163	*	40.6	−46	Corona Saltania, Ozieri	276½	4	39.4	+ 7½	Coineddu, Muravera
163	*	39.7	−47	Stessei, Nurri	285½	1½	39.8	+12½	Sa Omu 'e Nannis, Esterzili
163	*	40.1	−46½	Serra 'e Lizzos 1, Séneghe	335	7	39.7	+50	Guntruxoni, Nurri
163½	2½	40.2	−45	Iloi 2, Sedilo	350	0	39.8	+48½	Motroxu 'e Bois, Uséllus
164½	14	39.5	−34½	Sibiri, Gonnosfanadiga	353½	8	39.3	+58	Sa Domu 'e S'Orcu, Quartucciu
164½	0	40.5	−47½	[Nuraghic village E of town], Osidda					

*Altitude assumed to be 1° for the calculation of declination.

Table 12.7. Orientations of the Nuraghic temples.

Az. °	Alt. °	Lat. °	Dec. °	Temple
94	−0½	40.7	−4½	Alà dei Sardi
98	+0½	40.3	−6	Serra Orrios (small)
158	+3	40.3	−42½	Serra Orrios (large)
167	−0½	39.8	−50½	Esterzili
120c	+2½	41.1	−20½	Malchittu

Chapter 13. Tombs of Malta, Sicily and Pantelleria

13.1. Orientations of 15 dolmens of Malta and Gozo.

Az. °	Alt. °	Lat. °	Dec. °	Tomb	Az. °	Alt. °	Lat. °	Dec. °	Tomb
15½/105½	1/0	36.0	+52/−13	Gozo 1	144½	3	36.0	−39	Ta Hammut 2
35½/215½	0/0	35.9	+41/−41½	Bidni	155	4½	36.0	−43½	Ta Hammut 3
108	0	36.0	−15	Gozo 4 gallery	156	4	36.0	−44½	Ta Hammut 7
109	0	35.8	−15½	Wied Zubner	162	0	35.9	−51	Fuq Wied Filep 2
111	0	36.0	−17	Gozo 2	166	0	35.9	−52½	Fuq Wied Filep 1
113½	0	36.0	−19	Gozo 3	174	3½	36.0	−50½	Ta Hammut 1
139	3	36.0	−35½	Ta Hammut 5	264/344	0/0	35.8	−5/+50½	Misrah ta Syniura
141?	3	36.0	−37	Ta Hammut 4					

Data published courtesy of Giorgia Foderà Serio and Juan Antonio Belmonte.

13.2. Orientations (in degrees) of passages in the sesi of Pantelleria. Where no orientation is cited, no measure could be obtained, because of the condition of the monument or of the surrounding terrain. Tombs *not* marked with an asterisk may have passages in addition to the one(s) measured.

Tomb	Azimuths of Passages	Tomb	Azimuths of Passages
*1	48, 53, 96, 100, 122, 168, 265, 271, 304, 315; 344 and 35 [with common entrance]	22	–
		23	–
2	–	24	–
3	–	*25	110, 181, 351
4	–	*26	48, 170, 204, 338
5	99	27	139, 330
6	–	28	113, 159
7	81	29	–
8	–	30	264 and 351 [common entrance]
9	88	31	279
10	103	32	–
11	245	33	271
12	–	34	–
13	1, 99	35	191
*14	26, 155, 243, 342	*36	89, 133, 359
15	–	37	–
*16	340	38	71
17	158	39	–
18	–	40	–
*19	216	41	–
20	308	42	172
21	105		

Chapter 14. Tombs of Tunisia, Algeria and Morocco

14.1. Orientations of 13 dolmens at Beni-Messous, Algeria (lat. 36.7°).

Az.°	Alt.°	Dec.°	No.	Az.°	Alt.°	Dec.°	No.	Az.°	Alt.°	Dec.°	No.
86	2	+4	4	106	2	−11½	7	145	7	−35½	16
88	2	+2½	2	117	3½	−19	14	154	1½	−45	8
91	2	0	3	118	2	−21	15	158	7	−42	13
92	2	−0½	5	122	2	−24	1				
104	2	−10	6	127	2	−27½	11				

Data from J.-P. Savary, "L'architecture et l'orientation des dolmens de Beni Messous", *Lybica*, xvii (1969), 271–330.

14.2. Orientations of 34 'skylight-tumuli' at Foum al Rjam, Morocco (lat. 29.5°).

Az.°	Alt.°	Dec.°	No.	Az.°	Alt.°	Dec.°	No.	Az.°	Alt.°	Dec.°	No.
33	4½	+50	5	99	3½	−6	12	127	0	−32	26
80	2	+9½	7	99	2	−7	9	130	6	−30½	10
82	0½	+7	18	101	12	−3½	8	130	0	−34½	4
85	2	+5	1	105	3	−11½	11	132	0	−36	23
86	3	+5	5	106	0	−14	30	133	0	−37	27
91	0½	−1	19	110	0½	−17½	6	137	0	−40	33
93	4	−0½	13	114	0	−21	32	137	0	−40	34
94	1	−3	16	121	0	−27	28	141	0	−43	25
94	0½	−3½	2	122	1	−27	21	149	0	−48½	3
95	0½	−4½	22	122	0	−28	29	156	0	−53	24
96	14½	+2	14	123	4	−26	17				
98	1½	−6½	20	125	0	−30½	31				

Data from J. A. Belmonte *et al.*, "Pre-Islamic burial monuments in northern and Saharan Morocco", *AA*, no. 24 (1999), S21–34, authors' numbering. Tombs 1–14 are in the SE area of the necropolis, 15–23 in the NE area, and 24–34 in the NW area.

14.3. Orientations of 7 'chapel-tumuli' at Taouz al Qadim, Morocco (lat. 31.0°).

Az.°	Alt.°	Dec.°	No.	Az.°	Alt.°	Dec.°	No.	Az.°	Alt.°	Dec.°	No.
98½	1	−7	9	105½	1½	−12½	10	125	1	−29	6*
103	1	−11	3	106	1	−13½	1				
103½	1	−11	7	119½	1½	−24½	4				

*No interior chapel; orientation is of the gate of a large court.
Data from J. A. Belmonte *et al.*, "Pre-Islamic burial monuments in northern and Saharan Morocco", *AA*, no. 24 (1999), S21–34, authors' numbering.

Appendix: The Minoan Cemetery at Armenoi, Crete

A.1. Azimuths, altitudes of the skyline, and the corresponding solar and lunar declinations of tombs at the Late-Minoan cemetery at Armenoi, Crete (latitude 35.3°). Lunar declinations take into account the relative proximity of the moon to the earth and the fact that it is being observed from the surface rather than the centre of the earth.

Az. °	Alt. °	Solar Dec. ° ′	Lunar Dec. ° ′	Tomb	Az. °	Alt. °	Solar Dec. ° ′	Lunar Dec. ° ′	Tomb
52½	1.5	+30 33	+31 10	39	82½	8.5	+10 57	+11 28	208
53½	1.7	+29 57	+30 33	38	82½	8.0	+10 39	+11 11	98
		MLS: +29 00			82½	8.0	+10 39	+11 11	107
56	2.2	+28 23	+28 59	3	83	8.0	+10 15	+10 47	29
56½	2.3	+28 04	+28 40	43	83	8.0	+10 15	+10 47	90
57½	2.5	+27 26	+28 01	190	83	8.0	+10 15	+10 47	96
57½	2.5	+27 26	+28 01	191	83	8.0	+10 15	+10 47	154
58½	2.6	+26 43	+27 19	80	83	8.0	+10 15	+10 47	183
60½	2.8	+25 17	+25 52	175	84	8.5	+09 43	+10 15	209
61½	2.9	+24 34	+25 09	42	84½	8.0	+09 01	+09 33	41
		SS: +23 51			84½	8.0	+09 01	+09 33	192
63½	3.1	+23 07	+23 41	46	84½	8.0	+09 01	+09 33	196
64	3.2	+22 45	+23 19	44	85	8.5	+08 54	+09 26	204
64	3.2	+22 45	+23 19	45	85½	8.0	+08 13	+08 45	72
65	8.5	+25 11	+25 44	206	86½	8.5	+07 41	+08 13	LIII
65	3.3	+22 01	+22 35	25	87½	8.5	+06 52	+07 24	205
65½	3.3	+21 39	+22 13	199	87½	8.0	+06 35	+07 07	67
67½	3.5	+20 11	+20 44	37	88	8.0	+06 11	+06 43	16
67½	3.5	+20 11	+20 44	177	88	8.0	+06 11	+06 43	87
67½	3.5	+20 11	+20 44	198	89	8.5	+05 39	+06 11	207
68	3.6	+19 50	+20 24	182	89	8.5	+05 39	+06 11	210
68½	3.7	+19 30	+20 03	66	89	8.0	+05 22	+05 54	84
69	3.8	+19 09	+19 43	179	89	8.0	+05 22	+05 54	170
69½	3.9	+18 49	+19 22	180	89½	8.0	+04 58	+05 30	68
69½	3.9	+18 49	+19 22	181	90½	8.0	+04 09	+04 41	69
		mls: +18 42			91½	8.0	+03 20	+03 53	—
70½	4.1	+18 08	+18 41	168	91½	8.0	+03 20	+03 53	83
71½	4.3	+17 27	+18 00	33	91½	8.0	+03 20	+03 53	167
71½	4.3	+17 27	+18 00	76	92	8.5	+03 14	+03 46	202
71½	4.3	+17 27	+18 00	77	92	8.5	+03 14	+03 46	LIV
72	4.4	+17 06	+17 39	160	92	8.0	+02 56	+03 28	135
72½	4.5	+16 45	+17 18	47	92	8.0	+02 56	+03 28	136
72½	4.5	+16 45	+17 18	161	92	8.0	+02 56	+03 28	140
72½	4.5	+16 45	+17 18	172	92	8.0	+02 56	+03 28	149
73½	4.7	+16 04	+16 37	32	92½	8.0	+02 32	+03 04	24
73½	4.7	+16 04	+16 37	79	92½	8.0	+02 32	+03 04	70
74	4.9	+15 47	+16 19	36	92½	8.0	+02 32	+03 04	74
75	5.1	+15 05	+15 38	48	92½	8.0	+02 32	+03 04	81
75	5.1	+15 05	+15 38	95	92½	8.0	+02 32	+03 04	89
75	5.1	+15 05	+15 38	163	93	8.5	+02 25	+02 58	203
75½	5.2	+14 44	+15 17	78	93	8.0	+02 08	+02 40	28
75½	5.2	+14 44	+15 17	173	93	8.0	+02 08	+02 40	105
76	5.3	+14 23	+14 56	30	93	8.0	+02 08	+02 40	187
76½	5.4	+14 02	+14 35	26	93½	8.0	+01 43	+02 16	35
77	5.5	+13 41	+14 14	174	94½	8.0	+00 55	+01 28	—
77½	5.7	+13 23	+13 55	185	94½	8.0	+00 55	+01 28	—
78	5.9	+13 06	+13 39	31	94½	8.0	+00 55	+01 28	91
78½	6.1	+12 49	+13 21	40	95	8.0	+00 31	+01 03	—
78½	6.1	+12 49	+13 21	162	95	8.0	+00 31	+01 03	82
78½	6.1	+12 49	+13 21	176	95	8.0	+00 31	+01 03	186
81	7.3	+11 29	+12 00	—	95½	8.5	+00 17	+00 50	108
81	7.3	+11 29	+12 00	27	95½	8.0	+00 07	+00 39	20
81	7.3	+11 29	+12 00	65	95½	8.0	+00 07	+00 39	21
81	7.3	+11 29	+12 00	171	96	8.0	−00 17	+00 15	85
81½	7.5	+11 11	+11 43	1	96	8.0	−00 17	+00 15	169
81½	7.5	+11 11	+11 43	71	96½	8.0	−00 42	−00 09	22

Az.°	Alt.°	Solar Dec.° ′	Lunar Dec.° ′	Tomb	Az.°	Alt.°	Solar Dec.° ′	Lunar Dec.° ′	Tomb
97	8.5	−00 48	−00 15	152	112½	9.0	−12 39	−12 04	12
97	8.5	−00 48	−00 15	153	112½	8.5	−12 58	−12 23	110
97	8.0	−01 06	−00 33	17	112½	8.5	−12 58	−12 23	123
97½	8.5	−01 12	−00 39	148	113	8.4	−13 25	−12 49	63
97½	8.0	−01 30	−00 57	14	113	8.4	−13 25	−12 49	104
97½	8.0	−01 30	−00 57	19	113	8.4	−13 25	−12 49	117
97½	8.0	−01 30	−00 57	34	113	8.4	−13 25	−12 49	124
98	8.1	−01 50	−01 17	2	113	8.4	−13 25	−12 49	156
98	8.1	−01 50	−01 17	50	113½	8.3	−13 51	−13 15	127
98½	8.1	−02 14	−01 41	139	114	8.8	−13 55	−13 19	143
99	8.8	−02 15	−01 41	126	114	8.3	−14 15	−13 39	115
99	8.2	−02 35	−02 01	7	114	8.3	−14 15	−13 39	121
99	8.2	−02 35	−02 01	18	114½	8.2	−14 42	−14 05	133
99	8.2	−02 35	−02 01	131	115	8.7	−14 45	−14 09	10
99½	8.9	−02 35	−02 02	134	115	8.1	−15 08	−14 32	113
100	8.3	−03 18	−02 45	88	115	8.1	−15 08	−14 32	155
100½	9.1	−03 15	−02 42	130	116½	8.5	−16 00	−15 24	158
100½	8.4	−03 39	−03 06	49	116½	7.8	−16 28	−15 52	111
100½	8.4	−03 39	−03 06	73	117	8.4	−16 27	−15 50	197
101	9.2	−03 36	−03 02	119	117	7.8	−16 51	−16 14	109
101	9.2	−03 36	−03 02	128	117½	8.5	−16 45	−16 09	215
101	9.2	−03 36	−03 02	60	117½	8.3	−16 52	−16 15	132
101	8.5	−03 59	−03 26	6	117½	7.7	−17 17	−16 40	62
101	8.5	−03 59	−03 26	75	117½	7.7	−17 17	−16 40	147
101½	8.5	−04 23	−03 50	—	118	8.5	−17 08	−16 31	220
101½	8.5	−04 23	−03 50	L	118	7.6	−17 44	−17 07	56
102	9.4	−04 16	−03 42	146	118	7.6	−17 44	−17 07	100
102	8.6	−04 43	−04 10	52	118	7.6	−17 44	−17 07	114
102	8.6	−04 43	−04 10	165	119	8.1	−18 09	−17 31	9
102	8.6	−04 43	−04 10	201	119	8.1	−18 09	−17 31	194
102½	9.5	−04 36	−04 02	151	119½	7.4	−18 59	−18 22	58
103	9.6	−04 56	−04 22	150	119½	7.4	−18 59	−18 22	120
103	8.8	−05 25	−04 51	4	120	8.5	−18 37	−17 59	212
104½	9.5	−06 09	−05 35	122				mls: −18 42	
104½	9.1	−06 25	−05 51	13	121½	7.7	−20 16	−19 38	55
105	9.2	−06 45	−06 11	51	121½	7.7	−20 16	−19 38	15
105½	9.3	−07 05	−06 30	57	121½	7.2	−20 36	−19 58	129
105½	9.3	−07 05	−06 30	214	121½	7.2	−20 36	−19 58	138
105½	9.3	−07 05	−06 30	LI	121½	7.7	−20 16	−19 38	157
106½	9.5	−07 44	−07 10	193	122½	7.1	−21 24	−20 46	64
106½	9.5	−07 44	−07 10	200	122½	7.1	−21 24	−20 46	125
107	9.6	−08 04	−07 29	—	123	7.5	−21 32	−20 54	93
107	9.2	−08 17	−07 43	54	124	7.4	−22 20	−21 41	—
107½	9.1	−08 44	−08 10	102	124	6.9	−22 38	−22 00	101
108	9.6	−08 49	−08 14	23	124	6.9	−22 38	−22 00	137
108	9.6	−08 49	−08 14	141	125½	7.2	−23 31	−22 52	92
109	9.5	−09 39	−09 04	11	126½	8.5	−23 19	−22 39	216
109	9.5	−09 39	−09 04	189				WS: −23 51	
109	8.9	−10 01	−09 27	116	126½	6.4	−24 48	−24 09	118
109½	9.4	−10 06	−09 31	53	127½	8.5	−24 01	−23 21	213
110	8.8	−10 52	−10 17	106	127½	6.2	−25 39	−25 00	59
110½	9.3	−10 56	−10 21	94	127½	6.2	−25 39	−25 00	145
110½	9.3	−10.56	−10 21	LII	129	8.5	−25 04	−24 24	217
111½	9.1	−11 49	−11 14	86	130	5.8	−27 43	−27 02	144
111½	9.1	−11 49	−11 14	211	132½	8.5	−27 27	−26 46	218
111½	8.6	−12 09	−11 33	61	133	5.9	−29 43	−29 02	8
111½	8.6	−12 09	−11 33	112	135	8.5	−29 06	−28 24	219
112	9.1	−12 12	−11 37	159				MLS: −29 00	
112	8.5	−12 35	−12 00	103	—	—	—	—	178
112½	9.0	−12 39	−12 04	164					

mls: minor lunar standstill; MLS: major lunar standstill; SS: summer solstice; WS: winter solstice.
Numbers according to plan supplied by the excavator.

Index

*The page numbers of illustrations are in **bold** type.*